Knowledge Cities

Knowledge Cities

Approaches, Experiences, and Perspectives

Edited by

Francisco Javier Carrillo

ELSEVIER

AMSTERDAM • BOSTON • HEIDELBERG • LONDON
NEW YORK • OXFORD • PARIS • SAN DIEGO
SAN FRANCISCO • SINGAPORE • SYDNEY • TOKYO

Butterworth-Heinemann is an imprint of Elsevier

Butterworth-Heinemann is an imprint of Elsevier
30 Corporate Drive, Suite 400, Burlington, MA 01803, USA
Linacre House, Jordan Hill, Oxford OX2 8DP, UK

Recognizing the importance of preserving what has been written, Elsevier prints
its books on acid-free paper whenever possible.

Library of Congress Cataloging-in-Publication Data
Knowledge cities : approaches, experiences and perspectives / F.J. Carrillo, editor.
    p. cm.
    Includes bibliographical references and index.
    ISBN-13: 978-0-7506-7941-1 (pbk. : alk. paper)
    ISBN-10: 0-7506-7941-7 (pbk. : alk. paper)
    1. City and town life.   2. Intellectual life.   3. Metropolitan areas.   I. Carrillo, F. J.
HT255.K66 2005
307.76'01'1—dc22

                                                                        2005022281

British Library Cataloguing-in-Publication Data
A catalogue record for this book is available from the British Library.

ISBN 13: 978-0-7506-7941-1
ISBN 10: 0-7506-7941-7

For information on all Butterworth-Heinemann publications
visit our Web site at www.books.elsevier.com

Printed in the United States of America
05 06 07 08 09 10   10 9 8 7 6 5 4 3 2 1

"From now on, I will describe the cities myself" the Khan had said, "You, in your travels, will verify whether they exist."

But the cities visited by Marco Polo were always different from those conceived by the emperor.

"And nevertheless I have built in my mind a city model out of which all possible cities can be deduced," Kublai said. "It includes everything according to the norm. Since actual cities tend to diverge in different degrees from the norm, it is enough for me to foresee the exceptions and calculate the most likely combinations."

"I have also thought over a city model from which I can deduce any other," Marco replied. "It is a city made out of exceptions, exclusions, contradictions, incongruities, paradoxes. If a city like that is absolutely improbable, by diminishing the number of abnormal elements the likelihood increases that such city actually exists. Therefore it is enough that I subtract exceptions to my model, and however I proceed I will come to find myself before one of the cities that, even though made out of exceptions, they nevertheless exist. But I cannot take my operation beyond certain limits: I would obtain cities too plausible to be real."

Italo Calvino
The Invisible Cities (1972)

Table of Contents

Introduction: The Century of Knowledge Cities,
by Francisco Javier Carrillo   xi

Part One: Approaches   1

Chapter 1   An Emerging Pattern of Successful Knowledge Cities' Main
            Features
            Kostas Ergazakis, Kostas Metaxiotis, and John Psarras   3

Chapter 2   A Comparative Framework for Knowledge Cities
            Samuel David Martínez   17

Chapter 3   Global Research Centres: An Analysis Based on Bibliometric
            Indicators
            *Christian Wichmann Matthiessen, Annette Winkel Schwarz,
            and Søren Find*   31

Chapter 4   A Taxonomy of Urban Capital
            Francisco Javier Carrillo   43

Chapter 5   K-City and Society Entrepreneurship for Intellectual Capital
            Growth
            Leif Edvinsson   59

Chapter 6   Implementation of the Capital System for a
            Knowledge City
            Pedro Flores   75

Part Two: Experiences   85

Chapter 7 The Case of Singapore as a Knowledge-Based City
           Caroline Y. L. Wong, Chong Ju Choi, and
           Carla C. J. M. Millar   87

Chapter 8 Bilbao: From the Guggenheim to the Knowledge City
           Jon Azua   97

Chapter 9 Holon: Transition into City of Children
           Maya Levin-Sagi, Edna Pasher, and
           Hanah Hertzman   113

Chapter 10 UniverCities: Innovation and Social Capital in Greater
            Manchester
            Blanca C. García   123

Chapter 11 Greater Phoenix as a Knowledge Capital
            Jay Chatzkel   135

Chapter 12 A Capital System for Monterrey
            Francisco Javier Carrillo   145

Chapter 13 Rijeka: Increasing Efficiency of Intellectual Capital
            in City-Owned Companies
            Karmen Jelcic   167

Chapter 14 An Experimental Aesthetic Audit of a City Within a City:
            The Case of Christiania
            Raphaële Bidault-Waddington   177

Part Three: Perspectives   189

Chapter 15 How Much Does Urban Location Matter? A Comparison
            of Three Science Parks in China
            Stephen Chen   191

Chapter 16 Urban Concentration of European Business Services and the
            Role of Regional Policies
            Luis Rubalcaba and Rubén Garrido   205

Chapter 17 Knowledge Dissemination and Innovation in Urban Regions:
            An Evolutionary Perspective
            Jan G. Lambooy   223

Chapter 18 Knowledge Citizens: A Competence Profile
            América Martínez   233

Chapter 19 Knowledge City, Seen as a Collage of Human Knowledge
Moments
Ron Dvir 245

Chapter 20 Reconstructing Urban Experience
Francisco Javier Carrillo 273

List of Contributors 285
Index 287

Introduction: The Century of Knowledge Cities

Francisco Javier Carrillo

Few aspects of today's world may characterize better the dawn of the new millenium than the transformation of regions and cities into knowledge societies. The evolutionary significance of both the definite urbanization of the world's population and, above all, the *experience upgrade* of urban life in post-industrial economies is only beginning to be realized: *the 21st century society is post-industrial, the Knowledge City is its horizon.*[1]

On the one hand, the 21st century is being identified as the *Century of Cities.*[2] While massive emigration of rural populations into towns started with the Industrial Revolution, this is still an ongoing process even if very brief from a historical perspective. The couple of centuries since account for only about 0.5% of human existence on earth.[3] Yet, as recently as the 1980s, total urban population worldwide was less than 30%. Just now, the world's population living in cities is overcoming the 50% mark and is expected to become 75% by 2025 (a percentage already reached by most developed countries). Hence, the definite urbanization of mankind is happening right now, after 40,000 years of the appearance of our species. This is indeed the Century of Cities: "The urbanization of human experience is, as a dominant phenomenon, a reality of the new millenium."[4]

---

[1] Paraphrasing the opening sentence of Françoise Choay's tour-de-force of modern urbanism, *L'Urbanisme, Utopies et réalité.* Paris: Editions du Seuil, 1965: "The industrial society is urban. The city is its horizon."

[2] Charles Landry, *The Creative City.* London: Earthscan, 2000, p. xiii.

[3] F. J. Carrillo, Capital cities: A taxonomy of capita accounts for knowledge cities, *Journal of Knowledge Management*, Vol. 8, No. 5, October 2004, p. 29.

[4] Ibid.

On the other hand, the 21st century has also been identified as the *Century of Knowledge*[5] or the *Century of Learning*.[6] After World War II, over 50% of GDP in an increasing number of industrialized countries moved consistently from material-based to being knowledge-based. In the global arena, the United Nations,[7] the European Union,[8] the OECD,[9] and the World Bank[10] have all stressed the critical importance of the Knowledge Economy as a global reality established over the turn of the century. Taichi Sakaiya[11] and Peter Drucker,[12] amongst others, foresaw the end-of-century advent of the Knowledge Economy as the grounds for the foundation of the Knowledge Society. According to Sakaiya, we are inaugurating a new era: "It is my contention that we are entering a new phase of civilization in which the value attached to knowledge is the driving force."[13] We have entered the Century of Knowledge.

This book is about the convergence of these two emerging conditions of human civilization at the dawn of the new millenium: *The Century of Knowledge Cities*. Global urbanization and the advent of the Knowledge Society constitute each an unprecedented and complex reality. Each has exposed the limits of conventional disciplinary approaches to urban development and to social value creation, respectively. Both together, integrated in the Knowledge City, constitute one of the most complex phenomena ever faced by mankind and probably a critical one for its future evolution.

Conceptual and empirical studies on Knowledge Cities constitute an emerging, pre-paradigmatic, and multidisciplinary field. First, it is emerging insofar as not only a child of the new century, but also a fast growing one. The substantial amount of resources available now on this subject, as well as the existence of most elements of an institutionalized discipline (specialized journals, professional communities and networks, dedicated conferences) testify to that.[14] The *Knowledge Cities Clearinghouse* (www.knowledgecities.com) compiles lists of (i) glossaries, (ii) Knowledge-Based Development (KBD) initiatives, (iii) associations and international organizations, (iv) urban KBD value dimensions, (v) rankings, (vi) special editions, (vii) bibliography, and (viii) electronic references, related to Knowledge Cities (KCs) and KBD.

---

[5] Taichi Sakaiya, *The Knowledge-Value Revolution or a History of the Future*. New York: Kondasha, 1991, pp. xvii, 58. Also Peter Drucker, *The Post-Capitalist Society*, New York, Harper-Collins, 1994, pp. 3, 6–9 and *Management Challenges for the 21st Century*, New York: Harper-Collins, 1999, p. 135.

[6] N. Longworth, *Making Lifelong Learning Work: Learning Cities for a Learning Century*. London: Kogan Page, 1999 (p. 29).

[7] *Human Development Report 2001*. New York: UNDP, 2001.

[8] *Innovation Policy in a Knowledge-Based Economy*. Brussels: European Commission, 2000.

[9] *The Knowledge-Based Economy*. Paris: OECD, 1996.

[10] *World Development Report 1998/99*. Washington: The World Bank, 1999.

[11] Ibid.

[12] Ibid.

[13] Sakaiya, op. cit., p. 58.

[14] Cfr. González, Alvarado, and Martinez: A compilation of resources on knowledge cities and knowledge-based development. *Journal of Knowledge Management*, Special Issue on "Knowledge-based Development II: Knowledge Cities," Vol. 8, No. 5, 2004, pp. 107–127. From this work, the *Knowledge Cities Clearinghouse* originated.

Second, the emerging field of KCs can be characterized as pre-paradigmatic. While the interest on KCs is growing rapidly, the field still lacks a consensus regarding appropriate conceptual and methodological frameworks. Third, the new field builds upon established and novel disciplines. While KBD is a convergence of Economic Growth Theory and Knowledge Management (KM), KCs—a subfield of KBD—are a convergence of Urban Studies and Planning with KM. Both, like all KM, are founded on the Sciences of Knowledge (history, anthropology, biology, psychology, economy, political science, and sociology of knowledge). KCs, in particular, also benefit from geography and several areas of technology.

This book aims at contributing to shape the emerging field of KCs by collecting contributions from diverse disciplines, using alternative frameworks and methods, looking at different aspects of the same complex phenomenon. In doing so, the threads of dialog emerging in this book build on prior editorial projects carried out with the purpose to bride KM and New Growth Theory[15] on the one hand, KM and Urban Studies[16] on the other. Several of the authors of this volume also contributed to those exercises.

But, what is so special about KCs? What is so distinctive that requires a dedicated community and a new discipline? It would be worth if this book helped to answer these questions alone. In KCs, the city is the unit of analysis and KBD is the differentiating factor. Too often, the concept of KC is reduced to a constituent element, notably technopoles and innovation clusters, generally focused on regional GP growth. Yet, none of these concepts requires the idea of KC, since they all have existed independently and have evolved on their own accord. None of them aims primarily at the value dimensions, which are the *raison d'etre* of KM and KBD. In consequence, no urban development project, however strategic, justifies the use of the KC label if it aims primarily at economic development, or can be described in terms of available technoeconomic development frameworks.[17] This is in elementary consistency with the very concept of KBD as opposed to traditional economic growth theory and the now unacceptable dychotomy between economic welfare and overall social value.

The concepts of KBD and KC follow the realization that conventional economic analysis and economic growth theory fail to account for most of the distinctive value dimensions of knowledge-based production and overall social worth. It is the delibrated attempt by social agents to understand and manage

---

[15] See, e.g.: *Journal of Knowledge Management*, Special Issue on "Knowledge Based Development" (Vol. 6, No. 2, 2002). This *JKM* SI will be published annually as from 2006.

[16] See, e.g.: *Urban Studies*, Special Issues on "Cities, Enterprises and Society at the Eve of the 21st Century" (Vol. 32, No. 2, 1995) and "The Knowledge-based City" (Vol. 39, Nos. 5–6, 2002); and also the *Journal of Knowledge Management*, Special Issue on "Knowledge Based Development-II: Knowledge Cities" (Vol. 8, No. 5, 2004).

[17] They have their own unquestionable importance and have been quite ably dealt with. For example, Nicos Komninos (*Intelligent Cities*, London: Spon, 2002) provides a very complete account of the origin and perspectives of the technopolis, while Margaret O'Mara (*Cities of Knowledge*, Princeton University Press, 2005) draws from an analysis of Cold War Science a number of lessons on the development successful technopoles in the US, such as Silicon Valley.

such universe of value that characterizes KBD and KCs. Nevertheless, the novelty of the field implies a transition between the received, segmented approaches to KCs in terms of some of its constituent elements (notably Knowledge Infrastructure and Human Capital) and the emerging, systemic approach in terms of social value systems and holistic urban strategies.

Contributions to this volume have been selected with the aim to represent the diversity of theoretical and methodological approaches shaping the new discipline. From the empirical, analytical, and quantitative, to the conceptual, systemic, and axiological, all contributions form together a rich mosaic telling us more about KCs than any of its constituent chapters. The transition from the former socioeconomic analysis of KC components (technopoles, clusters, networks, etc.) to urban value systems as conceptual units is also evident.

The book is organized in three parts. *Part I: Approaches* contains several attempts to making sense of KCs. Chapter 1 by Ergazakis, Metaxiotis, and Psarras tries to identify some characteristics of successful KCs while Chapter 2 by Martínez compares existing frameworks and practices with regard to value dimensions involved. Matthiessen, Schwartz, and Find look in Chapter 3 at patterns of scientific productivity of urban research centers worldwide. In Chapter 4, Carrillo provides a taxonomy of accounts for social knowledge capital. Edvinsson, in Chapter 5, develops a view of KCs as communities of Intellectual Capital Entrepreneurs. Finally, Chapter 6 by Flores describes a Knowledge-Based Strategy process for developing KCs.

Part II: Experiences contains a number of KC-related initiatives at various levels. Chapter 7 by Wong, Choi, and Millar assesses the evolution of the city-state of Singapore into a KC. Azua, in Chapter 8, recounts the role of the Bilbao Guggenheim Museum in the KBD of the City and the whole Basque Country. In Chapter 9, Levin-Sagi, Pasher, and Hertzman describe the process of reinvention of Holon in Israel as a City of Children. The role of universities in the KBD of Manchester is explored by García in Chapter 10, while Chapter 11 by Chatzkel looks at the potential of Phoenix as KC and how this could be leveraged. In Chapter 12, Carrillo exemplifies with the case of Monterrey the taxonomy of urban capital introduced in Chapter 4. In turn, Jelcic explains in Chapter 13 how the improvement of city-owned companies in Rijeka, Croatia, have contributed to urban, regional, and national Intellectual Captial. Closing this part, Chapter 14 by Bidault-Waddington provides an aesthetical audit of Christiania in Copenhagen as a "city within a city."

Closing the book, *Part III: Perspectives* looks at some emerging issues in the context of KCs. Chapter 15 by Chen, analyzes the impact of urban location on the relative success of three science parks in China. In Chapter 16, Rubalcaba and Garrido assess the significance of urban business services concentration in Europe for KBD policies; while Lambooy, in Chapter 17, provides an evolutionary perspective of urban Innovation and Knowledge Dissemination. On a different ground, Martínez constructs in Chapter 18 a competence profile of the Knowledge Citizen while in Chapter 19 Dvir offers a conversational and pictorial account of the KC from "the user's" perspective. Finally, Carrillo in Chapter 20 addresses the question of what the essence of living in a City might be in the Knowledge Society.

In carrying out this collective effort, diversity was favored from the nation, gender, culture, discipline, sector, theory, method, and style insofar as possible. We aimed at the goal that this book somehow echoed the wealth of possibilities that are the fabric of KCs. I want to thank, first of all, each of the 27 authors who have vested their Intellectual Capital into this Knowledge Venture. Their collective wisdom constitutes probably the most complete and state-of-the-art account on KCs available up to now. I also want to thank Karen Maloney, our Publisher, Dennis McGonagle, Assistant Editor, Heather Furrow, Production Project Manager, and Priyaa H. Menon, Project Manager, for their professionalism and continued support in carrying out this project. They made the demands of editorial work a joyful experience.

I thank Mr. Juan Ignacio Vidarte, Director of the Guggenheim-Bilbao Museum, and Erika Barahona-Ede, Photographer and Rights and Reproductions Manager, for the permission to use a GBM photograph in the cover and their assistance in the process.

I hope all of our readers, both citizens and decision-makers, urban planners and policy analysts, academicians and practitioners, scientists and artists, students and professionals, find in these pages a mind-provoking and enabling welcome to the Knowledge City.

Part One: Approaches

Chapter 1

An Emerging Pattern of Successful Knowledge Cities' Main Features

Kostas Ergazakis, Kostas Metaxiotis, and John Psarras, *National Technical University of Athens, Greece*

Introduction

Over the past twenty years, there has been intensive discussions about the importance of knowledge management (KM) in the business world. Nowadays, knowledge is considered one of the most valuable assets of an enterprise, which has to be managed efficiently and effectively in order to gain a competitive advantage in the knowledge economy era (Ergazakis et al., 2004a).

Knowledge management has evolved into a strategic management approach, finding application not only in the business world but also in other areas such as education, government, and healthcare. The fact that major international organizations—such as the European Commission, the World Bank, the United Nations Organization and the OECD—have adopted KM frameworks in their strategic directions regarding global development clearly indicates that a new link exists between knowledge management and knowledge-based development (Carrillo, 2002, 2004; Metaxiotis and Psarras, 2004a,b).

This new link created the appropriate environment for the advent of the "knowledge city" concept that, nowadays, is a topic of high interest and discussion. Many cities globally claim themselves as being already knowledge cities while at the same time other cities have elaborated strategic and action plans in order to become one. However, as it also happened with the early stages of evolution of KM (Rubenstein-Montano et al., 2001), there is neither a coherent framework nor a unified methodology for the design and implementation of successful knowledge cities. The real success of knowledge cities is still under investigation in the research community.

Consequently, the identification of the characteristics that a successful knowledge city should have in real practice is more than necessary nowadays. This chapter aims to present and analyze these characteristics through an empirical evaluation of several case studies that have been successfully put in real practice. The key findings of this study are expressed as preliminary conclusions that may be helpful in building successful knowledge cities. Whether each case study supports these conclusions or not is discussed.

Key Concepts of Knowledge Cities: A Brief Overview

Basic Definitions

The concept of knowledge city is very broad and may refer to all aspects of social, economic, and cultural life of a city. According to Ergazakis et al. (2004b), "A knowledge city is a city that aims at a knowledge-based development, by encouraging the continuous creation, sharing, evaluation, renewal and update of knowledge. This can be achieved through the continuous interaction between its citizens themselves and at the same time between them and other cities' citizens. The citizens' knowledge-sharing culture as well as the city's appropriate design, IT networks and infrastructures support these interactions." This definition is also illustrated in Figure 1.

The process of developing a knowledge city is neither quick nor simple. Consequently, any effort to develop a knowledge city should have assured the active support of the entire society, i.e., local government, citizens, private sector, organizations, universities, etc. For this purpose, an in-depth analysis of the current situation, definition of a vision and strategy, and implementation of an action plan are required.

Figure 1

The Knowledge City Concept. Source: Adapted from Ergazakis et al., 2004b

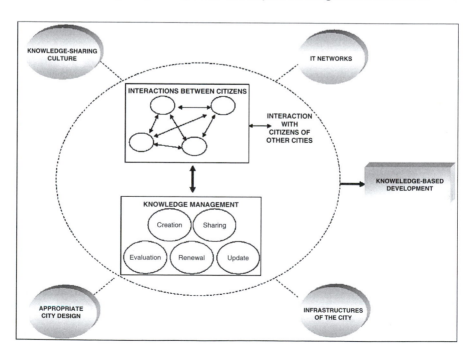

Main Benefits

Forecasts for future cities tend to take for granted the continuity of the industrial capitalist model that became dominant by the end of the 20th century. Cities, which are developing based on this model, become bigger and bigger, demanding increasingly greater inputs and generating growing outputs and waste. The end prospect for any such approach is inevitably the environmental, social, and economical collapse, as cities surpass the manageable limits for superimposed growth (Carrillo, 2004). It is obvious that this model of development is no longer functional. On the contrary, the advantages of knowledge-based development for human societies have been particularly emphasized in the literature during the beginning of the 21st century (Carrillo, 2002, 2004; Malone and Yohe, 2002). This development is environmentally sustainable, economically equitable, and socially responsible.

In this context, the main advantage of a knowledge city is that, by definition, it functions in such a way that is in favor of its knowledge-based development. The benefits of a knowledge city, on a more local scale, are the following:

- strong dynamics of innovation across all sectors of economic and social activity;
- better educational services;
- citizens are actively involved in their city's development, its identity, and its unique character;
- a more sustainable economy;
- creation of a tolerant environment toward minorities and immigrants, etc. (see Ergazakis et al., 2004b, for further details).

Moreover, a knowledge city contributes to the better functioning of democracy, by online knowledge-sharing among all citizens, by the provision of inexpensive, real-time access to consistent, up-to-date information facilities, by providing support for online debates, etc. The "digital divide" is replaced with "digital inclusion" and the benefits of technology flow to all members of the community.

Case Studies: Six Successful Knowledge Cities

Our study includes the analysis of six cities that are considered successful knowledge cities globally.

Barcelona (Ploeger, 2001)

In 1999 the Barcelona City Council, being aware of the new challenges imposed by the knowledge society, designed a strategic plan for the development of the city (Barcelona, 1999). The main target was to place Barcelona into the leading group of urban regions in the new information and knowledge society of the 21st century. A general council and an executive board were appointed as responsible for the implementation of the plan. All vital agencies in Barcelona were committed to this main goal and participated in the executive board with more than 215 representatives.

The executive board formalized the contents of the strategic plan, defined performance indicators, and identified which institutions would be responsible for implementation of the priority actions. Five strategic lines were chosen, with main points being "knowledge" and "own strengths" of Barcelona. Strategic line three involved the concept of "city of knowledge." It must be noted that in this strategic plan, culture was outlined as being the "motor of a knowledge city." A new councilor was added to the city's political structure, to work horizontally within the city administration and to be responsible for the project called "City of Knowledge." Its main task was to promote the development of Barcelona as a knowledge city, to make this concept an integral part of the policies of other departments—culture, tourism, and urban development—and to mobilize the entire system of stakeholders. Today, 1.6 million residents and more than 200 institutions are involved in developing and implementing the strategy (Montréal, 2003).

Private sector's initiatives and actions were important to the success of the whole effort. The City of Barcelona stimulated the private sector with two types of measures: by providing the necessary infrastructure—advanced communication networks, energy infrastructure, transport systems, etc.—and by encouraging the development of buildings for "knowledge businesses." Barcelona Activa, an autonomous company fully sponsored by the City Hall and responsible for the overall economic development of Barcelona, implemented a series of projects related to the "City of Knowledge" strategy (see Ploeger, 2001 for further details). Today, Barcelona is considered as one of the most successful knowledge cities globally (Montréal, 2003; Amidon and Davis, 2004).

Stockholm

The city of Stockholm worked in order to bring together the city, the business community, and the neighboring towns of central Sweden on a common agenda so as to make Stockholm the most exciting region in northern Europe. This agenda involved a series of measures, under the headings "Green City," "Knowledge City," "Events City," "Design City," and "IT City," and it also included an investment of €2 billion primarily in infrastructure and housing.

Under the heading of "Knowledge City," Stockholm is focusing on the development of the fields of biotechnology and biomedicine, in which it is already a European leader. In general, Stockholm is considered as the headquarters of some of the world's most important companies in high-technology sectors. The economic development policies are very knowledge oriented and aim to enhance the service provision toward innovative and new young entrepreneurs (Ploeger, 2001).

The mayor is cooperating with the University and with the business community to create a new urban development area, in the northern part of the city, with almost a thousand new working positions and new residential areas. This "Knowledge city for innovation" model is an integrated model combining the functions of a science park with city functions. This city section will have science, technology, and supporting activities as well as everyday city functions and residential areas side-by-side, and they are physically integrated. The cornerstones of this model are

- world-class science in several fields, as a basis for multidisciplinary collaborative efforts;
- research, innovation, and commercial activities exist in close proximity;
- natural meeting places, functioning as innovation engines;
- location attractive to international scientists and businessmen; and
- easy access thanks to excellent public transportation.

In 2004, Stockholm achieved a position as one of the world's most popular locations for congresses and other events. The city is also an international leader in IT and telecommunications. Moreover, in 2004 one of the city's municipal housing companies decided to provide access to low-cost broadband services to 90,000 citizens. Today, Stockholmers are already the most connected population globally.

Munich (City of Munich, 2003)

There are many different clusters in Munich, consisting of research and development establishments for the documentation and transfer of knowledge. Thanks to its flourishing business environment, Munich enables the continuous transformation of knowledge into business ideas and activities, attracts people with different qualifications, and in this way, mutually advances knowledge and its implementation.

Numerous companies, institutions, and organizations are dealing professionally with knowledge. They produce, organize, transmit or store knowledge. Munich is also the center of many public administration organizations, services, and supplies, mainly those provided by the municipality and also by the state of Bavaria, the federal government, etc. The departments and service centers of the city gather knowledge in important areas for the population and for the companies. Moreover, important public corporations and interest groups from the business sector are located in Munich. They function as contacts, advisers, and knowledge pools for their members. This knowledge is available through the Internet. The whole city is equipped with broadband Internet connections, and the ratio of connections to the Internet is higher than any other major German city.

Research and development in universities, companies, and specialized institutions have a distinguished tradition in Munich. Research and knowledge-intensive firms are grouped into a variety of clusters such as IT, medicine, biotechnology, telecommunications, environment, etc. In addition, the city has a network of over 700 libraries that function as keepers of knowledge and tries to strengthen their role as transmitters of this knowledge.

The city has become a financial center for implementing entrepreneurial ideas. The technology transfer centers promote the transfer of knowledge in various technological areas and ensure that intensive networking takes place between the research and the business sector. In Munich, there is also a dense network of organizations that provides support to people in setting up businesses and new firms.

Finally, there are many museums, galleries, exhibitions, theatres, and art scenes. It is also an international culture and art city. This variety reveals the diversity of the city with respect to the collection and transmission of cultural knowledge.

Montréal (Montréal, 2003)

Montréal has a rich industrial history. However, it has experienced profound changes in recent decades as these industries have gradually been shifted to countries that offer cheaper labor. Montréal, as well as other major urban centers, has been investing increasingly in leading-edge sectors that are driven by innovative, knowledge-based activities. It possesses a concentration of high-knowledge industry segments and professions, a strong number of high-technology fields, and a significant core of creators in arts and culture fields. It also possesses a series of knowledge assets and networks of expertise, such as universities, research centers and numerous institutions and laboratories devoted to creativity and innovation. In the last five years, a number of investments have been made in the Montréal university community. For example, the University of Montréal as well as the Engineering School will operate soon in a new building. This structure will foster interaction of expertise and enhance Montréal's potential as a key center for research into the next-generation products and services.

In terms of innovation capability, Montréal ranks number one in Canada. This high concentration of knowledge-based activity, combined with the climate that is conducive to the production and dissemination of new ideas, also generates a strong culture of creativity and innovation. Moreover, it possesses an employment base capable of attracting and retaining knowledge workers and fostering strong dynamics of innovation.

The existence of universities, high-tech industries, and cultural institutions from different disciplines, the synergy between them, and the overall quality of life position Montréal as one of the successful knowledge cities. This is also the finding of the Montréal's Knowledge City Advisory Committee. However, according to the report of the same Committee, Montréal should leverage its knowledge assets and focus on a series of priority actions and strategies in order to strengthen its status globally as a successful knowledge city.

Dublin (Montréal, 2003; Dublin Chamber of Commerce, 2004)

Dublin overcame considerable handicaps in positioning itself as a knowledge city. The initiatives of Dublin were aimed at positioning the city as a pole of knowledge. These initiatives combined traditional investment with new modes of capitalization and have led to remarkable success.

At the end of the 1980s, Dublin was an industrial city in decline. The unemployment rate was high, and the level of education was low. The challenge of changing this situation and positioning Dublin as a knowledge city was prodigious. The city succeeded in its transition by organizing forces of change around the local development agency and the mayor's office, with support from the Irish Government. Two convergent strategies were followed: the attraction of high-tech multi-national companies and investments and the offering of inexpensive, well-trained labor and tax incentives.

Dublin exploited smartly the advantage of Ireland's membership in the European Union, acquiring access to considerably large amounts of funding in order to aid the financing of the abovementioned strategies. EU membership was also an advantage to Ireland in rendering the country as one of the preferred business destinations for multi-national companies. Dublin also invested in effective e-government initiatives.

The Irish Government played a structure-enhancing, balanced role toward Dublin. It issued powerful guidelines to support the transformations under way, in particular by inciting other Irish cities to follow Dublin's lead and by promoting the creation of local development agencies. Moreover, partnership between the public and the private sectors was vital and a driving force for the success. Despite the fact that Dublin managed to overpass a series of problems and to be developed as a successful knowledge city, it continues its efforts to strengthen its position as one of the leading knowledge cities globally. The Dublin Chamber of Commerce (2004) has, at the time of writing, set a strategic agenda in order to make it possible.

Delft (Kraaijestein, 2002)

Delft has a long tradition in industrial activity. The difficulties that the industrial companies faced during the 1970s and 1980s have resulted in a significant drop of employment. The response of the local government to this decline can be distinguished in three phases:

- **Phase 1 (end of 1970s):** During this phase, the objective was to maintain the number of jobs. An active policy was necessary. The importance of the local University of Technology and of TNO (research institute) in the direction of offering business in Delft was recognized. However, this importance was not translated into specific policy measures.

- **Phase 2 (1980s):** Unemployment increased considerably. The city needed to have a clear vision for the future. The project known as "View of Delft" set a new direction. Delft, as a modern center of knowledge, was considered to be one of the strong points for future development.
- **Phase 3:** A study implemented for the city, by TNO-INRO (TNO-INRO, 1990; Knight 1995), named "Delft, the Knowledge City," offered an extensive analysis of the strengths and weaknesses of Delft economy. The main conclusion was that knowledge was one of its strongest points. According to this report, the local government had the responsibility of transforming Delft into a knowledge city, through the promotion of networks linking local business, the university, research institutions, and the local government as partners. In order to bridge the "traditional Delft" and the knowledge sector, a change in culture was needed. Citizens, companies, and social organizations should be actively involved in this cultural shift. In 1996, Delft City Council adopted a main strategy to further develop it as a knowledge city. This strategy could not be accomplished by the city on its own. Practitioners from the "knowledge industry" were invited to take part in the planning process. Knowledge players in town were asked to help define the mission and develop an action plan, financed by the $3 million fund that was made available. Since then, 60 projects have been carried out. The city clustered its knowledge-intensive projects in five streams, which reflect Delft's strengths:

  - Water and Soil
  - Design and Architecture
  - Information Technology
  - Innovative Transport Systems
  - Environmental Technologies.

During the implementation of the strategy, the intention was to strengthen these points and thereby increase employment levels in Delft as well as the familiarity of Delft as a brand. At the time of writing, it was decided to develop a Research and Development Park for high-tech companies at the Technical University campus.

Key Findings and Observations

The results of our comparisons are presented in Table 1. The "Common Features" column includes qualitative statements that seem to be the common features among successful knowledge cities. These statements are either derived from literature or based on our own observations. The "Source" column provides the literature source for each qualitative statement. It is certainly difficult to track the ultimate origin of each observation in the literature. Consequently, we have presented those studies that have discussed a given statement.

A "+" means that the case study supports the statement, while a "−" means that it does not support it. Our findings and observations are divided into two main categories: development and operation. The features that belong to the "Development" category are considered by the authors as being of crucial importance for the design and development of a knowledge city. The features belonging to the operation category are also of major importance for the successful operation of a knowledge city. The features belonging to the "Operation" category are also of major importance for the successful operation of a knowledge city.

Table 1: Common features among knowledge cities

Common Features	Source	Barcelona	Stockholm	Munich	Montréal	Dublin	Delft
Development							
Political and societal will is indispensable	Montréal, 2003	+	+	+	+	+	+
Strategic vision and development plan is crucial	Montréal, 2003	+	+	+	+	+	+
Financial support and strong investments are necessary	Montréal, 2003	+	+	+	+	+	+
Setting-up of agencies to promote the development of knowledge-based regions is essential	Engels, 2003	+	+	+	+	+	+
International, multi-ethnic character of the city is necessary	SGS Economics, 2002 and Florida, 2002	+	+	+	+	+	+
Metropolitan website is very important	Montréal, 2003	+	+	−	−	+	−
Value creation to citizens is indispensable	Montréal, 2003	+	+	+	+	+	+
Creation of urban innovation engines is significant	Dvir, 2003	+	+	+	+	+	+
Assurance of knowledge society rights of citizens is substantial	Viale, 2004	+	+	+	+	−	−
Operation							
Low cost access to advanced communication networks is imperative	SGS Economics, 2002; Dublin Chamber of Commerce, 2004	+	+	+	+	−	+
Research excellence is indispensable	SGS Economics, 2002;	+	+	+	+	+	+
Existence of public libraries' network is necessary	Barcelona, 1999	+	+	+	+	+	+

Development

Political and Societal Will Is Indispensable

In all the cases examined, there was a sense of social urgency, a belief in the necessity for change, in order to reposition the city in the knowledge era, as a response to difficult situations such as the decline of traditional industries (e.g., industrial sector in Dublin) or the scarcity of local resources (e.g., raw materials are absent in Stockholm) (Montréal, 2003). This societal will for change, which can be characterized as the spark for any further action, must be translated into political will. A city cannot succeed in its effort to develop as a knowledge city without clear support from higher levels of government and local leadership.

Strategic Vision and Development Plan Is Crucial

Any attempt to transform a city into a knowledge city is doomed to failure if it is not guided by a clear strategic vision. This strategic vision should incorporate and take into account the entirety of in-depth knowledge concerning the city status. Therefore, it is compiled by community leaders and actors being responsible for the city's future and results to a set of specific objectives and a series of measures and actions. Top-tier knowledge cities typically choose to target a few sectors only, but set ambitious goals for each. They also seek to balance the interests of these sectors against available resources and the competitiveness of the metropolitan area. Finally, they target at the development of a quality system of higher education, quality of citizen's life, and advanced social services (Montréal, 2003). All the cases examined in our study had this common feature.

Financial Support and Strong Investments Are Necessary

Other major conditions for success are the financial support and strong investments for the implementation of the strategic goals. Before the implementation of any actions or measures related to the strategic plan, the appropriate funding of the initiatives should have been ensured. Through marketing actions, the city can attract outside investments (Montréal, 2003). In all the cases examined, the cities have obtained financial support from public and private resources, by applying various tax schemes and by attracting public funding at the national and supranational level.

Setting-up of Agencies to Promote the Development of Knowledge-Based Regions Is Essential

According to Engels (2003), the setting-up of agencies that promote the development of knowledge-based regions is essential for a knowledge city to succeed. These agencies can be technology foundations, research centers and institutions, technology parks, universities, etc. They may be involved in different kinds of activities such as designing and implementing projects, conducting of research and strengthening of scientific co-operation and knowledge sharing, attracting and retaining knowledge workers, sustaining economical development, marketing of the knowledge city concept, etc. In all the cases examined, there were agencies responsible for the promotion of the development of knowledge-based regions.

International, Multi-Ethnic Character of the City Is Necessary

For a knowledge city to succeed, it must also be built on diversity. Florida (2002) explains that creatively talented individuals prefer to live in cities with populations characterized by diversity, tolerance, and openness, because such an atmosphere stimulates cross-fertilization of ideas and practices and promotes faster flow of knowledge. Consequently, it is a fundamental aspect of any knowledge city. In addition, according to a technical report derived from a research project (SGS Economics, 2002), the success of many knowledge cities can be traced back to positive attitudes toward immigration. Knowledge cities know how to listen and find ways to support the different backgrounds, views, cultures, and experiences of their citizens, which make a real contribution to new ideas and innovations. All these characteristics can be found in the cities examined.

Metropolitan Website Is Very Important

Effective metropolitan website development, which responds in an integrated way to citizens' needs and expectations in their search for information and their desire to assimilate into different communities, is also important (Montréal, 2003). A knowledge city's creativity and appeal are reflected in the quality of its website, and, according to the same Committee, should have the following features:

- a single portal, instead of several sites for the various municipal bodies;
- a modern, visually appealing site, responding to usability criteria;
- offering of effective e-government services.

Our study generally verified this conclusion, but some cities' websites do not have the characteristics referred above. However, in their strategic plans it is stated that they will proceed in their transformation toward this direction.

Value Creation to Citizens Is Indispensable

According to the Montréal Knowledge City Advisory Committee (2003) one of the indispensable pre-requisites of a successful knowledge city is to offer opportunities for value creation to its citizens. Examples of such practices are creation of "microcosms of creativity," establishment of spaces for ongoing societal dialog, and building of comprehensive, high-quality websites and networks among knowledge cities. According to the same Committee, a knowledge city is also distinguished by the pace of assimilation, use, dissemination, and sharing of new types of knowledge, the promotion of which in turn ensures that they rapidly acquire economic and social value. Fully agreeing with this observation, we also realized that the value creation to citizens is highly appreciated by them and can render them active supporters of the knowledge city concept.

Creation of Urban Innovation Engines Is Significant

According to Dvir (2003), "an urban innovation engine is a system that can trigger, generate, foster and catalyze innovation in the city." It is a complex system that includes people, relationships, values, processes, tools, and technological, physical, and financial infrastructure. Some examples of urban constructs that can serve as innovation engines are the Library, the Café, the Stock Exchange, the Town Hall, the University, the Museum, etc. However, not every such construct plays the role of a true innovation engine. There is always a unique combination of intangible factors that turn a specific ordinary urban construct into an innovation engine. This, for example, might include a strategic intention, an explicit vision to use it as innovation engine, an urgent need or challenge, a stimulating physical space, etc. (Dvir, 2003; Dvir and Pasher, 2004). The analysis of the case studies indicates that, indeed, the creation of urban innovation engines was of major significance for their success.

Assurance of Knowledge Society Rights of Citizens Is Substantial

According to Viale (2004), a knowledge-based city must ensure, among others, the following information and knowledge society rights of its citizens:

- **Accessibility rights.** The city must guarantee access to broadband networks for all citizens.
- **Information rights.** Accessibility to user-friendly, highly understandable, complete, diversified, up-to-date, transparent public information must be ensured.
- **Education and training rights.** All citizens must have rights to training in order to effectively benefit from services and available knowledge, through information and communications technology (ICT).
- **Participation rights.** Citizens should have the right to a transparent public administration at all levels of decision-making. Public administration must be committed to fostering citizen's participation and to strengthening civil society.

In the case of Dublin and Delft, the strengthening of the accessibility and participation rights of their citizens is still one of their strategic goals.

Operation

Low-Cost Access to Advanced Communication Networks Is Imperative

Knowledge cities must ensure low-cost and integrated access to advanced communication networks and broadband services for all citizens. Well-developed communication networks sustain the nurturing of knowledge. Connectivity is an essential feature of a knowledge city, and it is facilitated by broadband services equally accessible for organizations and individuals at all rungs of the economic ladder (SGS Economics, 2002; Dublin Chamber of Commerce, 2004). Almost all of the cases examined have this common feature.

Research Excellence Is Indispensable

Research excellence concerns the capacity to create new knowledge principally but not exclusively, in the areas of science and technology. Research excellence provides the platform for new knowledge-based goods and services (SGS Economics, 2002). A successful knowledge city is primarily notable for the wealth of its acquired knowledge, which essentially revolves around its research centres and learning institutions. Knowledge production proceeds largely from what are known as a city's engines of economic development such as its research centres and universities (Montréal, 2003). In the cases examined, the cities' efforts to become knowledge cities were always accompanied by systematic efforts to develop advanced research capabilities in different clusters.

Existence of Public Libraries Network Is Necessary

According to the 3rd Strategic Plan for the Development of the City of Barcelona (Barcelona, 1999), a basic attribute of a knowledge city is the existence of a public libraries network. Libraries are not only about archiving the intellectual achievements of past generations but can also serve as a place of innovation. They can be active, lively places, where knowledge may be created and exchanged, ideas may be generated through conversations, and innovation can occur (Dvir and Pasher, 2004).

Conclusion

The advantages of a knowledge city on global and local scales are really substantial and attractive, which cannot be ignored by the policy makers and researchers. In this way, this concept has begun to attract the interest of the research community and practitioners.

Our main effort in this chapter is to draw a pattern of recurrence of significant features among knowledge cities. For this purpose, our study was focused on the analysis of six successful knowledge cities. The key findings were expressed as 12 preliminary conclusions for building successful knowledge cities. Most of these statements are of crucial importance for the design and development of a knowledge city, while the others are of major significance for the successful operation of a knowledge city.

In terms of future research, it would be interesting and useful to deepen the analysis made by several researchers and look for more fundamental reasons behind these observations. The development of such theory will give more confidence to the observations and provide a general framework where the results of case studies can be positioned.

References

Amidon, D. and Davis, B. (2004). Entovation: Get in the zone, *Knowledge Management Magazine*, vol. 8, issue 2, pp. 26–28, available at: http://www.kmmagazine.com/.

Barcelona. (1999). Pla Estrategic Economic Social de Barcelona (en la perspective 1999–2005), *Associacio pla estrategic de Barcelona & Ajuntament de Barcelona.*

Carrillo, F. J. (2002). Capital systems: Implications for a global knowledge agenda, *Journal of Knowledge Management*, vol. 6, no. 4, pp. 379–399.

Carrillo, F. J. (2004). Capital cities: A taxonomy of capital accounts for knowledge cities, *Journal of Knowledge Management*, vol. 8, no. 5, pp. 28–46.

City of Munich. (2003) *Munich, City of Knowledge*, Department of Labour and Economic Development, Munich.

Dublin Chamber of Commerce. (2004). *Dublin 2020: Our Vision for the Future of the City*, April.

Dvir, R. (2003). Innovation engines for knowledge cities: Historic and contemporary snap shots, available at: www.knowledgeboard.com.

Dvir, R. and Pasher, E. (2004). Innovation engines for knowledge cities: An innovation ecology perspective, *Journal of Knowledge Management*, vol. 8, no. 5, pp. 16–27.

Engels, R. (2003). The Berlin Strategy: Develop our strengths – manage our weaknesses, *Presentation to the Value of Cities International Conference*, Deputy Managing Director, IHK Berlin.

Ergazakis, K., Karnezis, K., Metaxiotis, K. and Psarras, J. (2004a). Knowledge management in enterprises: A research agenda, *Intelligent Systems in Accounting, Finance & Management* (accepted paper, under publication).

Ergazakis, K., Metaxiotis, K. and Psarras, J. (2004b). Towards knowledge cities: Conceptual analysis and success stories, *Journal of Knowledge Management*, vol. 8, no. 5, pp. 5–15.

Florida, R. (2002). *The Rise of the Creative Class*, New York: Basic Books.

Knight, R. (1995). Delft Kennisstad concept, Knowledge-based development: Policy and planning implications for cities, *Urban Studies*, no. 2, pp. 243–245.

Kraaijestein, M. (2002). Delft: From industrial city to knowledge city. Local economic policy in Delft, the Netherlands, *Urban History Conference*, Edinburgh.

Malone, T. F. and Yohe, G. W. (2002). Knowledge partnerships for a sustainable, equitable and stable society, *Journal of Knowledge Management*, vol. 6, no. 4, pp. 368–378.

Metaxiotis, K. and Psarras, J. (2004a) E-Government: New concept, big challenge, success stories, *Electronic Government, an International Journal*, vol. 1, no. 2, pp. 141–151.

Metaxiotis, K. and Psarras, J. (2004b) Applying knowledge management in higher education: The creation of a learning organisation, *Journal of Information and Knowledge Management*, vol. 2, no. 4, pp. 1–7.

Montréal Knowledge City Advisory Committee, Montréal, Knowledge City. (2003). Report prepared by the Montréal, Knowledge City Advisory Committee, available at: http://www.montrealinternational.com/docs/MtlSavoir_En.pdf.

Ploeger, R. (2001). Innovation and new entrepreneurship: A cross national survey of policies in 13 European cities, *Technical Report*, Amsterdam study centre for the Metropolitan Environment, available at: http://www.ez.amsterdam.nl/eurocities/.

Rubenstein-Montano, B., Liebowitz, J., Buchwalter, J., McGaw, D., Newman, B. and Rebeck, K. (2001). SMARTVision: A knowledge-management methodology, *Journal of Knowledge Management*, vol. 5, no. 4, pp. 300–310.

SGS Economics and the Eureka Project. (2002). Towards a knowledge city strategy, *Technical Report prepared for Melbourne City Council.*

TNO-INRO (Instituut voor Ruimtelijke organisatie). (1990). Delft Kennisstad concept, *Technical Report*, 1990, Delft.

Viale, J. (2004). TeleCities – a framework for the Knowledge Based Society: A way forward?, *Presentation at Global Forum*, Malmo.

Chapter 2

A Comparative Framework for Knowledge Cities

Samuel David Martínez, *Department of Computer Sciences, Tecnológico de Monterrey, México*

Introduction

During the last two decades of the 20th century, worldwide economies have experienced deep changes in structural terms. These changes are mainly related to the way in which the economy creates value originating in the so-called knowledge-based economy.

The knowledge-based economy operates in parallel with the traditional economy, and in many cases intersects directly with it. This allows the continuous innovation of products and services. The knowledge-based economy has resulted in new organizational structures that promote the sharing of human capital expertise. However, what truly differentiates today's knowledge-based economy is the acceleration and intensification of the production, use, and dissemination of new knowledge and new technologies (Michaud, 2003).

Alain Lapointe (2003) of HEC Montréal wrote, "The new economy is characterized by acceleration of the trends that have led us to transform our modes of production and organization." He remarks that the knowledge-based economy is part of a historical evolution. Within that context, in recent years many cities around the world have started up initiatives that involve debates, shared efforts and set strategies in order to improve their competitive position at a national, continental, and international scale from a knowledge-based perspective. Richard Florida (2002) believes the economic competition criterion for cities with the new economy is based on their capacity to attract, hold, and integrate talented and creative individuals.

As a result, cities compete in three main areas:

(1) The quality of local culture (a city with unique cultural vitality, ethnic diversity, and social tolerance);
(2) A dense labor market (job abundance and additional opportunities for knowledge workers);
(3) The presence of local facilities and attractions which are highly valued by knowledge workers (access to outdoor activities and artistic events).

The initial direction followed by cities in the era of knowledge generally consists of investments in high technology, investments in traditional infrastructure, and strategic investments in arts and culture. Each city is different with regard to investments and implementation methods.

The main purpose of this chapter is to establish a comparative framework among the different knowledge cities' initiatives around the world from the Capital Systems model's perspective (Carrillo, 2002). This analysis will also compare some of the different denotations the term "Knowledge City" (KC) has been assigned with, and how this has influenced diverse cities' initiatives. In addition, two other models are also briefly described. Based on these, KCs are compared. Finally, there is a brief comparison about strategies and stakeholders that had been involved in the development of KC initiatives.

This chapter draws on the exercise reported by González et al. (2004) with regard to existing public information and databases regarding KCs and Knowledge-Based Development (KBD). As a follow-up to that report, the Knowledge Cities Clearinghouse (http://www.knowledgecities.com) continues to offer probably the richest source of information on KCs worldwide, across eight categories:

(1) glossary of KC- and KBD-related terms,
(2) KC and KBD initiatives,
(3) related international agencies and organizations,
(4) KC and KBD value dimensions and indicators,
(5) related international rankings,
(6) special editions on KCs and KBD,
(7) bibliography, and
(8) related websites.

Concepts, Definitions, and Contexts of a Knowledge City

The cities' knowledge context is the first significant factor to better understand the dynamics and diffusion of a KC initiative. Therefore, it is necessary to consider the following significant aspects according to Angehrn (2004):

- **Context:** Urban communities normally have heterogeneous populations (in terms of individual competitions, incentives, and objectives), as well as a great variety of relationship networks (like families, neighbors, and professional networks) and a government mechanism (electing or appointing its representatives, having processes for making decisions at a regional, national, or international level, depending on the type of democracy, or some other type of government).
- **Creation of knowledge and its dynamics of exchange:** In urban communities, knowledge is regularly linked and influenced by remote or recent history, and this is reflected in the existing social and architectonic spaces.
- **Dynamics of exchange:** In urban communities, aside from revolutions, change is typically slow—a gradual process determined by power relationships among the community members, their representatives, and their main agents.

The second factor to be considered is recognizing that the concept of KC is a vital component in strategic plans for cities. In one way or another, the KC idea is discussed in several strategic and vision plans, as well as in the statements of policies for different cities.

Below, you will find some of the most common terms used by different authors to describe a KC or closely related initiatives:

Technopolis

Joe Horn and Scott Henson provide alternative ideas of this term, as quoted by Okubo (1998). For Joe Horn, it is a euphemism for the creation of a national industrial policy. For Scott Henson, it reflects the vision of liberal economic and social planners to create a new form of city-state centered around high-tech industry. Okubo himself suggests the following as characteristic criteria for features of a technopolis: "Incorporates technological advances in a basic infrastructure and utilities; comprises institutions and resources that hasten the application and diffusion of technological innovation; enhances or protects the quality of life and overall human condition; and links the inhabitants of the technopolis globally for the widest possible range of forms of communication and transaction."

Intelligent City

Toh (1999), from the Infocomm Development Authority (IDA), claims that in an Intelligent City, the government has the responsibility to ensure that the community has access to advanced information and communication services. Additionally, she suggests that Intelligent Cities work toward positioning their citizens, businesses, and public-sector to prosper in the Information Age. She also thinks that this kind of cities embrace the growth industries of tomorrow and work to create the advanced infrastructure of telecommunications and IT needed to gain a competitive edge in attracting these growth industries that create a knowledge-based economy.

An alternative perspective has been offered by Komninos (2002). He defines intelligent cities as islands and communities where innovation processes meet the digital world and the applications of the information society.

Knowledge Society

In a Panel on the concept of "knowledge society," Venkatasubramanian (2003) mentioned that a Knowledge Society makes greater use of technology of information and communication technologies and increases skills and knowledge of people to achieve social and individual development. Drucker (1994) suggests that in the knowledge society the access to the acquisition of knowledge will no longer be dependent on obtaining a prescribed education at any given age.

Learning City

Meg Holden and Sean Connelly (2004) indicate that the learning city is a city that approaches sustainable development as an ongoing educational process. This kind of learning is an essential social function of the city. Although social learning needs to occur throughout the city, the urban institution best suited for reinvigorating the learning city is the school. The learning city has four critical dimensions: partnering, serving, designing, and teaching.

Knowledge City

For the Australian firm SGS (2002) the term "KC" is shorthand for a regional economy driven by high value-added exports created through research, technology and brain-power. Edvinsson (1999) defines Knowledge City as "a city that is purposefully designed to encourage the nurturing of knowledge."

Michaud (2003) claims that a knowledge city is notable primarily for the wealth of its acquired knowledge, which essentially revolves around its learning institutions, research centers, businesses and creators. Carrillo (2004) defines a Knowledge City as a permanent settlement of relatively higher rank in which the citizenship undertakes a deliberate, systematic attempt to identify and develop its capital system in a balanced, sustainable manner.

In this study we will use Carrillo's definition of a KC, as I consider it to be the most comprehensive. Eventually other concepts like Technopolis, Learning City, etc., may be recognized within the encompassing notion of a Knowledge City.

Models for a Comparative Framework

Knowledge cities' initiatives carry out the transition of the cities' current status, from economies based on physical production to requirements of the knowledge-based economy. To do this, models that allow the measurement, administration, comparison and the upcoming development of strategies this new economy become necessary.

Next, three of these models are to be described, highlighting their connection with the Capital System Model to be used later in the comparison of knowledge cities' initiatives.

1   IC Navigator Model for Municipalities
This model is based on the Skandia Navigator model (IC Navigator model) initially created and applied by Edvinsson and Malone (1997) in the Swedish Insurance Company Skandia. Nowadays, this model is not just an IC model for companies, but also a model that evaluates the IC of a country or city.

The IC Navigator model provides a balanced and holistic outlook of both financial and intellectual capital (Figure 1). According to this model, there are four areas of focus with regard to intellectual capital:

(1) **Market Capital:** These are those markets with which the city has national and international contacts. Assets in this focal point include customer-city loyalty, the satisfaction expressed by strategic customers, the value of brands.

(2) **Process Capital:** Cooperation and flow of knowledge require intellectual structural aspects (software, information systems, databases, laboratories, an organizational structure, and a management structure), which keep and increase the level of human capital.

(3) **Human Capital:** This refers to the knowledge, experience, intuition and skills individuals have to complete the tasks and goals of the city. They also include cultural values and the city's philosophy. Human Capital is the individual's property, not the city's.

(4) **Renovation and Development Capital:** This reflects the city's capacity, the current investment in its future development, and its renovation through the exploitation of its competitive strength in future markets. Renewal and Development assets include investments in research and development, patents, trademarks, start-up companies.

This model has been applied to the evaluation of countries like Sweden and Israel and the countries in the Arab region.

Figure 1

IC Navigator House Metaphor. Source: Edvinsson and Malone, 1997

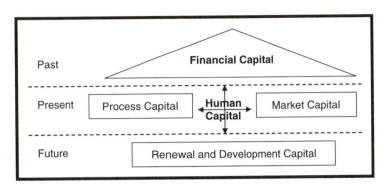

2   Cities Intellectual Capital Benchmarking System (CICBS)

The CICBS is a methodology and framework to evaluate and manage the cities' IC and it is highly dependable of IC Navigator model for countries (Viedma, 2004).

The CICBS has two approaches (Figure 2). The first, called Cities General Intellectual Capital Model (CGICM), is a transversal approach that covers all of the economical activities carried out at the city or all of the economical microclusters for which the economical activities are performed. This goes through the following stages: vision, core activities, core competencies, indicators and intellectual capital categories. These IC categories cover the following value dimensions: financial capital, human capital, process capital, market capital, and renewal and development capital.

The second approach, "Cities Specific Intellectual Capital Model (CSICM)," is a longitudinal one, which is established with each of the city's important economical activities or with the relevant economical microcluster, in a particular and distinctive way. Factors included in microclusters are as follows: vision, demand segment, output, products and services, processes, core competencies, and professional core competencies.

This model has been applied the City of Mataró in Spain.

3   KC Capital System

The model was originated as a Generic System of Capitals following the Knowledge-based Value Systems approach to Knowledge Management and Knowledge-Based Development (Carrillo, 1998). From the perspective of the generic system of capitals, and considering several possible levels of analysis (e.g., age and history, endogenous forces vs. exogenous forces, critical incidents, relative level of development), as well as the specific dimensions of capital for each city, it is possible to create a taxonomy of capitals for knowledge cities (Carrillo, 2004).

The Capital System model builds upon prior inductive IC approaches to try and integrate a basic set of capital categories from which all possible variations can be derived. The CS model has been applied to both organizational and social entities.

Table 1 is a summary of a Capital System for any Knowledge City, which can be classified in a more detailed way depending on the city. Chapter 4 in this book explains in further detail the KC Capital System.

Figure 2

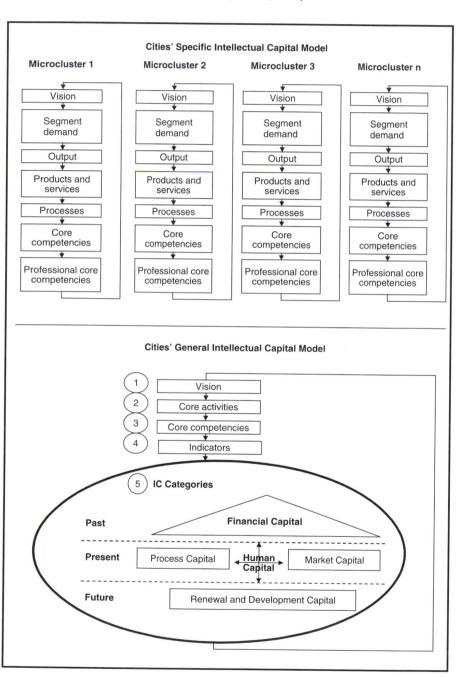

CICBS Model (Viedma, 2004)

Table 1: Basic categories of a Capital System (Carrillo, 2002)

Metacapitals

- Referential
  - Identity: clarity and differentiation.
  - Intelligence: external entities and events.
- Articulation
  - Relational: social integration and cohesion.
  - Financial: economic sustainability.

Human Capitals

- Individual base
  - Health: biological inheritance and physical development.
  - Education: holistic personal development.
- Collective base
  - Live Culture(s): wealth of cultural inheritance.
  - Evolutive capacities: cultural fitness.

Instrumental Capitals

- Tangible
  - Natural: exiting before the settlement.
  - Artificial: created or incorporated by settlers: infrastructure.
- Intangible
  - Organization and production systems in: non-electronic repositories.
  - Organization and production systems in: electronic repositories.

This model has been used to assess the knowledge capital of cities like Manchester in the UK, Legazpi in Spain and Monterrey in Mexico. It will be used as a knowledge value framework for making the comparison among cities in this analysis.

Comparative Framework

In order to carry out a comparison of knowledge cities' initiatives, the work carried out by González et al. (2004) was updated. That report identified the value dimensions taken into account by some cities, countries and international organizations around the world willing to engage in formal knowledge-based development initiatives.

It is important to stress that the results of this comparison are limited to information available in public sources, revealing plans of the knowledge cities' initiatives. Nevertheless, it is conceivable that restricted information to which we had no access may include a greater level of detail and possibly alter results.

The first point of comparison is made from the perspective of the System of Capitals at the most aggregated level (Level 1) which includes only 3 categories: (1) Metacapitals, (2) Human Capital, and (3) Instrumental Capital (Figure 3).

Figure 3 shows that most knowledge cities' initiatives consider Instrumental Capital as the base for the development of their strategic plans. Considering this, it is possible to suggest that we might be talking about KC's initiatives of a Technopolis type, where traditional investments on physical infrastructure give the city international prestige (financial centers, convention centers), and high technology is a fundamental element. We have clear examples of these initiatives in Chicago, Pittsburgh, Cleveland, Barcelona, and Dublin.

Figure 3

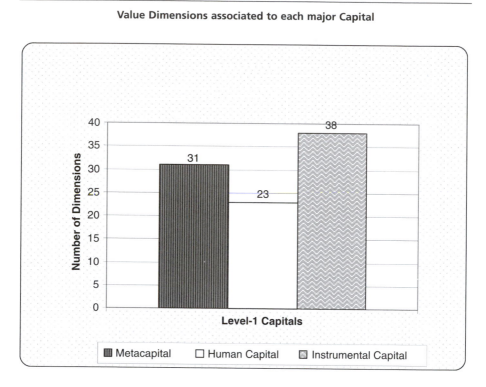

Value Dimensions associated to each major Capital

With regard to human capital, the figure shows that this is the less considered issue by most initiatives, but this may be rather misleading, since, if we were to subsume within human capital the 18 value dimensions related to relational capital found in metacapitals, then value dimensions in metacapitals would be minimal. Therefore, Human Capital is the second most common approach in number of initiatives, as it is later shown in Figure 5. Here the concept of a Learning City where activities for the development of knowledge generation and transfer institutions (higher education institutions, R&D centers, technology transfer centers, community development institutions, etc.) and educational options for life are of particular relevance. Some examples of related initiatives are found in Austin, Boston, Munich, Dublin, Seattle, and San Francisco.

Regarding metacapitals, as we can see, there are very few instances to be found within the initiatives under study. This circumstance is mainly due to the prevailing views on KM which are still object-centered and, at most, subject-centered (Carrillo, 1998), thus leaving the broader and strategic context-centered approaches largely out of the current scenario. In third-generation, context-based KC initiatives, metacapitals are deliberately and extensively developed, placing emphasis in activities for participating in democratic life, street life and cultural and historical value dimensions. Preliminary examples of initiatives pursuing a wider KC sense are Zaragoza and Melbourne.

Another comparison with greater level of depth is observed in Figure 4. This shows the System of Capitals at the next level of dissaggregation (Level 2) which allows a clearer idea of the approach taken by each Knowledge City's initiative. In this Level, we are able to see the three abovementioned categories, but now expanded into:

    1.1.1) Identity Capital
    1.1.2) Intelligence Capital
    1.2.1) Relational Capital
    1.2.2) Financial Capital
    2.1) Human Capital Individual Base
    2.2) Human Capital Collective Base
    3.1) Tangible Instrumental Capital
    3.2) Intangible Instrumental Capital

Figure 4 shows that Instrumental Capital, in its tangible component, continues to be the most important aspects of the initiatives. But, even more interesting is the fact that the initiatives consider Relational Capital as a very important one in their plans. This involves aspects like social cohesion, equality and legality, national and international image, and both, national and international treaties and agreements. On the other hand, Intelligence Capital is the most generally neglected. This capital focuses on aspects like current and future trends, both internal and external. Another capital that most initiatives do consider is Identity Capital, even though reduced to basic historical, current, and future reference basis for the city.

Figure 5 shows a comparison with regard to the holistic or integral degree of the initiatives under study.

Here, results show that most of the initiatives have in their Instrumental and Human Individual Base Capitals the angular aspects for the development of their initiatives, and all the other capitals are merely complementary poles for that central axis. At this point, it is important to compare the results of the Figures 3 and 4, where we can see that most of the initiatives' current focus is on Instrumental Capital, perhaps in

Figure 4

Value Dimensions associated to each capital: Level-2

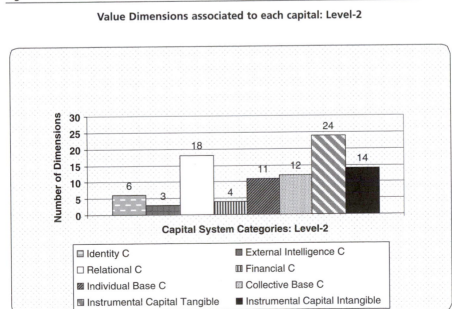

Figure 5

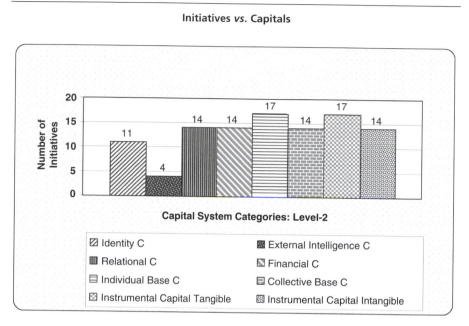

Initiatives *vs.* Capitals

order to improve Human Capital levels. Then, it may be observed that Instrumental Capital is mainly the means for developing and improving the capacities of the Human Capital, and that they are closely interrelated.

A last element of comparison in current analysis shows the value dimensions identified by each initiative and how they are structured according to the System of Capitals (Table 2).

In this table, knowledge cities' initiatives like Barcelona, Malaga and Bilbao are not only highlighted as the most intensive ones with regard to the number of value dimensions in their specific contexts, but as the most integral ones from the System of Capitals' perspective, since all the capitals have been taken into account.

Nevertheless, it is important to note that the absence of value dimensions in certain capital may be due to the fact that a particular initiative is not considering this as an explicit strategic factor. Certainly, the particular Knowledge City concept adopted by such initiatives, like the alternative concepts introduced at the beginning of this chapter, also determine the value dimensions to be considered.

Comparison of the development of strategies for implementing knowledge cities' initiatives is given in Table 2.

Finally, when comparing different Knowledge Cities' initiatives from around the world, a common element, more than a differentiator, is the way in which these initiatives have been carried out. It is possible to identify, in a general way, the following actions to carry out knowledge-based development strategies for those cities:

(1) Embrace Knowledge-Based Development as a conceptual and value framework.
(2) Integrate all major stakeholders from the initiative's birth throughout its development.
(3) Recognize all major value elements (Capital System).

Table 2: Knowledge cities comparative table

City/Organization	Metacapitals				Human Capital		Instrumental Capital	
	Referential		Articulation					
	Identity 1.1.1	External Intelligence 1.1.2	Relational 1.2.1	Financial 1.2.2	Individual Base 2.1	Collective Base 2.2	Tangible 3.1	Intangible 3.2
Buenos Aires	•••	•	•••	•	•••	•••	•	••••
Andalucia Cities	•		•••	••	•••	•	••••••••••	•••
Bilbao	••••	•	••••	•	•••••	•••	••••••••••	••
Birmingham			••••••••••	••	•••••••	•••••	••••••••	
Barcelona								
Sao Paulo	•••		•	•	••••••	•••••	•••••	•••••
Boston								
Edinburgh	•		••••	•	•••••••	•	•••••	•••
Korea								

Table 2: Knowledge cities comparative table (*Continued*)

City/Organization	Metacapitals				Human Capital		Instrumental Capital	
	Referential		Articulation		Individual Base 2.1	Collective Base 2.2	Tangible 3.1	Intangible 3.2
	Identity 1.1.1	External Intelligence 1.1.2	Relational 1.2.1	Financial 1.2.2				
London	•		••	••	••	•	••	•
Manchester	••			•	•		••	••
Malaga		•	•••	•	•••	••	•••	••
Munich			•••				••	•••
Mataró	•••	•	••	••	••	•	••	••
Progressive Policy Institute			••	•	••	••	•	••
Philadelphia	•		•		••	••	••	•
Tucson				•	•	•	•••	•
Global Urban Observatory					•		•••	
World Bank	•			••	•	•	••••	•

(4) Structure and understand those value elements (where they are, how are they produced, and how they can be maximized).
(5) Advance in the quality of operationalization as understanding advances.
(6) Carry out measurements.
(7) Diagnose gaps between current condition and desired conditions.
(8) Develop strategies for closing gaps or developing capitals potential. Strategies should always include the following: required resources, work plan, key success and failure factors, quality assurance procedures.
(9) Create a monitoring and evaluation system.
(10) Select and appoint evaluation agents.

Some other elements identified in the implementation of strategies in the selected KCs under study are given below:

Intended city development must be influenced by a desire of continuous improvement having as main axes innovation and competitiveness, as well as the commitment of participation and collaboration of all agents involved, particularly citizens themselves.

It is also evident that most of the initiatives are led by local government. Often, the agency leading the KC project is the same one coordinating urban and economic development activities in conjunction with associated councils and committees, including private sector and other voluntary organizations. Therefore, the role of government with regard to the management of strategies is crucial, and the shared responsibility of other agents should not be overlooked.

In this sense, a further common element present in all initiatives is the sharing of responsibility with all stakehoders. This is essential to jointly build support and consensus, and even include those agents who do not agree with the initiative, so that they all together, with their constructive contributions and reflexive analytical attitude, communicate and actively participate. Legitimation and alignment need to be built if the initiative is going to have any chance of succeeding.

A key feature of several ongoing initiatives is a well-designed and massive campaign organized by government which includes: what is to be changed, how is it to be changed, who is involved, and how, and expected results. Such an exercise builds public awareness and makes evident the intention of an initiative that is meaningful to all critical agents.

The inclusion of further initiatives or government's projects under the umbrella of the Knowledge City has been found to be common as a leverage factor. Finally, the willingness to make adjustments along the way is another element often foreseen by the initiatives that have been implemented.

Conclusion

This preliminary analysis indicates that although at the moment we can find many city initiatives that call themselves Knowledge Cities, there is an enormous difference in the approaches each of them have taken. The great majority is still working, albeit in a more intensive way, in the development of Technopoles, which seems to constitute an entry level for each city, and may eventually evolve into a distinctive Knowledge City.

On the other hand, although many of the initiatives set a great amount of value dimensions within Instrumental Capital, it is also true that most of the initiatives are actually wider, since they include at least some value dimensions that belong to other capitals. As KCs gain greater understanding and capacity to discriminate the value dimensions involved in knowledge-based development, these dimensions will become explicit and deliberate categories in their frameworks and plans. In this sense, even though the importance of working on Instrumental Capital infrastructure is recognized, this also shows that for all initiatives the key element is the development of Human Capital in its individual base.

This indicates that in the past the cities' views and goals were determined by the tangible components as a factor of development. Nowadays, in the era of knowledge, intangible assets are gradually becoming fundamental and every month more cities added to the known list of formal knowledge cities or knowledge-based development initiatives.

Consequently, future studies will have access to further and deeper information on all significant Knowledge Cities' initiatives. As our understanding of the distinctive value innovated by KCs becomes clearer and more widely recognized, so will our frameworks to describe, develop and assess true knowledge cities.

Acknowledgment

This Chapter would not have been possible without the active support of Carolina Maribel Martínez.

References

Angehrn, A. (2004). Learning-by-playing: Bridging the knowing-doing gap in urban communities. *Intellectual Capital for Communities*, Elsevier/Butterworth-Hienemann.

Carrillo, F. J. (1998). Managing knowledge-based value systems. *Journal of Knowledge Management*, vol. 1, no. 4.

Carrillo, F. J. (2002). Capital systems: Implications for a global knowledge agenda. *Journal of Knowledge Management*, vol. 6, no. 4, October, pp. 379–399.

Carrillo, F. J. (2004). Capital cities: A taxonomy of capital accounts for knowledge cities. *Journal of Knowledge Management*, vol. 8, no. 5.

Drucker, P. (1994). *Knowledge Work and Knowledge Society*, Harvard University, John F. Kennedy School of Government.

Edvinsson, L. (1999). IC of nations for future wealth creation. *Journal of Human Resource Costing and Accounting*, Stockholm University.

Edvinsson, L. and Malone, M. S. (1997). *Intellectual Capital. Realizing Your Company's True Value by Finding its Hidden Roots*, New York: Harper Business.

Florida, R. (2002). *The Rise of the Creative Class*, New York: Basic Books.

Holden, M. and Connelly, S. (2004). *The Learning City*. Urban Sustainability Education and Building Toward WUF Legacy, Simon Fraser University, March 2004, World Urban Forum 2006.

The Knowledge Cities Clearinhouse. Available at http://www.knowledgecities.com.

Komninos, N. (2002). *Intelligent Cities*, London: Spon Press.

Lapointe, A. (2003). La Performance de Montréal dans l'Économie du savoir: unchangement de politique s'impose, Cahier de recherche HEC No. IEA-03-03.

González, R., Martinez, S. and Alvarado, A. (2004). A compilation of resources on knowledge cities and knowledge based development. *Journal of Knowledge Management*, vol. 8, no. 5.

Michaud, P. (2003). *Montréal: Knowledge City*. Report prepared by the Montréal, Knowledge City Advisory Committee.

Okubo, M. (1998). *Future Technopolis Changes its Form-from Visible to Invisible*.

SGS economic & planning (2002). *Knowledge Cities*, Bulletin Urbecon.

Toh, J. (1999). Singapore Awarded First-Ever "Intelligent City" Award by World Teleport Association and Telecommunications Magazine.

Venkatasubramanian, K. (2003). *Knowledge Society*, Elcot.

Viedma, J. M. (2004). Cities' Intellectual Capital Benchmarking System (CICBS): A methodology and a framework for measuring and managing Intellectual Capital of Cities – a Practical Application in the City of Mataró.

Chapter 3

Global Research Centres: An Analysis Based on Bibliometric Indicators

Christian Wichmann Matthiessen, *Institute of Geography, University of Copenhagen, Denmark*

Annette Winkel Schwarz and Søren Find, *Technical Knowledge Centre of Denmark, Denmark*

Recent shifts in industrial geography combined with the advancement of regional and urban competition set focus on different themes. In this chapter, research strength of the major research metropoles of the world is analyzed in general terms because the importance of this theme in regional and urban competition is generally recognized although relations between urban and regional economic growth and knowledge level are far from clear. The present chapter also analyzes the interrelations between the centers using coauthorship as indicator. The aim is to identify the nodal cities of the global research community.

Universities, research institutions, firms, and leaders of (large) urban agglomerations interact at a growing rate in creating a solid knowledge base for their city. They do so because they share the view that the local knowledge base is of increasing importance for urban economic growth and change. They do so also because a high and growing level of investments in research and development is worthwhile for activating the region. And they do so in spite of the "common belief" that distance plays a less and less important role and that access to information is almost universal in the "information society." There has indeed been a remarkable decrease in communication and transportation costs in the latest decades, giving way to networking over long distances. And if one asks scientists about their individual pattern of contacts they will often point out that it is international or even global. However, when added up for scientists of a given region it turns out that the "gravity model" gives the best explanation of contacts with other regions. This implies that short physical distance between scientists is still an important criterion for cooperation. Synergies between ideas and direct face-to-face communication still are major factors of research productivity.

Castells and Hall (1994) write in their book on technopoles of the world: "Cities and regions are being profoundly modified in their structure, and conditioned in their growth dynamics, by the interplay of three major interrelated, historic processes: a technological revolution based on information technologies, the formation of a global economy that works as a unit in a worldwide space for capital, management, labor, technology and markets, and the emergence of a new form of economic production and management characterized by the fact that productivity and competitiveness are increasingly based on the generation and distribution of new knowledge." They also remark that no region can prosper without some level of linkage to sources of innovation and production, and that a new industrial geography with different levels of specialization and diversity of markets is advancing rapidly. In a world economy whose productive infrastructure more and more is made up by information channels, cities and regions are increasingly becoming critical agents of economic development. Cities and regions thus throw themselves into the roles of entrepreneurs. Venturelli (2004) even says that the source of wealth is no longer found in mineral resources and in the creation of capital in plant equipment and manufactured products, but in a different capital: intellectual and creative ideas distributed in different forms over information networks. Creation of wealth in an economy of ideas is derived far less than we imagine from the technological hardware and infrastructure. Rather it is dependent upon the capacity to continually create content or new forms of widely distributed knowledge, for which there is a need to invest in human capital throughout the economy.

Metropolitan regions do concentrate on knowledge. Creative industries are more and more looked upon as the drivers especially of metropolitan growth. Howkins (2002) demonstrates how creative clusters in the United States have impacted economic growth, and Florida (2002) has argued that regions and urban areas with the best economic performance have the largest number of creative workers. The important factor is crossover and integrative effects acquired through proximity and networking. Many authors have discussed methods of measuring creativity, ranking from patents to economic output from the creative economy (publishing, design, software, TV and radio, film). The concentration of human capital, knowledge, and creative capacity in cities has given rise to the terminology of the knowledge-based city (Simmie and Lever, 2002). Lever (2002) distinguishes between tacit knowledge, codified knowledge, and knowledge infrastructure, correlating some composite measures of these three knowledge-base attributes with the economic performance of 19 European cities.

From the first analysis of the strength, interrelations, and nodality of global research centers based on Science Citation Index (SCI) data for 1997–1999, which was presented in Matthiessen, Schwarz, and Find (2002), we found a pattern of research output highly concentrated to a small number of urban units. We also found structured networks of cooperation within the research community with a few strong nodes and identified leaders and followers. We focus on the scientific part of knowledge production as an indicator of creativity. Science Citation Index, 2002–2004, registered 3.1 mio. papers worldwide of which 1.1 mio. had at least one author located in one of the 30 largest research centers. We present an analysis of the structure and geography of the globally top-level research centers. We identify and examine patterns of winners and losers measured absolutely using time series of data pertaining to 1996–1998, 1999–2001 and 2002–2004. We further present and discuss cooperation patterns in the peer communities using data on coauthorship 2002–2004.

Data

Scientific wealth can be analyzed in terms of the fast growing number of research papers and documents. Nations are often taken as units of analysis since statistics are presented on a national scale and can be used as input data. Another reason is that many quantitative studies of research production use the large bibliographic data banks directly. When doing so, the obvious registration unit is again the nation because it is easy to identify the nation in the address of the author of a given publication. In a frequently quoted study, May (1997) used the national research output as a reference to compare productivity and specialization. But in a world of rising importance of regions and cities as sites of competition and as producers of strategic plans, they are also of interest, especially for investors, local planners, and people "selling" cities to identify comparative positions in scientific strength.

In this chapter, a geographical urban delimitation is combined with a systematic use of SCI to derive an arguably significant list of important research centers measured by research output registered under the address of author's institution. Thomson Scientific (Philadelphia, PA) produces the SCI database along with a number of related products. It records, for over 6,300 journals leading in their field and for a large number of conference proceedings and other research publications, all contributions with full bibliographic description, all authors with affiliations, subject codes for journals and references (citations) to the research literature. The on-line version is available as "SciSearch" on major hosts, e.g., DIALOG and STN. Details are given on http://www.isinet.com/products/citation/citsci.html. Recently, a version with extended search facilities has been launched as "Web of Science." Details are given on http://www.isinet.com/prodserv/citation/wosprev.html. There is a large literature on applications of these databases. A number of indicators useful for comparative analysis of R&D productivity and other forms of complex data analysis are discussed in Schwarz et al. (1998). Compilation of data on research is discussed in reports from Eurostat and OECD and the method used here is related to this latter work. Several publications contain definitions and recommendations concerning data compilation with a view to establish indicators for uniform and internationally comparable measures of input, processes, and output of regional R&D and innovation. Starting from OECD handbooks on national indicators, in particular the "Frascati Manual" (OECD, 2002) and the "Oslo Manual" (OECD, 1997), the reports extend the scope to cover regional aspects (Eurostat, 1996, 1997).

The present analysis covers 74 urban units (Matthiessen and Schwarz, 1999; Matthiessen, Schwarz and Find, 2002 for method). They represent the largest scientific centers of the world, measured by output of SCI-registered papers of 2002–2004 in science, medicine, and engineering. International bibliographic databases are useful tools for study of many aspects of the international research system, but the data are not unproblematic, due to various biases of coverage, to different publication patterns in different disciplines and to technical intricacies, like multiple authorships (Schwarz et al., 1998). Multiple authorship is registered so that each author is attributed one bibliographic unit. This implies that papers with several authors count as equally many items in the statistics. While distorting the actual count of papers produced, it accounts for the collaboration links in terms of persons involved. In spite of such problems, our conclusion is that analyses based on bibliometric data can give indications (but indications only) of a quantitative nature and that interpretations must give heed to the shortcomings and biases inherent in the data.

Delimitation of Urban Units

There exists no easy way to obtain comparable data on large cities. National statistical offices delimit urban units by different philosophies—postal services do not provide lists of place names or postal numbers clustered to comparable functional urban units. A series of attempts at constructing a European counterpart to the metropolitan region concept of the United States is still short of results, which can be used for the purpose of comparing the scientific base of large cities. Organizations like NUREC (1994) and the Reclus-Datar group (Reclus-Datar, 1989; Cattan et al., 1994) work on this. Reclus-Datar, a French group, has done the original work on categorizing and analyzing the urban system of the European Union. Also in connection to the "European Union Spatial Planning Mobilization," a contemporary delimitation of functional urban units is discussed (Bengs, 2002; ESPON, 2004). In general, the closest one comes to a generally acceptable definition of the urban unit is the United Nations' urban area concept, but it is purely physical and based on distance between buildings. This widely used UN-definition is actually an anachronistic delimitation of greater urban units, especially when it comes to comparative studies, because distance between buildings does not determine function, although distances influence function. Extension and density in urban regions differ due to tradition, legal factors, physical layout, and development stage.

In default of a general formal or functional definition, we have used a physical concept based on density of population as the basis for identifying a borderline for each large agglomeration conceptualized as a "greater"-urban region. We have used the NUREC-concept and thus added neighboring local units to the urban area defined by the UN-method, and further added additional local units when densities of urbanized areas on detailed topographical maps indicated suburbanization. We have checked this with population figures to find an acceptable extension of the single agglomeration. Delimitations for areas, not included in the NUREC atlas, are estimates. Homogeneity of estimates has been given priority but no precise method has been used. We have further combined neighboring agglomerations to units when transport time between city centers can be judged to be below 45 minutes. This way of delimiting units in a rather generous manner and using a strict rule to aggregate the units combines similar cities which interplay at large (for example, the units of the Rhine–Ruhr area), but also puts together dissimilar cities of little interplay (for example Oxford and Reading). We have been careful not to let our different level of knowledge on the cities influence the exercise.

Research Output: Megacities of the World

For the years 1996–1998, SCI registers 2,792,459 papers on a world basis. Out of these large numbers of papers, 917,708 relate to the 30 largest centers. It must be noted that the two figures can only be compared with caution since papers with authors from more than one city will appear in the statistics for all cities in question. In comparison, the figures for 1999–2001 were 2,930,628 and 995,957, and for 2002–2004, these figures were 3,143,283 and 1,086,453 respectively. As SCI is a dynamic database constantly incorporating new journals and proceedings, growth in figures does not necessarily correspond to a real growth of production. Anyhow, the pattern of concentration is not biased by the dynamics of SCI. The 30 largest cities of the world represented 32.9% of research output for 1996–1998, and 34.6% for 2002–2004. It can be concluded that concentration to the large urban units is an active process.

The top-30 research centers are listed and ranked in Figures 1–3. Concentrations of research output form a distinct pattern, with North America, the northwestern part of Europe, and Japan in dominating positions. National patterns of concentration are obvious, relating to differences in policy over centuries. Nations with a tradition of urban concentration, like France and Russia, demonstrate a very centralized pattern of research output, and nations with a tradition of deconcentration like Germany, Great Britain, and the United States demonstrate a decentralized pattern also for the production of research papers. There are also clearly differences affected by university location policy, ranging from the university-town or campus philosophy, with Cambridge as an example, to the capital-city university structure with Washington, Rome, and Madrid as examples. Size of research output of a city, measured by number of papers produced by scientists located in the greater urban area itself, clearly demonstrates a pattern that deviates fundamentally from the way the large cities of the world generally are conceptualized. Even relatively small cities like Cambridge or Stockholm-Uppsala present themselves as megacities when it comes to research output. Clearly a pattern of economic development stage is also reflected in the ranking of the centers. What must be remarked too is the very high number of large research centers located in Great Britain and the United States.

Ten urban regions constitute the top level when it comes to research output 1996–1998 (Figure 1). London and Tokyo-Yokohama are outstanding as number one and two. The San Francisco Bay area, Paris, Osaka-Kobe, Moscow, and Boston follow them. Also New York, Amsterdam-Hague-Rotterdam-Utrecht, and Los Angeles join this super-league. The next group of 8 metropoles is led by Philadelphia and Berlin followed by Chicago, Copenhagen-Lund, Baltimore, and San Diego. Also Stockholm-Uppsala and Houston belong to this primary league. The rest of the cities on the list form a secondary league with 12 participants. This group is dominated by European cities. Also 3 United States centers and 2 Canadian cities are found here. In Figure 2, the top-30 for 1999–2001 is registered. The list is almost identical to the list in Figure 1. Three cities, Beijing, Seoul, and Milan, have entered the list, which Cambridge, Montreal, and Dortmund-Düsseldorf-Cologne have left. The top-level

Figure 1

Ranking of the 30 largest global research centers, 1996–98

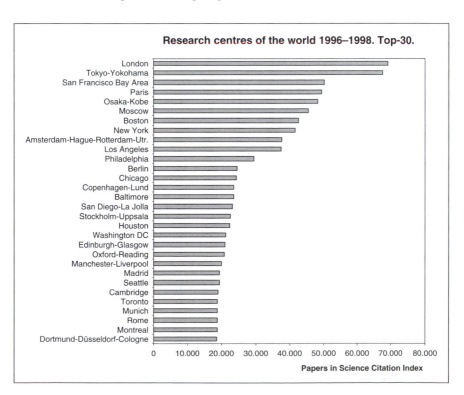

Research centres of the world 1996–1998. Top-30.

Figure 2

Ranking of the 30 largest global research centers, 1999–2001

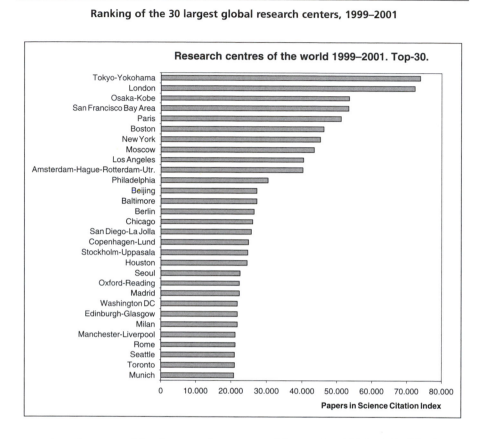

comprises the same cities, but not the same ranking as for 1996–1998. The largest concentration of research output is now found in the Tokyo region. The second level now represents 9 centers as Beijing has joined the group. In the 2002–2004 data (Figure 3) Cambridge reentered the top-30 list at the expense of Washington DC. The top-level now comprises 11 cities, with Beijing as the newcomer. On the second level, Seoul is the new member of the group of 9 cities.

Winners and Losers

Growth in research output from 1996–1998 to 2002–2004 has been calculated for all the 74 metropolitan units we have registered. These are not the 74 largest units in the world, but we are confident that few other cities could find their way into this list as higher ranking in research output than any of those included. Average growth has been 13% and individual growth ranges from 170% (Shanghai) to −10% (Moscow).

In Figure 4, growth percentages for all units are indicated. The big winners are Asian cities. Arranged in order, they are Shanghai, Beijing, Seoul, Singapore, and Hong Kong. These are followed by two South American cities, Sao Paulo and Rio de Janeiro. Then comes New Delhi followed by Melbourne, Mexico City, and Buenos Aires. The losers also present a distinctive picture. Their ranking from bottom-up is: Moscow,

Figure 3

Ranking of the 30 largest global research centers, 2002–2004

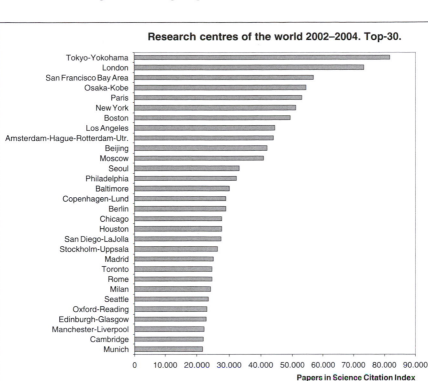

St Petersburg, Washington DC, Basel-Mulhouse-Freiburg, St Louis, Stuttgart, London, Paris, Edinburgh-Glasgow, and Detroit. They are North American and European, and they are large capital cities, some of them with old and decreasing manufacturing centers. A new picture of research location is emerging. The old centers of Europe and North America are lagging behind when it comes to growth, and the new actors in world economy are taking over as locations of rapid upgrading. If this growth pattern is sustained, a globally much wider distribution presents itself than we were used to just a decade ago.

Research Cooperation: Coauthorship Patterns

The ways researchers work together follows many paths and reflects cooperation on different levels and of different types. With focus on intercity links, we use coauthorship between authors from different cities as an indicator and present two analytical steps. Intercity coauthorship reflects generally the total of national and international patterns, while intercity coauthorship between researchers from different nations indicates the international pattern. The interaction pattern of researchers mirrors the flows of ideas and reflects attraction patterns and traditions of cooperation. It is influenced by similarities and differences of many types and also reflects different kinds of barriers for contacts. Research cooperation contributes to the status of a given city and demonstrates the nodal position of the centers in question.

Figure 4

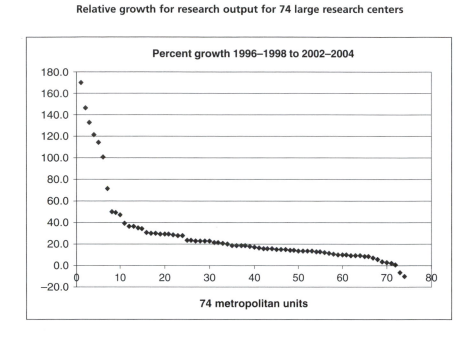

Relative growth for research output for 74 large research centers

Percent growth 1996–1998 to 2002–2004

74 metropolitan units

The geography of coauthorship is indicated on two similar map-type diagrams (Figures 5 and 6). The position of the cities on these maps is not in any way precise. Latitude and altitude, scale, and direction differ all over the maps. The maps only give

Figure 5

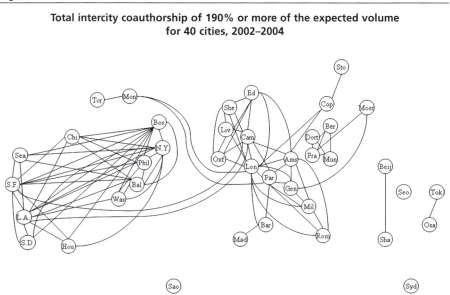

Total intercity coauthorship of 190% or more of the expected volume for 40 cities, 2002–2004

Figure 6

International coauthorship of 200% or more of the expected volume for 40 cities, 2002–2004

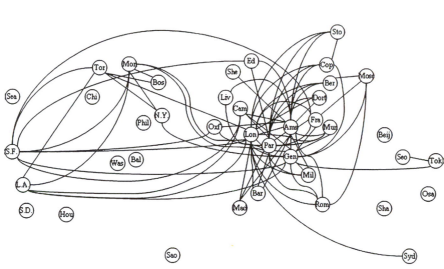

primitive but recognizable gross pictures of the world. Observed coauthorship is linked to expected level of coauthorship between scientists (authors) of two cities estimated from statistical averages across intercity links considered. For a set of city pairs (e.g., London and Paris or Berlin and the San Francisco Bay area), expected number of coauthorships is defined as the total number of papers published in the smallest city of that pair divided with total number of observed coauthored papers of the whole matrix. Observed coauthorship is then subtracted from expected coauthorship and calculated as a percentage of expected coauthorship. We have made calculations on coauthorships for the 40 largest research centers of the world 2002–2004.

Total intercity coauthorship numbers 498,472 cases. The highest level of intercity coauthorship is presented by the Tokyo Bay region with Osaka-Kobe-Kyoto, and then follows London with Oxford-Reading, London with Cambridge, Los Angeles with the San Francisco Bay region, and Manchester-Liverpool with Oxford-Reading. The major links are demonstrated in Figure 5, where the 83 links of 190% or more of the expected coauthorship between two cities are indicated. The diagram is dominated by national intercity-links within the United States, with major nodes being Los Angeles, Boston, New York, and the San Francisco Bay area. National patterns of Great Britain and Germany are also evident and some additional strong urban interrelations within nations are presented by Canada, China, Japan, Spain, and Italy. London, Cambridge, Paris, and Amsterdam-Hague-Rotterdam-Utrecht are the major European nodes. Clearly, German and British scientists (except those from London and Cambridge) are as nationally focused as are researchers from the United States. Only four intercontinental links are strong enough to be indicated on the diagram. The eight centers mentioned above represent the top-level of intercity relations of coauthorship and are thereby characterized as major nodes in terms of the total (national plus international) research network. Cities located in Asia, Australia, and South America are not well related to the research communities of other cities, and cities like Toronto, Madrid,

Stockholm, Tokyo, and Osaka are linked heavily to only one other city. Although new centers have entered the top global lists of research giants, they are not yet in good connection with the outside world research community.

International intercity coauthorship numbers 308,866 cases. The highest level of international intercity coauthorship is presented by London with Amsterdam-Hague-Rotterdam-Utrecht, and then follows London with Paris, Paris with Amsterdam-Hague-Rotterdam-Utrecht, the San Francisco Bay area with London, and Paris with Genéve-Lausanne. The major links are demonstrated in Figure 6, where the 80 links of 200% or more of the expected international coauthorship between two cities are indicated. The diagram differs fundamentally as expected from the diagram in Figure 5. European cooperation dominates the picture of strong international inter-relationships. Only 15 strong links are intercontinental and most of them between European and North American cities. Four cities stand out as top international nodes. London, Paris, Amsterdam-Hague-Rotterdam-Utrecht, and Genéve-Lausanne (where the international science cooperation facility CERN is located). The second level comprises San Francisco, Montreal, and Frankfurt together with Cambridge, Copenhagen-Lund, Los Angeles, Rome, and Toronto. These 12 centers are the strongest nodes in the international intercity relationship pattern of coauthorship. The research community of many cities is not particularly strongly oriented toward international relations.

Global Research Centers

In this chapter we have identified the largest research centers of the world measured in general terms of research output and we have calculated growth rates. The pattern of cooperation between the large units has been analyzed and we have looked at two dimensions of cooperation links. One dimension is represented by the total of intercity relations, the other by the international parts of these links. Synthesizing the analysis to a simple picture of the major global system and identifying nodes of research is as complicated as all summaries of categories are. Through the 9 years, the data span over there has been a concentration of research output to the 30 largest global centers. The top level is almost identical for the three periods analyzed. Only Beijing has joined this group of now 11 cities. London has lost its top-position to Tokyo-Yokohama and Moscow is moving rapidly downward. The other members of the top-level are the San Francisco Bay area, Paris, Osaka-Kobe, and Boston. Also New York, Amsterdam-Hague-Rotterdam-Utrecht, and Los Angeles join this super-league. When we look at growth percentages and use a larger number of cities (74), we find Asian cities in the lead with South American and Australian units coming just after. The losers are North American and European, and they are heavy capital cities together with old and decreasing manufacturing centers. The old research centers of Europe and North America are lagging behind when it comes to growth, and the new world is taking over as the location of rapid upgrading. If this growth pattern is sustainable, a globally much wider distribution is presenting itself than what we were used to in the 1990s. When we look at networks and sum up the total of national and international intercity links we can identify the nine major research nodes, which are London, Los Angeles, the San Francisco Bay area, Boston, and New York followed by Cambridge, Paris, Baltimore, and Amsterdam-Hague-Rotterdam-Utrecht. The United States, England, and France are in the lead. When we turn to the international dataset and point out the international nodes, four cities stand out as top international nodes: London, Paris, Amsterdam-Hague-Rotterdam-Utrecht, and Genéve-Lausanne, and the second level comprises San Francisco, Montreal, and Frankfurt together with Cambridge, Copenhagen-Lund, Los Angeles, Rome, and Toronto.

In this chapter, the nodal function of the large research centers has not been directly linked to their economic performance, but the structure of—and the links within—the network of research represents important aspects of contemporary economic geography and gives rise to some additional observations. The picture demonstrated in this chapter confirms that economic and political connections, language, and distance play roles in the pattern of research networks. By analyzing the data set we further find that even for the major research centers, national links in general dominate over international links. We also find a much more nationally centered pattern of links within the United States and Great Britain than we expected tentatively. And we observed that centers of small European nations like Switzerland, the Netherlands, and Denmark play important roles as international nodes.

Acknowledgments

The authors would like to thank N. B. Olsen (DTV) for his valuable and imaginative contribution to bibliometric data collection and analysis.

References

Bengs, C. (ed.) (2002). *Facing ESPON*. Stockholm. Nordregio R2002:1.
Castells, M. and Hall, P. (1994). *Technopoles of the World*. London and New York: Routledge.
Cattan, N., Pumain, D., Rozenblat, C. and Saint-Julien, T. (1994). *Le systeme des villes europeennes*. Paris: Antropos.
ESPON. (2004). *Espon in Progress*. Denmark. Available at: www.espon.lu.
Eurostat. (1997). Research and Development in Europe.
Eurostat. (Annual Statistics). Research and Development.
Eurostat. (1996). F&U- og Innovationsstatistik. Set i Regionalt Perspektiv. Regionalhåndbog.
Florida, R. (2002). *The Rise of the Creative Class*. New York: Basic Books.
Howkins, J. (2002). *The Creative Economy*. Penguin Press.
Lever, W. F. (2002). Correlating the Knowledge-base of Cities with Economic Growth. *Urban Studies*, vol. 39, nos 5–6, pp. 859–870.
Matthiessen, C. W. and Schwarz, A. W. (1999). Scientific centres in Europe: An analysis of research strength and patterns of specialisation based on bibliometric indicators. *Urban Studies*, vol. 36, no. 3, pp. 453–477.
Matthiessen, C. W., Schwarz, A. W. and Find, S. (2002). The top-level global research system, 1997–99: Centres, networks and nodality. An analysis based on bibliometric indicators. *Urban Studies*, vol. 39, nos 5–6, pp. 903–927.
May, R. M. (1997). The scientific wealth of nations. *Science*, vol. 275, pp. 793–796.
NUREC: Network on Urban Research in the European Union. (1994). Atlas of Agglomerations in the European Union, vol. I–III, Duisburg.
OECD. (1974). Proposed standard practice for surveys of research and experimental development.
OECD. (1992). Proposed guidelines for collecting and interpreting technological innovation data.
OECD. (1997). *Proposed Guidelines for Collecting and Interpreting Technological Innovation Data: Oslo Manual*. Paris: Organisation for Economic Cooperation and Development.
OECD. (2002). *The Measurement of Scientific and Technological Activities: Proposed Standard Practice for Surveys of Research and Experimental Development*. Paris: Organisation for Economic Cooperation and Development.
Reclus-Datar. (1989). Groupement d'Intérêt Public RECLUS: Les villes Européennes. Montpellier.
Schwarz, A. W., Schwarz, S. and Tijssen, R. J. W. (1998). Research and research impact of a technical university – a bibliometric study. *Scientometrics*, vol. 41, no. 3, pp. 371–388.
Simmie, J. and Lever, W. F. (2002). Introduction: The knowledge-based city. *Urban Studies*, vol. 39, nos 5–6, pp. 885–857.
Venturelli, S. (2004). *From the Information Economy to the Creative Economy*. New York: Center for Arts and Culture.

Chapter 4

A Taxonomy of Urban Capital

Francisco Javier Carrillo, *The World Capital Institute and The Center for Knowledge Systems, Tecnológico de Monterrey, México*

Introduction

The role of knowledge-based value or "Intellectual Capital" (IC) in business perform-ance and consequently in the economic understanding of the firm has been one of the major drivers in the emergence of Knowledge Management (KM).[1] It continues to be one of its major challenges. Even if a substantial effort has been carried out to explain and manage the value of IC from a number of perspectives, there is much to be advanced before a common framework for the understanding and development of IC is developed (Marr and Chatzkel, 2004; Marr, 2005).

Such diversity of approaches has been transferred into the realm of Social Knowledge Capital (Bounfour, 2005; Edvinsson, 2005). A necessary condition for the identification, classification, and valuation of social—and organizational—knowledge-based value is a taxonomy that has enough completeness and consistency to account for all possible cases. Only so, the common reduction of IC management practices into traditional economic thinking (Augier and Teece, 2005) can be progressively overcome.[2] The intention to reduce IC into monetary capital or the continued dichotomy between labor and capital or between economic and social policy are only a few common examples. At the Social Knowledge Capital level, this is evident in the continued tendency to dissociate the economic and social agendas.

This chapter builds upon previous work where the conceptual basis and formal requirements for a capital system have been outlined.[3] The first section of this chapter

---

[1] The "Three Drivers of the KM Movement" are discussed in Carrillo (1999).

[2] This became evident at the recent First World Conference on Intellectual Capital for Communities held at the World Bank Office in Paris, June 20, 2005.

[3] See Carrillo (1998, 2001, 2002, 2004).

summarizes the foundational elements of the Knowledge-based Value System approach. The second section constructs the idea of capital systems as Productive Value Structures and identifies their elementary components. The third section describes the generic structure of capital systems as applied to the social domain.

Developing Knowledge-Based Value Systems

The Knowledge-based Value System approach[4] is based on the assumption that all forms of value as individual and social constructs constitute homogeneous domains, i.e., value systems. Such systems span the individual, organizational, or social levels of experience. Basically, the so-called Knowledge Economy or Knowledge Society is a transition from predominantly material-based value-production systems to predominantly knowledge-based value-production systems. As it unfolds, such transition pervades and transforms the way in which the development of individuals, organizations, and societies is understood and managed. Figure 1 shows how the value domain at each level has been understood and operationalized, i.e., its previous domain and previous measurement. It also shows the new broad element incorporated and the corresponding redefinition of both domain and measurement.

Although the recognition of these new "knowledge-based" elements into the individual, organizational, and social value domains took place mostly throughout the second half of the 20th century, the resulting transformation in ideas and practices is far from complete. The material-based value paradigm characteristic of the Industrial Society still pervades most individual and collective behaviors. In order to evolve into a true knowledge-based society, a fundamentally new paradigm still needs to penetrate wider levels of individual conscience and collective culture. What follows are some of the basic realizations that could contribute to the social construction of a Knowledge Culture.

Knowledge Events: Objects, Agents, and Contexts

First, the relational nature of knowledge needs to be acknowledged: it constitutes an event rather than a mere object or record (Assudani, 2005). This realization is parallel to the crisis that modern physics experienced at the dawn of the 20th century by

Figure 1

Social, organizational and personal terms of transformation into a Knowledge Society.
© F J Carrillo, 1999

	Previous domain	*Previous measure*	*Added element*	**New domain**	**New measure**
Individual	Analytic intelligence	Intellectual coefficient	Emotional intelligence	Whole person	Integrated Capacity Profile
Organizational	Business strategy	Financial states	Intellectual Capital	Whole organization	Integrated Value Report
Social	Economic development	Gross National Product	Quality of life	Whole society	Social Knowledge Capital Accounts

---

[4] See Carrillo (1998) for further explanation.

"de-materializing" itself. It need not imply a dualism. On the contrary, it involves an epistemological shift from matter-centered to a monistic relation-centered natural base. It sets the ground for a continuous, homogeneous ground between "physical" and "knowledge" capital, i.e., between material objects and their representations. Indeed, it is difficult to see how KM and Knowledge-Based Development (KBD) could rest on any rational grounds—including how "intellectual capital" and "stock of knowledge" can acquire managerial and political significance—unless such natural continuity is established.

This epistemological stand opens up a search for the basic elements in a "k-event" (Figure 2). The first and most obvious is the one most people identify knowledge with: the k-object or that which is known. K-objects can be things, representations of things (images, words), people, events—actually any portion of the perceived universe.

Second, there is the k-agent: her/him who knows. Agents in a k-event can be human individuals, groups, and arguably animals, automata, and extraterrestrial life forms. Let us stay for the time being with human individual and groups. An agent/object interaction must take place, but that is not enough for a k-event to happen.

Third, there is the k-context which provides significance, i.e., selects a specific agent/object interaction from potentially infinite possibilities. This element has a referential nature, i.e., constitutes a value or a preference criterion.

Thus, the necessary and sufficient elements for knowledge to take place are: an object, an agent, and a context, all of which must be "process capable," i.e., have the qualities that enable a particular k-connection to occur. For example, all objects must be perceivable, all agents must be active, and all contexts must be discernible.

In a simplified sense, all KM, including KBD, involves the identification of relevant values, agents, and objects in a system and the alignment of these. In mainstream KM, not all three aspects have been given due attention. During the initial years (early 1990s), most KM practice focused on object-management activities such as yellow pages, document management, organizational memories, and other archival, bibliographical, and IT tasks.

As early k-managers learnt, adequate user interface, motivation and skills were critical for the effectiveness of k-bases. During the second half of the 1990s, the transactional aspects of k-agents and objects, such as k-transfer, collaboration, etc., received increasing attention. Hence, flow-cycle second-generation KM models gained prominence.

Figure 2

Three components of a knowledge event. © F J Carrillo, 1998

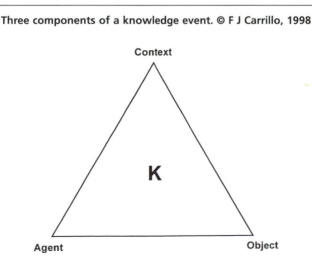

Up to this point, value is attributed to knowledge in terms of its accumulation (as in organizational memory) and distribution (as in shared practices). Stocking and circulating become the mechanisms for capitalizing on knowledge. This tends to prevail until the third element of k-events, context, is taken into consideration.

Context is the element that grants semiotic status to a k-event. The economic significance of knowledge does not become apparent until an agent/object interaction is framed in a value context. Take any k-object (e.g., a treasure map, a company memo, a technique description) and give a competent agent (e.g., one proficient in the language in which the object is recorded) access to it. Unless that agent has enough contextual elements to adequately interpret the object and determine the proper course of action, the value realization of that agent/object interaction will be impaired.

Hence, the first and most critical task for managing knowledge is to determine and operationalize the value framework of the systems whose capacity to attain its goals are to be maximized. Value alignment become the primordial KM function. Once the value framework is expressed into a manageable structure—the capital system—the other two components of k-events can be adequately selected, developed, and assessed.

Three Generations of KM

From this perspective, the plethora of available KM definitions can be organized into three generations. Each generation is recognizable in terms of (a) what is to be managed (the nature of knowledge), (b) what is to be maximized (the nature of management), and (c) what is the consequent approach (the nature of KM). Whereas there is a sequence in this evolution, these three families have coexisted, albeit in very different proportions.

Object-centered KM was from the start, and still is, quantitatively dominant, but decreasing in proportion. Agent-centered KM emerged with great strength and advanced rapidly during the late 1990s. Context-centered KM, even if anticipated in some early contributions, only in later years became a true alternative. Each subsequent family has subsumed the former elements.

Figure 3 shows how each generation can be identified according to the aforementioned features: concept of knowledge, capitalization process, and KM definition. This categorization implies no value judgment as to which approach is "best" in an absolute sense. Each approach capitalizes on specific attributes of a k-system and is therefore valuable in specific circumstances (i.e., "situational KM").

Figure 3

Three KM generations. © F J Carrillo, 1999

KM Approach / Feature	I Generation: Object-centered	II Generation: Agent-centered	III Generation: Context-centered
Knowledge concept	Record	Flow	Alignment
Capitalization process	Keeping and accumulating stock	Facilitating and increasing circulation	Attaining sustainable value balance
KM definition	KM is a *tool* for identifying, storing, keeping, organizing and retrieving the organization's k-base	KM is a *method* to identify, codify, structure, store, retrieve and diffuse experience	KM is a *strategy* to identify, systematize and develop the organization's value universe

A context-centered approach aims at expressing all significant forms of capital, including object-capital and agent-capital. Therefore, this approach involves the following three core KM processes.[5]

- **Alignment and strategic consolidation of capitals.** Determining, systematizing, and operationalizing the value universe of an organization;
- **Agent capital management.** Determining and developing the value-generating capacities of productive individuals and teams, as well as those of the organization as a whole;
- **Instrumental capital management.** Determining, implementing, and developing the optimal array of conditions and resources to leverage the value yield of all elements in the organization.

These three KM processes and generations of KM approaches can be extrapolated to identifiable KBD processes as in Figure 4. Further discussion and examples are available elsewhere (Carrillo, 2002).

- **First-Generation KBD: Distributing Instrumental Capital.** Most KBD strategies start by focusing on the most immediate area of impact—the instrumental base that would enhance the capacities of productive agents. Hence, G1 initiatives focus on knowledge infrastructure such as S&T parks, educational facilities, and public information services.
- **Second-Generation KBD: Developing Human Capital.** One of the earlier lessons learnt by major development agencies was how ineffective mere fund allocation was in promoting development in more depressed economic regions. Such capital flow involved a dual perversion of purpose: lack of transparency in local fund management and profiteering by contractors, often from the same donating countries. The old Chinese proverb, "do not give fish to the hungry man; teach him how to fish" also gained increasing empirical support. Human-capital KBD policies are now strongly favored by New Growth Theory (NGT). Education, self-managed learning, technology transfer, expertise assistance, experience sharing, and other forms of k-flow are now a central issue in development programs.

Figure 4

Three KBD generations. © F J Carrillo, 1999

Label / Atribute	*I Generation:* *Object-centered*	*II Generation:* *Agent-centered*	*III Generation:* *Context-centered*
Knowledge concept	Information record	Capacity flow	Value alignment
Capitalization and development process	Accumulate and retain stock	Facilitate and increase circulation	Dynamically adjust to a sustainable value balance
KBD definition	KBD is a *infrastructure* to increase the social stock of knowledge	KBD is a *policy* to propiciate the social flow of knowledge	KBD is a *development strategy* based on the identification, systematization and sustainable balance of social k-capital

---

[5] Further disaggregation available at the CKS website: www.knowledgesystems.org.

- **Third-Generation KBD: Developing Capital Systems.** When it gets to value-based KBD, we can make reference to some ideal specifications (those identified above), and to a vision, but to no actual instances. A Global Capital System that is complete, consistent, systematic, and inclusive is the framework for the global KBD we seek.

Most of these efforts tend to patch traditional economic and accountancy methods in view of their increasing incapacity to determine individual, organizational, and social wealth. These "new measures" usually tend to complement the hard traditional measures with some form of soft addendum. What we get is a compound of heterogenous indicators carrying different axiological assumptions, defined within different theoretical frameworks, obtained through different methodological rules, and compiled under an inevitable umbrella of eclecticism. This circumstance pervades current practices to determine k-capital at individual, organizational, and social levels.[6] While such gross comparisons may be of use at some early point, they cannot be the basis for a systematic development strategy at the organizational or social level.

Attempts to assess the widest human value system, our planet, face the same restrictions. Interestingly though, it is at this newer and most ambitious level that the system's perspective is more naturally adopted. This is exemplified through the attempt by some international development agencies to define "global public goods" (GPGs). A GPG is one that "must be supplied through the joint effort of nations or international agencies, beyond a single government and that constitutes a benefit for the inhabitants of the whole planet."[7] The UN Program for Development (UNPD) distinguishes three kinds of GPGs: natural ones, such as the ozone layer or the atmosphere; man-made such as universal norms and cultural baggage; and political ones, such as international market efficiency, financial stability, security and peace, environmental sustainability and health (ibid.). This important development initiates the collective capitalization of the global commons. But it is still different from the concept of a system of global capital, which would include the value universe of our planet, including all forms of value currently possessed or managed by any individual entity, those that are managed jointly through some form of cooperative alliance, and those that so far are not claimed or managed by any identifiable entity.[8] Only such a domain would correspond to the complete, consistent, and operational global capital system we are searching for.

Like any formal system, capital systems must aim to fulfill two fundamental criteria: completeness and consistency. The first requirement means that it covers all significant categories; the second, that the inclusion of one does not imply the exclusion of another. It is also required that the capital system be operational in the scientific and managerial tradition by which an element is defined in terms of the operations required to measure it. These three requirements also imply—unlike most existing

---

[6] At the organizational level, Intellectual Capital constitutes mostly an addendum to *real* accountings. At the international level (not yet a global one), a new and growing branch of soft or k-based benchmarks is getting wider recognition. *Fortune Magazine* has added profiles of *Most Admired Companies* and *Best Companies to work for* to its traditional *Fortune 100* and *Global Fortune 500* listings. In the US, the *Metropolitan New Economy Index*, developed after *The New Economy Index* and *The State New Economy Index* sponsored by the Progressive Policy Institute, is part of a program aimed at developing *"a new set of economic indicators to illustrate the structural foundations of . . . the New Economy."*

[7] (Carrillo, L., 2002). Note this is not the chapter's author.

[8] This is the value domain aimed at by the World Capital Institute.

knowledge capital indicator inventories—that the categories must be homogeneous, i.e., that all categories are generated from a well-defined set of dimensions. In particular, financial and material capitals must be included in the same universe of natural dimensions as all other social knowledge capitals.

In the next section, the evolution of KM and KBD IC is analyzed from the normative perspective of these three requirements. The introduction of the capital system approach suggests new directions for IC management at the organizational, social, and global levels.

Capital Systems

The Inductive Phase of IC

As mentioned earlier, one of the economic drives for the fast expansion of the KM movement was the realization of the weight intangible assets have in companies, particularly public ones. The huge economic implications of this realization led to an intellectual gold rush aimed at identifying, measuring, and capitalizing on such intangibles. As in the early stages of other conceptual fields, efforts have been predominantly inductive, resulting in arbitrary collections of IC "indicators." The variety of IC models and categories has been documented, (e.g., Flores, 2000; Sullivan, 2000; Bontis, 2001; Marr and Chatzkel, 2004; Marr, 2005). More often than not, such arrays are inductive and, hence, heterogeneous (with a mix of dimensions from different planes). One discovers that when attempting to value IC, very few of those arrays abide by basic canons of metrology. Even fewer attempt to differentiate k-based value dynamics (e.g., Thoreson and Blankeship, 1996).

While IC has become one of the most fertile areas of KM, to what extent the basic dimensions describing k-based value generation have been grasped remains an open question. What follows is an attempt to identify a distinctive knowledge-based value dynamics on the basis of the concepts discussed above.

Productive Value Structures

The evolution of production systems throughout history may shed some light on the nature of k-based value systems. Although a production system is not exclusively one aimed at increasing the stock of goods, services, and exchange capital, we will refer mainly to these for the time being. Production systems aiming at furthering esthetic, epistemic, and ethical value do include mechanisms for such enhancing or development. Such mechanisms, common to all value systems, will be identified as a production function.

Hence, looking at how humans have organized throughout history in order to obtain a positive differential of goods, services, investments, and savings at the end of a working cycle, we recognize how productive systems have evolved. Nomadic tribes, by far the longest prevailing form of human society, were based on hunting-gathering. Under that scheme, a bare minimum of tools was kept to maintain effective and efficient hunting, collection and other basic life-preserving and community building functions. Oral tradition was a dominant mechanism for preserving knowledge and transmitting it from generation to generation (Ives, Torrey and Gordon, 1998).

The emergence of human settlements is associated with the advent of agriculture, and was to become the dominant production system for several millennia, coexisting with remnant forms of hunting and gathering. In agricultural societies, land was a prime capital, inputs such as water, seeds, and fertilizers, very important productivity formulas, and a relatively invariant technological stock. The agricultural cycle provided landmarks to cultural and religious frameworks. Recorded symbolic language became a vehicle to knowledge, with the advent of printing as epitome.

The degree of human penetration on and transformation of the natural landscape increased as productive systems evolved. From surface-bound hunting-gathering to land manipulation and landscape transformation in agriculture, human incidence on nature deepened. Extraction of natural resources, which started as nomadic tribes moved along territorial paths, increased as urban settlements allowed for more powerful tools and techniques. The combination of agriculture with extractive production and compatible hunting-gathering prevailed for most of documented history.

In the scale of human history, modernity has just happened. One of its more significant outcomes, the industrial revolution, under such a time scale, is right before today. At that critical point, production systems undergo a major change. Extracted raw materials and energy are transformed through mechanical and chemical processes,[9] using machinery and equipment to generate manufactured goods. Technology begins to change at an accelerating rate. The value-added manufactured goods supersede that of agricultural production. Commercial mobility increases, reaching today's breathless flow of goods, services, financial capital, and technological innovations at a global scale.

As modern Economic Science took hold, it became concerned with the way in which production factors combine into the most effective and efficient arrays. What the necessary and sufficient production factors are for a given system is a question that Economic Theory of the Firm addresses (Bontis, 2001; Marr and Chatzkel, 2004). Through dynamic systems modelling, k-based alternatives to business design and development are being explored (e.g., Guevara, 2002).

Contemporary Theory of the Firm is a child of industrialization. It responds to the logic of production which is conatural to manufacturing. Even service industries are conceived under the same fundamental logic. Certainly, many issues which could be associated with k-based production have been addressed by recent economic analysis, but only marginally. The dominant economic rationale is still founded on the distinctive value dynamics of mechanical and chemical transformation of matter and energy and the associated hierarchy of human labor, management, and investment (Cyret and March, 1992).

K-Based Value Structures

Certainly, there are continuities in the transition from material-based to representational-based production, as there were from hunting-gathering, to agricultural, to industrial societies. Economic phenomena are a manifestation of a combinatory of objects, agents, and contexts. Economic principles are an abstraction of such a combinatory. Physical and chemical conditions inextricably constrain that combinatory, determining possible economic outcomes. In general, the properties of underlying natural phenomena predetermine the economic behavior of production systems.

Continuities in economic processes from industrial to k-based production are bound to happen insofar as material elements are involved and they do not get subsumed by k-processes. Human labor as production factor will behave in the same way it has as long as it is regarded primarily as a mechanical, muscle-bound activity. Even

---

[9] Simultaneously, modern physics and chemistry are born.

work in the service industry will be similarly regarded insofar as it is measured in traditional output units.

But there are also discontinuities in the economic behavior of production systems once the predominant factors are representational or k-based. Indeed, this is the very raison d'etre for KM and for the whole spectrum of k-based development. How old and new factors will combine is an open question. While some of the most visible characteristics of the k-based economy have been pointed out (Choi et al., 1997; Woodwall, 2000; OECD, 2001; The European Commission, 2000), they still need to be formally structured and empirically tested. Beyond those currently under debate (e.g., increasing marginal returns), other received concepts such as intellectual property and the capital/labor dichotomy need to be redefined.

The bet on the distinctiveness of k-production factors rests on the physiological, psychological, and social strata of k-events. While there are causal interdependencies between material and represented objects (as there are between physical, chemical, and biological processes) there are also behavioral patterns idiosyncratic to each level. Once we enter the domain of represented objects or events, the combinatory is singular and as a consequence so is the spectrum of economic outcomes. This is the main point. For the purpose of the overall argument it is enough to raise such a possibility. What exactly are those natural differences and how they determine economic outcomes is a major question which we are only beginning to grasp.

Productive and Metaproductive Capitals

Production was identified above as a generic function of all value systems. Such a function aims at preserving and enhancing the total worth of the system. "Worth" does not necessarily mean an increase in size or an accumulation of stock, but a preferred state relative to a specific value structure.

In the construction of a well-defined capital system—whether for a company, a government office, an NGO, or a city—it becomes necessary to look at the generic array of value elements that are required to sustain the production function. Simplified to the irreducible form of an input/process/output system, all production systems consist of (i) an input capital that is the given value base with which the system begins to operate (in the case of cities, the set of favorable circumstances that led to the foundation of a city—water supply, orography, climate, etc.); two process capitals—(ii) the agent capital which performs production (in the case of contemporary cities, basically its functional population) and (iii) the instrumental capital, which constitutes all the means of production (in the case of cities, most of the traditional objects of urban planning such as layout, water supply and sewage, etc.); finally, some form of value exists as (iv) product capital (surplus yield from primitive farming was simultaneous to the transition from nomadic to urban societies). To sum up, all value-creation systems include an input capital, process capitals (agent capital plus instrumental capital), and an output capital.

Hence, all human societies can be described as capital systems. All operate on the basis of an input, an agent, an instrument, and a product capital (Figure 5).

Figure 6 compares major production systems throughout history along these categories. Early service industries are regarded as transitional into the knowledge economy and, hence, not differentiated in this comparison.

As the output of production systems needed to be represented for practical reasons, currencies and records were developed. This alone multiplied the value combinatory of material products. Thus, material production systems generated a form of metacapital,

Figure 5

Minimum capital system. © F J Carrillo, 1998

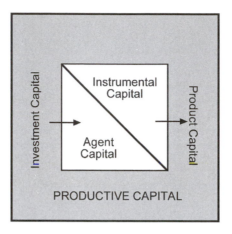

one which served as representation of all other forms of production value and allowed for its quantification, recording, and exchange. This combination of material and financial capital has been the dominant realm of economics (Figure 7).

Once "representational" or "k-based" production factors became increasingly relevant and the Intellectual Gold Rush exploded, the need for not only a new structure of production factors, but also of its combination rules became apparent.[10] Figure 8 shows a generic arrangement of such factors, followed by their definition. Whereas any of these can include k-capital, the best identified forms (internal elements) are still related to production capital, such as instrumental (mostly, k-objects) and agent (mostly, human competencies). The most elusive or ignored so far are new metacapitals

Figure 6

Dominant factors of major production systems. © F J Carrillo, 1999

	Production type	Input	Process		Output
			Agent	Instrument	
Physical Era	Hunting-gathering	Natural habitat	Human and animal	Hands and primitive tools and techniques	Game, fish and collected natural goods
	Agricultural	Land, water, seeds, fertilizers	Human and animal	Agricultural equipment and techniques	Agricultural goods
	Extractive	Natural deposits	Human and animal	Mining equipment and techniques	Stones, metals, minerals
	Industrial	Raw materials and enery	Human and automata	Industrial machinery, equipment and techniques	Manufactured goods and industrialized products
	Physical-based production	Matter and energy	Muscular strength and sensory-muscular dexterity	Physical tools, equipment and techniques	Physical goods
Knowledge Era	Knowledge-based production	(Relative) lower-level K-input	Rationality and Emotion	K-processing tools, systems and networks	(Relative) higher-level K-output

---

[10] See Carrillo (1999).

Figure 7

Productive capitals and financial metacapital. © F J Carrillo, 1998

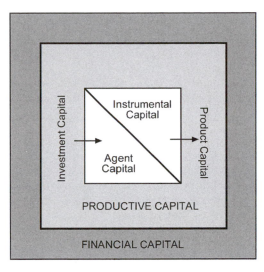

Figure 8

Generic Capital System. © F J Carrillo, 1998

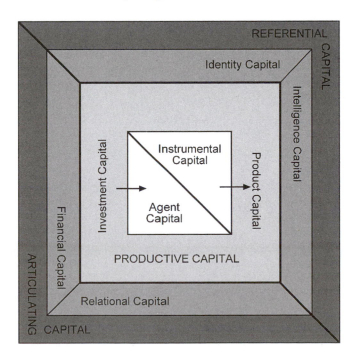

(external elements), those which are not directly productive but which determine the overall productivity of the system. Amongst these, two major categories emerge: referential and articulating capital. The first has a function to focus and align, like a compass or lighthouse. It includes endogenous (identity) and exogenous (intelligence) capital. Articulating capital has the function of interconnecting all other forms, like glue or cement. It includes financial (the first form of metacapital) and relational capitals.

Basic Assumptions of a Generic Capital System

On the basis of the previous analysis, the following assumptions summarize the rationale for a Capital System:

(1) All value systems involve a production function. This refers to the system's capacity to achieve and sustain value balance.

(2) All production functions involve an input, an agent, an instrument, and a product. These are all Productive Capitals. Productive capitals account for all forms of material-based value systems.

(3) In the course of history, metacapitals have been generated to multiply the value-generating potential of productive capitals. The creation of currencies allowed for the representation and exchange of productive capitals, multiplying their potential in space in time. Hence, Financial Capital was created.

(4) In knowledge-based production, two major forms of metacapital are involved. Referential Metacapital mutiplies the effectiveness and efficiency of the system by providing focus, thus diminishing error (through increasingly precise internal and external feedback). This includes Identity and Intelligence Capitals. Articulating Metacapital multiplies the productivity of the system by providing cohesion, thus diminishing transaction costs and redundancies. It includes Financial and Relational Capitals.

Generic Capital System Definitions

The previous analysis leads to the following definitions of the generic elements of all capital systems:

GENERIC CAPITAL SYSTEM

The taxonomy of a system's value categories

- Metacapital
  - Referential Capital (Value elements which allow the identification and alignment of all other value elements)
    (i) Identity Capital (endogenous value referents)
    (ii) External Intelligence (exogenous value referents)
  - Articulating Capital (Value elements which allow the interconnection or exchange amongst value elements)
    (i) Relational Capital (status of interaction amongst significant agents)
    (ii) Financial Capital (aggregate monetary expression of value elements)
- Input Capital
  - Investment Capital (Value element from another system which is brought in as an input)

- Production Capital
  - Agent Capital (Those value-generating capacities of individuals—animal, human and automata—and their groupings, as well as those from the organization as a whole to improve its own performance)
  - Instrumental Capital (The means of production through which every other capital leverages its value-generating capacity)
- Output Capital
  - Product Capital (The inventory of values generated by all other value elements which has not been realized yet in another form of capital)

Where we were able to capture completely and consistently the capital system of any given entity, we would be representing its "value blueprint," the state of the system with reference to its ideal state. Such an ideal state would be one where each of the value elements existed just in the right proportion to achieving full balance. Hence, value systems are unique, as unique as personalities or cultures. And, therefore, capital systems are as diverse as the multiplicity of systems amenable to a singular description. This would apply to every individual, every organization, and every society.

The emphasis on metaproductive values helps us understand that production does not have primacy in all systems. Indeed, no single form of value has primacy: it is only the perfect equilibrium of all value elements (whatever their relative weights) that becomes an ideal for probably all existing systems.

A Taxonomy of Capital Accounts for Knowledge Cities

From the generic capital system described above, and considering the levels of analysis as well as the specific capital dimensions of cities discussed before, a general taxonomy of urban capitals can be constructed. To conclude this chapter, a taxonomy of urban capital is deployed to the fourth level of disaggregation only (further disaggregation is not manageable within this chapter). In fact, some value dimensions become evident only at further levels of disaggregation. Thus, the following fourth-level taxonomy can be best read in reference upwards to the generic capital system described a few paragraphs above and downwards to Chapter 12 where this taxonomy is taken to the lowest levels of disaggregation as applied to the City of Monterrey. The more disaggregated it gets, the more specific it becomes. A specific city's capital system would be unique in its structure and specificity. Yet, it could be compared with any other city at the sufficient level of aggregation and, certainly, at the uppermost levels of the generic urban capital system.

TAXONOMY OF URBAN CAPITALS

The generic classification of city categories as a value system

1   METACAPITALS
   1.1   Referential capital. Value elements that allow the identification and alignment of all other capitals
      1.1.1   Identity capital. Internal value referents
         1.1.1.1   Inherited identity. Formal and informal elements, accumulated through the city's history, that contributed to determine its identity
         1.1.1.2   Current identity. Formal and informal elements, contributing to determine its current identity
         1.1.1.3   Prospected identity. Formal and informal elements composing its future vision

      1.1.2   Intelligence capital
          1.1.2.1   City intelligence system. Quality of the city's systems to sense, make sense of and respond to agents and events which are significant to the city's welfare
          1.1.2.2   City future center. Quality of the city's system to foresee and foster its future
  1.2   Articulation capital. Value elements which make possible the interrelationship or exchange of value elements
      1.2.1   Relational capital. The quality of the interaction between the city's internal significant agents, as well as between the city and its external significant ones
          1.2.1.1   Internal. State of the interaction between significant internal agents
          1.2.1.2   External. State of the interaction with significant external agents
      1.2.2   Financial capital. Monetary denomination of all or some production value dimensions
          1.2.2.1   Macroindicators. Set of economic indicators conventionally used for basic international comparisons
          1.2.2.2   Public accounts. The official city accounts

2   PRODUCTIVE CAPITALS
  2.1   Investment capital. Any value element contributed as a new production input
      2.1.1   Local investment. R&D Expenditure and private/public proportion
          2.1.1.1   Private sector
          2.1.1.2   Public investment
      2.1.2   Foreign investment
          2.1.2.1   Direct foreign investment
          2.1.2.2   Fund allocation by international agencies
          2.1.2.3   Creation of technology-based businesses
          2.1.2.4   Risk capital investment
          2.1.2.6   Attractiveness of human capital
  2.2   Human capital. Value generating capacity of individual and collective social agents
      2.2.1   Individual base. Value generating capacity of individuals
          2.2.1.1   Organic. Aspects of the individual's physical constitution, its developments and health condition which are determined by the environmental and social conditions and determine its organic integrity and overall potential
          2.2.1.2   Intellectual. Aspects of intellectual and emotional development of individuals which are determined by the environmental and social conditions and determine its organic integrity and overall potential
      2.2.2   Collective base. Collective and team-based value generating capacities
          2.2.2.1   Organic. Structural human dispositions having an impact on the constitution of organizations or on their functions
          2.2.2.2   Intellectual. Knowledge-based, including emotional and cultural collective capacities
  2.3   Instrumental capital. The means of production through which other capitals leverage their value generation capacity
      2.3.1   Tangible. Material-based means of production through which other capitals leverage their value generation capacity
          2.3.1.1   Geographic
          2.3.1.2   Environmental
          2.3.1.3   Infrastructural

    2.3.2   Intangible. Knowledge-based means of production through which other capitals leverage their value generation capacity

        2.3.2.1   Social organization structure. Structural capacities of social subsystems

        2.3.2.2   Information and telecommunications infrastructure. Structural capacities, traditional and ITC-based for information, and communications

2.4   Product. Output of the economy as a whole, and of its most important aggregated factors

    2.4.1   City product

        2.4.1.1   GDP

        2.4.1.2   GDPc

        2.4.1.3   GDP index

        2.4.1.4   GDP annual variation

    2.4.2   Productivity. By worker, unit of investment, and resource

    2.4.4   Sector product

    2.4.5   Tax collection. Coverage of taxable base

        2.4.5.1   Net tax collection

        2.4.5.2   Percentage collection per tax category

As the system disaggregates further and further, it becomes more and more specific to a given city. Hence, these categories have general applicability only at the uppermost levels. At the lowermost, they become the value blueprint or "soul" of that city. They also provide the most subtle level of knowledge and are, therefore, of strategic significance to a given city. Chapter 12 provides an instantiation of this generic capital system for the specific case of the City of Monterrey.

To conclude this chapter, it may be convenient to list some of the most obvious benefits of a capital system for a city:

- To provide the "Knowledge Accounts" or "State of The City" report of the Knowledge City
- To provide a systemic perspective of the complex interdependencies between the many and diverse dimensions of urban value categories
- To facilitate an understanding of the variables affecting the life of the city at most significant levels of experience
- To help building consensus on priorities and policies based on a wider public understanding of the city's realities
- To focus action and public accountancy of all development initiatives
- To sense the city's "soul" by revealing its value structure and thus helping to evolve its identity.

References

Assudani, Rashmi H. (2005). Catching the chameleon: Understanding the elusive term "knowledge". *Journal of Knowledge Management*, vol. 9, no. 2, pp. 31–44.

Augier, Mie and Teece, David J. (2005). An economics perspective on intellectual capital. In Bernard Marr (ed.) *Perspectives on Intellectual Capital*. Elsevier/Butterworth-Heinemann, pp. 3–27.

Bontis, N. (2001). Assessing knowledge assets: A review of the models used to measure intellectual capital. *International Journal of Management Reviews*, vol. 3, no. 1, pp. 41–60.

Bounfour, Ahmed. (2005). Modelling intangibles: Transaction regimes versus community regimes. In Ahmed Bounfour and Leif Edvinsson (eds.) *Intellectual Capital for Communities–Nations, Regions and Cities*. Elsevier/Butterworth-Heinemann, pp. 3–18.

Carrillo, F. J. (1998). Managing knowledge-based value systems. *Journal of Knowledge Management*, vol. 1, no. 4, junio, pp. 280–286.

Carrillo, F. J. (1999). The knowledge management movement: Current drives and future scenarios. *Memorias del 3rd International Conference on Technology, Policy and Innovation: Global Knowledge Partnerships: Creating Value for the 21st Century*. Austin, University of Texas. Agosto 30–Septiembre 2, 1999.

Carrillo, F. J. (2001). Meta-KM: A program and a plea. *Knowledge and Innovation: Journal of the KMCI*, vol. 1, no. 2, enero, pp. 27–54.

Carrillo, F. J. (2002). Capital systems: Implications for a global knowledge agenda. *Journal of Knowledge Management*, vol. 6, no. 4, October, pp. 379–399.

Carrillo, F. J. (2004). Capital cities: A taxonomy of capital accounts for knowledge cities. *Journal of Knowledge Management*, vol. 8, no. 5, October 2002.

Carrillo, L. (2002). *Enfrentan rezagos desde globalización*. El Norte, Monterrey, México, March 31, p. 5A.

Choi, S., Stahl, D. and Whinston, A. (1997). *The Economics of Electronic Commerce: The Essential Economics of Doing Business in the Electronic Marketplace*, Indianapolis, IN: Macmillan.

Cyret, R. and March, J. (1992). *A Behavioral Theory of the Firm* (2nd edn), New York: Blackwell Business.

Edvinsson, Leif. (2005). Regional intellectual capital in waiting: A strategic intellectual capital quest. In Ahmed Bounfour and Leif Edvinsson (eds.) *Intellectual Capital for Communities–Nations, Regions and Cities*. Elsevier/Butterworth-Heinemann, pp. 19–34.

European Commission. (2000). *Innovation Policy in a Knowledge-based Economy*. Brussels: European Commission.

Flores, P. (2000). Relación de enfoques y modelos de Capital Intelectual, *Guía del Módulo 2: Sistemas de Capitales*, Diplomado en Administración del Conocimiento, Monterrey: CSC.

Guevara, D. (2002). Modelo de Negocios Basado en Conocimiento a partir de la Teoría de la Firma. *Tesis de grado: Maestría en Administración de Tecnologías de Información*, Monterrey: Tecnológico de Monterrey.

Ives, W., Torrey, B. and Gordon, C. (1998). Knowledge management: An emerging discipline with a long history. *Journal of Knowledge Management*, vol. 1, no. 4, pp. 269–274.

Marr, Bernard. (ed.) (2005). *Perspectives on Intellectual Capital*. Elsevier/Butterworth-Heinemann.

Marr, Bernard and Chatzkel, Jay. (eds). (2005). IC at the crossroads: Theory and research. *Special Issue of the Journal of Intellectual Capital*, vol. 5, no. 2.

OECD. (2001). The new economy: Beyond the hype. Final Report on the OCDE Growth Project, Meeting of the OCDE Council at Ministerial Level. Available at: http://www.oecd.org/EN/home/0,EN-home-33-nodirectorate-no-no—33,FF.html.

Sullivan, P. (2000). A brief history of the ICM movement. *Value-driven Intellectual Capital; How to convert Intangible Corporate Assets into Market Value*. Wiley, pp. 238–244. Available at: http://www.sveiby.com/articles/icmmovement.html.

Thoreson, J. D. and Blankeship, J. H. (1996). *Information Secrets: Metrics and Measures for Valuing Information*. Richardson, Texas, USA: Valuable Information.

Woodwall, P. (ed.) (2000). Survey: The new economy. *The Economist*, 21 September.

Chapter 5

K-City and Society Entrepreneurship for Intellectual Capital Growth

Leif Edvinsson, *UNIC, Stockholm, Sweden*

Quizzics for the Knowledge City

The open space in between intelligence (what we know) and ignorance (what we do not know that we do not know) might be seen as the opportunity space for knowledge navigation of the knowledge city of tomorrow. This is also the opportunity room for society entrepreneurship adding to the evolution of knowledge cities. Quizzics, as the art and science of questioning, might be an initial mind-stimulating dimension. What are the most critical questions to ask to stimulate the thought process for the insights of Knowledge Cities (K-cities)? Here are some suggestions:

What dominates today? What we know about K-cities versus what we do not know? What are the major characteristics or distinctions of a K-city? What drives the evolution of a K-city, the so-called demand factors or supply factors? If you were to migrate into another city, what are you looking for? If you were to stay, what do you appreciate most? What makes your city attractive for the creative class of knowledge workers? How do we transform the traditional harbor of goods into the knowledge harbor? What kind of social innovations do we see today in K-cities? If your city were up for sale, would you buy it? Is there another value logic emerging, calling for another, active intelligence and society entrepreneurship. What might be the future earning capabilities, or roots for the fruits of a K-city?

Futurizing and Longitude

The core distinction of Intellectual Capital (IC) is Future Earnings Capabilities, i.e., not historical costs, but rather trying to hedge—capability to think ahead and to go from harvest and subtracting value to nourishing and adding value. This calls for another type of leadership role than traditional management as well as a refined perspective beyond the linear value chain. This is futurizing.

For city leadership it is essential to look out, ahead, up, and backwards. This is a time and longitude perspective. Leadership might also contain an interesting historical meaning. According to a story/myth, leadership is related to the navigator in front of a Viking ship loading or measuring the depth of the water. The task of the corporate board as well as a city board is to navigate the future of its constituency.

The common practice of most board work of today is around fulfilment of legal requirements related to maintenance. Society innovations and society renewal will become exceptions. For society leadership, it is essential with an amplified focus on renewal and intelligence. It is a continuous process to be informed and alerted, and hedging what is around the corner. In other words, an intellectual capability for futurizing.

This extended perspective might also be called a longitude perspective, beyond the traditional perspectives of the balance sheet and financial economy. "Longitude" emerges from Latin, *longitudo*, meaning length. It has a distinction as degree of length, or the angle between the meridian where you are at the moment and another selected meridian of origin.

Today we assess mainly present position—and resources used to get here. This present position, can be assessed and appreciated, but not changed. That value is in other words a given asset, shaped by historical activities. The measurement unit of longitude is time. And the key indicator is the angle for futurizing, i.e., time to move onwards and turn the future into an asset. The core of it is the capability to perceive and relate to the surrounding context. It is about the sustainability, ecology, and meaning making.

The longitude perspective is also very much based on the intangible dimensions and investments into knowledge and highlights the cultural context for value creation. The future image is in our brains. This is a visionary foresighted value. It might also be seen as capital in waiting, as opportunity room for the K-city. It might even be regarded as sustainability wealth in waiting. But as such it needs continuous city renewal or continuous society innovations.

The most essential for city futurizing is not cash flow but time flow or knowledge advantage based on intelligence. As long as the city or enterprise has this intelligence advantage they have a time monopoly that represents a value. Therefore one of the core distinctions of a longitude board is not to give advice, but to refine strategic questions, raising the level of intelligence, also called quizzics.

The way to get around this is to initiate a supplementary intelligence force to the traditional board of directors, as a kind of longitude board. This could be a temporary group of navigators with outsights, networks, relationships, etc. to be able to chart the course. Another longitude role might be to have a chief venture officer for initiating tangible prototypes of tomorrow.

Knowledge City Context and Intangibles Investment

For this city renewal and society innovations, we have to look at the shift of global investment flows into intangible and knowledge. The investment into intangibles among 18 countries in OECD countries in 2000, according to M. Khan at OECD, varied from 2 to 7% of GDP, with Sweden and USA at the top end. This figure is based on a narrow definition of expenditure for R&D, education, and software investments. With a broader definition, the figure would grow for the knowledge-intensive economies to be beyond 10% of GDP. Furthermore in those countries, the intangibles investments seem to be more than 60% of total investments. A major proportion of these investments go into urban areas.

The total expenditure on R&D for 2000 for the countries in OECD is estimated to be US$563 billion. The distribution among major regions is that USA stands for 47%, EU for 31%, and Japan 17%. Sweden is reported to invest 3.9% and Finland 3.4% of GDP. The average for OECD countries is reported to be 2.4%. Adding to these investments educational investment would raise the amount with more than 5%. The software investment has recently grown but still to be around 1.4% of GDP of OECD countries. To that comes the intangible impact of bioinformatics and genetics research.

In Europe this has also resulted in a quest for promoting the competitive investments into intangibles, also called the Lisbon agenda, from the European Union summit in Lisbon, Portugal in 2002.

The aspiration is to lift the investment of especially R&D to the level of 3% of GDP for EU's 12 countries. How will this magnitude and shift of intangible investments impact the evolution of knowledge-intensive regions and cities?

Top List of IC of Nations

Intellectual Capital contains three major dimensions, human capital, organizational structural capital, and relationship capital. The focus of IC is now not only for individuals, but also for enterprises, public as well as private, and the larger context of structural capital from cities, communities, and nations are being looked into.

The results from a study in January 2005 of IC of European Union versus USA and Japan, based on statistics up to 2001, by Dr. D. Andriessen and C. Stam, are shown in Figure 1.

Figure 1

IC Assets of the European Union. Source: Andriessen and Stam (2005), www.intellectualcapital.nl

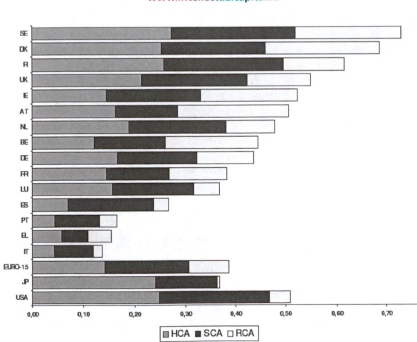

The top list of IC countries in the EU are:

- Sweden
- Denmark
- Finland
- UK
- Ireland
- Austria
- Netherlands
- Belgium
- Germany
- France.

This list is summarizing the assets of IC including the three major components of Intellectual capital, human capital (HCA), structural capital (SCA), and relationship capital (RCA). The strategic map can be refined even more regarding investment of IC and its effects on wealth and welfare of EU (see www.intellectualcapital.nl) But with a benchmarking perspective it clarifies the opportunity space for many countries to address. In that opportunity space the knowledge-intensive regions and cities will be the spark plug.

Ragusa, a City of Intelligence

Ragusa is an interesting historical bench learning case as K-city. It was both a city and a republic on the coastline Mediterranean, more precisely the Adriatic coastline. It had one of the highest standards of living for 500 years. It sustained its independency throughout five centuries. In a 2002 article, "Ragusa intelligence and security 1301–1806: A model for the twenty-first century?" the late professor Stevan Dedijer, known as the "father of social intelligence," elaborated on the key success factor for Ragusa. I have rephrased it to sustainability factors for knowledge regions.

Ragusa, according to R. Harris, was legendary for its diplomatic expertise; its political stamina was extraordinary, its merchants trading throughout the huge Ottoman Empire, enjoyed privileges denied to other Western states. A politicaly skilled and commercially enterprising ruling class took every opportunity to maximize the Ragusan Republic's Wealth. At the end of the 15th century, it had the largest fleet of merchants in the Adriatic Sea. During the second half of the 18th century it established 60 ambassadors or intelligence offices in almost all major cities in the Mediterranean. In 1806 for the first time in its history Ragusa was occupied by the forces of Napoleon, and in 1808 it ceased to exist. Today the city is called Dubrovnik in the nation of Croatia.

The sustainability factors for Ragusa have been extracted in a research by one of my Master students at Lund University: D. Radovanovic. They can be summarized as follows:

- Organized strategic intelligence and security (According to Dedijer, the first European function for Intelligence and Security emerged in Ragusa in 1301.)
- Political stamina and governmental diplomacy
- Spirit of the city and cohesiveness
- Diversity with intensive immigrations in a quest for collective wealth
- Rich cultural life, and multi-linguistic with writings in three languages
- Scientific environment and cultivated knowledge tradition
- Favorable geopolitical position and infrastructure for transports and communication.

One of the most intriguing learning is this capability to develop inside as well as outside knowledge navigators as "eyes and ears" for the future sustainability. In Ragausa they were among others educating special dragomans for the role as knowledge navigators or more formally titled ambassadors. Ragusa then used its overseas and international contacts to detect signals from the surrounding world to learn and adapt rapidly. How could such knowledge navigators be able to establish a longitude board of the intelligent K-city?

Intelligent Knowledge City

More and more cities are declaring themselves as intelligent and knowledge cities, where the political agenda is developing the context or structural capital from human capital growth to collective wealth. Here is a list of some of the emerging key cases:

- Singapore
- Barcelona
- Manchester
- Copenhagen/Malmoe
- Dubai
- Melbourne
- Shanghai
- Monterrey.

Most of the distinctions of Intelligent Cities are emerging from an information technology perspective. The World Teleport Association has a special interest group on Intelligent Communities with an award to the Intelligent City. According to them, the following critical success factors form the intelligent community—broadband infrastructure, knowledge work force, and innovative digital democracy. A list can be accessed on www.intelligentcommunity.org with among others Singapore, Dubai, and Osaka on it.

One distinction of intelligent cities has been offered by N. Komninos (2002) in his book on Intelligent Cities. He defines intelligent cities as islands and communities where the innovation processes meet the digital world and the applications of the information society. The functions of an intelligent city are those related to production of knowledge such as R&D, technology transfer, innovations, and networking. These functions are taking place in real space by human interactions and in virtual space via ICT. He is highlighting three basic components of an intelligent city:

(1) islands of innovations e.g., Cluster of industries and services
(2) virtual innovation system including knowledge tools e.g., Science parks and telemetric
(3) integrations, i.e., connection between real and virtual innovation system.

Another distinction that connects the concept of intelligent city with the intellectual capital paradigm is coming from G. Bugliarello, Chancellor at Polytechnic University in Brooklyn, N.Y. He argues that an intelligent city is one that has the ability to successfully self-adapt to threats and to change and renew. It is rather close to the dimensions of Ragusa as elaborated by professor S. Dedijer in terms of social intelligence. Bugliarello also argues that the city must be efficient in its use of resources. He also highlights the importance of education as a core element of civilization. This is very close to the dimensions of both A. Pulic on IC efficiency and N. Bontis' research on the drivers for regional IC.

Figure 2

The Intelligent City K-Recipe. Source: Leif.Edvinsson@unic.net

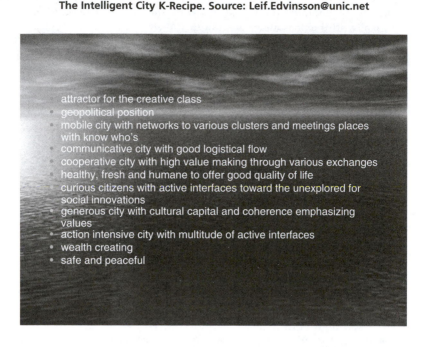

- attractor for the creative class
- geopolitical position
- mobile city with networks to various clusters and meetings places with know who's
- communicative city with good logistical flow
- cooperative city with high value making through various exchanges
- healthy, fresh and humane to offer good quality of life
- curious citizens with active interfaces toward the unexplored for social innovations
- generous city with cultural capital and coherence emphasizing values
- action intensive city with multitude of active interfaces
- wealth creating
- safe and peaceful

Based on among others learning from Ragusa, I would like to characterize an intelligent city by the following attributes—knowledge-recipe for City Intelligence (Figure 2):

According to the research on Ragusa three major sustainability factors can be grouped as clusters for further elaborations

- Intelligence, being well organized to relate to the external structural and human captial
- Governmental leadership for providing structural capital as precondition for wealth creation
- Community spirit or values for bonding human capital with different structural institutional capital for the larger common good of the city.

So my emerging definition of a K-city might be: A city purposely designed for encouraging and nourishing the collective knowledge as capabilities to shape efficient and sustainable value creating actions of welfare.

The City as Knowledge Harbor or Knowledge Exchange

One of the most intriguing aspects for evolution of the K-city might be found in the roots of a city. According to research on the origins of cities it was to address the cost of exchange of goods, and to reduce the transaction cost. Consequently the harbors emerged as a core space for the flow of goods. Copenhagen might be illustrative. The meaning of its name is a harbor (hague) for procurement (copen). In cities of today we still see the growth of shopping centers and malls. However this might in the knowledge economy be challenged by the evolution of trade of intangibles, knowledge, and thoughtware. Here I suggest another design for knowledge harbors or knowledge exchange to reduce the friction cost of relationship capital growth. This is still a concept in evolution and prototyping, as a space for the new urbanism.

The major characteristics of a knowledge harbor might be related to:

- trade of knowledge and thoughtware as context
- migration and flow of knowledge workers as the tools
- quality of life and ergonomics as the outcome and impact.

A knowledge harbor is a kind of society innovation based on the triple helix collaboration of society, academia, and business community. It is based on the logistics of knowledge flow. It is a tool for the growth of regional intellectual capital. The K-city as an exchange or harbour is then a knowledge tool.

The value of a K-harbor emerges in the interaction of the flow of knowledge and the knowledge arenas; for example, knowledge cafés. The K-harbor emerges as a meeting space for brains. It has a lot of similarities to the Future Center concept I have developed, as a space for experiential knowledge exploration. The currency that emerges is relationship capital. As such it can be measured as customer relations as well as supplier relations. However K-harbor is based on the structural capital of the K-city; for example, the architecture and design of the knowledge arena.

One of the most essential structural capital dimensions for the knowledge migration of today is airports. According to research by J. Poort, Holland, NYFE, and data from Eurostat, there is a very strong and positive correlation between regional airport activity and regional economic growth. A 1% growth in airport activity boosts regional economic growth by 0.17% on average. Between 1991 and 1998 the top 100 European airports grew twice the speed of regional economics, or 6.7%. Furthermore, airports are like small cities in terms of numbers of employees. The airport of Stockholm Arlanda today has more than 16,000 employees. So if airports have such impact as catalysts, just imagine what leverage an explicit knowledge port design might give for the future knowledge economy.

The knowledge harbour acts as a bridge for relationship development. As such it is acting as an intellectual capital multiplier for the human capital leveraged by good structural capital. In recent research this can be assessed as a space full of joy, or in other terms a campus area of endorphins. This is something we have been prototyping at the CMM—Centre for Molecular Medicine—as the Happy Restaurant. The purpose is to nourish the interaction and contractility of the researchers to cultivate the innovations and continuous renewal.

In its extension, K-harbor might be resulting in another emerging concept for urban design—En2Polis, the knowledge city of the future. Some of the major features might be—gateway to world knowledge, knowledge bank, knowledge exchanges, knowledge olympics, knowledge tourism. See more on www.entovation.com.

Knowledge City Measurement

Why is measurement or mapping so important? It is because the absence of systematized intelligence and communicable information will affect trust. Such missing intelligence will also have an impact on the efficient supply and distribution of future resources for wealth. What is needed in a growing complexity is a clarifying measurement system to sensitize our minds to perceive the best options. In other words, we need an accounting system to assure us on the angle of longitude navigation into the future. It might be illustrated by the gap between blindfold observations (e.g., News) and insightful seeing (e.g., Social intelligence), resulting in either crises or opportunity perspectives.

What measurement systems can support this sea change in orientation? Certainly the contribution from the essential associated intangibles such as trust, brain efficiency, and healthy collaboration are well beyond the scope of conventional accounting systems. The value of relationships needs to be measured, as does the contribution from knowledge recipes. As the new economical value is both intangible and in the longitude, i.e., lateral dimensions instead of vertical dimensions, we have to develop more lateral, comparative, and benchmarking accounting of value creation potential of intangibles. We have to acknowledge such new intangible indicators and get the accountants to audit those, as well as annual reports to present transparency of such intellectual capital, to be able to navigate these new organizational value creations. See the Danish Guidelines on www.vtu.dk/icaccounts.

One of the most refined such IC reports, following very much the experiences from my prototyping IC reporting at Skandia, has been presented in 2002 by Seibersdorf Research Center, and IC pioneering colleagues in Austria. During 2003 a law has been implemented in Austria requiring all universities and colleges to publish a knowledge capital report annually, showing knowledge goals, knowledge processes, and knowledge indicators. The very first prototype for university reporting was done by University of Kremz, Austria. How will the first such IC report for a K-city look like?

In 2004 the Ministry of Science and Work in Germany has run a prototyping project on Knowledge Reporting. See www.wissenskapital.info or www.akwissensbilanz.org. The core of this approach is to visualize the key drivers for IC development and also to make an IC decision map for alternative investment choices.

Furthermore in Japan the Ministry of Economy, Trade and Industry launched in 2004 the first version of guidelines for reporting on intangible assets. In USA the AICPA—American Institute of Certified Public Accountants—are working on similar guidelines. In December 2004 a High Level Expert Group to which I belong, had been appointed along with the European Commission to look into developing guidance for IC reporting for knowledge intensive enterprises, especially the R&D sector.

Several methods for regional IC have been presented by, among others, Dr. Nick Bontis, Canada, Professor Ante Pulic, Croatia, Professor José Viedma, Spain, and Professor Ahmed Bounfour, France, for regional mapping and measurement approaches. In Sweden and Norway there is also a special municipality instrument called Kommun kompass. It is focusing on key quality areas.

Intelligent Capital rating is also a relevant assessment tool, in progress since 1997. It is focusing the IC components for future earnings potential. It might be seen as complimentary to Standard & Poor's rating of financial capital. IC rating is about benchmarking 3 major perspectives of:

(1) efficiency
(2) renewal
(3) risks.

The scale is 10 grades from AAA to D. See more on www.intellectualcapital.se. It is now used by more than 200 organizations both in Europe and Japan. The IC-rating gives both a map for benchmark versus best in class, but also a platform for assessing how to release the future earning capabilities and best option, thereby creating an intelligence trust for the future. It seems to be especially interesting for public organizations such as schools and hospitals that do not have the public stock market as a grading reference point. This approach is now also being applied for regional rating of IC of cities and regions. For a K-city to look only at the financial bottom line will give blindfold intelligence, as the major proportion of the key resources for a K-city is invisible intangibles.

One example of such municipality IC rating can be shown in Figure 3. The map shows in this city a strong internal management focus and the weaker external relationship capital nourishment. It visualizes the balance between management efficiency of the present and the renewal for the future. It also highlights as city intelligence map, the present position and forthcoming high-risk areas. So this kind of City IC rating might be a very complementary mapping to the administrative and economic perspectives of a city. The alternative might be a city of ignorance rather than intelligence. A K-city not continuously renewing the wealth-creating context for its citizens will erode. So the social intelligence has to focus on indicators to release the potential of collaborative efforts between the stakeholders of politicians, municipality staff, and its citizens.

By applying such approaches for intangibles it has shown that municipalities in Sweden might have a major hidden value potential. According to PwC—Price Waterhouse Coopers, Sweden—there is at least an efficiency gain in resource utilization to be gained, estimated to around 10% of total economic volume! Further prototyping on mapping IC of municipalities might also reveal a correlation of value growth related to the relationship capital dimensions. Such prototyping has also highlighted the issues of commuting knowledge workers. They live in one municipality and work in another. How do we refine the map to capture this dynamic flow for urban value creation?

Figure 3

Norway: Municipality – Development. Source: www.intellectualcapital.se

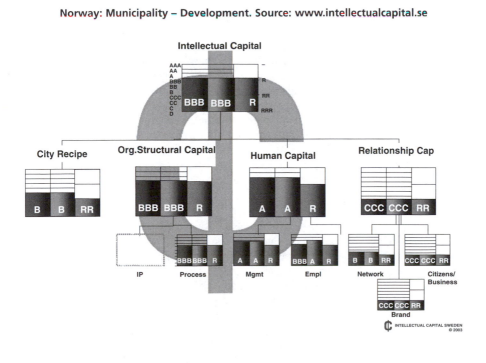

Figure 4

CMM IC reporting model. Source: Center for Molecular Medicine, Stockholm (2004), www.cmm.ki.se

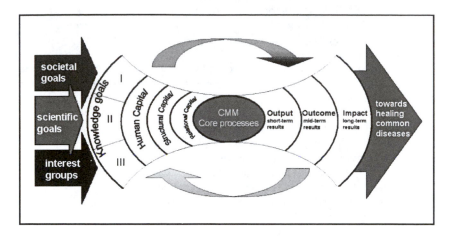

This might be related to the earlier observation that the flow of relationships, also called migration, is of critical importance while mapping for knowledge intensive regions. It also indicates that value-creating trade is taking place in the so-called twilight zones, or border regions; among others, characterized by diverging thought processes, instead of converging thinking. It might be illustrated by the prosperous historical Hansa period with extensive trade in the Baltic Sea between the surrounding states. Today it can be illustrated by the Oresund, the sea channel between Sweden and Denmark, where among others the life science sector is clustering into global excellence and called the Medicon Valley.

The core of IC reporting is to extend the time perspective to go beyond input–output perspectives, to also include the medium-term outcome as well as the long-term impact. For city leadership this kind of longitude perspectives might also be extremely essential. What is the long-term impact of the political leadership and voting of today? Is the value equivalent to input, or is it more in line with outcome or even is the impact visible only over time longer than the accounting cycle? In Sweden the very first prototype for such innovation-oriented R&D institutions was launched by CMM. See Figure 4 and www.cmm.ki.se.

Arena for Cultivating Leadership

The new strategic units of analysis in the knowledge era will be renewal, learning, innovations and sense making. This might reconnect to the ecology of the knowledge economics. It is about the roots meeting their context. It is about cultivating spaces for both such meetings to happen and to release the brainpower potential when it happens. It is about the intangible enablers for knowledge exchange and knowledge interactions by longitude leadership. Traditional offices or shopping centers might not be the solution, but rather knowledge cafés as the exchanges for new thought leadership. Development of such arenas will be important tools and landmarks for the K-city. This is, among others, visible in both Barcelona and Dubai.

Value of intellectual capital is created in the interaction between people (human capital) and the organizational structural capital. Nonaka (1994) is referring to this as knowledge creating dialectics. He also referred to them as "Ba," which literally is said to mean a space for appreciation in Japanese. The recent emerging way of addressing future challenges in Japan is called chi management. The innovative chi management involves a thought leadership, integrating and optimizing knowledge sharing, enabling wisdom and a conscious mind in harmony with the context. This might be of critical importance to be able to attract and nourish the globally migrating creative class. The creative class is the well-educated globally migrating people, according to Florida and Tinagli (2004), looking for where and how to connect to other talents, through technology and tolerance.

The importance of Ba for a knowledge city has been further refined by Baqir and Kathawal (2004). However, they are more focused on futuristic technologies as pillars for knowledge home, which when acting together collectively, constitute a knowledge city. In my experience, it is the combination of structural capital as technology together with the cultural and relationship dimensions that will leverage the human capital. I call this the IC multiplier effect.

In Skandia's case the arena was labeled Future Centre. The Skandia Future Centre (SFC), established in 1996, focused on the value creation by experiential knowledge exploration. It became an arena where employees could enter into the future and then return to the present with new insights and aha's for a more intelligent dialog and knowledge sharing. SFC, with its focus on prototyping knowledge exploration, might also be described as an arena for intellectual entrepreneurship, as labeled by professor Kwiatkowsky. The SFC also became an arena to prototype the impact of space design for, among others, knowledge well being and reducing the fear of innovation. In other words to nourish the entrepreneurial courage. SFC has now been followed by many more similar arenas.

In February 2002 the Ministry of Economics in Denmark launched Mind Lab. It is a center with the aim to nourish knowledge management in the public sector, see www.mind-lab.org. A similar innovation platform has now been launched by the Dutch government and its ministries for knowledge nourishment. The Ministry of Finance, Ministry of Social Affairs, the Ministry of Agriculture, Ministry of Taxation, and Ministry of Transportation (see among others www.molbilion.nl) all have a very challenging public agenda for the arena.

In 2004 there was another such knowledge idea lab, called Momentum, established for regional development on North Zealand in Denmark, see more on www.Momentum-nord.dk. In 2006 there will be another 7-floor building called LabLand by Innovation Lab launched in Aarhus, in Denmark. See www.labland.net.

What seems to be essential in these new K-spaces is, among others,

- the creative context
- networking space
- quality of relationships and mind satisfaction.

Research at University of Gothenburg show the high importance of psychosocial dimensions for the knowledge work. In that we find the architecture, and contextual design to stand for around 20% of the health impacting factors. Furthermore Dr. Reza Emdad, at Karolinska Institute in Stockholm together with several colleagues, has looked into the impact and intervention approaches, derived from modern brain research, to prevent work-related brain stress and transformation of intellect into IC at work.

Consequently the new psychosocial ecosystem for cultivating leadership will require a combination of both new accounting approaches with new intangible indicators related to values and mind cultivating spaces for value creation. In Sweden, the work of prototyping the holistic accounting, health management, and cultural knowledge space design for intangible strength is going on at the time of writing. See www.bottomline.se.

Knowledge Zones as Super Brains

Urban design becomes a sustainability factor for attracting, insourcing, and retaining talent. In the 21st century innovation-based knowledge zones are emerging, with a more amplified dimensions collaborations and quality of life for its citizens. According to Dr. Debra Amidon (2003) a Knowledge Zone is a geographical region, segment, or community of practice in which knowledge flows from the point of origin to the point of need or opportunity. She sees an evolution from the 1980s with various academic, industrial and governmental technology park-oriented training-based initiatives. In the 1990s this was replaced by more learning-based science parks.

What is evident is the clustering of talent to special places, for knowledge specialization. The creative class will migrate to knowledge center on a global scale with a good living. This is where both financial capital and intellectual capital will accumulate. Efficient societies are shaped to attract, retain, and cultivate the brains. This also relates to the core of urban design to reduce the transaction cost of flow of goods in the old days, and in the knowledge economy to reduce the friction cost of knowledge flow.

This evolution of organized knowledge capital can also be viewed from emerging insights of neuroscience. During the last decade more and more research have shown how the brain is evolving, and has been growing to the present size and capability. Billions of connections and neurons are shaping the evolutionary biological base for intellectual capital. The society is such an organized collaborative thought processor. The brain is in evolutionary growth since millions of years. The cultural competitive process and migration of talent into super brains is described by professor emeritus G. A. Karlsson. The K-city becomes a hub both for the creative class but also an intelligence center, like hippocampus. From pedagogical research by Hemlin, Allwood and Martin (2004), in Lund we can learn that creativity needs joy and vice versa. From neuroscience we might also learn about the importance of brain stilling and joy. Where do we find the joyful hippocampus of the K-city full of endorphins? In the shopping center, plaza, school, or amusement park for edutainment?

Society Entrepreneurship

Society development and urbanism might be the key sustainability factor for the future. The social construct of the firm as well as the city design is emerging as key organizational capital among others with urban design as social innovation, like in the case of Barcelona. The key question for the innovative approaches might be related to what is valued over time by the citizens.

Research on how wealth is being created in the knowledge era, by Dr. Nick Bontis, points to a leadership or governance agenda focused on the following priority order:

- research and development initiatives
- educational initiatives
- networking and trade development
- industrial efficiency.

One of the most challenging future roles related to this agenda will then be Society Entrepreneurship. It is a kind of intellectual entrepreneurship, hunting for the opportunity room. Sometimes it is described as the 4-th sector, on the intersection of public, private, and idealistic sectors. The space for this work will definitely be in the twilight zone between public and private sector. For example, the transformation of old idle airfields into modern airports for low cost tourism together with Ryan Air. Therefore it is also referred to as PPP—public–private partnerships. It is about nourishing a cross-over prototyping. This is an opportunity space, with a lot of IC in waiting, for society and social innovations. It will be an intellectual challenging process to optimize both the non-traditional thought processing and the new value flows.

The space for K-city renewal and Society Innovation by society entrepreneurship might be illustrated as in Figure 5. It is to address the process dimensions as well as the social capital dimension, as labeled by Putnam (2000). He refers to social capital as the social networks and the interactive reciprocity that might be vivid in those. The structural organization capital stays behind when people migrate. Process capital corresponds to the core processes of the region, often culturally driven, for wealth creation. The collective innovation capital will flourish in the right context. Just look at Silicon Valley, Paris, Milan, and Barcelona. Furthermore, Anne Tsui (2005) shows the importance of refined network analysis of social capital to include also the moderating role of cultural context. Her distinction of social capital is the advantage an individual gets for from being in certain types of social networks, i.e., cities.

This new space for society innovations might also be referred to as the Creapreneurship ©, based on the combination of creative entrepreneurship. This is a concept in development by L. O. Landin in Sweden (see www.ebc.se). Among others it is highlighting the emotional intelligence to get to a higher level of FQ—fantacy quota. But most of all it is about looking for the continuous renewal.

In Sweden a special project to award, in 2005, the most innovative municipality has been initiated by PwC. So far 16 municipalities have been nominated. The society innovations vary from collaborative concepts, democracy approaches, visionary attraction, administrative efficiency tools, organizational system to impact health, leadership quality development, local competency brokerage, knowledge tourism, etc.

In the growing complexity we need to highlight the transparency for the IC multiplier, or in other words look for what kind of strategic structural capital will leverage the human citizen capital, for organizations as well as regions or cities. Technical innovations might be more related to the organizational capital, for example Internet, while social innovations relate more to the relationship capital dimensions, for example city design

Figure 5

Society Innovation Spaces. Source: Edvinsson and Radovanovic, 2004

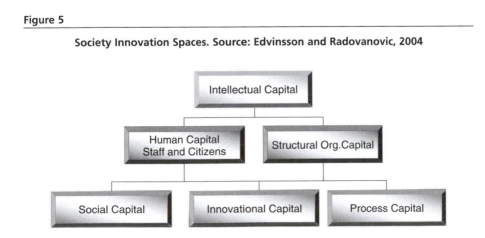

for quality of life. Barcelona made this very explicit in its transformation process with its special social construction company of 22@.

Conclusion

The K-city can be regarded as a tool, or partial arena to nourish the transformation and renewal into the knowledge economy. For this Future Knowledge Society we need to develop the infrastructure for migration and flow of people as well as the cultivation of relationship capital. This will call for society entrepreneurship as a prime mover role. If Ragusa was good at Social Intelligence we need to be prime movers of prototyping a good IC multiplier effect by focusing the collective brain potential for continuous society and social innovations. This will be resulting in sustainable wealth.

What we now need is a deeper intelligence to understand and follow the wave of knowledge economics for K-city design and IC urbanism by:

- ecosystem for knowledge sustainability
- space for attracting and shaping quality of life and health for knowledge workers
- relationship spaces for continuous renewal and society and social innovations.

Some Links for Further Reading

www.corporatelongitude.com
www.intellectualcapital.se
www.wissenskapital.info
www.akwissensbilanz.org
www.iccommunity.com
www.entovation.com
www.ebc.se
www.vtu.dk/icaccounts
www.kmcluster.com
www.bontis.com
www.minez.nl
www.blev.stern.ny
www.vaic-on.net
www.intellectualcapital.nl.

References

Amidon, D. (2003). *The Innovation Superhighway – Harnessing Intellectual Capital for Collaborative Advantage*. Oxford: Butterworth-Heinemann.

Andriessen, D. and Stam, C. (2005). The IC of the European Union, Measuring the Lisbon Agenda.

Baqir, M. N. and Kathawala, Y. (2004). Ba for Knowledge cities: A futuristic technology model. *Journal of Knowledge Management,* vol. 8, no. 5, pp. 83–95.

Bontis, N. (2002). *National Intellectual Capital Index: Intellectual Capital Development in the Arab Region*. NY: United Nations.

Danish Ministry of Industry. (2001). *Guidelines for Knowledge Accounts*. Denmark: Copenhagen.

Dedijer, S. (2002). Ragusa intelligence and security 1301–1806. *International Journal of Intelligence and Counter Intelligence*, vol. XV, no. 1, Spring.

Dedijer, S. (2003). Development & Intelligence 2003–2053. Working Paper 2003/10, Lund: Research Policy Institute.

Edvinsson, L. and Grafstrom, G. (1999). *Accounting for Minds*. Stockholm, Sweden: Skandia, ISBN 0749917679.

Edvinsson, L. and Radovanovic, D. (2004). *Intelligence and Lund*. Lund: Lund University.

Emdad, R. (2002). The theory of general, and job-related EPOS: Emdad's pyramid of stress (demand, effort, satisfaction), Stockholm, Karolinska Institute, National Institute for Psychosocial Factors and Health, ISBN 91-85910-25-2.

Hemlin, S., Allwood, C. M. and Martin, B. (2004). *Creative Knowledge Environments*, UK: Elgar.

Florida, R. and Tinagli, I. (2004). *Europe in the Creative Age*. London: Demos.

Karlsson, G. A. (1991). *The Competitiveness of Super Brains*. "Superhjärnornas kamp–om intelligensens roll i samhället" (Fischer & Co, 1997) Sweden: Stockholm.

Komninos, N. (2002). *Intelligent Cities*. London: Spon Press.

Nonaka, I. (1994). A dynamic theory of organizational knowledge creation. *Organization Science*, vol. 5, no. 1, pp. 14–38.

Poort, J. (2004). On the intimate relationship between airports and regional growth. In *Innovative City*. Germany: Hagbarth Publications.

Pulic, A. (2003). *Efficiency on National and Company Level*. Zagreb: Croatian Chamber of Commerce.

Putnam, R. (2000). *Bowling Alone: The Collapse and Revival of American Community*. New York: Simon&Schuster.

Viedma, J. M. (1999). *ICBS Intellectual Capital Benchmarking System*. Canada (Paper): McMaster University.

Tsui, S. A. (1992). *Being Different: Relational Demography and Organizational Attachment*. USA: Administrative Science Quarterly.

Chapter 6

Implementation of the Capital System for a Knowledge City

Pedro Flores, *Center for Knowledge Systems, Tecnológico de Monterrey, México*

Introduction

One of the economy's tasks is to find a way of combining the factors of production in the most effective manner. This implies defining which factors of production are necessary for a specific value creation system, and to what extent. As Lev comments, nowadays we can observe, in a great number of organizations, that the representation of knowledge as a factor of production is becoming stronger and stronger (Lev, 2004).

Carrillo (2002) refers to knowledge as an event, where the basic elements are the object of knowledge that is known (ideas, images, and representations), the subject of knowledge (the agent that performs the action on the object) and the context of knowledge (providing meaning to the event's possible relations). This last one has a referential nature. Knowledge-Based Development (KBD) involves an identification of categories related to value, agents, and objects, in a knowledge system.

According to Carrillo (2002), Knowledge Management (KM) has difference definitions depending on the knowledge event that it manages. The simplest form of KM focuses on the object, which is basically information. A second form of KM is the use of the object by an agent, meaning, the transfer and assimilation of knowledge. Under a third approach, KM adds the context, which gives economic meaning to the internal relationships between object and agent. The basis for this chapter, where KM is proposed as a strategy for managing the complete set of capitals or value dimensions of an entity. In this case, the entity is a city.

In a previous work (2000), I mentioned that value can be recognized as tangible and intangible objects of preference for a certain community, in their material as well as artistic and/or relational aspect. Production as the basis of a social organization is formed by activities that increase social value. On the other hand, Carrillo (2004) affirms that all forms of human organization constitute systems to provide all their individuals with a value balance including everything from minimum health and survival elements to an increase in intangible capital such as education, culture, and other forms of human development.

At the same time, Carrillo (2004) says that the key factor for a city to exist consists of a significant community of people organizing life around a system of recognizable value. Due to today's transition—from industrial production to knowledge-based production—cities as collective values are also emerging as knowledge-based value systems. He also comments that the units that form a city (citizens, companies) have the possibility to remain in a determined city, depending on its particular value balance and the perceived development alternatives.

This chapter describes a process for detecting, understanding, and strategically applying a city's assets, which are viable for the construction of a differentiated value proposition for its types of customers: citizens and companies. This process has been developed under the principles of a KM approach focused on the strategic capitalization of knowledge (context–agent–object), basically on the Capital System (CS) model developed by Carrillo (2002). First, it is important to understand some elements of Knowledge-Based Strategies (KBS) for a city. Next, we must cover the CS model, its basis and implementation plan. Last is a description of the process that I propose for instrumenting a KBS through the CS, for a city. This chapter proposes a detailed description of the process, and its objective is to serve as a reference for the implementation of this process.

Knowledge-Based Development

For Dickinson, KBS needs to be built on the pillars of knowledge. The first pillar states that current services and products have incorporated knowledge. The second pillar states that intangible assets become a channel through which tangible assets are capitalized, increasing their productivity and maintaining sustainable efficiency. The task is to give added value to the tangible assets through performance practices focused on value-creation attributes (Dickinson, 2001).

Considering the previous statements, it seems to me that an organization may have a combination of intangible assets over which it may create differentiators for certain customers. I think that it is important to consider a new platform in order to understand the task of tangible and intangible assets in the creation of value—their individual contribution as well as connectivity with others.

A KM approach based on the capitalization of knowledge assets is available for cities. Understanding intangible variables may provide a wider context for approaching a community's efforts toward a future position. It is my opinion that the task of a knowledge-focused city is to maximize interactions between agents and available means, toward a balanced approach of value creation. Communicating these interactions is vital in motivating and attracting people and companies with better attributes, for building the city's different proposition.

According to Bounfour, today's development theories form solid arguments focused on the integration of knowledge and technology for the understanding of growth dynamics. These theories provide reasons to consider research, education, and learning as key elements for a community's growth. The foundations of a society are supported by forms of knowledge, such as culture, values, and participation. In today's economy, development initiatives must integrate these attributes (Bounfour and Edvinsson, 2005).

Lev affirms that knowledge assets are the essence of competition in today's organizations. However, most of those who are in charge of competition management in these organizations underestimate these assets (Lev, 2004). According to Kaplan and Norton (2002), this situation is more noticeable in public organizations, as is the case of a city, where the sought-for results are not of a financial nature, but are more related to impact on customers.

An economic factor to consider for the development of KM is the importance of intangible assets or Intellectual Capital (IC) in organizations. In a previous work (2000), I mentioned that IC management is based on the identification and measurement of intangible assets under a strategic implementation approach. Its initiation and development is a merger of two trends, one of which comes from organizations that acknowledged that the main contribution to their value proposal came from intangible assets, such as staff competence, use of technology, brand, and the creation of customer loyalty. The second trend comes from social entities (cities, regions, countries) that assimilated a social policy of KBD with special attention given to education, innovation processes, ecology, and technological development. For Bounfour and Edvinsson (2005), this last trend constitutes one of the initial steps toward the formation of a city through KBD.

The IC has a great number of lines of development for strategic identification, categorization, measurement, valuation, and interpretation. Each of these lines has been connecting effectively, in relation to the objective of managing the IC of each organization. Some organizations have focused on understanding each intangible asset regarding its strategic use (Flores, 2000). I consider that the details of this process are important for this work, having in mind the implementation of KBD for a city.

Kaplan and Norton mention that investing in intangible assets generally produces medium and long-term results. This limits the vision of public organizations, which are generally pressured by medium- and short-term results and are mostly focused on increasing their physical infrastructure. However, on the other hand, some cities' managements have identified knowledge as the asset that makes a city's value proposal toward integral development different. In their strategic management proposal to public and private organizations, Kaplan and Norton mention that intangible assets may contribute to the creation of value. Nevertheless, several factors prevent the strategic management from understanding and linking these assets (Kaplan and Norton, 2002):

(1) **The value is indirect.** Intangible assets rarely have a direct impact on major results. Improvement of intangible assets affects the results through cause–effect relationship chains that have intermediate stages.

(2) **The value is contextual.** The value of intangible assets depends on context and strategy. The assets cannot be valued separately from the processes that transform them.

(3) **The value is potential.** Intangible assets have potential value but they do not have market value. Processes are required to transform the potential value of the intangible assets in products and services that do have tangible value.

(4) **The assets are grouped.** Intangible assets rarely have value by themselves; they must be grouped along with other assets.

Understanding knowledge assets in any type of organization allows making better investment decisions (Lev, 2004). I consider that, in the case of public entities, understanding comes from a measurement of values attached to the entity's context, meaning that values are not general. Some experiences, like Toronto, Barcelona, and Charlotte, have made evident that the key lies in not thinking of knowledge as an object, but rather of its conversion capacity, meaning, understanding, and connecting all forms of knowledge through a strategy. Such interaction requires the representation of knowledge as capital.

Knowledge City

For Dedijer, a city with a knowledge approach represents an intelligent entity whose management uses its contacts for the detection of signs of development in order to learn and adapt as quickly as possible. In order to provide sustainability, a city must focus on innovation. One of the aspects of this type of innovation is social intelligence, which is a society's ability to learn from its environment, its context, and itself, in order to build its future. Social intelligence is not only limited to being informed, but also to understanding and connecting the variables, focusing on sustainable behavior (Dedijer, 2002).

From Komninos's point of view, the task of an intelligent city is focused on the production of knowledge, in the form of investigation, technology transfer, innovation, and networking. These interactions have both real and virtual spaces through digital technologies. The basic attributes of this type of cities are: the creation of clusters or innovation communities, the use of tools for virtual work, and the capacity of integration among physical and virtual communities (Komninos, 2002). On the other hand, a wider approach of intelligent cities displayed by Dedijer is regarding their capacity to understand, to adjust, and to generate growth through the efficient use of all types of resources and, mostly, by pushing education as an element that differentiates a society (Dedijer, 2002).

In his work regarding managing IC in order to develop a Knowledge City (KC), Edvinsson creates a composition of the outstanding attributes of an intelligent city (Bounfour and Edvinsson, 2005):

- Attraction toward knowledge workers
- Favorable geological position
- Established networks for high-knowledge capacity communities and spaces
- Flow and logistics for an effective community
- A cooperative society with high quality levels of exchange
- Quality of life: health, beauty, security, and cohabitation
- Culture and high social value experience
- Focused on the creation of value.

For Bounfour and Edvinsson (2005), bringing together and locating clusters of talent results in the specialization of certain knowledge areas. An increase in creative class or knowledge workers may be achieved through migration to knowledge regions. These areas will have potential characteristics for the accumulation of financial and intangible capital; also, they must be efficient in attracting, retaining, and cultivating the creative class.

Some cities have preferred the slogan "Intelligent City" instead of "Knowledge City." In my point of view, the first slogan's approach is integrated into the second slogan, which I describe later on under the proposal of the Capital System model.

One aspect is defining the concerns and attributes of a knowledge or intelligent city as described earlier. Another aspect is strategically translating these concerns and attributes into a management model. Kaplan and Norton (2002) comment that cities normally have problems to operationally define and translate their strategy. Strategy-related exercises are carried out that have nothing to do with the results that the city is trying to obtain. Most cities' strategies are focused on operational efficiency. The cities consider their mission as a given thing and attempt to do their work with utmost efficiency: reducing expenses, making fewer mistakes, and doing everything quickly. It is unusual to find a city centered on leadership strategy focused on value attributes for its customers: citizens and companies.

Currently, there are cities that have developed and translated a strategy focused on a series of strategic subjects interrelated in order to create value. According to Kaplan and Norton (2002), cities have had difficulties in representing their results, because financial success does not capture their essential role. A city's results must be focused on the customers: citizens and companies. In a city, the customer can be one of two, the one who supplies a resource and the user. In many cases, the customer plays both roles, supplying resources when paying for the services (installments, rents, taxes), and receiving a social service as a user. For Kaplan and Norton, it is important to get to know the customer in both ways, develop capital for both, and identify the processes that will create a supply of value that will cover all expectations.

For Kaplan and Norton (2002) it is necessary to consider long-term objectives in order to form a city's strategy; objectives that have an important impact on the society, where the city itself takes on a distinctive role, like for example reducing poverty, reducing illiteracy, improving the quality of life or the environment. I believe that when taking on KBD, these long-term objectives constitute the formation of specific actions for the development of a city's knowledge capital.

In their strategic city management works applied to the city of Charlotte, Kaplan and Norton (2002) comment that a city has three high-level perspectives that it can attend to in its strategy:

(1) **Created value.** Identifying benefits created for the citizens. Some examples of measurement to represent created value may be the percentage of students who acquire a specific knowledge, the density of contaminant agents in the water, mortality rates in a population, perception rates regarding public security and transportation quality rates.

(2) **Legitimating support.** Insuring the continuous financing of activities. The city must make an effort to fulfill the objectives of its sources of income: the public administration, the companies and the citizens.

(3) **Cost of supplying services.** Emphasizing the importance of operative efficiency. The measured cost must include the city's expenses and the social cost imposed on citizens and other organizations through their operations. The city must minimize direct and social costs required for producing its mission's benefits.

I believe that the principles to create a strategy-based organization are also applicable to a city. A city's quality strategy requires a more precise definition of its customers and their attributes. The customers must be the focus of major objectives, given that providing them with services accounts for the city's value proposal.

A KC's development factor is attracting knowledge workers (creative class) that will cover better the citizen's profile. According to Florida, this type of citizens is characterized by having a higher level of education, being well-informed, participative, critical, and politically active; constantly searches for a better quality of life, has healthier habits and is less dependent on consumerism; significantly values artistic and cultural representations; has a diverse, tolerant position; is competent in human relations (Florida, 2002).

Edvinsson speaks about several current cities that may be taken as reference in KC initiatives. Minneapolis–St. Paul occupies the first position in the competitiveness index based on knowledge activities in North America. Barcelona is focused on a superior urban design to attract knowledge workers based on a higher level of quality of life and development. Vancouver emerged in 2004 as the best city to live and work in due to a balanced combination between urban infrastructure and development capacity (Bounfour Edvinsson, 2005).

The Capital System Model Applied to a Knowledge City

I have identified the Capital System (CS) model as the technical element that forms a Knowledge-Based Strategy (KBS). This model has been developed in a practical environment, which makes its importance valid for organizations. Carrillo (2002) affirms that in today's economy a theory of the firm has been redefined, in which the organization builds a new type of competitive advantage regarding knowledge discovery, access, mobilization, and leverage along its areas. According to Carrillo, the CS helps represent all the dimensions of value for collective and aligned decision-making on behalf of any organization, private or public.

Consequently, knowledge is not only accumulative (object) and transactional (flow), but it is also referential and relational (context). I have suggested (2000) that different forms of knowledge need adequate, specific techniques for their management, and one must not focus on object and flow only.

It is only the contextual dimension of knowledge, above the object and the agent dimensions, what provides meaning to object-based and agent-based transactions and what realizes the value content of any knowledge event. Therefore, it is this value dimension what provides the strategic significance to KM (Carrillo, 1998).

Considering that knowledge-based capital has become obvious in the creation of value in any type of entity (Lev, 2004), I believe that a new structure is required to combine the assets and the rules to do so. It is my opinion that this structure is included in the CS model proposal. In developing the Capital System, Carrillo (2004) defines the CS as a system's taxonomy of value accounts. The system's operation and understanding is not associated to the nature of the accounts (tangible or intangible), but to the form in which they participate in the generation of value. As the physical assets have been integrated into a city's urban planning, intangible assets start having a presence thanks to their distinction within a society. Both types of assets are integrated into a structure that includes all significant forms of social value: the city as a Capital System.

In the construction of a CS, it is necessary to analyze the entire generic arrangement of value elements that are needed to sustain production. This task in its simplest form includes an investment, a process and a product.

Carrillo (2004) suggests that this task may land on a city through the CS. The investment capital represents the grounds over which a system begins to operate— favorable conditions for the city's formation: orography, water availability, climate, etc. The process capital is the productive part. It is divided in two: the agent capital, which performs production activities (actor) and the instrumental capital, which represents the means of production used by the agents. For a city, the agent capital would be within its population's capacities and the instrumental capital would be in urban planning models, infrastructure, technologies, etc. Last, the product capital represents the results of the production process, in a city this may be physical assets or higher living conditions.

Due to the existence of different types of knowledge (object, flow, context), a city may have different approaches. The parameters that characterize knowledge will position a city as a KC. Carrillo (2004) comments that, from a KBD approach, developing a KC strategy consists of specifying the value system under which the city will operate, identifying the system's critical dimensions (critical knowledge) and converting these dimensions into a system that will allow its operationalization (indicators, policies, initiatives). Considering all of the above, we can understand that a city's CS becomes the central instrument for designing and implementing its strategy.

I consider that a city's CS has to have a scheme for understanding other cities' practices and evolution in order to shape the city's behavior. Comparison is a must in the evaluation of performance, and it is a tangible measure of a city's development capacities.

Following is a proposal of the value account of a CS for a KC disaggregated into three levels, based on the work of Professor Carrillo. It is important to point out that each city has the privilege and responsibility to create and develop its value proposal through its CS, there is no general rule for combining capital.

(1) Metacapital
  - Referential (value elements that allow identification and alignment)
    —Identity (endogenous): definition and differentiation
    —Intelligence (exogenous): comprehension of and response to external events
  - Articulation (value elements that allow interconnection or exchange)
    —Relational (strata of interaction with meaningful agents): social integration and cohesion; equity and legality
    —Financial (monetary expression of value elements): financial statements
(2) Human (individual, group, and organizational capacities translated into performance)
  - Individual basis
    —Ethnic diversity
    —Health
    —Education and learning
    —Social economy
  - Collective basis
    —Culture
    —Evolutional abilities
(3) Instrumental (production means through which the different types of capital strengthen their value multiplication capacity)
  - Tangible
    —Geography
    —Environment
    —Infrastructure
  - Intangible
    —Public institution systems and procedures
    —Private institution systems and procedures
    —Information platforms
    —Entity's memory

Instrumentation of the Capital System for a Knowledge City

The steps that I propose for the process of implementing a KBS through the instrumentation of the CS for a KC are as follows:

(1) **Defining an objective.** It is essential to convince oneself of the importance of knowledge in the creation of value. The objective may be to leverage the level of attractiveness, quality of life, or to form technology centers. The objective must focus on the strategic use of knowledge in a concrete differentiation line. For example, in the city of Barcelona (Barcelona, 2005), this objective is focused on attracting technology-based companies and the creative class. The initiative that stands out is Poblenou 22@BCN, dedicated to transforming economies based on manufacturing into knowledge economies based on services, business incubation, and technological development.
(2) **Defining the identification route.** The city's government can follow the path it considers best for identifying and understanding the city's CS. This may be through identity, axiology, services plan, procedures model, development

segments, among others. In order to create a proposal for Charlotte (Kaplan and Norton, 2002) as an ideal city to live, work, and have fun in, the team took as reference the knowledge integrated in each one of the services that the city must provide to its citizens and companies. On this path, the team found types of critical knowledge to include in the city's strategic themes, in relation to its proposal.

(3) **Forming a work team.** It is necessary to have a collection team that will help identify and interpret every asset of the CS. This team may have city government and non-government members. The team's objective is to accomplish an understanding of the city's forms of knowledge: how they are being used, how they relate, and what results they produce. In the case of Toronto (Salazar, 2005), in its knowledge-based social development project, in addition to the city's government, the team was made of citizens' representatives, business chambers, companies, universities, the State of Ontario, non-profit entities, and students. Each member contributed an interpretation of how to achieve the city's task in a balanced manner.

(4) **Identifying the CS accounts.** Identifying and describing each capital that significantly supports the city's value proposal. How to detect the city's knowledge? It is necessary to interview critical agents; review documents, projects, initiatives, and learned lessons; review the operational experience; speak to clients; speak to providers; analyze the work teams; investigate internal networks; review external news, etc. In the case of the city of Charlotte (Kaplan and Norton, 2002), the team carried out interviews with regard to the role of the government and users, different agents involved with the city, like artists, businessmen, writers, tourists, professors, religious representatives, parents, students, children, and elders. The city's historical and statistical information was also analyzed. The task was to identify and describe knowledge assets that had an impact on the fulfillment of the city's objective.

(5) **Measuring the CS.** Understanding the behavior of each knowledge asset through assessment of performance and gap identification. It is necessary to define the context for it to have sense, before beginning measuring. Measuring must be a process of interpretation of every asset's importance for the city. This will contribute a substantial basis for understanding the strategic role of each asset from an individual perspective and as a group. Measuring also requires the definition of goals, either endogenous, through the evaluation of capacities, or exogenous, through the measuring of other cities. In Barcelona (Barcelona, 2005) a very complete work was carried out to describe every knowledge capital that influences in attracting companies and the creative class. It included everything from indicators of economic opportunity to quality of life. In their work, they grouped measurements in order to communicate a flashier proposal, like the increasing of the levels of culture in relation to the transformation of the economy from manufacture to technological development.

(6) **Understanding the CS.** The team has the information and the means to strategically describe the performance of each knowledge capital in the city's value proposal. It is possible to identify the relation of each capital to development variables. The task of understanding consists of comparing capital indicators with results and financial variables. After completing this detailed relationship description, it is possible to identify the CS's breaches, its actors, how it can be leveraged, and how to care for its strategic alignment with the city's critical themes. In the case of Charlotte (Kaplan and Norton, 2002), the process of understanding knowledge capital was carried out through strategic

maps. Cause–effect relationships were used for the unveiling of the impact of every asset and of the entire capital on tangible results that represented an ideal city to live, work, and have fun in. In a very logical and transparent manner, citizens were briefed regarding the way in which good education, an integral health service, active citizen participation, and culture fomentation had an impact on the reduction of insecurity and increase of quality of life.

(7) **Developing the CS.** Once we have an understanding of the CS, we know what we have to do with it in order to maximize the city's value proposal. Specific initiatives or actions are targeted with the objective of connecting, formalizing, and explaining the CS within a previously defined development context. Every initiative aims at developing an asset that is relevant for the city's value proposal. Returning once again to the case of Toronto (Salazar, 2005), it was identified that the basis for social development was the citizen participation capital. This capital was interpreted as the integration of the city's participants (government, enterprise, citizen) for a higher quality of life. The main initiative of the city of Toronto is forming this participation through everything from activities as visible as the formation of committees, to the integration of a learning program for children in which, through an ecological proposal, children are informed of ways in which they must participate in order to form a better city toward the future.

Conclusion

The objective of a KBS is to understand how to connect the meaning and attributes of each capital with the integral performance of a CS. The KBS must have a tangible and identifiable starting point in the city—this is the first step to motivate participation. A KBS is based on social behaviors; forming a focused, aligned, and integrated work team is the basis for a good management of the strategy. The CS development has a strong investment of cultural change; using knowledge in a strategic manner requires learning new forms of management, thinking in a systematic, relational manner, mostly when speaking about society-related goals. The development of KM may contribute to cities understanding their intangible assets' task of creating value. If the city goes through the exercise of understanding its knowledge, and applies it, it is possible that its position will become more and more sustainable because it will be able to systematically manage the capital that supports the operation of value creation for its customers: citizens and companies.

References

Barcelona, Ayuntamiento (2005). Webpage, www.bcn.es.

Bounfour, Ahmed and Edvinsson, Leif (2005). *Intellectual Capital for Communities*, Burlington, MA, USA: Elsevier Butterworth-Heinemann, pp. 3–34.

Carrillo, Francisco (1998). Managing knowledge-based value systems. *Journal of Knowledge Management*, vol. 1, no. 4, pp. 280–286.

Carrillo, Francisco (2002). Capital systems: Implications for a global knowledge agenda, *Journal of Knowledge Management*, vol. 6, no. 4, pp. 379–399.

Carrillo, Francisco (2004). Capital cities: A taxonomy of capital accounts for knowledge cities, *Journal of Knowledge Management*, vol. 8, no. 5, pp. 28–46.

Dedijer, Stevan (2002). Ragusa intelligence & security (1301–1806): A model for the twenty-first century, *International Journal of Intelligence and Counter Intelligence*, vol. 15, No. 1, pp. 101–114.

Dickinson, Emily (2001). *The Wealth of Knowledge*, Thomas A. Stewart: Nicholas Brealey.

Flores, Pedro (2000). Modelo de medicion de valor de una empresa a traves de sus ordenes de capital, Tesis de Maestria en Administracion de Tecnologia de Informacion, ITESM.

Florida, Richard (2002). *The Rise of the Creative Class: How It's Transforming Work, Leisure, Community and Everyday Life*, New York, NY, USA: Basic Books.

Kaplan, Robert and Norton, David P. (2002). Como utilizar el cuadro de mando integral, Gestion 2000.

Komninos, Nico (2002). *Intelligent Cities*, London: Spon Press.

Lev, Baruch (2004). Sharpening the intangibles Edge, *Harvard Business Review*, June, pp. 109–116.

Salazar, Carlos (2005). Ciudades Competitivas y Gobierno Local: Una perspectiva Canadiense, *Seminario de Retos y desafíos: el rol del municipio en el siglo*, XXI, Escuela de Graduados en Administración Pública, Instituto Tecnológico de Monterrey, www.mty.itesm.mx/egap.

Part Two: Experiences

Chapter 7

The Case of Singapore as a Knowledge-Based City

Caroline Y. L. Wong, *Australian National University, Australia*
Chong Ju Choi, *National Graduate School of Management, Canberra, Australia*
Carla C. J. M. Millar, *University of Twente, Enschede, The Netherlands*

Introduction

In the post-industrial economy, knowledge-related activities have become central to creating national wealth and sustaining economic growth in the so-called "knowledge economy," also variously known as "knowledge-based economy" (KBE), "knowledge-driven global economy," "new networked economy," or the "new economy" (Ofori, 2003). The OEDC (1996) defines a KBE as one in which the production, distribution, and use of knowledge are the main drivers of growth, wealth-creation, and employment for all industries. In that regard, many authors identify information and communication technology (ICT) and globalization as key drivers of the knowledge-based economy (Economic and Social Council, 2000) as the rise of ICT gives the KBE a new and different technological base that changes significantly the conditions for the production and distribution of knowledge (Chia, 2000). The emergence of the new economy with its ICT development has also stimulated considerable interest among governments and policy communities within the Asia-Pacific including Singapore, Japan, Malaysia, Hong Kong, and China (Hutton, 2004). Hutton (2004) noted that ICT is deployed as a key instrument of urban transformation and modernization with both substantive effects (like higher productivity and value-added production) and "symbolic" outcomes (like re-imaging of local/regional societies and economies). For example, Singapore and Vancouver exercise an explicit strategy that fosters developmental synergies between technology (especially ICT), culture (in the form of creative and design service industries), and "place" as expressed in the innovative milieu of the inner city (Hutton, 2004: 55).

Singapore makes for an interesting case study for a knowledge-based city because of its paradigm shift from a city-state with an image of conservative ideology and strict censorship toward a free-spirited dynamic creative hub in the making. It also displays many characteristics typical of a KBE, such that people, their ideas, and capabilities are the key sources of wealth and opportunities (Chia, 2000). The many international accolades achieved in the first five years of the millennium account for the dynamic business environment that has spawned a well-established IT and telecommunications infrastructure serviced by over 6000 multinational companies (MNCs) and over 100,000 local enterprises comprising small and medium-sized enterprises (SMEs) and large local corporations (EDB Singapore, 2003).

In 2001, the Swiss-based Institute for Management Development ranked Singapore 3rd in R&D in its Global Location Attractiveness Rankings. The World Economic Forum (WEF) pointed out that Singapore was evidently an economy that had the greatest innovative ability in the world and a solid macro economy (EDB Singapore. Why Singapore? Singapore: Your Choice Business Location). Singapore has been consistently ranked as one of the most competitive nations and best places for business in the world. Rankings in years after 2000 include

- 2nd place in World Competitiveness Yearbook, 2003—International Institute for Management Development (IMD)
- 4th place in the Global Competitiveness Report, 2002–2003—World Economic Forum
- 2nd most profitable place for investors, Investment Climate—Global, 2003—BERI
- Best business environment in Asia-Pacific, 2004–2008—EIU Country Forecast, October 2003
- One of the five least corrupt countries in the world and least corrupt nation in Asia—Transparency International, August 2002
- Top in Asia for Intellectual Property Rights Protection, Protection of Intellectual Property—Global, 2003—World Economic Forum and IMD
- 2nd most globalized nation in the world, 2004—4th Annual AT Kearney and *Foreign Policy* magazine globalization index, 2004
- 2nd most network ready country—Global Information Technology Report, 2003–2004.

(Source: EDB Singapore—Why Singapore? Singapore Rankings in http://www. sedb.com/edbcorp/sg/en_uk/index/why_singapore/probusiness_environment.html.)

In "The Rise of the Creative Class," Florida argues that the business of today is about access to talented and creative people, as highly skilled creative people gravitate to places that are centers of creativity, places that are multifunctional and diverse, and full of stimulation and cultural interplay. He recognizes that creative people are going to be the "critical resource of the new age" and that high human capital individuals are the key to success in this new era of economic growth. There is an international pool of more than 90,000 professional expatriates living and working in Singapore, bringing with them their unique cultures and perspectives (EDB Singapore, 2003). Sixty percent of the 6000 multinational companies or 3600 foreign firms have located their regional headquarters here. More than three-quarters of these companies use their regional headquarters in Singapore to service not only the Southeast Asian region, but also the Greater China region (EDB Singapore: Newsroom, 28 May 2002).

The impressive economic growth record of Singapore in the last four decades has been achieved through continuous industrial re-structuring and technological upgrading (Wong, 2001). The knowledge-based industries as defined by the OECD have contributed to an increasing GDP, from 48% between 1983 and 1985 to 56% in 2001 (APEC, 2003). Singapore's commitment to KBE development during 1995–2005 has enabled it to make a rapid and successful transition to a newly industrialised economy. The future growth of sectors such as healthcare, ICT, education services, photonics, and nanotechnology, identified by the Economic Review Committee, is dependent on

Singapore's knowledge capabilities. This is where knowledge creation, acquisition, dissemination, and application interact with each other in the economy to create the main drivers of growth, wealth creation, and employment across all industries (APEC Economic Committee, 2000).

As will be discussed in this chapter, Singapore's information society development trends have been shaped by its developmental state (Wong, 2004), and though this has reaped benefits for Singapore in many ways, it has also negatively constrained its development in other ways.

Historical Development of Singapore's Economy

Singapore has been transformed from a fishing village in the early 19th century to a highly developed and successful free market economy in the 21st century, enjoying a remarkably corruption-free environment, stable prices, and one of the highest per capita GDPs in Asia—US$25,979 in 2004 (Singapore Department of Statistics, 2004). Singapore's economic strategy proved to be a success and the economy grew at an average annual rate of over 8.5% from 1965 to 1997, before the regional financial and economic crisis of 1997–1998 (Chia, 2000). Since its independence in 1965, the economic restructuring of the city-state is very much government-directed and not market-driven.

Singapore's economy is very much a product of inter-linkages among the development vision, institutional setup, and the business environment (Loo et al., 2003). This is in part due to domestic constraints on growth (small population base and lack of natural resources) and a rapidly changing external environment.

The development model has taken Singapore from an industrialization strategy in the 1970s to a higher, sophisticated manufacturing one, which included computer peripherals and software packages (Loo et al., 2003). The manufacturing sector continued to be an important contribution to the economy as its share of GDP remains above 25% for most years since 1980s (Wong and Singh, 2004).

The 1980s saw a strategic shift toward the technology-intensive sectors and from the early 1990s it was one focused on high knowledge-intensive companies (Loo et al., 2003). By the late 1990s, the state was fully aware of the growing trend of globalization, technology, and competition and that the ability to acquire, process, and apply knowledge and information would be a key competitive advantage (*Sunday Times*, 1998). There was already recognition by the government that knowledge would become a strategic asset due to technological advances and globalization.

The government acknowledges the need to forge an environment that is conducive to innovations, new discoveries, and the creation of new knowledge and one that harnesses the intangibles such as ideas, knowledge, and expertise to add value and create new value in the knowledge economy (Ministry of the Arts and Information, Renaissance City Report, 2000). The Committee on Singapore's Competitiveness (CSC) was therefore formed in 1997 to address Singapore's competitiveness as a knowledge economy within the next decade. Its vision is for Singapore to become an advanced and globally competitive knowledge economy with manufacturing and services as its twin engines of growth (Committee on Singapore's Competitiveness Report, 1998). It is therefore not surprising that the concept of the KBE has generated increased discussion and recognition in the late 1990s. A study conducted by Toh et al., (2002) indicated that the continued growth of the Singapore economy would require growth from the production, dissemination, and application of knowledge. As a result, in the last few years there have been substantial efforts made at the educational and industry level (especially R&D) to link learning to knowledge creation and business creativity. The educational and cultural economic policies are tailored according to global economic restructuring and reflect the state's ideology of pragmatism and developmentalism (Kong, 2000).

Likewise, Singapore's model of information society development has been distinctively shaped by its MNC-leveraging economic developmental strategy (Wong, 2004).

Technology

Research findings by Loh (1998) and Wong (1995, 1998) show that Singapore has from the 1970s made substantial progress within the catch-up or simple learning phase through an MNC-induced technology transfer route through the FDI process. The idea was to promote investment by global companies and leveraging them to generate direct and multiplier economic growth (Wong, 2004). This involved heavy investment in public infrastructure, manpower development, and relevant incentives to support the development of industries and establishing government-controlled companies (also known as government-linked corporations or GLCs) to operate in strategic sectors ear-marked by the government (Wong, 2004). At the time of writing, Singapore's manufacturing output has been mainly derived from MNCs and more than 60% of equity in this sector was also foreign-owned (Wong, 2004). This high dependence on foreign firms had contributed to the lack of a critical mass of indigenous entrepreneurial firms for the global economy (Wong, 2004). It has hence reached a developmental stage where it needs to develop its own science, technology, and innovation capabilities.

The CSC was instrumental in recommending specific plans for key sectors such as manufacturing, finance, and telecommunications so as to transform Singapore into an advanced and globally competitive KBE (CSC, 1998). One of the strategies recognizes the strong linkage between manufacturing and services as the twin engines of growth. Singapore will continue to attract foreign MNCs and local enterprises to produce high-value-added products and to provide manufacturing-related and headquarters services to the region. The Singaporean government also recognizes the need to nurture small and medium local enterprises and to build up a core of world-class companies with core competencies, which can compete in the global economy (CSC, 1998). As such, the Economic Development Board (EDB) of Singapore launched a 10-year plan to develop Singapore into a vibrant and robust global hub of knowledge-driven industries in manufacturing and traded services with emphasis on technology and innovation capabilities. The idea is to encourage MNCs to locate more of their key knowledge-intensive activities in Singapore and for local companies to embrace more knowledge-intensive activities and become world-class players.

Amongst the many recommendations to develop the manufacturing sector, the following are closely tied to Hutton's exposition of an explicit strategy exercised by Singapore that fosters developmental synergies between technology (especially ICT), culture (in the form of creative and design service industries), and "place" as expressed in the innovative milieu of the inner city (Hutton, 2004). Strategies recommended by the Competitiveness Report (1998) included

- Integrating Singapore into the global economy to leverage on international talent, knowledge, and technology;
- Providing an entrepreneurial environment that tolerates business failures and allows freedom for the generation of ideas;
- Embracing innovation to generate new business and growth;
- Grooming world-class local and foreign companies in niche areas;
- Positioning Singapore as the premier regional hub to attract foreign MNCs and local enterprises to use Singapore as a production base for high-value-added products and to provide manufacturing-related services for their subsidiaries in the region.

Singapore's KBE is therefore characterized by a strong knowledge acquisition capability. According to findings made by APEC (2003), knowledge acquisition based on current trends will continue to grow and will remain the main source of new knowledge in the medium term.

The widespread emphasis on ICT infrastructure and education means that Singapore has scored high in knowledge dissemination capability. Although Singapore has created a stronger base for knowledge creation from 1995 onwards, there is still a considerable gap between Singapore's R&D output and that of the more advanced KBEs (APEC, 2003). There is a lot that Singapore has to catch up within the area of knowledge application as entrepreneurship and tertiary education are found to be the weakest links (APEC, 2003). For example, in the 2004 Global Entrepreneurship Monitor (GEM) report, experts ranked Singapore's environment for entrepreneurship as above average on all dimensions. However, there is still a need to address the cultural values and mindsets of the population, as many do not regard entrepreneurial activity as a good career choice and therefore do not accord high status to new business success (Wong et al., 2004). Statistics released by the recent 2004 GEM report shows that Singapore lacks behind the OECD and East Asian countries in their choice of starting business as a career—49.1% versus 59.5% (Wong et al., 2004).

There is a need now to move away from an MNC-propelled industrialization past to one that embraces an indigenous pool of technological and entrepreneurial expertise (Koh, 2000). As such, the educational system was re-structured in the last few years in order to foster greater creativity and instill higher-order (i.e., analytical, creative, and systems) thinking skills amongst its school children. There is now a substantial reduction in curriculum content and student assessment in favor of team learning, problem-solving, and process skills acquisition (Loh, 1998). This recent quest to restructure and inject critical thinking skills and greater creativity into its educational agenda has been sparked off by the need to reduce reliance on the multinationals and to provide a broader base for future growth. Efforts at educational restructuring have as their targets, the production of a future intelligent workforce (i.e., today's school children) that is capable of advanced, continuous learning, un-learning, and re-learning (Koh, 2000). This educational restructuring is beginning to pervade the entire spectrum of students ranging from elementary school right through to the university level (Koh and Pakir, 1999). In the long term, these efforts aim at having a future workforce that is capable of advanced learning, knowledge creation, and creativity leap-frogging.

Singapore's research institutes are also working at the forefront of technology to deliver better value for industry. In 2001, the Swiss-based IMD ranked Singapore 3rd in R&D in its Global Location Attractiveness Rankings. The WEF pointed out that Singapore was evidently an economy that had the greatest innovative ability in the world and a solid macro economy (EDB Singapore. Why Singapore? Singapore: Your Choice Business Location). The Agency for Science, Technology and Research (A*STAR) ensures that Singapore's R&D efforts are world-class. It has under its wing 12 research centers that focus on a range of disciplines from info-communications technology and nanotechnology to manufacturing technology. The A*STAR is building a diverse community of local and foreign researchers, and has already attracted some of the best and brightest minds from the US, Europe, Australia, and Asia.

Concerted efforts are being made to strengthen R&D collaboration between research institutes, universities, and industry. The strong links and fluid exchanges between industry and academia make Singapore attractive to international companies as a key location in their global R&D network (EDB Singapore. Why Singapore? Ample R&D Resources). Measures to promote greater enterprise formation continued to show favorable results. The number of new high tech companies and businesses registered with the

Registry of Companies and Businesses (RCB) grew from 3502 in 2001 to 3578 in 2002. They came from areas like info-communications and media, engineering and electronics, and other technical and engineering services. Specifically, the number of foreign high-tech companies also doubled in 2002, signifying Singapore's growing attractiveness as a global hub for enterprise and innovation (EDB Singapore. In the News: Early Efforts in Innovation and Enterprise Bear Fruits for Singapore, 5 February 2003).

Nonaka (1991) argues that the "successful companies are those that consistently create new knowledge, disseminate it widely throughout the organization, and quickly embody it in new technologies and products." An economic survey carried out by Toh et al. (2002) reveals that Singapore's KBE is comparable to that of the OECD countries especially in the areas of knowledge creation, acquisition, dissemination, and application (Toh et al., 2002). In that regard, Singapore has continuously relied primarily on knowledge transfers through the attraction of multinational corporations and foreign talents (Toh et al., 2002). Singapore has also demonstrated an ability to adopt a comprehensive, integrative approach to technology diffusion promotion that combines incentives to individual businesses to adopt and use the identified new technologies or innovations and the strategic use of the public sector as a lead-user or early adopter of new technologies (Wong, 2004: 12).

Since 2000, many efforts have been channeled to enhance the base of its knowledge economy through its national innovation system, entrepreneurship, and educational capability (Toh et al., 2002). There is a need, however, to address the issues that attract or embed mobile professionals who make up the knowledge workforce to a quality place rich in physical and cultural amenities and ideas. This is where culture and place have to be expressed in the innovative milieu of the inner city (Hutton, 2004: 55).

Culture and Place

Sharon Zukin (1995) maintains that culture has become more and more the business of cities and that it will form the basis of a city's tourist attractions and its unique competitive edge. The production of cultural events and symbolic goods is becoming predominant in many cities today and a new economy characterized by flows is emerging—flows of information, images, goods, and people that are increasingly connected and that circulate even faster. The growth of cultural consumption (of art, food, fashion, music, tourism) and its related industries will become more visible (Zukin, 1995: 1–2) as cities continuously seek to engage in urban redevelopment strategies. In recent years, urban growth in places like London and New York has been significantly driven almost exclusively by the importance of cities as centers of innovation, creativity, and cultural/social activity.

Various other studies done by Castells (1996), Simmel (1907), and Pratt (1998) highlighted the importance of geography, place, and location in defining the new economy. Castells (1996) in his work on network society focuses on the spatial logic of the cultural economy by paying attention to the ways in which locational concentration enhances both a city's competitive performance and its creative potentials. Michael Porter (2000) writes that places where creative clusters and networks are found are gaining competitive success overall.

The fact that capital and people cross borders frequently makes the Singapore government realize that something more creative is needed for economies to remain productive. Studies have shown that it is the presence of human capital, or knowledge professionals and creative talents, which in turn attracts innovative, technology-based industries (Brooks, 2000; Glaeser et al., 2001; Bassett et al., 2002; Florida, 2002). Studies have also linked the growth of cities to human capital as cities bring together and augment human capital (Lucas, 1988; Glaeser et al., 2001). Florida (2003) reiterates that successful regions are places where creative people gravitate and gather, in a conducive setting, to generate and implement a constant flow of new ideas—new products and services, new firms, new and better ways of doing things within the existing firms.

The then Prime Minister of Singapore Goh Chok Tong articulated the need for a culturally vibrant city to attract global creative talents in the KBE. The focus is on expanding local creativity in addition to attracting global creative personnel and retaining entrepreneurs in an effort to create a more cosmopolitan city-state (Goh, National Day Rally, 2002). It is therefore not surprising that the current economic policies, which aim at Singapore becoming a renaissance "city of the arts," reflect the pragmatic and developmental model (Kong, 2000) of the city-state. The role of public policy has hence shifted to one that emphasizes human capital, talent, knowledge professionals, and the role of cultural and creative endeavors.

Recognizing that knowledge management and creativity were important for development of cultural capital, the Creative Industries Development Strategy was the outcome of findings conducted by the Economic Review Committee (ERC) in 2002 to enable Singapore to compete in the global knowledge economy (ERC Report, September 2002). As a result, the creative sector will be given due prominence in the economy and the creative industries are slated to be a growth engine of the Singapore's economy (6% of GDP by 2012). The Singapore government has set aside more than 200 million Singapore dollars (US$116 million) over the next five years to invest in the arts sector (Forbes, 2004). The developmental strategy adopted by the Singapore government aims at Singapore becoming a creative city in the league of creative cities such as San Francisco, London, and New York. By focusing on the emergent arts and culture scene, the Singapore government hopes to expand local creativity in addition to attracting global creative personnel and retaining entrepreneurs in an effort to create a more cosmopolitan city-state (Goh, National Day Rally, 2002). For example, a number of regional and foreign firms in the creative sector have established their regional headquarters in Singapore, including a leading Indian firm—DLM Digital studios and the production studio of Lucas Film, a company founded and owned by *Star Wars* director, George Lucas. And in late 2002, the iconic arts center—the Esplanade—Theatres on the Bay—built at a cost of S$590 million was opened. Drawing from the experience of other performing arts centers such as Toronto's Harbour Front Centre, the Esplanade features programs that allow for collaboration and exchange between local and foreign performing arts groups (Wong et al., 2005). It has staged many internationally renowned programs ranging from music to ballet and orchestra performances.

Some critics have pointed out that the cultural capital injected into the Singapore cultural scene is basically the "hardware" or the tangible side of the equation, which includes cultural facilities, programs, and festivals. There is a need to also nurture the "software" or intangible and intrinsic aspects of cultural capital. This relates to the presence of a multifaceted cultural environment that accepts highly divergent views within the film, art, and theater circles (Sigurdson, 2000). There is also a greater need for the government in Singapore to open up sources and flows of information into the city-state if it were to maintain its leading position in Asia.

Conclusion

To a large extent, Singapore's efforts in creating an "intelligent island" through knowledge acquisition (via the MNC-led approach) and dissemination (through its national innovation system and educational capabilities) since late 1990s is a very laudable effort and its developmental path provides useful guides for other developing countries. There is a need to work further on capabilities such as knowledge creation and application especially when they are applied to the entrepreneurship scene in Singapore. This is where social and cultural mindsets would have to embrace individual creativity, diversity, and community-led initiatives.

Urban and regional planning researchers have also analyzed the importance of the social interactions at the individual level as driving value creation and the concentration within cities of creative talent (Florida, 2002) or knowledge professionals. The presence of human capital, or knowledge professionals and creative talents, in turn attracts innovative, technology-based industries (Brooks, 2000; Glaeser et al., 2001; Bassett et al., 2002; Florida, 2002). Moreover, the heritage of a city or the meanings attached to the past and present form the foundations of social, political, and cultural knowledge, which in turn can help attract such talented individuals and human capital to global cities (Cochrane and Passmore, 2001; Escobar, 2001; Graham, 2002).

Singapore's long-term success will also hinge upon how it deals with long-standing development questions relating to economic and social sustainability, gentrification and local displacement, exclusionary practices and local identities (Tay, 2004). That is a challenge for the city-state especially if Singapore seeks to reposition itself as a creative city in the KBE.

References

Asia-Pacific Economic Cooperation. (2003). The Drivers of New Economy in APEC: Innovation and Organizational Practices. Available at: http://www.apec.org. Accessed Date: 16 March 2005.

APEC Economic Committee. (2000). Towards Knowledge Based Economies in APEC, APEC Secretariat in Asia-Pacific Economic Cooperation, The Drivers of New Economy in APEC: Innovation and Organizational Practices, in http://www.apec.org. Accessed Date: 16 March 2005.

Bassett, K., Griffiths, R. and Smith, I. (2002). Cultural industries, cultural clusters and the city: The example of natural History film-making in Bristol. *Geoforum*, vol. 33, no. 1, pp. 165–177.

Brooks, C. (2000). Knowledge management and the intelligence community. *Defence Intelligence Journal*, vol. 9, no. 1, pp. 15–24.

Castells, M. (1996). *The Rise of the Network Society*. Oxford: Blackwell.

Chia, Siow Yue. (2000). Singapore: Towards a Knowledge-Based Economy, in http://www.tcf.or.jp/data/20000127-28_Siow-Yue_Chia.pdf. Accessed Date: 10 March 2005.

Cochrane, A. and Passmore, A. (2001). Building a national capital in an age of globalization: The case of Berlin. *Area*, vol. 33, no. 4, pp. 341–352.

Committee on Singapore's Competitiveness Report. (1998). Singapore: Ministry of Trade and Industry. Available at: http://www.mti.gov.sg/public/NWS/frm_NWS_Default.asp?sid=42&cid=177. Accessed Date: 10 March 2005.

Economic and Social Council. (2000). Development and International Cooperation in the Twenty-First Century: The Role of Information Technology in the Context of a Knowledge-Based Global Economy. *Report of the Secretary-General*, New York.

EDB Singapore. (2003). Media Releases: New Headquarters Program Launched for Companies Across All Industries and Geographies, 7 January. EDB Singapore: Newsroom. Headquarters available at: http://www.sedb.com/edbcorp/browse.jsp?cat=40&type=2&parent=36&root=36). Accessed Date: 10 March 2005.

EDB Singapore. (2003). Media Releases: Early Efforts in Innovation and Enterprise Bear Fruits for Singapore, 5 February. Available at: http://www.sedb.com/edbcorp/browse.jsp?cat=40&type=2&parent=36&root=36). Accessed Date: 10 March 2005.

EDB Singapore. Media Release/2003/03 June 2003 available at: http://www.ida.gov.sg/Website/IDAContent.nsf/0. Accessed Date: 10 March 2005.

Escobar, A. (2001). Culture sits in places: Reflections on globalism and subaltern strategies of localization. *Political Geography*, vol. 20, no. 2, pp. 139–174.

Florida, R. (2002). Bohemia and Economic Geography. *Journal of Economic Geography*, vol. 2, no. 1, pp. 55–71.

Florida, R. (2003). *The Rise of the Creative Class*, Cambridge: Harvard University Press.

Forbes. (2004). *Singapore Wants to Double Arts and Media*. Associated Press, 07.24.2004 in E:\creative industries\Forbes_com. Singapore Wants to Double Arts and Media.htm. Accessed Date: 10 March 2005.

Glaeser, E., Kolko, J. and Saiz, A. (2001). Consumer city. *Journal of Economic Geography*, vol. 1, no. 1, pp. 27–50.

Goh, C. T. (2002). Remaking Singapore—Changing Mindsets. National Day Rally Address, Singapore Government Press Release, MITA, University Cultural Centre, NUS, 18 August.

Graham, B. (2002). Heritage as knowledge: Capital or culture? *Urban Studies*, vol. 39, no. 4, pp. 1003–1017.

Hutton, A. T. (2004). Service industries, globalization and urban restructuring within the Asia-Pacific: New development trajectories and planning responses. *Progress in Planning*, vol. 61, pp. 1–74.

Koh, A. T. (2000). Linking learning, knowledge creation, and business creativity: A preliminary assessment of the East Asian quest for creativity. *Technological Forecasting and Social Change*, vol. 64, no. 1, pp. 85–100.

Koh, A. T. and Pakir, A. (1999). Twenty-first Century Higher Education: The Role of a Liberal Arts Education in Singapore. Paper presented at the 1999 ASAIHL (Association of Southeast Asian Institutions of Higher Learning) Seminar, Hong Kong.

Kong, L. (2000). Culture, economy, policy: Trends and developments. *Geoforum*, vol. 31, no. 4, pp. 385–390.

Loh, L. (1998). Technology policy and national competitiveness, in M. H. Toh and K. Y. Tan (eds), *Competitiveness of the Singapore Economy: A Strategic Perspective*, Singapore: Singapore University Press and World Scientific Publishing Co.

Loo, L. S., Seow, E. O. and Agarwal, A. (2003). Singapore's competitiveness as a global city: Development strategy, institutions and business environment. *Cities*, vol. 20, no. 2, pp. 115–127.

Lucas, R. (1988). On the mechanics of economic development. *Journal of Monetary Economics*, vol. 22, pp. 3–42.

Ministry of Information and the Arts. (2000). Renaissance City Report, March, available at: http://www.mita.gov.sg/renaissance. Accessed Date: 10 March 2005.

Nonaka, I. (1991). The knowledge-creating company. *Harvard Business Review*, November–December.

OEDC. (1996). Organisation for Economic Cooperation and Development. *The Knowledge-Based Economy*, Paris.

Ofori, George. (2003). Preparing Singapore's construction industry for the knowledge-based economy: Practices, procedures and performance. *Construction Management and Economics*, vol. 21, pp. 113–125.

Porter, M. (2000). Location, competition and economic development: Local clusters in a global economy. *Economic Development Quarterly*, vol. 14, no. 1, pp. 15–34.

Pratt, Andrew. (1998). A "Third Way" for the creative industries-hybrid cultures: The role of bytes and atoms in locating the new cultural economy and society. *International Journal of Communications Law and Policy*.

Sigurdson, Jon. (2000). Singapore Means to turn into a Knowledge-Based Economy. Paper prepared as Visiting Professor at the Centre for Management of Innovation and Technoprenuership (CMIT), National University of Singapore, May–July.

Simmel, G. (1978 [1907]). *The Philosophy of Money*, London: Routledge.

Singapore Department of Statistics. (2004). Singapore Statistics available at: http://www.singstat.gov.sg/keystats/annual/indicators.html. Accessed Date: 21 February 2005.

Sunday Times. (1998). Report from the Committee on Singapore's Competitiveness (CSC), 8 March.

Tay, Jinna. (2005). *Creative Cities in Creative Industries*, in John Hartley (ed.), UK: Blackwell Publishing.

Technology, Talent and Tolerance: Attracting the Best and Brightest to Memphis. A Report by the Memphis Talent Magnet Project available at: http://www.creativeclass.org/av.htm. Accessed Date: 14 October 2003.

Toh, M. H., Tang, H. C. and Choo, Adrian. (2002). Mapping Singapore's knowledge-based economy. *Economic Survey of Singapore*. Third Quarter.

Wong, P. K. (1995). Technology transfer and development inducement by foreign MNCs: The experience of Singapore, in K. Y. Jeong and M. H. Kwack (eds), *Industrial Strategy for Global Competitiveness of Korean Industries*, Korea Economic Research Institute, Seoul, Korea.

Wong, P. K. (1998). Upgrading Singapore's manufacturing industry, in M. H. Toh and K. Y. Tan (eds), *Competitiveness of the Singapore Economy: A Strategic Perspective*, Singapore National University Press and World Scientific, Singapore.

Wong, P. K. (2001). The role of the state in the industrial development of Singapore, Chapter 1 in P. K. Wong and C. Y. Ng (eds), *Re-thinking the East Asian Development Paradigm*, Singapore University Press.

Wong, P. K. (2004). *The Information Society and the Developmental State: The Singapore Model*, National University of Singapore (NUS) Entrepreneurship Centre Working Papers.

Wong, P. K. and Singh, A. (2004). Country Survey Report: Singapore, Report prepared for ECLAC/IDE (JETRO) Joint Project, Comparative Study on East Asian and Latin American IT Industries.

Wong, P. K., Lee, L., Ho, Y. P. and Wong, F. (2004). *Global Entrepreneurship Monitor GEM: Highlights in Singapore*, NUS Entrepreneurship Centre, National University of Singapore.

Wong, Caroline, Kim, J. B. and Choi, J. C. (2005). Global cities and creative capital with its applications to Asia. *Paper presented at the proceedings of the 32nd Annual Conference of the Academy of International Business*, Bath, UK, 7–8 April.

Zukin, S. (1995). *The Cultures of Cities*, Cambridge, MA: Blackwell Publishers.

Chapter 8

Bilbao: From the Guggenheim to the Knowledge City

Jon Azua, *Chairman, Enovatinglab, Bilbao, Spain*

All around the world, museums and other elements of culture sprawl as drivers for new regional and urban economic development processes. Strategic development of cities can no longer take place without a relevant role for culture and knowledge.

Cities, city-regions, or new spaces arise, ever more, as relevant units of analysis for human communities. These new spaces or territories carry a critical role in enhancing the new policies of competitiveness and well-being. They have stopped being mere passive holders of physical resources to become true active agents. Additionally, knowledge and culture have evolved from the static productivity factors (together with capital and manpower) and comparative advantages of the past, to a dynamic component of the competitive advantage of a nation, region, or city.

Unique and differentiated cities face the challenge to retain and attract strategic resources (capital, companies and mainly, talent) to guarantee their connectivity along the world and to favor the development and ownership of live networks. This is a new answer to the old simplistic debate of "Global vs Local." A new, complex, and diverse mode of interrelation, challenge, and opportunity opens up in the horizon.

These new cities are the main nodes of leadership for ideas, culture, technology, economy, and society. They have become the critical spaces of coexistence, solidarity, and creativity.

But the received view of urbanism is rendered obsolete when trying to develop this new role for territories. The traditional disciplinary approach to creative nodes as driving forces of competitiveness needs to give way to mutidisciplinary perspectives as well as to public–public and public–private dialogs and also to multi-agent solutions. In doing so, cities and regions must rethink their purpose, their structure, their management, their financing and their insertion in a country-region-city strategy. Above all, they should focus on how to attract and retain talent through knowledge. To achieve this, would-be Knowledge Cities have a long road to travel. A basic path is learning from experience to build a unique future for themselves.

Within this framework, the case of Bilbao contributes to this learning process, through the success story of Guggenheim Bilbao.

Understanding the Bilbao-Guggenheim Effect

As Frank O. Gehry once said, art museums are, both literally and figuratively, points of interaction or cross-roads, in all of the world's large cities. The location of the new museum he designed was just at a bend of the river running through Bilbao and provided him the opportunity for creating one of those intersections and become a privileged agent of the revitalization, renewal, and transformation of the city.

Guggenheim-Bilbao was not an isolated building but a relevant element of an ongoing—at the time—strategic puzzle to "open, modernize and internationalize the Basque Country and its economy."

Bilbao-Guggenheim: A Cultural Project . . . and Something Else

We need to place the Guggenheim-Bilbao project within the framework of a complex cultural process, which is impossible to interpret until it is first understood.

I once had the opportunity to meet Evan Dobelle, at the time a University President.[1] The motive for this meeting was his interest in knowing "What makes Bilbao different from other cities of the world, so that it encourages the current popularity and success of such a singular project as that mentioned earlier." His reflections were as straightforward as they were reasonable and interesting: "Today, there are hundreds of cities in the world completely immersed in a revitalizing process. All these share instruments, ideas and even 'leaders and planners.' Why does Bilbao, with one visible project, have such an impact?" and he added: "The answer cannot be the Museum. We know the Solomon R. Guggenheim Foundation (SRGF), we have collaborated with it for many years, it is important but it is not the number one in New York. Therefore, there must be something else." Along these years, after the Bilbao-Guggenheim's opening, hundred's of similar international visitors repeated similar stories and arguments.

Finding that "something else" is what motivates this chapter. We will try to find it from the point of view of culture and the humanities, as well as economics and city-region development. This great avant-garde center of modern and contemporary art will allow us to better understand a natural community, that of the Basques, which confronted a serious epoch of crisis with the necessary creative tension to invent a new model, a new city and, also, a new museum. But at the same time, this should allow us to understand additional relevant issues:

(1) How and why strategy is relevant for culture, business, industries, institutions, governments, and cities?
(2) The role of culture as a driver for economic development and creativity in an extended knowledge basis
(3) The key role of the new *glokal* dialogue.[2]

Bilbao is the heart of the Basque nation. Since its foundation—705 years ago—this port city has driven the history of this vigorous industrial community, which found itself, in terms of epoch's theory, in a period of chaos. Its continued identity crises, of belonging to various political-administrative powers (several kingdoms, Spain, France), the succession of wars that it has endured throughout its history (the most recent, the Spanish Civil War

---

[1] President of Trinity College, Hartford, CT, USA.
[2] Glokal, Jon Azua (Enovatinglab). Permanent coopetition with many agents involved, dialogue/contradiction between global and local spaces and the "k" factor (Knowledge's Technology).

Figure 1

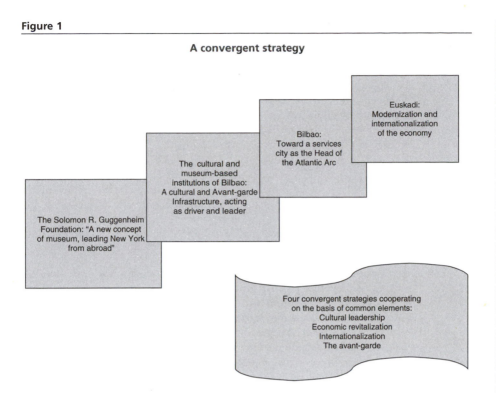

A convergent strategy

1936–1939 as preamble to World War II), the lack of territorial unity (seven Basque provinces divided between two autonomous regions in Spain—the Basque Country and Navarre—and three in France), the process of recovering its language, Euskera (the oldest language in Europe), whose use was prohibited during Franco's dictatorship, and its profound industrial economic crisis during recent periods (1975, 1980, 1992) which obliged it to transform its industrial base characterize the starting point of our story.

Therefore, it is not surprising that once a time of stability arrived, with Franco's dictatorship having come to an end and the process of recovering self-government having recommenced,[3] there emerged: (a) innovative proposals, (b) new structures of government and economic management, and (c) new administration, economics and education philosophies, and intellectuals. It is here that we can see the emergence of what we might call a Convergent Strategy (see Figure 1) as a context for this case.

A Convergent Strategy

The Basque Country was embroiled in a strategy for the modernization and industrialization of the economy in the context of the forthcoming European Union. The new framework would not only generate economic and social tensions but could also

---

[3] Following the death of dictator Francisco Franco in 1975, Spain began a process of transition toward democracy. In 1980 this process led to the creation of the Basque Government and Parliament, opening the way to a long process of devolution of sovereignty. Today, Euskadi (the Basque Country) is the Autonomous Region that enjoys the highest degree of self-government in Spain and one of the highest in Europe.

leave the Basque society—by virtue of it being a peripheral region—outside the main axes of European development. In parallel, Bilbao, home to 50% of the Basque population, was suffering a deterioration that is characteristic of industrial cities, caught up in a process of decline, losing its motivation and its capacity to attract new projects, and thereby accentuating the well-known infrastructure deficits suffered by large cities. Furthermore, cultural institutions themselves had to endure severe abandonment, with scarce available resources, limited creativity and artistic-cultural promotion and minimal non-public initiatives, so that the cultural infrastructures were the only elements in the Autonomous Basque Region that were below the Spanish average.[4]

At the same time, the SRGF was living through its own bitter crisis. With its leading museum in New York being closed for renovation and with the failure in the financing of the project to open a new museum in Salzburg, Austria, it sunk in a profound operating deficit and it required an innovative project and a renewed strategy. Thus, visions and opportunities encountered a common space for a convergent strategy involving the following:

(1) A new museum concept capable of leading the contemporary art world of New York, gaining that position from abroad
(2) The provision of new cultural and avant-garde museum infrastructures, acting furthermore as driving and leadership symbols
(3) The revitalization of a city, reconverting it from industry toward advanced services, as functional capital of the European Atlantic Arc[5]
(4) The modernization and internationalization of the economy (and people's mentality)
(5) The background of a new European space currently under construction.

Therefore, four convergent strategies coincided, cooperating on the basis of a series of common elements:

(1) The search for cultural leadership
(2) Economic revitalization
(3) Internationalization
(4) An avant-garde vocation.

Hence, a cooperation project between two substantially different cultures and communities started. On the one hand, the North-American culture, in the form of an international institution rooted in the creative world of contemporary art and, on the other, a variety of political-administrative institutions coming from a nationalist ideology and culture that was committed to recovering the identity and personality of a small society in a changing world apparently overtaken by Globalism.[6]

---

[4] "Ekonomiaz." Synthetic Index: Amenities and Infrastructure 1980–1990. The Basque Government.

[5] The Atlantic Arc: an integrating space made-up of the peripheral regions of Europe that face the Atlantic and comprising the Canary Islands, the Portuguese Coast, the coasts of Galicia, Asturias and Cantabria in Spain, the Basque Country, the United Kingdom, and France.

[6] Namely, the single-mindedness that seems to inspire present economic thinking at world level. According to this, we are witnessing an unstoppable "globalization of the economy," where domestic economies have lost their reason for being, free market rules society and global governmental institutions (political, financial, etc.) emerge.

The differences are clear. However, the same cannot be said of similarities. So, the success of Guggenheim-Bilbao is due to the happy convergence of a number of strategic initiatives based on the following:

(1) A regional strategy for the modernization and internationalization of the Basque economy
(2) A strategy for revitalizing Bilbao and its metropolitan area and transform it from one based on the manufacturing industry to one based on the service sector
(3) Guggenheim's own strategy for museum leadership and innovation
(4) A cultural strategy based on Guggenheim-Bilbao as the powerhouse behind the change toward cultural management and education in the Basque Country.

As a result, Guggenheim-Bilbao is much more than a museum, more than just a building, thanks to the creative genius of an architect.

Thus understood, we may identify some key factors that were decisive in the shaping of the Bilbao Model:

(1) Generating a vision shared by a whole range of leading players in a new expansion project (Guggenheim, the city, a strategic objective, the actual cultural and economic organization to be created)
(2) A strategic context (city-region) in which the project was a major part and not just "something else" or the minimum to be done
(3) Public and private commitments throughout all relevant phases:
    (a) Decision
    (b) Ownership
    (c) Financing
    (d) Construction
    (e) Control
    (f) Management
    (g) Operation
(4) Mix of cultures and multiple coalitions of interest
(5) Strategic, organizational, budgetary, and management coherence
(6) Suitability of Guggenheim to the new situation (new members and fellow travelers, new cultural communities, new structures).

These general ideas were reinforced by a series of mutual benefits that have made the SRGF, the Bilbao Museum, and the city of Bilbao (and, by extension, the Basque Country as a whole) "winning partners."

A Long Road to Travel

As if we were trying to return to ancient Athens, after searching for areté,[7] trying to achieve competitiveness in solidarity, so Basque nationalism, through its institutions of self-government, was laboring to construct a new socioeconomic and, at the same time, cultural project in a fully democratic concept, whilst, as Isocrates[8] said with regard to the people of Greece,[9] Basque people suffered—and still do—a

---

[7] A Greek term equivalent to the diligent search for excellence.
[8] Isócrates (380 BC), an Athenian orator.
[9] "The name Greek is no longer a mark of race, but of outlook, and is accorded to those who share our culture rather than our blood."

Table 1: Benefits deriving from this relationship

Benefits for SRGF (excluding the initial contribution)

- Presence in Europe
- First example of international institution
- Association with prestige architecture
- Association with urban development through culture
- Unique exhibition spaces
- Program synergies
- Operational synergies
- Presentations from the Permanent Collection and temporary exhibitions which cannot be exhibited in New York
- Enlarge Permanent Collection through acquisitions
- Increase the value of the Guggenheim brand
- Use the Bilbao success as a magnet (more than 100 requests worldwide)

Benefits for GMB

- International presence
- Access to Program (Permanent Collection and temporary exhibitions)
- Access to know-how
- Internationally recognized brand

Benefits for city-region

- International fame
- Vanguard image, technological, and urban development leadership, etc.
- Powerhouse behind revamped economic and cultural activity
- New investment and development opportunities

---

lack of their own territorial, administrative, and political space where they could set up their own nation. Inspired by the Platonic principle[10] of people's commitment by way of politics, the Basque people became engrossed in a modernizing strategy that would allow them to reach the much desired, but at that time still distant, new 21st century Europe.

Figure 2 reflects the objectives and basic pillars of the strategy put into effect. It rested on five elements which, from the point of view of associated human values and principles, contributed in the following manner:

(1) **A competitive context**, which, as mentioned earlier, is inspired by the search for excellence. Not a question of doing as well as the rest, but better than them. This is the basic principle of competitiveness and the only one that guarantees the survival and permanent increase of welfare.

(2) **A social welfare state**. Far from liberal ideas, which rely on market for demi-perfect allocation of resources, policies implemented within the framework of

---

[10] Plato. *The Republic*: All citizens are obliged to participate in politics and in the government of their nation.

Figure 2

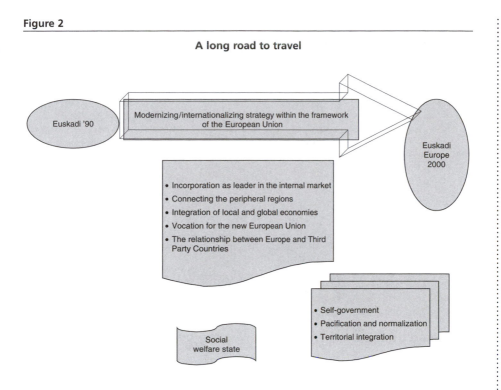

A long road to travel

this strategy favor solidarity. That is why the basic pillars are a support network of welfare for the community, including

(a) *Health.* Universal, free health coverage.
(b) *Education.* A system of economic agreements guaranteeing free compulsory education (up to age 16) with free choice on the part of the parents, regarding public or private education.
(c) *Social services.* A minimum social wage for all the population that has no alternative income. This first level of provision is complemented with an efficient network of social assistance, particularly for the handicapped and the elderly.

(3) **Self government.** All policies, or instruments applying them, are preceded by the spirit of self-government. The mood prevalent today is strengthening the ideas and values which underlie the principle of self-government, endowing it with maximum efficiency and efficacy.

(4) **Peaceful dialog.** In an atmosphere of turbulence, disrupted by marginal terrorism committed by one part of the population that has adopted a position of confrontation and argues for the use of violence in the name of politics, the strategy of modernization and internationalization promoted by democratic Basque nationalism has clearly opted for peace and the normalization of the country. This makes dialog the basis for cohabitation and the instrument for the progressive recovery of the political autonomy and sovereignty that cannot be renounced.

(5) **Territorial integration**. By way of democratic routes, conviction, and time, the recovery of cultural identity and the new concepts associated with virtual spaces give this element a new value in the implementation of the strategy. It is here that we once again find a certain parallel with the values of ancient Greece, in the sense that we can speak of this period as being characterized by the presence of the following values that accompanied the development of the Greek arts:

   (a) *Optimism*. A strategy infussed with faith and optimism; conscious of the great difficulties but with belief in the strengths of people who are capable of overcoming the adversities of history, as well as their own problems and contradictions

   (b) *Freedom*. An everlasting vocation, accompanying all individual and collective activities

   (c) *Self-respect*. The Guggenheim project results are accelerating the recovery of self-respect and pride for this community, reinforcing its capabilities and strengths so that it may confront new projects

   (d) *The search for excellence*

   (e) *A historic legacy*. With a deeply rooted history, it faces a new future that does not renounce its own cultural identity.

Focusing on a City: A City-Region Strategy for Excellence

It was mentioned before that global cities, by contrast with the historic cities, capitals, ports, or industrial metropolis that preceded them, will not be determined by locational or geographical considerations, but by their capacity to adapt to change and to offer continuity and order in a turbulent environment. Clearly, "many cities, and particularly those national capitals, international financial centers of the first order, priority ports or historical centers, have the potential to transform themselves into global cities, but not all of them will be successful. The process is one of self-selection, mission and local initiatives."[11]

These words perfectly define the underlying spirit of the revitalizing project for Bilbao and its metropolitan environment. Just as in the Middle Ages, cities are now essential for the development of civilization. We may repeat, in light of the success achieved by the Guggenheim-Bilbao project, the words of Robert C. Lamm[12] when he wrote that "agriculture is the business of rural areas and culture is the business of cities." Such spirit translates into the mission and objectives contained in Figure 3.

Committed to this strategy, the Basque society has opted for the creation of new regional spaces that will form a type of Euskopolis[13] (or Euskal Hiria), adopting the structure of a metropolis of the different conurbations that make up the Basque Country, in a new time frame (15–20 years), and in which the infrastructures and technologies, combined with the coexistence and culture of

---

11 Richard Knight and Gary Cappert: "Cities in Global Society."
12 Robert C. Lamm: "The Humanities in Western Culture." McGraw Hill, 1996.
13 A term employed by the author and in general use in the Basque Country to refer to a conglomerate made up of the Basque capitals of Bilbao, Vitoria-Gasteiz, Donostia-San Sebastian, Irun, Pamplona, and Bayonne. Today, the well-known writer Bernardo Atzaga generalizes its use.

Figure 3

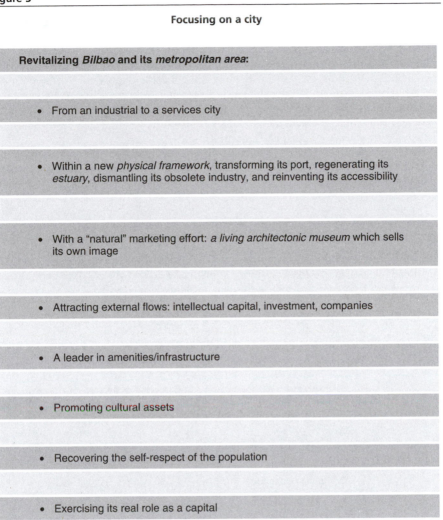

Focusing on a city

Revitalizing *Bilbao* and its *metropolitan area*:

- From an industrial to a services city

- Within a new *physical framework*, transforming its port, regenerating its *estuary*, dismantling its obsolete industry, and reinventing its accessibility

- With a "natural" marketing effort: *a living architectonic museum* which sells its own image

- Attracting external flows: intellectual capital, investment, companies

- A leader in amenities/infrastructure

- Promoting cultural assets

- Recovering the self-respect of the population

- Exercising its real role as a capital

citizens, will provide it with continued competitiveness. This "New City" will have to become a center for

(1) Innovation
(2) Education, research, and social assistance
(3) Culture, recreation, sport, and tourism
(4) Transport, logistics, and trade
(5) Market and qualified labor
(6) Production, industrialization, and generation of advanced services.

The revitalizing strategy for Bilbao would be directed at these objectives-functions by way of a symbolic, essential, and driving project, namely the Guggenheim-Bilbao Museum.

Implementing a Driving Project

In this context, the agreement between the Basque institutions and the SRGF gave birth to a unique cultural project: the Guggenheim Museum in Bilbao (GMB).

The GMB provides Basque and European societies access to one of the largest and richest collections of modern and contemporary art in the world, the capacity for "contagious education" in the vast field of arts, and the opportunity of access to a new form of understanding the exhibition, promotion, and financing of the arts. Yet, the Museum also offers a unique opportunity of integrating different cultures and, above all, constitutes a landmark of global architecture, a unique statement marking the frontier between the 20th and 21st centuries.

Beyond all that, the driving character of this project and its natural fit within the revitalizing structure of Bilbao helps the city to draw closer to the objectives mentioned earlier which will govern the economic spaces of tomorrow. Figure 4 summarizes the basic characteristics of the project.

Toward a New Cultural Epoch? New Avenues

It was mentioned earlier in the chapter that knowledge of history allows us to prepare the future. We also suggested a possible parallel between the Middle Ages and the current moment of construction of the European Union. Similarly, as we have noted the

Figure 4

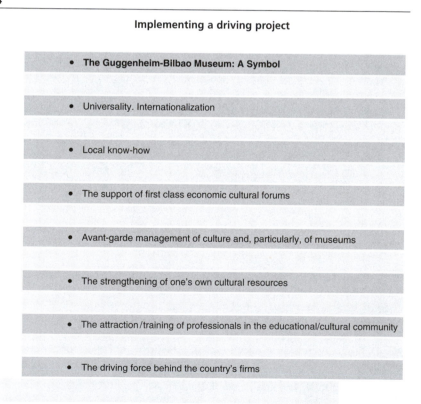

Implementing a driving project

- **The Guggenheim-Bilbao Museum: A Symbol**

- Universality. Internationalization

- Local know-how

- The support of first class economic cultural forums

- Avant-garde management of culture and, particularly, of museums

- The strengthening of one's own cultural resources

- The attraction/training of professionals in the educational/cultural community

- The driving force behind the country's firms

values that the Guggenheim-Bilbao Museum symbolizes for the new century and its economic alternatives, it is worth trying to draw some comparisons in the history of art and the humanities.

The earlier mentioned Robert C. Lamm has said with respect to the art of the 1990s[14] that it has ceased to be a bohemian activity and that New York is no longer the primary center of artistic activity. It is the proliferation of styles, fashions, and artists that stands out, reinforcing the importance of the individual and of the specific work above movements or schools. The resulting difficulty in identifying the author/work school seems to challenge the generalization of ideas, principles, and criteria beyond certain general aspects. While one may or not agree with Lamm, new initiatives along the world are enhancing culture and opening up new ways to teach, promote, conserve, and exhibit art as well as engaging individuals, governants, and institutions in a new culture–economy binomium.

In light of the new avenue opened by the Guggenheim-Bilbao project, a fresh epoch of positive crisis-adjustment marks the dawn of the 21st century. Art museums and other related issues become redefined. Figure 5 indicates some of the innovations that this project has required, also identifying the cultural values that lie behind. Thus, the creation of Frank O. Gehry[15] represents the mixture of individual creativity (an essential

Figure 5

Opening new avenues

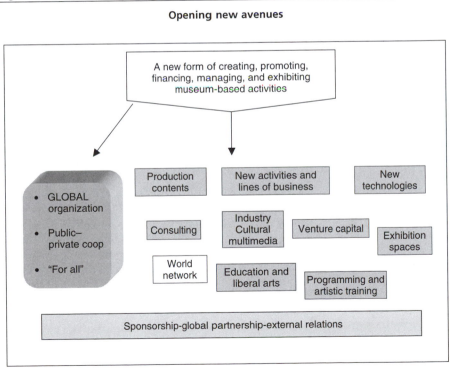

14 Robert C. Lamm: "The Humanities in Western Culture." McGraw Hill, 1996.
15 A Canadian architect and the artistic creator of the Guggenheim Museum Bilbao.

presence in all works of art) with a functional focus (to exhibit the art of our time, on a large scale, and in a free and open manner), its communication and permanent complicity with the city and its people, and where this mixture can be compared to the different materials he employs (steel, titanium, stone, glass), and the historic landscape of the Country.

The project also exemplifies a unique experience in co-management, co-ownership, and co-financing of the building itself, the Foundation, and the artistic collection. In this way, private investment shares responsibilities and successes with public Basque institutions. Above all, it has achieved what few mega-projects have succeeded in doing, namely gaining the support and adherence of everyone.[16] Consequently, other local museums and culture institutions are transforming their organization and management.

Finally, in tune with the new times, culture is also a source of wealth and employment. Numerous business spinouts were generated by this cultural project, contributing to strengthen the Country's economy.

Before reviewing the current impact of this strategy, let us go back a few years from the time of writing, just to remember what the leaders of this initiative explained before BGM's opening:[17]

> The Bilbao-Guggenheim Museum will be opened in 1997. Designed by architect Frank O. Gehry, it aims to become one of the main museums of modern and contemporary art in Europe. To this end, in addition to having the Guggenheim collection, considered the finest private collection of modern and contemporary art in the world, it will be housed in a building that seeks, in its architectural excellence, to become emblematic of the City.

Also,

> ...the project is one of the initiatives being taken by the various Basque Government Bodies with a view, on the one hand, to contributing to the renewal of the economic structure of the Basque Country and, on the other, to enhancing the possibilities of converting Metropolitan Bilbao into a reference point for the Euro-region that has come to be called the Atlantic Axis. (Ibid.)

And finally,

> ...the inauguration of the Bilbao Museum will mark a new and important era in the history of Guggenheim, and will provide our institution with an international scope unique among cultural institutions—Tom Krens. (Ibid.)

Such vision finally overcame substantial opposition coming initially from many fronts—media, local artists, and almost all political parties: "cultural imperialism"; "they will never come to the Basque Country"; "the museum is unbuildable"; "there will not be either art or the Guggenheim's Collection"; "no one is coming to visit it"; "Basques are not going to accept the project"; "too expensive"; "more job creation and less museums" ... and so on.

---

[16] Following the rejection, criticism, and attacks faced by almost all mega-projects, soon after its opening, the Museum obtained practically unanimous support, hence becoming the City symbol.

[17] Summer 1997. An official booklet edited by Guggenheim Bilbao to promote and advertise the Opening.

Beyond Art . . .

As mentioned before, understanding the decision process backing Bilbao-Guggenheim, requires us to visualize several converging strategies:[18]

(1) A country-building strategy (region, space, etc.)
(2) A revitalizing strategy to transform a city
(3) An innovative strategy in search of a new way to create/develop the Museum and culture industry
(4) An entrepreneurial strategy for a new type of Museum.

Four consistent strategies, resting on the interaction not only of Guggenheim and Bilbao, but other agents (public and private) as well. Four strategies aligned in a specific context to converge in a unique project.

To better understand what we call a "country-building strategy," it will be necessary to go back to 1980, when the Basques recovered a considerable part of their decision-making capacity and self-government at the end of the Franco dictatorship, when democracy began to be regained in Spain.

At that time, when they had yet to join the European Economic Community and were in a clearly peripheral situation, far removed from competitive, promising regions and centers, and led by a fledgling, inexperienced public administration, the new Basque institutions embarked on a fast changing "process of strategic interaction," focused on changing the rules on behalf of Basque citizens, along with the changes and transformations taking place in the economy and society.

Against this background, and with its own framework of economic, fiscal, and financial relations with the Spanish government, the Basques undertook a number of major strategic initiatives. In 1991, with industry in full recession and unemployment soaring way out of control, the "country-building strategy" included a number of opportunities and challenges making up a "strategy to modernize and internationalize the Basque Country," based on the following key factors:

(1) **Image:** a negative image, resulting from economic recession, violence ravaging the Country, and the general impression that nationalism was synonymous with negative isolation, confrontation, etc., became both a cause and consequence in a vicious circle generating discouragement, unwillingness to take forward-looking decisions, inability to attract foreign investment and a justification for policies having an adverse effect on the development of the country.

(2) **Reinvention of the economy:** a regional economy based on outmoded, heavy industry overly concentrated in just a few sectors (steel, shipbuilding, etc.) made it necessary to marshal our real and historical competences and build a new entrepreneurial culture, incorporating new promising industries, creating new industrial relations frameworks and preparing the human resources that the new economy would need.

(3) **Infrastructures:** the Basques started lacking both physical and intellectual infrastructures, meaning that they would have to multiply their efforts to provide enormous investments and imaginative programs. It should be noted that by the time the Guggenheim project started, with the exception of "cultural infrastructures," all other synthetic indicators placed the Basque Country (in relative terms) above the Spanish average.

---

[18] Jon Azua, "Netting Coopetitives Strategies: Business, Government and Innovative Regions" (Enovatinglab ed. 2003).

So, within this overall strategy, the Basque Country, and mainly the city of Bilbao (50% of the country's population) used culture as a key driver or "strategical intent," providing not only a major physical renewal, but also a new injection of self-esteem on the part of the population.

Culture played a dual role in strategic considerations:

(a) Culture per se as something intrinsic to mankind and, above all, to society in the special process of regaining self-esteem and values, a sense of identity and of a region capable of lending strength to all forward-looking projects.

(b) The binomial culture—development, which has become a key factor in the economy and development of the country.

The "K Factor"

In view of this "strategic convergence" and clockwork operation, we now look for those unique components that have been present along the process.

First, we observe a permanent interaction of coopetitive agents (business, governments at different levels, public and private sector), sharing a vision and implementing innovative ways to apply a strategy, as well as individual leaders coping with the dialogue/contradiction between the global and the local. Similarly, we must stress the crucial role of "K factors": technology (particularly IT) and other forms of knowledge. While the "global economy" requires us all to forge a minimum space, or new playing field, which we can see either as inevitable or as an enriching new space for opportunities, the "Local" factor is increasingly important to the success or failure of any strategies we devise. However, as we have seen, the "Local" must also be transformed so that it becomes what we have schematically defined as "LoKal," where the "K" stands for the inclusion of a number of differentiating k-elements:

(1) "Konnectivity," made inevitable by the need for interdependence, communication, cooperation, and competition with all other spaces involved.

(2) "AttraKtiveness" for recruiting talent, capacities, resources, and economic-financial flows able to enrich local space, so that all available resources can be strategically engaged in sustained competitiveness.

(3) "TeKnology" able to extend the "e" of the digital economy to the economy as a whole (e-business, e-commerce, e-government, e-ducation, e-innovation).

(4) "Kommunity spirit," fostering solidarity and participation in a true natural community where all the institutional, political, economic, academic, and social agents work together to develop a differentiated, successful platform of their own.

These K-factor elements, present along the whole process, expand into the new global–local dialog in open interactions:

(a) Where the space is the container and active promoting agent of the so-called competitive socio-economic platform, we suggest instead the creation of a spatial region-city strategy for excellence.

(b) In a context of regional strategy for success, business and industry are called upon to devise (and implement) their own collaborative strategies with governments and communities.

(c) Interdependence between the different platforms generates an internationalization process where specific strategies are required to take advantage of new spaces for opportunity.

The GloKal model (representing K-factor components) has been present all along this story: from a long-term strategic thinking dreaming a new scenario for the country and the art industry; leading all stakeholders into new spaces (for business, employment, knowledge and life), creating coopetitive alliances and instruments among agents through a genetic code associated with the attributes of the city, netting all elements (internal and external), enhancing intellectual capital, building new spectacular and efficient infrastructures (both hard and soft), and using IT to enable new businesses and industries.

Building a Smart City: K-Bilbao

But the story goes on! Figure 6 shows how, since recovering self government within a new political framework, the Basque Country (and Bilbao) have experienced a great transformation.

Within that new context, Bilbao continues its renovation into a smart city. In order to achieve this new goal, main challenges involve people, talent, and knowledge focused on creativity and innovation.

A number of City differentiators have been identified (Figure 7), stressing some basic attributes for all areas of opportunity:

(a) **An attractive city:** The City's ability to attract and hold talent and individuals who can contribute to a balanced development economy, housing, town planning, social concerns, and leisure.

(b) **A revitalized city:** Whose people rediscover hope in the future, a city in which old degraded areas are recovered and reinvented.

(c) **A connected city:** In connection to various agents working together toward the development of the city, creating and managing networks along the world

(d) **An innovative city:** Which welcomes and encourages all new ideas regarding technology, public–private management, town planning, leisure, art, culture and social improvement.

Entering the Knowledge Society, Bilbao-Basque Country (Euskal Hiria) works to establish itself as an innovative knowledge territory, a scenario and source of new

Figure 6

Basque Country GDPc, 1980–2003. Source: EUSTAT, Alderdi and Azua

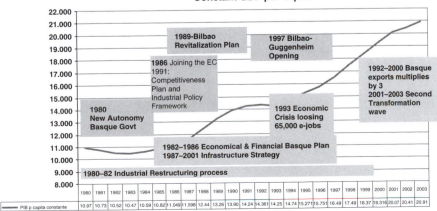

Figure 7

Bilbao differentiators

University City
Financial center
The port
The river
Public–public cooperation
Public–private cooperation
Entrepreneurial culture
Related innovative services
Political and institutional system
Active public agents
B&G&C interaction
Geo-strategic location
Strategic process culture
Social network
Ability to re-invent Guggenheim, culture, design

products and services, technology and talent. This will be the future of Bilbao, Knowledge City as part of the interdependent world network. In the same way as other nodes of the emerging global/local Knowledge Society, it faces new challenges:

(1) Insertion in the infrastructure system and in physical and telematic networks
(2) Sensitive, sustainable dialog with the environment and landscape
(3) Materials and solutions consistent with the principles of sustainability, promoting bio-climatic initiatives for new urbanism and architectures
(4) Energy self-sufficiency and diversification favoring alternative and renewable sources
(5) Quality and variety of public relationship space (parks, boulevards, streets, sport fields, logistic and industrial areas, etc.)
(6) New multiuse meeting spaces, residential spaces, and areas of economic creativity
(7) Unique spaces to live, think, have a good time, create, and work
(8) Diverse residential and productive typologies (innovation cubes, offices, lofts, shops, villages and business parks)
(9) Last-generation digital infrastructure
(10) Complete cycle management of water and other basic utilities
(11) Intelligent residuals management
(12) New governance
(13) Above all, vision, strategy, and knowledge.

Chapter 9

Holon: Transition into City of Children

Maya Levin-Sagi and Edna Pasher, *Edna Pasher Associates, Tel-Aviv, Israel*
Hanah Hertzman, *Municipality of Holon, Israel*

Introduction

Many cities around the world are dying. One of the main problems they face is stagnation. Some cities have reached the point where they no longer renew their services, implement their infrastructures or invest in human capital. Hence, they are losing their overall appeal to citizens in general and specifically to the younger educated group. The result is a process in which citizens are leaving the city where they went to school, grew up and felt at home.[1]

Elizabeth Curid who graduated from Carnegie Mellon University's Heinz School of Public Policy and Management wrote this article before leaving her hometown, Pittsburgh.

> Pittsburgh is a city stuck in its transitional phase. It has the insight and prudence to shed the glory of its past for its potential in the 21st century, yet it lacks the gusto to take the final leap and risk investing in the type of amenities and goals that influence regional growth in today's economy.
>
> Pittsburgh needs to see what is truly worthwhile: It has one of the largest student populations in the country. It is home to world-class medical research facilities. Carnegie Mellon is on the forefront of the most innovative and progressive of high technologies, and Pittsburgh is a city that is home to an ethnically and racially diverse student body . . . [Pittsburgh's] future has a stockpile of raw materials finer than Silicon Valley could ever dream of . . . [yet] it is [not] a city that is willing to take risks and invest in the intangible, like the arts, creativity, and human capital. (Curid, 2002)

Knowledge cities aim at stopping this stagnation. Among the different definitions one finds for a knowledge city, there lies a generic definition of the concept, which

---

[1] Examples of such cities are Philadelphia and Jerusalem, two very different cities with some similar problems. http://www.philly.com/mld/inquirer/11397700.htm; http://www.jpost.com/servlet/Satellite?pagename=JPost/JPArticle/ShowFull&cid=1113358705106&p=1006953079865.

focuses on the strategic objective of a knowledge-based development of a city "by encouraging the continuous creation, sharing, evaluation, renewal and update of knowledge . . . achieved through the continuous interaction between its citizens and simultaneously their interaction with citizens of other cities. The citizens' knowledge sharing culture as well as the city's appropriate design, IT networks and infrastructures support these interactions" (Ergazakis et al., 2004). In other words, a knowledge city promotes and enables constant exchange and renewal of knowledge both within the city, between its residents, and outside the city borders, and between the populace of different knowledge cities. At the core of knowledge cities is the capability to generate and apply knowledge onto the creation of new ideas and innovations, which stimulate the making of competitive products, services, and procedures for the advancement of the city (Amidon, 1993).

The key source for competitive advantage among cities, as well as any other organization, is the knowledge rooted in people, its intellectual capital (Kotkin and Devol, 2001). This is why urban centers must access, create, and utilize human capital. A knowledge city does so by defining a clear vision and aiming at continuous revitalization in order to carry out this vision. Cities that hold knowledge assets, such as educational and research institutions, cultural centers and green spaces, benefit their residents by strengthening the satisfaction, interest, and involvement of everyone in the city's life. Moreover, this process improves the quality of life between the city borders, resulting in becoming appealing to knowledge workers, such as researchers and highly skilled individuals to live, learn, and care for their city.

Through the establishment of knowledge networking and urban innovative engines, the city is enabled to implement and achieve sustainable development and renewal (Dvir and Pasher, 2004). Nevertheless a society must consist of three generations to use these tools. In order to make the most of knowledge management the collaboration should aim to be between those of the same generation and those of a different generation. The older generation holds experience and knowledge that the young have yet to acquire. While the younger generation hold knowledge that is more technologically oriented, up to date, and innovative. The youngest generation is to learn from the former generations and at the same time come up with initiatives that the elders do not dare think of. Together they make up a multifaceted group that exchanges methods, lessons learned, new ideas, technological advances, and initiatives to better foster responsible urban revitalization. That is why a city must be perceived as an attractive entity to both its own residents and outside knowledge workers, especially to the younger generation, which is newly educated and skilled and is seeking to find a home which best suits its aspirations.

Holon's Initiative

Holon, with 180,000 residents, is a city located in the center of Israel. In the 1990s, this major Israeli city was encountering the problems mentioned above. It was looked at condescendingly and was considered a place that offers little to its populace. It found its younger generation fleeing the city and moving to more attractive neighboring towns. What was once an appealing metropolis was becoming stagnant, neither alluring to a new, young well-to-do population, nor keeping its original young residents.

In response, the new mayor, Motti Sasson, initiated a new approach to the city's management, by proposing that the city, as all organizations, implement a client-and-supplier relationship with the population. In order to execute this new approach the reasons for the rising problem had to be found. The municipality of Holon, led by its

CEO, Hanah Hertzman, conducted benchmarking and comparative analysis regarding demographics and citizens' satisfactions, needs and expectations from the city and its services. This was done initially by conducting surveys to discover the attitudes of the public toward Holon in the broader Tel-Aviv metropolitan area, and through surveys on the municipal demographic, economic, cultural and social profile of Holon. The results of the research led to the development and deployment of a new strategy, which was to make Holon a knowledge city. It started out by adopting a new identity, City of Children. This identity was to illustrate the new vision of the city—a focus on the intellectual capital of Holon made to encourage the nurturing of knowledge. This vision helped the city focus on a goal that would aim at drawing in the younger generation by providing it with the services, attractions, and infrastructures that would serve them and their children.

The implementation of the new strategy was brought about in different ways. First, by enhancing the city's educational environment and infrastructures, creating new and unique cultural institutions and activities with a major emphasis on children's activities aimed at enabling children to be exposed to and to learn different facts and ideas in various fields. The city found several ways to execute these, such as in the Israeli Children Museum, a unique museum in Israel and in the Middle East that uses advanced technologies and offers an interactive experience for both children and their parents. Another example is "Meets the Eye," a center for experiencing art through advanced technological means, as part of a municipal community view, aimed at enriching children's culture and intellect and introducing them to the language of art. Through the opening of the Center for Digital Art, or the establishment of the Inter-Domain Center associated with the Weizmann Science Institute, kids can receive scientific knowledge through an interactive experience. In addition, Mediatech, a theater center for young people, was found. These and many many more activities and establishments were to introduce and enlighten children and grownups on different sciences, on culture and heritage.

Second, the city applied its vision by emphasizing the importance of developing a unique and esthetic urban appearance and environment. This was done by developing natural green surroundings, turning Holon into one of the leading green cities in Israel, and through investing in public art gardens such as the Storybook Garden, integrating cultural knowledge in a natural setting. Third, Holon aimed at providing economic development opportunities. Fourth, the city put its vision into practice by insuring the constant improvement of municipal services and the municipal workforce.

Part of the city's pioneering and creative ideas for transformation into a knowledge city was in the realization by the Head of the Educational and Cultural Administration, Rami Hochman, that the process should be accompanied by an ongoing measurement of its performance as a knowledge city. One way it chose to do so was by creating an Intellectual Capital Report of the Educational and Cultural Administration of the city of Holon. This tool showed the city's competencies in these areas. The study was led by the Educational and Cultural Department assisted by Edna Pasher PhD and associates who specialize in measuring Intellectual Capital of organizations, communities, and nations. Intellectual capital is the overall knowledge, wisdom, abilities, and expertise that give a person, an organization, a community, and a city a relative advantage in comparison to others. Assessing an organization's Intellectual Capital helps identify and picture its hidden values, enabling the organization and other stakeholders to obtain an integrated and comprehensive view of all of the organization's assets, to learn about its potential for future growth, and to navigate the organization toward the realization of its goals and vision.

What is the Skandia Model for Measuring Intellectual Capital?

The Skandia Model provides a balanced and holistic picture of both financial capital and intellectual capital (Edvinsson and Malone, 1997). This model, which measures the intellectual capital, uses "the house" as a metaphor for an organization, a nation, and a city (Figure 1). The financial capital constitutes the roof of the house and reflects the organization's history and achievements of the past, which do not necessarily enlighten us in terms of future achievements. The supporting columns are process capital and market capital, and they are the areas upon which the present operations of the organization/city are based. Renewal and development capital, which is situated in the foundation of the house, measure how the organization/city prepares for the future. Human capital, which is found in the center of the house, interacts with all the different focal points. The human capital is the heart of the organization/city, i.e., the capabilities, expertise, and wisdom of the people. It is the role of the organization/city to assist, guide, and support its people toward realization of their vision and strategic goals.

The Focal Areas of the Model

The value chain, according to Professor Edvinsson, expresses the various components of market value on the basis of the following model (Figure 2):

$$\text{Market Value} = \text{Financial Capital} + \text{Intellectual Capital}$$

Human Capital

This includes knowledge, wisdom, expertise, intuition, and the ability of individuals to realize national/local tasks and goals. This focus also includes the values, culture, and philosophy of the organization/nation/city. Human capital is the property of individuals, not of the organization/city.

Figure 1

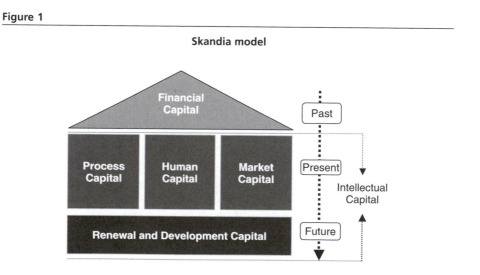

Skandia model

Figure 2

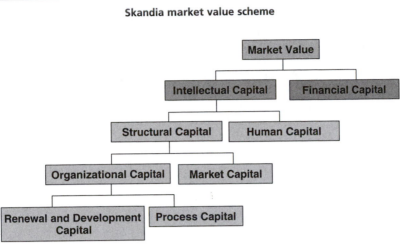

Skandia market value scheme

Process Capital

Cooperation and the flow of knowledge require structural intellectual assets, i.e., information systems, hardware, software, databases, laboratories, an organizational/city infrastructure and a management focus—which sustain and amplify the output of human capital. Process capital is, and remains, in the organization/city hands.

Market Capital

Market assets reflect the general assets imbedded in the interrelationship between the organization/city and its customers. The indicators in this focal point include customer/resident loyalty and the satisfaction expressed by customers and brands.

Renewal and Development Capital

It is not enough to manage knowledge assets; it is impartial to create new knowledge. Renewal and development assets include investments in research and development, new initiatives, using innovative technologies, using and exploiting new products and devices, etc. Renewal and development capital shows the readiness of the organization to deal with the future and what it brings with it. It reflects the organization's ability and investments in the development of innovation for future growth.

Preparing Holon's Educational and Cultural Administration's Intellectual Capital Report

After establishing a steering committee headed by Rami Hochman and his team in the Educational and Cultural Administration, there was a need to launch the project in all parts of the administration, and to motivate and commit the employees to take an active role in the process.

Accordingly, Knowledge Café sessions for employees and managers and other stakeholders were organized. Knowledge café is a distinct method that enables conducting effective brainstorming sessions with a large group of people. At this forum employees from all parts of the organization discuss strategic and management issues, as they sit in small groups over a cup of coffee. This is a knowledge-sharing junction that enables a wide discussion, which at the same time is held at a personal level. The gatherings usually start with a presentation of one or more management dilemmas turning them into the topic of each table's separate conversation. After these discussions are over, a representative from each table presents the findings of his group to the other participants. The knowledge cafés held focused on evaluating what should change and what should not change in Holon, how to constantly contribute to the renewal and revitalization of the city, and what areas the city should focus and invest in.

The outcome of the knowledge cafés' discussions resulted in the finer definition of the Educational and Cultural Administration's vision:

> To be the leading administration in Israel and in the world in innovative thought and actions and in the development of educational and cultural needs, from birth till old age.

This meant a commitment to a client-and-supplier relationship, and to holding and carrying out acts of quality, excellence, innovation, creativity, and organizational learning. Moreover, it meant being obligated to Holon's residents to accomplish certain outcomes. These included residents' satisfaction, service development, and an equal opportunity for all inhabitants to use these, and creation of original, special, and creative solutions regarding community obligation. Furthermore, it included a commitment of municipality employees to specific goals. These goals incorporated fostering a highly qualified creative and professional team, highly motivated and proud of its workplace, and giving all employees a high degree of freedom to initiate, design, and implement their goals in a unique way. In addition to the administration's commitment to achieve ongoing improvement in all measures, it focused on a high level of service.

After creating and defining Holon's vision, the second step in the process, which was identifying the core competencies needed to realize the vision, was begun. This step was also accompanied by interviewing many different city personnel and city residents. It dealt with different issues and questions such as, which types of knowledge will you develop within the organization and which will you outsource? What are the competencies which form a relatively continuous advantage in comparison to other cities, and which of these will differentiate the city from existing and potentially rising cities? Fourteen different competencies were found to exist:

(1) Autonomous and professional management of the educational institutes, which also emphasizes collaboration and teamwork within and between departments and their different costumers. Constantly aiming toward improvement, through repeated reviews and by enhancing creativity in problem solving.
(2) Quality treatment of students starting in kindergarten up to high school graduation with the help of different divisions concentrating on each step in the students' path.
(3) Development of experimental and innovative schools and school programs such as the Democratic School focusing on democracy and its values.
(4) The ability to organize, supervise, and match the educational institutions to a pedagogic perception. Through the combination and collaboration between the IT, construction, engineering, and infrastructure departments.

(5) Development of knowledge networks between the community and the Educational and Cultural Administration on all levels (schools, higher management, teachers, parents, students, etc.), encouraging communal involvement and taking it into account while making decisions.

(6) Development of external knowledge networks with academic institutions in order to improve educational standards and teaching methods, and also to encourage kids to continue in academic studies and to enrich their areas of interest.

(7) Combining formal and informal education with leisure culture by grasping the overall importance of all forms of knowledge, education, and culture (sport centers, museums, libraries, playing grounds, etc.).

(8) As a result of understanding the importance of human capital as a key to future success, the administration has chosen to develop and foster a qualified and high standard instruction faculty. Thus the teaching force has turned into one that emphasizes processes and research in order to develop an independent researcher.

(9) Investment in new technology as part of the learning environment, adjusting it to the computer era, and enabling better learning, supervision and management.

(10) Becoming a learning organization by holding, on a regular basis, training sessions for department managers, school principles, teachers, and others in order to enhance their professional and managerial skills and capabilities.

(11) Employees hold a strong obligation to the system and find it to be their second home. They enjoy a strong and attractive work place and social activities that are offered after working hours such as trips, parties, and promotion opportunities.

(12) Combining the secular and religious educational systems, presenting educational pluralism and liberalism by giving everyone an opportunity to express their individual uniqueness through cooperative activities.

(13) Investment in research and development. The administration believes in an ongoing investigation and a constant search for new channels, guiding progress and enriching what already exists.

(14) Socializing "veteran" immigrants with "new immigrants" in order to better integrate immigrants into the society, by specially training teachers and through integrating immigrant kids in cultural activities, projects, and youth centers.

The next step was to measure Holon's Educational and Cultural Administration Intellectual Capital. The following were found:

Financial Capital

It was found (Figure 3) that the overall budget of the Educational and Cultural Administration was the highest of the entire city budget.

Human Capital

In accordance with Holon's vision, the key indicators of success regarding human capital include the professional level of educational workers and the learning institutions. It was found that the educational work force constantly improves itself through regular seminars and educational programs guiding the teachers and the managers and promoting them professionally and personally.

Figure 3

Percentage of the Educational and Cultural Administration from the overall city budget

		Percentage from the overall city budget
Year 2000	Formal education	28.7
	Culture	7.7
Year 2001	Formal education	28.3
	Culture	8.0

The Educational and Cultural Administration emphasizes in particular the effect that education may have in the long run on the city and on society, it works toward educating for social and value-oriented goals, and encourages critical thought and taking an original perspective on different issues. Educating for the adoption of values is a long and complicated process, which eventually aims at designing beliefs and opinions. Therefore, the administration influences youth to volunteer for their peers through collaborative programs between the schools, instructors, students, the community, and different institutions within the city. These programs have helped involve youth in making decisions on issues that force them to deal with their personal, social, and national obligations.

Additionally, the administration works toward nonstop revitalization and improvement. Thus, it encourages its workers to initiate creative and innovative ideas. The administration nurtures the workers by sending them professional articles in their specific field once a month. A meeting is also held between the Head of Administration and its employees once a month, accompanied by a lecture on a professional subject by an outside source.

Process Capital

The process capital represents the ability to transform the collaborating knowledge from human capital to structural capital. It includes a variety of infrastructures, computer systems, teaching programs, and organizational and structural procedures. The Educational and Cultural Division has created and built unique cultural centers such as museums, interactive science and art centers, theaters, outdoor art centers and reading gardens. It has also developed communication channels within the department and with other stakeholders (residents, suppliers). It is currently also working on implementing an online network that will supply information to everyone in an organized, easy to use, accessible, and clear format.

The administration has also initiated many joint projects and steering committees on a variety of issues involving the civil servants as well as the city community. Furthermore, Holon fosters and encourages academic pursuits through providing many scholarships to students, according to financial needs and excellence.

Market Capital

The city's "market" is made up of students, the elderly, parents, teachers, kindergarten teachers, Israel's Ministry of Education staff, the community of Holon and the whole Israeli nation. The obligation of the Educational and Cultural Administration is serving its clients "from the cradle to the grave." Fulfillment of the clients' needs and servicing them affect their satisfaction, their involvement in the city, and their loyalty to it.

In addition to the "grownups," youth also have an important part in shaping the informal education and the leisure culture. Many committees enable youth to take a vital part in the community. These activities make them caring and involved citizens.

Renewal and Development Capital

Holon's municipality invests in the development of creative and educational thoughts and initiatives. It encourages different unorthodox ways of conceptualization and adoption of alternative and original directions to problem solving. It does so by allocating specific funds for innovative initiatives.

Innovative ideas and programs have already been implemented as mentioned earlier, for example in Holon's Israeli Children's Museum, The Center for Digital Art, The Inter-Domain Center, and in the Mediatech. It is also implemented through school programs that foster innovation through work with UNESCO, community television, art therapy, etc.

In conclusion, Holon has been the first to initiate the creation of a city's Intellectual Capital Report. The city used the Intellectual Capital Report as a tool to assess and visualize the overall ability, potential, and actions of the Educational and Cultural Division. It has been found that Holon has invested significantly more in education, culture, and the environment than other municipalities. The municipality's initiatives, actions, and interactions have allowed the exchange, evaluation, update, development, and creation of knowledge, thus transforming Holon into a knowledge city.

Foremost, this process has helped stop the emigration of Holon's inhabitants to other urban areas, demonstrating that a knowledge city serves and benefits its individual residents and communities, and is rewarded with their loyalty. Secondly, Holon, as a knowledge city, constantly aims both at improving the existing and at creating new knowledge networks, actions that generate and foster innovation within the city and throughout the nation in varies domains. All these are proof of the total commitment in action, of the Educational and Cultural Division and municipality as a whole, to make it a "city purposefully designed to encourage the nurturing of knowledge" (Henley, 2003).

References

Amidon, D. (1993). Knowledge innovation: The common language. *Journal of Technology Studies*, Fall.

Curid, E. (2002). Why this 24-Year-Old is Leaving Pittsburgh, http://www.newcolonist.com/leaving_pitt.html.

Dvir, R. and Pasher, E. (2004). Innovation engines for knowledge cities: An innovation ecology perspective. *Journal of Knowledge Management*, vol. 8, no. 5.

Edvinsson, L. and Malone, M. S. (1997). *Intellectual Capital – Realizing Your Company's True Value By Finding Its Hidden Brainpower*. Harper Business.

Ergazakis, K., Metaxiotis, K. and Psarras, J. (2004). Towards knowledge cities: Conceptual analysis and success stories. *Journal of Knowledge Management*, vol. 8, pp. 5–16.

Henley (2003). Henley Knowledge Management Conference, Annual 2-day conference, 3–4 June, UK: Henley Management College.

Kotkin, J. and Devol, R. C. (2001). *Knowledge-Value Cities in the Digital Age*. CA: Milken Institute. http://www.philly.com/mld/inquirer/11397700.htm; http://www.jpost.com/servlet/Satellite?pagename=JPost/JPArticle/ShowFull&cid=1113358705106&p=1006953079865.

UniverCities: Innovation and Social Capital in Greater Manchester

Blanca C. García, *Institute for Development Policy and Management (IDPM), School of Environment and Development, University of Manchester, UK*

Introduction

It has been only since late 1990s that Manchester and the Northwest of UK are openly documented as a potential knowledge city-region and as a crucial economic engine for a decentralized England. Neglected for decades by central policy, Manchester has turned the corner over an initial 15-year process of property-led regeneration, awakening into the service-oriented knowledge economy of the new millennium. Seemingly, such an infrastructure investment process has triggered a step change in the city's development strategies, moving from its traditional-industry past into creative knowledge-based development. These efforts have strongly shaped and influenced one of the city-region's most prominent social capital: its universities. As part of a regional strategy, two of them have recently merged into a European "super-campus," with research-intensive, world-class aspirations, and some scholars would expect the new university to become a nerve center, a powerhouse for social development in the region (Georghiou and Cassingena-Harper, 2003: 9).

It is also only since late 1990s that a number of the city-region stakeholders (such as authorities, policy-makers, private sector investors, and social organizations) have adopted an explicit Knowledge City (KC) strategy for policy deployment and practice, which makes the city-region a field of analysis for pioneering knowledge-based development frameworks. In this chapter, we are aiming to characterize present and future university life in Manchester under the KC model. By presenting a case study and a summary of recent literature on universities from "knowledge factories" to "a source of civic leadership" (Wolfe, 2004), this chapter offers an overview of policy and action for development taken in Greater Manchester in key areas such as its universities, key repositories of the human and social capital of the city-region.

Living, Learning, and Working in a Knowledge City

During lunch time, while enjoying the delicacies of Chinese Dim Sun at Tai Pan Restaurant on Upper Brook Street, Andy finds himself discussing the particulars of holographic optical technology. An animated conversation on information storage challenges can be heard from Andy's table, in which five other people of Asian, North American, and European origins share some amusing insights and jokes. Through the restaurant windows, Andy sees in front of him the impressive building that houses the laboratory of the Photon Science Centre, in the newly refurbished Schuster Building of the University of Manchester (Unilife, February 2004: 1/1/16). That is where he will be heading to after lunch time today, to see some of his project partners.

Andy Hill is one of the many graduates who stayed at the merged University of Manchester, landing in a good development opportunity in one of its new faculties. He earned a Master of Enterprise in Computer Science and developed some interest in visual computing. In less than five years, Andy has moved on through the University's compulsory life-long learning career path into being responsible for one of the Information Systems (IS) research groups. He was recently appointed the IS leader of a multidisciplinary, multinational team running the Fujitsu Innovation Incubator developments at Central Park, New East Manchester (MCC, 2004: 216), in partnership with the university. As part of his own personal development, Andy has been learning some Japanese language and culture at the fully virtual campus of the Japan Centre North West on Oxford Road (May and Perry, 2003), which is allowing him to better understand the context of the project-related, international people he deals with everyday, mostly on-line.

Andy can be described as the typical knowledge citizen; living, learning, and working in a KC. He is well informed, participative, critical, and politically active (Carrillo, 2004: 40). He is careful with his investments and lives with his partner in his city center accommodation in Hulme, as it is not as expensive as other newer areas. He wanted to remain at the heart of some of the well-regarded re-generation developments started at the beginning of the millennium.

However, he has spotted a good investment opportunity at the Manchester Millennium Village, in New Islington, New East Manchester. In less than five years, the promise of a varied community and urban development could materialize for his family at a reasonable cost of investment, although the English Construction partnerships have estimated its construction value in £240 million (MCC, 2004: 220). The Millennium Village has been the next most strategic phase of the Manchester city regeneration after the re-vamp of the inner city and surrounding areas during the first ten years of the initiative, back in 1994. Now Andy could think of a long-term residence in the city, something that former generations would not have considered, given the meager employment and development opportunities in the region.

But several factors have made a difference. The infrastructure and investments made in the city, plus a number of instrumental and social capital developments have made Manchester a true option for living. One of them has been the Project Unity initiative, which has transformed the University of Manchester into the key research-intensive institution in the region and a real strategic partner of the former Golden Triangle institutions (London, Oxford, and Cambridge). As if sensing these are new times, the Oxbridge universities have been accepting the University of Manchester as their peer in a number of research partnerships without too much of the traditional southern polite dismissal.

This is more than good news for Andy, as he not only has the possibility of a steady job and decent wages but also a realistic possibility of managing his career development in the right environment.

By now income is being generated for universities as the majority of knowledge-based businesses in Manchester are fully aware of the services and partnerships the universities can offer them (Georghiou and Cassingena-Harper, 2003: 15). Today, there is a wide network of knowledge workers interfacing at a personal level throughout the city-region. Andy is indeed one of them. He is fully engaged in using the wireless and broadband infrastructure, and also the mass transport policy developed in the city in recent years. He visits his partners regularly, but keeps in touch on a daily basis through the Internet and intranets habilitated for communications purposes. This not only keeps Andy informed but also interested in life-long learning opportunities within the university and beyond, and links him with the practice and reality his students face everyday as they learn at their own pace on-line following the new e-learning policies of the University. He enjoys e-moderating, and before dinner time today, he will be tutoring a group on-line for the MSc module he is leading this term, with local and international students alike.

But dinner time will be a different story today. Andy will go Indian at the Shimla Pink, in the City center to bid farewell to a couple of his partners departing from Manchester. The mostly tidy city center, the River Irwell boats, the spicy food, and the impressive views of the dazzling Spinningfields Riverside new developments on Bridge Street will probably erase some first impressions: rough streets near the University of Salford, the homeless beggars on Deansgate Street, and the insidious rain of the last three days. Andy acknowledges to himself that there are still a lot of regeneration, inclusion, and development to work on in Manchester's inner city . . . and the rest of the North West for that matter. But it has only been half way practice of most of the initiatives planned for a decade, due for completion in 2015. Andy is optimistic. This is only 2008 after all.

Knowledge and the City

Indeed, "Great universities and great cities go hand in glove: both are driven by knowledge and innovation" says Professor Eric Thomas, Vice-Chancellor of the University of Bristol (Work Foundation, 2005). So are social networks, social capital, and the quality of life in a city, as present and futuristic scenarios are demonstrating in the context of the knowledge economy (Burt, 2000). From Weber's classical definition of a city as "a settlement that does not live on agriculture but on trade and services" (Weber, 1958: 66), cities as units of analysis for research are progressively being understood primarily as productive entities (Amin et al., 2003: 3; Carrillo, 2004: 29). Following this worldview, Andy is living in what has been defined as a Knowledge City, which is "short hand for a regional economy driven by high value added exports created through research, technology and brain power" (Melbourne City Council, 2002; in Ergazakis et al., 2004: 6). As a city "purposefully designed to nurture knowledge" (Edvinsson, 2002 in Dvir and Pasher, 2004: 17), a KC is "a city in which its citizenship undertakes a deliberate, systematic attempt to identify and develop its capital system, with a balanced and sustainable approach" (Carrillo, 2004: 34).

But although the terminology is new, there are a number of historical examples of cities that follow the KC pattern. In its own way, Andy's story might be evoking in 2008 historical elements of core cities of the past, where open, informal places were the space for knowledge to be liberally shared. As modern Agora, Knowledge Cities encompass the underlying assumption that knowledge and ideas are created mainly through conversations (Dvir and Pasher, 2004: 17, 21).

Such assumption positions learning, innovation, and clustering at the core of some theories of knowledge-creation, strongly influenced by Michael Porter's work (1995). Not surprisingly, recent literature on the role of universities in the knowledge-based economy tends to highlight three essential functions: the training of highly qualified personnel, the performance of research, and the transfer of knowledge for economic growth (Wolfe, 2004). It is argued in this literature that "the joint production and transmission of new knowledge occurs most effectively amongst economic actors located close to each other" (Wolfe, 2004: 16). It is also thought that "synchronous face-to-face interactions matter for transmitting (non-bit string) knowledge" (Quah, 2002: 39), as

> Researchers must work somewhere and so might well cluster geographically because communication of tacit knowledge, not digital goods, is most efficient in close physical proximity. (Quah, 2002: 36)

In the case of Manchester, the dynamics of learning and clustering are encouraging knowledge-intensive universities, characterising them as "engines of innovation" and major agents of change and economic growth (Wolfe, 2004: 1). And innovation is progressively understood as "knowledge innovation" or the creation and application of marketable goods and services for the advancement of society as a whole (Amidon, 1993 in Dvir and Pasher, 2004: 17). In the UK, Glasgow (Scotland) was to become a self-appointed example of earlier conceptualizations of learning cities (Florida, 1995; Porter, 1995) by reclaiming the renewal of its social capital. Warwick Science Park (Warwickshire) is virtually the only recorded success story to date in the science-park movement, in terms of its spill-over and upward shifts in the innovation learning curve (Cassingena-Harper, 2003). But still only few UK cities can claim the ownership of the capitals that characterize a KC: seemingly only London and Manchester have been short-listed (University of Salford, 2003; Work Foundation, 2002).

Indeed, amongst the almost 80 explicit initiatives around the world for a city to become a KC (Ovalle et al., 2004: 170), Manchester follows a singular pattern, amongst "UniverCities" (Peters and May, 2004: 270; Berg and Russo, 2004: 18). Shaped by its geo-historical conditions, the citizenship in the Manchester city-region have developed different forms of social capital, but clearly, not everyone has had equal access to information, learning, social networks, and/or power (Healy, 2002: 84), as any brief geo-historical portrait of the city could convey. As a potential KC, a quick review of the wealth of its heritage is imperative.

From Industrial to Entrepreneurial City

Greater Manchester is a conurbation with a population of two and a half million people living within 12 miles (20 km) of the city center. It regroups the two cities of Manchester and Salford and the neighboring boroughs of Bolton, Bury, Oldham, Rochdale, Stockport, Tameside, Trafford, and Wigan. The city-region has a present GDP of £18 billion, which makes it, in size and importance, second in UK after London, which is situated 183 miles (300 km) to the south west (MIDAS, 2004).

Situated at the edge of the Roman Empire, Manchester was founded by a Roman legion as Fort Mamucium (MSIM, 2004). Seen as a "frontier" territory by the ruling south, it was only incorporated as a town in 1838; the Industrial Revolution being the engine to bring rapid change to the city (Worthington, 2002).

By 1850 with a population of 316,000, Manchester became Stephen Blackpool's twin town, "a town of machinery and tall chimneys. It had black canal in it, and a river that ran purple with ill-smelling dye, and vast piles of buildings where the piston of the steam-engine worked monotonously up and down, like the head of an elephant in a state of melancholic madness" (Dickens, 1854: 27). "But the most horrible spot lies on the Manchester side, with masses of refuse, offal and sickening filth lie amongst standing pools in all directions; the atmosphere is poisoned by the effluvia from these, and darkened by the smoke of a dozen tall factory chimneys" (Engels, 1845: 98). "A horde of ragged women and children swarmed about here . . . while a conversation was heard: 'neighbour,' said she, 'your man is dead. Guess yo' how he died?' 'He were found drowned,' said Mrs Boucher, feebly . . . 'He were coming home very hopeless o' aught on earth . . . He 'as left me alone wi' a' these children!' (Gaskell, 1845: 292).

A Social Capital for Manchester

Indeed, by becoming a "Cottonopolis" and the leading UK northern center for commerce, industry, and communications during the Industrial Revolution, Manchester also became the "Shock city" (Briggs, 1963, quoted in Peck and Ward, 2002). A place where the alienation of the well-known "satanic mills" of the textile industry and the worst working-class living conditions of its time were rampant (Desai, 2003). Manchester was perhaps an unusual birthplace to capital development, but historically, it has been indeed the singular context where "the process of globalisation was unleashed, liberalising trade" (Desai, 2003). Such Mancunian liberal tradition covering different aspects of life has been the utmost element of social capital of all settlers in this city-region.

Manchester, as a bastion of various forms of radicalism, home of (once) a large industrial working-class population, and the cradle of the modern Labor movement, "has always been located at the leading, or bleeding edge of change" (Robson, 2002). It is argued that Manchester's multiculturalism and its geographical distance from historical urban centers has given birth to an independent, resilient spirit that constitutes a core value of the Mancunian identity (Worthington, 2002). Such spirit has risen in critical moments such as the attacks during war times or IRA's bombings. This latter "became a pivotal moment in the city's revolution of partnership and revitalisation" (Holden, 2002: 135), which mobilized Manchester's entrepreneurial dynamism and innovation spirit. For some, it was a case of "explosive entrepreneurialism":

> The institutional and political processes that accompanied the rebuilding of Manchester city centre precipitated three forms of opportunity: space for redesign and redevelopment in line with plans (City Pride); legitimacy and image for entrepreneurial partnerships between public and private funding bodies, affirmed MCC as an innovative, entrepreneurial core partner within local governance. (Holden, 2002: 136)

However, the heritage of the traditional-industry economy made the UK North West, and Manchester in particular, be desperately late for regeneration tasks. The city-region (with East Manchester in particular) still includes the nation's poorest and most disadvantaged areas (Work Foundation, 2002). As a former center for traditional manufacturing industry, Manchester suffered particularly badly from the economic recessions of the 1970s and 1980s. It lost 60% of its employment base between 1975 and 1985. In some neighborhoods, large areas of idle, ex-industrial open space can still be seen as well as the effects of high levels of unemployment. Poverty, crime and the fear of crime, poor health, poor working skills, low educational levels, and a lack of facilities are clearly the heritage of such recessions (MCC, 2004).

In this context, creating learning-rich environments, not only in places designed for formal instruction and accredited learning, but also in workplaces, local communities, and places were people meet and interact (Healy, 2002: 84) is a major challenge for the Manchester city-region of the new millennium.

Entrepreneurial Partnerships

In 1997, New Labour attempted a new turn into regionalism, following the OECD and European Commission agendas, aiming to tackle regional inequality by "unlocking the wealth of regions." The strategy was based on "the promise of local connectivity (in clusters and value chains, between institutions and through local relations of trust and reciprocity)." Its key assumption was that "regions can be a basic unit of economic organisation" and therefore an engine for innovation (Amin et al., 2003: 22). These knowledge-based models are putting the policy emphasis on direct measures,

> to boost local economic competitiveness, including programmes to stimulate inno-
> vation and learning within firms, strengthen clusters of inter-related industries, and
> upgrade the infrastructure for education, training and knowledge transfer and
> communication. Regions have been told to plan for clusters and local innovation
> systems. (Amin et al., 2003: 22)

And although still a matter of debate and contestation, such views on inter-related infrastructure brings the essence of a social capital definition at the operational level that includes those structures such as distribution channels and networks, as has been proposed by the OECD Report on The Well-being of Nations: The Role of Human and Social Capital. The report has defined social capital as "the total of social networks together with shared norms, values and understandings that facilitate cooperation within or amongst groups" (OECD Report, 2001, in Healy, 2002: 78). Social capital is thus "a metaphor about advantage" and the contextual complement of human capital (Burt, 2000: 3) and human capital is potentially a close complement of social capital (Healy, 2002: 78).

Following such worldview, the UK central government has emphasized programs and initiatives to address the causes and consequences of poverty and social exclusion. Education Action Zones, Health Action Zones, and New Deal for Communities are all active in Manchester. These initiatives have been broadly welcomed as "positive and participatory, albeit modest, attempts to extend local partnerships and develop a cross departmental, bottom-up approach to solving entrenched social problems" (Herd and Patterson, 2002: 196).

Although heavily criticized by scholars such as Armstrong (2001: 525, in Taylor, et al., 2004: 229), successive UK governments have also adopted some "infusions of enterprise" to higher education, aiming to tackle an absence of entrepreneurial culture. For instance, in 1991, the (then) Victoria University of Manchester and the University of Manchester Institute of Science and Technology (UMIST) applied jointly for the Enterprise in Higher Education (EHE) funding initiative launched by central government. They were awarded a £2 million contract over five years from October of that year. It was expected that the program would introduce the concepts of EHE to about 50% of the student population. Although staff resistance to change was identified ("universities exist to educate, not to train"), the principles of partnerships between staff, students, and employers were established as well as the need for champions on a voluntary basis for the realistic implementation of programs of this nature (Wolfenden, 1995: 19). Likewise, some key reports and white papers have shaped the strategies in educational and university settings. Such is the influential Dearing report, commissioned by the emerging New Labour government in 1997. In his report to the Committee of Enquiry into Higher Education, Sir Ron (now Lord) Dearing highlighted the importance of centralization of data, networks, and information technologies in the learning process. He made recommendations to educational institutions, from student admissions to teaching and assessment of students, which have shaped strategies at the national level in recent years (Hazemi and Hailes, 2002).

Also, having identified technology transfer as a particularly weak area in HEIs, successive white papers from the Department of Trade and Industry (DTI) have identified an enterprise deficit as the cause of poor technology transfer (Taylor et al., 2004: 229). In 1998, the white paper on Competitiveness (DTI, 1998) led to the Science Enterprise Challenge initiative, which in turn led to the participation of the Manchester Metropolitan University (with Plymouth and Greenwich) to pilot an enterprise program on developing and sustaining the UK's enterprise culture (Taylor et al., 2004: 229). After the initial success of the pilot program, which "enabled individuals from socially deprived areas to gain confidence and skills to participate in mainstream business activity," the proposal is being rolled out into an increasing number of universities (Taylor et al., 2004: 232).

KC UniverCities

Later, the white paper on enterprise, skills, and innovation (DTI, 2001) portrayed universities as powerful drivers of innovation and change, as "producers" of people with knowledge and skills (Wolfe, 2004), and a hub of business networks and industrial clusters of the knowledge economy (Peters and May, 2004: 268). Also, the white paper Investing in Innovation: A strategy for science, engineering, and technology (OST, 2002) would be more emphatic on knowledge transfer programs linking universities with business projects. In the North West, this policy context is reflected in several recent developments promoting a KC model of "excellence with relevance" clearly inviting universities to "embrace the wider ethos of the enhancement of human and social capital" (Peters and May, 2004: 270).

In terms of research, the support and funding from central government are key for the entrepreneurial activity in all three Manchester universities. Examples of good practice are the North West Japan Center (in all Universities), Ventures (in University of Manchester, UM) and Community Finance, Academic Enterprise, and Salford Money (in the University of Salford) (May and Perry, 2003: 43).

Also, in partnership through the Contact Group and the North West Universities Association (created in 1999), the universities have built a unified vision for their participation in the KC strategy, working increasingly closer with the North West Development Agency (NWDA), the umbrella organization overseeing the regional initiative. In a report prepared by the SURF research centre, interviewees of each university seemed to recognize the roles their institutions were to play in the knowledge-based scenario. For the merged University of Manchester, "further evidence of an innovative milieu" would take place in KC initiatives, with a capacity to attract high-profile students and staff as its distinctive strengths in the knowledge economy. For the Manchester Metropolitan University (MMU), an institutional growth and transformation were the aspirations for its role in the KC communicated in the report, with the KC model as a "means to continually cultivating relationships between the University, city and region." Salford, on its side, came across in the report as "a university with a focus on innovative engagement with business, industry and commerce, being vocational, real world and linked to industries" (May and Perry, 2003: 30). And even though the awareness of KC processes in universities remains at senior management level, it is expected to cascade down at all levels within the next three years.

Moreover, in October 2004, a purposeful creation of a super-campus by merging the two major universities in the region is seemingly part of the deployment strategy of local and national authorities to smooth the progress into a KC-type of development. The "Project Unity" between the Victoria University of Manchester and the UMIST is aiming to fulfil the third of five best-case scenario aspirations of universities' contribution to the KC initiative: to become a world-class institution. In the scenario for success at Andy Hill's university (2008), the following five indicators of success in KC universities were agreed by a number of Manchester's stakeholders (Georghiou and Cassingena-Harper, 2003). The emerging university would

(1) have an intelligent infrastructural development and management
(2) be a net importer of high quality brains
(3) be a world-class university
(4) trigger massive inward investment
(5) develop intelligent networking.

Likewise, Professor Alan Gilbert (from Melbourne, Australia), President and Vice-chancellor of the University of Manchester, has mentioned that "by elevating Manchester into the premier league of world universities over the next decade, we will also make the University a dynamic contributor of wealth-creation and employment growth in Manchester, the North West and the UK" (Unilife, 2004/2/6). Seemingly, a new type of university is emerging. Some scholars have called it the "enterprise university" with the fundamental mission of advancing the prestige and competitiveness of the university, with key examples of a culture of economic consumption observed in Australian universities (Marginson and Considine, 2000: 5).

Most of all, there is an aspiration of city renewal and an emphasis of the university as a local source or research, expertise, and innovation, that enables KC citizens to thrive in the global economy (Peters and May, 2004).

The Sustainable City

Hence, in some international observers' opinion, Manchester has made an "entrepreneurial turn" by embracing the KC models that will shape the city-region economic community, including its universities. However, despite an effective marketing strategy to promote the city, "Manchester remains a much divided city since the 1990's presenting a complex story of poverty characterised by deprivation in tight geographical areas lying in close proximity to relative affluence" (Herd and Patterson, 2002: 191). A number of initiatives have taken place since 1995, led by the North West Development Agency (NWDA), and are being evaluated in 2005. Regeneris, an independent agency, has performed an independent evaluation of the regeneration initiatives undertaken by the NWDA within a five-year time frame.

The Agency has reported some successes and also significant gaps in the areas of human and social capital in the city, amongst the most acute needs of the city-region. The North West has

(1) A significant skills gap. It has 120,000 more people than England's average with no qualifications.
(2) An undoubted enterprise gap. It needs 40,000 businesses more to mirror the national average.
(3) An innovation gap. Its knowledge base is still too small compared to the most advanced economies.

(4) A knowledge-sector gap, with 10% fewer people employed in these sectors than the national average.

(5) An employment gap, with 80,000 fewer people than England's average.

Clearly, this corresponds almost exclusively to the human and social capitals challenged in an atmosphere of deprivation which has been in the Manchester city-region for over two-hundred years. Having such disadvantages in the areas of human and social capital, the Manchester strategy is significant in terms of inclusive education and development for the young population as well as for the tertiary sector for life-long learning (Regeneris, 2005).

"However, social capital can never become the Trojan Horse to deliver economic and social progress. Likewise, the promotion of higher skills, knowledge and learning in schools, organisations and communities alone cannot deliver sustainable economic and social progress" (Healy, 2002: 85). In spite of this sheer realism, some authors have hope in the future of Knowledge Society, "in which an old discourse of equity and opportunity—access and participation in the context of education—is reborn in the language of social inclusion; the recognition of community, its strength, value and sheer utility, is re-discovered through various notions of social capital" (Duke, 2002: 160).

Indeed, the expected outcome of the knowledge-based initiative within universities is to promote and provide widespread lifelong learning and inclusion of disadvantaged groups in learning activity may provide one of the most effective ways for public policy to renew social capital in the future (Healy, 2002: 86). These aspirations of development are placing human and social capital in an integrative meaning of knowledge; as it is becoming progressively apparent for KBD scholars that "there is a convergence between the 'sciences of development' and the 'sciences of knowledge' as together, they refer to the whole domain of human experience and potential" (Carrillo, 2002), therefore bringing multiple possibilities.

Seemingly, in recent years Manchester has shaped most of its core social capital through its partnerships, as this chapter attempted to demonstrate. The city-region's partnership network with local public, civic, and private stakeholders is already having a positive impact in key areas of its socioeconomic infrastructure. Also, by means of its social capital, Manchester's citizenship is also building partnerships with other UK cities, the central government, the European Union representatives, and other European cities. In the future, it is expected that this capital would actually bring significant moments in Manchester's journey into becoming a KC.

But most importantly, its citizenship is in the process of redefining the nature of their relationships amongst their multiple stakeholders: the city's researchers, authorities, students, and all citizenship who work, live, and learn in a city like Manchester. By doing so, the city's identity, potential, and aspirations are being reinvented. Universities and communities are also in a radical process of reinvention. In a moment in time such as this, Manchester's citizenship is confronted with the possibility of reconceptualizing its regional development, and thriving in the global economy by radically increasing its social capital, against the odds of the last two-hundred years. Indeed, of all cities in the UK, Manchester has the best chance to come up with the utmost radical solution to such challenge.

References and Bibliography

Amin, A., Massey, D. and Thrift, Nigel (2003). Descentering the nation: A radical approach to regional inequality, *Catalyst Paper 8*, September. Available at: www.catalystforum.org.uk

Berg, L. van den and Russo, A. (2004). The student city, *Strategic Planning for Student Communities in EU Cities*. Hants: Ashgate.

Briggs, A. (1963). Manchester, symbol of a new age, *Victorian Cities*, London: Odhams Press.

Burt, R. (2000). 'The network structure of social capital', in Sutton, I. and Staw, B. M. (eds), *Research in Organisational Behaviour*, vol. 22, Greenwich, CT: JAI Press.

Carrillo, F. J. (2002). Capital systems: Implications for a global knowledge agenda, *Journal of Knowledge Management*, Special issue on Knowledge-based Development, vol. 6, no. 4, pp. 379–399.

Carrillo, F. J. (2004). Capital cities: A taxonomy of capital accounts for knowledge cities, *Journal of Knowledge Management*, Special issue on Knowledge-based Development II: Knowledge Cities, vol. 8, no. 5, pp. 28–46.

Carter, A. (2000). 'Strategy and partnership in urban regeneration', in Roberts, P. and Sykes, H. (eds), *Urban Regeneration: A Handbook*, London: Sage.

Cassingena-Harper, J. (2003). Improving links between tenant companies and HEIs, *Report on Exploring Emerging Scenarios for Manchester Science Park, PREST*. University of Manchester and Manchester Science Park Ltd. Available at: http://les.man.ac.uk/PREST/Publications/universities_sciencepark.htm

Desai, Lord (2003). Manchester and Development: Trade, Growth and Markets, in Third Manchester Lecture in International Development. (Master Conference in the occasion of the opening of University of Manchester's Harold Hankins Building, and the 45th Anniversary of IDPM). Manchester, UK, 29 October. Lord Desai is Director of the Centre for Global governance at the London School of Economics.

Department of Trade and Industry (DTI) (1998). *Our Competitive Future: Building the Knowledge Driven Economy*. Cm4176. London: HMSO.

Department of Trade and Industry (DTI) (2001). Opportunity for all in a world of change: A White Paper on enterprise, skills and innovation. Available at: www.dti.gov.uk/opportunityforall/

Diamond, J. (2002). Strategies to resolve conflict in partnerships: Reflections on UK urban regeneration, *The International Journal of Public Sector Management*, vol. 15, no. 4, pp. 296–306.

Dicken, P. (2002). 'Global Manchester: From globaliser to globalised', in Peck, J. and Ward, K. (eds), *City of Revolution: Restructuring Manchester*, Manchester: Manchester University Press.

Dickens, C. (©1854). *Hard Times*, London: Penguin Books.

Duke, C. (2002). 'Universities and the knowledge society', in Instance, D., Schuetze, H. G. and Schuller, T. (eds), *International Perspectives on Lifelong Learning. From Recurrent Education to the Knowledge Society*. Milton Keynes: Society for Research into Higher Education (SRHE) and Open University Press.

Dvir, R. and Pasher, E. (2004). Innovation engines for knowledge cities: An innovation ecology perspective, *Journal of Knowledge Management*, Special issue on Knowledge-based Development II: Knowledge Cities, vol. 8, no. 5, pp. 16–27.

Engels, F. (©1845). *The Conditions of the Working Class in England*. London: Penguin Books.

Ergazakis, K., Metaxiotis, K. and Psarras, J. (2004). Towards knowledge cities: Conceptual analysis and success stories, *Journal of Knowledge Management*, Special issue on Knowledge-based Development II: Knowledge Cities, vol. 8, no. 5, pp. 5–15.

Florida, R. (1995). Toward the Learning Region, *Futures*, vol. 27, no. 5, pp. 527–536.

Gaskell, E. (©1845). *North and South*, London: Penguin Books.

Georghiou, L. and Cassingena-Harper, J. (2003) Contribution of Universities to the Knowledge Capital, *Report on the Success Scenario Workshop, PREST/IOIR*, University of Manchester and Manchester Science Park Ltd. Available at: http://les.man.ac.uk/PREST/Publications/universities_knowledgecapital.htm

Hazemi, R. and Hailes, Stephen (2002). *The Digital University. Building a Learning Community*, London: Springer-Verlag.

Healy, T. (2002). 'From Human Capital to Social Capital', in Instance, D., Schuetze, H. G. and Schuller, T. (eds), *International Perspectives on Lifelong Learning. From Recurrent Education to the Knowledge Society*. Milton Keynes: Society for Research into Higher Education (SRHE) and Open University Press.

Herd, D. and Patterson, T. (2002). 'Poor Manchester: Old problems and new deals', in Peck, J. and Ward, K. (eds), *City of Revolution. Restructuring Manchester*. Manchester: Manchester University Press.

Holden, A. (2002). 'Bomb sites: The politics of opportunity', in Peck, J. and Ward, K. (eds), *City of Revolution. Restructuring Manchester*. Manchester: Manchester University Press.

Hylton, S. (2003). *A History of Manchester*, Chichester, West Sussex, UK: Phillimore & Co. Ltd.

Manchester City Council (MCC) (2004). *Manchester: Shaping the City*. London: Riba Enterprises Ltd.

Manchester City Council and Knowledge Capital Partnership (2003) Manchester: Knowledge Capital, in Gyroscope Manchester, June 2003.

Manchester Investment and Development Agency Service (MIDAS) (2004). Available at: www.manchestercalling.com.

Manchester Science and Industry Museum (2004). Exhibit at the MSIM, in Central Manchester. Visit in February 2004.

Marginson, S. and Considine, M. (2000). *The Enterprise University. Power, Governance and Reinvention in Australia*, Cambridge: Cambridge University Press.

Maskell, P. (2001). 'Growth and territorial configuration of Economic activity' paper presented in the DRUID Conference: Danish Research Unit for Industrial Dynamics, 12–15 June 2001, in Copenhagen, Denmark. See abstract on line at: http://www.druid.dk/conferences/nw/paper1/maskell.pdf

May, T. and Perry, B. (2003). Knowledge capital: From concept to action, *Report to the Contact Partnership Group*, May. SURF Centre for Sustainable Urban and Regional Futures. University of Salford. Available at: www.thecontactpartnership.ac.uk, Knowledge City, key documents.

Office of Science and Technology (OST) (2002). Investing in innovation: A strategy for science, engineering and technology. Available at: www.ost.gov.uk/policy/science_strategy.pdf

Ovalle, Gonzalez, R., Martinez, S. and Alvarado, A. (2004). A compilation on knowledge cities and knowledge-based development, *Journal of Knowledge Management*, Special issue on Knowledge-based Development II: Knowledge Cities, vol. 8, no. 5, pp. 28–46.

Peck, J. and Ward, K. (2002). *City of Revolution. Restructuring Manchester*, Manchester: Manchester University Press.

Peters, M. A. and May, T. (2004). Universities, regional policy and the knowledge economy, *Policy Futures in Education*, vol. 2, no. 2. Available at: http://wwwords.co.uk/pdf/validate.asp?j=pfie&vol=2&issue=2&year=2004&article=4_Peters_PFIE_2_2_web&id=130.88.205.96

Porter, M. (1995). The competitive advantage of the inner city, *Harvard Business Review*, May–June.

Portes, A. (1998). Social capital: Its origins and applications in modern sociology, *Annual Review of Sociology*, Palo Alto, vol. 24, pp. 1–12.

Quah, D. (2002). Digital goods and the new economy, Centre for Economic Performance, London School of Economics. Available at: http://cep.lse.ac.uk/pubs/download/dp0563.pdf

Regeneris Consulting (2005). North West Economic Baseline: Issues Report. *Report to the North West Development Agency (NWDA)*, March. Available at: http://www.regeneris.co.uk

Robson, B. (2002). Mancunian ways: The politics of regeneration, in Peck, J. and Ward, K. (eds), *City of Revolution. Restructuring Manchester*, Manchester: Manchester University Press.

Taylor, D. W., Jones, O. and Boles, K. (2004). Building social capital through action learning: An insight into the entrepreneur, *Education and Training*, vol. 46, no. 5, pp. 226–235.

University of Manchester (2004). *Unilife*. Student & Staff Magazine of the University of Manchester, vols 1 and 2, February–November.

University of Salford (2003). 'Manchester—The UK's only Knowledge Capital outside London', *Campus Report*. Student Magazine of the University of Salford, Autumn, pp. 3–4.

Wallis, J. and Killerby, P. (2004). Social economics and social capital, *International Journal of Social Economics*, vol. 31, no. 3, pp. 239–258.

Weber, M. (1958). *The City*. New York/London: The Free Press, Macmillan Publishing Co.

Wolfe, D. (2004). 'The role of higher education in regional innovation and cluster development', in Jones, G. and McCarney, P. (eds), *Creating Knowledge, Strengthening Nations*, Toronto: Toronto University Press. Available on line at: http://www.utoronto.ca/progris/pdf_files/higher_education_UofTPress.pdf

Wolfenden, R. (1995). Experiences of enterprise in higher education within two research-led universities, *Education and Training*, vol. 37, no. 9, pp. 15–19.

Work Foundation (2002). *Manchester: Ideopolis? Developing a Knowledge Capital*. Prepared by Andy Westwood and Max Nathan. London: The Work Foundation.

Work Foundation (2005). *The Ideopolis: Knowledge City Consortium*. Research Project. March 2005–February 2006. Available at: http://theworkfoundation.com/research/ideopolis.jsp

Worthington, B. (2002). *Discovering Manchester*, Cheshire, UK: Sigma Press. Update available at: www.sigmapress.co.uk

Chapter 11

Greater Phoenix as a Knowledge Capital

Jay Chatzkel, *Progressive Practices, Phoenix, Arizona, USA*

> Becoming a knowledge capital requires a conscious decision to achieve a network of knowledge-based entities that strategically interface with the world

What is a Knowledge Capital?

A "knowledge capital" is a region that bases its ability to create wealth on its capacity to generate and leverage its knowledge capabilities. In a knowledge capital, enterprises and people link to form knowledge-based extended networks to achieve strategic goals, cultivate innovation, and successfully respond to rapidly changing conditions. A knowledge capital recognizes that its ability to grow, capture, leverage, and share its knowledge is the basis for both its competitive advantage in the world and its quality of life.

As we emerge from the Industrial Era, physical and financial resources still are important, but it is now knowledge, and actionable knowledge specifically, that is the most powerful factor of production. Physical and financial resources have become commodities that are relatively easy to obtain or replicate. The knowledge factor differentiates a region by uniquely producing the ability to generate, capture, and leverage the knowledge necessary to mobilize the other resources and yield remarkable outcomes.

The Engine of a Global Network

The reason to pursue becoming a knowledge region is to create the capacities for great gain. In fact, every country or company that has made great leaps has built a knowledge base as its springboard. This is no less the case for Greater Phoenix or any other potential knowledge capital at this point in time. The driving enablers for this transformation will be the revamping of the institutions of the region (private, not-for-profit, and public) to become knowledge-based enterprises, as well as mapping out an overall set of strategic goals for the region and a knowledge strategy to achieve those goals.

A knowledge capital is the center point of ultimately a network with global reach. Prince Henry the Navigator set the stage for Portugal to become the wealthiest commercial force in the world for two centuries through establishing a knowledge capital. Captain James Cook used a seaborne knowledge capital to chart out the future British Empire during his voyages in the 1700s. Those involved in forging 21st century knowledge capitals must embark on similar expeditions to map the new territories of the next half century. These expeditions will be to bring into being new territories of the mind which will be part of extended knowledge-based enterprise networks. To be sure, a knowledge capital will not serve its people if it is purely local or even regional in scope. It must see itself operating as a global wealth-generating actor.

The advent of the computer and the Internet, coupled with growing global competition and hyper-exponential change, has changed the recipe for creating and sustaining a successful enterprise and region. Knowledge is directly in the hands of all members of an enterprise who can communicate much more freely via the Internet anywhere, any time to anyone. Physical and political boundaries mean far less, and are far more permeable. At this point in history no enterprise can consider itself effectively insulated from global competition. In fact, in an increasingly wireless world, that competition can arise from any place on the globe where there are adequately educated people and sufficient technology.

While in previous decades it was manufacturing jobs with lower skill requirements that became footloose, relocating to areas of least expensive labor, at the beginning of the 21st new century, white collar professional and technical jobs are equally in play and can wind up anywhere. The result is the high levels of current angst of many who thought they had privileges of seniority, benefits, and a secure future in their enterprises, only to find out that their jobs were outsourced to India, China, the Philippines, or Poland. The rate of change is not just growing or growing exponentially, but it is growing hyper-exponentially, as John Seely Brown[1] has said. We have been led to expect that we will be encountering a continually changing environment, but the velocity of change is hyper-accelerated due to the convergence of new technologies, new availabilities of those technologies, and the universal incidence of those technologies.

In conjunction with these dynamic challenges, we are beginning to realize that approaches and technologies that we believed were good and progressive are actually value neutral. The attacks of September 11, 2001, showed that all of these technologies and approaches, such as intellectual capital and knowledge management, can be used for good or ill. As wealthy in physical resources and powerful as the United States was, it turned out to be vulnerable to a small number of people with a minimal, and barely adequate, amount of technology training, but a fierce will, who used the physical resources of United States against itself. The lesson here is that organizations, and even city/regions and nation-states, must not only actively cultivate their intellectual capital and knowledge management capabilities, which is usually an internally focused, self-improvement type of effort. They also have to have the ability to be acutely sensitive to the whole range of possible competitive forces at play globally that can affect them. We live in a world where any advantage is temporary, and the challenges to the status quo are disruptive and ongoing. It is a world where dominance of purely physical resources does not make the difference, but rather where the capability to shape the whole range of physical, financial, human, and technological resources to respond to ever changing conditions is what matters. In a word, it is the intangible capabilities and the ability to navigate and reshape recipes for transformation, which create the competitive edge.

---

[1] Presentation at the 2001 BrainTrust Conference, February 13, San Francisco, CA.

The Knowledge Capital Advantage

Knowledge capitals have a unique advantage in this world. They are the dynamic centers where new knowledge is created, brought in use, and leveraged. Just as the great merchant/trading cities of the Renaissance, such as Venice, were the catalysts and focal points for generating wealth and power, and the New York and Chicago of the early 20th century where society's problems were both most intense and at the same time freshly resolved,[2] knowledge capitals of the 21st century will be where the critical problems of the planet are met and responded to. And, it is the tackling of those problems that yields new, breakthrough opportunities. Knowledge capitals are singularly able to meet these challenges and forge new opportunities because they have the concentrations of human capital, infrastructure, and the other requisite resources, as well as the values and the entrepreneurial orientation to bring to bear to create solutions and implement these responses. While nation-states will continue to exist, it is the knowledge capitals that will negotiate their future with each other. It will, over time, turn out that knowledge capitals across North America, South America, Europe, Asia, and Africa will have more in common and be better and more directly linked than will be their host nation-states.

Will these knowledge capitals be the same as traditional cities of the past century? What will continue to be true is that knowledge capitals will be where the action is. The actual physical and other characteristics will vary from place to place determined by regional requirements. For example, knowledge capitals may have downtowns or not, but even if they do, these will not be conventional downtowns in any case. The dominant elements of a knowledge city are an intensity of interaction and high levels of performance. The Silicon Valley, the technology corridors around Washington DC, the Research Triangle in North Carolina, and the clusters of office complexes in Bangalore may be good indicators that it is clustering, connectivity, proximity, and intimacy that matter more so than traditional downtown locations and physical structures.

Bringing a Knowledge Capital into Existence

There are two dimensions in the development of a knowledge capital. Internally enterprises must be in a continuous process of transformation in order to be at one with and respond to changing conditions in the world. At the same time, the region needs to formulate overall strategies that build upon and capitalize on its unique strategic advantages. These strategies guide the development of the knowledge city's technological, physical, and social infrastructure across enterprises, and extend out into the world.

From the internal perspective, Knowledge Era organizations need to generate extended enterprise structures for operating. This means that the enterprise must reground itself in its business strategy, customer strategy, organizational strategy, and knowledge strategy. The business strategy is the largest context and each other strategy nests in, is aligned with and reinforced by the larger business strategy.[3]

The business strategy maps out the place of the enterprise in the world and denotes its competing areas such as niche markets, customized offerings, and service packages. The customer strategy targets selected customer foci and concentrates on the nature and levels of relationship and service level, as well as the goods and services that

---

[2] Jane Jacobs (1970), *The Economy of Cities*, Vintage, New York.
[3] Hubert Saint Onge and Charles Armstrong (2004), *The Conductive Organization: Building Beyond Sustainability*, Butterworth-Heinemann, Woburn, MA.

would be developed and supplied to discrete customer groupings. The organizational strategy looks at the internal operations of the organization, articulating types of human capital functional abilities and experience and the processes that are necessary to support the customer and business strategy. The knowledge strategy deals with the kinds of knowledge leadership, staff, suppliers and customers need, tied to the technology that is critical to achieve business strategy goals.

As part of that internal perspective, the enterprise must move beyond the old social contracts which were temporary truces between the antagonistic interests of management versus labor. That type of social contract is now in tatters. Enterprises can no longer support work rules and benefit agreements geared to an era of gradual growth and long-term relationships. Rapidly changing and newly emerging requirements demand new skills and ever changing offerings and have made traditional arrangements obsolete and counterproductive.

In the emerging knowledge capital recipe, the management, the workforce, suppliers, and customers all have to collaborate in an extended supplier/producer/customer network or else do not survive. This is not an easy or simple process. It requires that each individual build and use a strong set of negotiating skills to flesh out the specific characteristics of their deals with the enterprises they work with. Autonomous members of the workforce must negotiate with enterprise managers to forge these new "social contracts" where individuals "invest" their capabilities so that the enterprise's strategic goals can be reached. Just as financial investors bring their financial capital to the table to invest and work out the best deal for themselves, all individuals in the workforce are investors of their own human capital and seek the best return on investment for themselves.[4] The enterprise shapes the context for these "deals" so that the human capital resources are used to achieve strategic targets. Everyone has to participate in negotiating these deals. Frontline employees, supervisors, and senior leadership all have to seek the best outcome for both the enterprise and the workforce. The same holds true in the relationship between the enterprise and the customers of its outcomes, with products and services being cogenerated with inputs from users.

Secondly, there are a range of strategic policy choices that leadership of enterprises and city/regions must make. Becoming a knowledge capital requires a conscious decision to achieve a network of knowledge-based entities that interface with the world. It then requires a set of strategic goals and commitment of resources to build the infrastructure and engage the talent that is necessary to design and implement the related dimensions of the knowledge enterprise and region. While this is happening, all parties need to search out existing and emerging opportunity areas that can be new centers for innovation and service that take the knowledge capital to new levels of achievement and performance.

Building a knowledge capital further entails understanding that this is a long-term undertaking. Projects can be the impetus and catalyst to establishing a new basis for the economy and society, serving as stepping stones to the larger transformation.

For a knowledge capital to be fully successful all elements of the population need to participate. This requires extensive and continuous communications across all sectors and to all populations about the transformation. In the end, everyone in the city/region (i.e., business leaders, politicians, school teachers, artists, students, retirees, and office workers) needs to grasp that the shift to a knowledge era economy and

---

[4] Thomas O. Davenport (1999), *Human Capital: What It Is and Why People Invest It*, Jossey-Bass, San Francisco, CA.

society is well underway and to understand that knowledge is the currency of this new era. A knowledge capital cannot afford to leave anyone out.

Further, a knowledge capital is not just about communication. It is about education as well. Since knowledge capital is rooted in knowledge-abilities, everyone needs to participate in a lifelong education process. This is not an option but rather a core way of operating and providing the basis for generating new wealth.

There is a tendency for some in the knowledge capital movement to emphasize the development of a strategic action framework, while others concentrate on making individual enterprises increasingly knowledge-based enterprises. The truth of the matter is that there is a fundamental bond between creating a strategic action framework through which the city/region moves to reposition and reframe itself as a knowledge capital and the simultaneous development of enterprises built on principles of responsiveness, speed, transparent values, continuous learning, and high performance. It can be said that the relationship is Janus like, where each is necessarily an embodiment, reflection, and manifestation of the other but with a different face. In the end, it is the same brand, the same quality of intelligence and level of performance that is brought to bear on the global scene.

Can the Greater Phoenix Region Become a Knowledge Capital?

The Greater Phoenix region has major elements that can enable it to become a Knowledge Capital. The region has a number of educational institutions at the university, community college, and technical school level, which are interested in creating the technological basis for knowledge enterprises. It is the political capital of Arizona, with certain agencies that have developed themselves into world-class operations. Further, people from all over the United States and the world are drawn to live and vacation in remarkable climate in Greater Phoenix, with its numerous resorts and legions of continuously developing communities for people of all ages. Its climate, along with relatively inexpensive development and operating costs, drew a core group of technology companies to the region. Beyond that Greater Phoenix has clusters of cultural organizations and is also a gateway to many of the most outstanding recreational areas in the United States. It has a transportation network, primarily of highways, that gives it access across the region and country, and an international airport that provides connections to anywhere in the world.

At the same time, Greater Phoenix is a living contradiction. It banks heavily on tourism, a continuing construction boom, and a low-wage service economy. All of these economic pillars are vulnerable. The tourism industry is still recovering from the attacks of September 11, 2001, and can be equally affected by any similar incident or downturn. The real estate development industry can experience an unpredictable rise in interest rates that could starkly cut the market for its offerings. And finally, its low-wage service work is increasingly under pressure since major elements of it, such as call centers, are easily outsourced offshore. The result is that, based upon these three economic drivers, it is difficult for many residents of the Greater Phoenix region to build satisfying and sustainable standard of living. Table 1 provides a brief profile of Phoenix city.

A Knowledge Conversation: Building the Basis for Making the Leap

A knowledge capital is a result of a continuing conversation of the major participants in the region. The people who join in this conversation map out the strategic goals for the region and determine the knowledge strategy. This conversation focuses on determining

Table 1: Phoenix profile

- Phoenix is the fifth largest population city in the United States with 1.3 million people
- It is surrounded by nine other cities in Maricopa County that have populations of 100,000 people or more
- The overall population for Maricopa County is 3,500,000 people, growing 45% over the last decade
- The Phoenix-Mesa metropolitan area increasing in population by 45% during that same period
- 34% of the City of Phoenix population is Hispanic/Latino, and 25% of Maricopa County population is Hispanic/Latino
- The Phoenix metro area is just over 9000 square miles in area

Source: US Bureau of Census Data.

the basic requirements for becoming knowledge-based enterprises and the need to set goals for the region to achieve so that it can win in the global competitions over the next five decades.

There are two basic, overall approaches to a knowledge strategy. One is enterprise-wide and the other is project-specific. In some cases there is a basis to mobilize the entire region network of enterprises, as was done in Singapore, to make it a "wired," highly educated country with institutions that have a common goal of furthering the Singapore "brand." Areas as diverse as its ports, airline, and defense department were each focal points for transformation, supported by a well-educated and outwardly focused government and people.

Another approach is more project-based. While the operating principles of both are the same, the project-based approach specifically targets opportunities, gradually building up a constituency and over time weaving the links into a full-scale knowledge capital enterprise.

This project-based approach may make the most sense in the Greater Phoenix region. There are numerous opportunities to create projects that are catalysts for broader transformation in the region.

An example of one such opportunity is that Greater Phoenix is in a unique position to establish a Center for NAFTA Performance Excellence. Phoenix is a major American city that stands near Mexican border and has a strong Canadian presence. Such a center could both draw on and build the academic capabilities required to study international trade issues, be a focal point for how enterprises could markedly improve their performance, and be a generator for the kinds of industries that could actively and beneficially participate in cross-border activities. This is an issue for small to medium businesses in Arizona, across Canada, and in Mexico as well. They are simply not geared nor have the strategic frameworks and networks to step up readily to engage in international trade activities.

A Center for NAFTA Performance Excellence could also be a springboard for Greater Phoenix becoming an international trade center similar to the role that Miami, Florida, plays in its region. The related opportunity is to establish an International Trade Center near the region's Sky Harbor International Airport. This center would have the potential for being an educational, informational, and meeting center as well as carrying out conventional international business trade agenda activi-ties. The various consulates that are located in the Phoenix region, trade associations, and trade consultants could be located there to facilitate trade requirements, along with components of international business schools that would offer graduate and enterprise-tailored educational programs and conferences.

The International Trade Center could also be an enabler for Phoenix to be seen as the intellectual capital and organizational venue center for the triangle of Asian/Mexican/North American transnational trade. In this schema after basic work is completed in Asia, goods would be shipped to western Mexico ports where value added work is done in nearby regional areas and then forwarded across the US border to the Phoenix region for both more efficient and less congested routing into the American markets. The reverse is true as well, in that North American commodities and goods could be sent more easily and competitively to Asian markets.

There is room for many additional centers that can serve as catalysts for raising the level of service, performance, and knowledge in the Greater Phoenix region. These centers would generate ripple effects to stimulate a broader reframing of regional institutions to become a network of knowledge-based enterprises. The centers would build on the already existing infrastructure to transform and enhance their current offering to a world-class level. Some centers are:

- **Center for Technology and Innovation:** A cross-enterprise endeavor of educational and private enterprise institutions to name and nurture technologies that introduce new opportunities and support higher levels of performance in regional enterprises. This center would be a neutral body to work with the private sector, educational institutions, and the investment community to forge the kind of powerful presence that would command resources and develop new and lucrative markets.

  There are many excellent undertakings that exist in the Phoenix region, yet there is very little regional benchmarking or using of current successes to foster the degree role modeling and prototyping that could leverage these outstanding efforts and acknowledge them as the norm for which all enterprises need to strive.

- **Center for Enterprise Performance:** This center would focus on availing the new and innovative perspectives and skills that are needed in all types of enterprises across the region. The goal would be to foster world-class levels of performance. This performance would be characterized by an attitude of autonomy, collaboration, and investment among the workforce and the development of strategic capabilities in enterprises.

  No one type of business or sector will make the region successful. It will take all types of organizations becoming customer-centric, strategic, and capability-rich to power the engines for continuing competitive advantage. This center will engage organizations from all sectors (public, for-profit, and not-for-profit) to create an upward spiral of quality, effectiveness, and innovation.

- **Center for Hospitality and Tourism:** The Tourism and Hospitality sectors are well developed, having true world-class capabilities and a strong national and international presence. Yet there is no center at the university or advanced degree level to grow the broad range of leadership and technical skills needed to make Greater Phoenix a destination region and not largely a pass-through to competing cities like Las Vegas that it has become. In a word, Greater Phoenix has to capitalize on its current robust capabilities and cultivate itself to be experienced as one of the most compelling attractions in the world.

- **Center for Construction and the Environment:** Although construction and real estate is a prime driver in the Greater Phoenix region, the emphasis has been the gains from development of inexpensive land and related resources and not developing itself as a cutting edge center for design and construction of sustainable environments. Urban design and architecture, coupled with explorations on how to imaginatively, sensitively, and economically build on the Greater Phoenix region's unique Sonoran desert setting would create an exciting, living legacy for all ranges of the regions population, across all income levels. It would also build a legacy of housing and commercial building stock that is not geared to deteriorate but rather to be ongoingly renewed and valued over a multiple decade timeframe.

- **Center for Citizen Participation:** Retirees and others have vast amounts of experience and talent that can be drawn upon to invest themselves as volunteers in the gamut of non-profit, for-profit, and public enterprises of the region. A fundamental shift in approach would be that the volunteer experience is designed as a continuous process of learning and enrichment for participants. This large group of people is a set of human resources that is currently barely tapped or appreciated. In addition to engaging already the resident population into value-creating community endeavors, this center's work could also be an attractive beacon to large numbers of people who want a place to move to for a meaningful, engaging retirement. A further dimension is to reframe regional institutions to know how to utilize this reservoir of unpaid staff power to significantly benefit both the institutions and its volunteers.

- **Center for New Citizens:** The Greater Phoenix region is faced with a critical problem and opportunity. There is a vast legion of Latino and other immigrants to the region, which needs to be integrated into the overall fabric of its communities. The issue of illegal immigration rages in the region and is typical of similar situations throughout the world where people with little opportunity swarm across the borders of their more affluent neighbors for a chance of a decent life. Conventional tightening of borders and legal restrictions are less than successful despite large boosts in funding, manpower, and advances in surveillance technology. In the end this is a human problem and may be significantly addressed as legal and even illegal residents learn how to best become productive citizens of the region and nation. Beyond being a social welfare agency, such a center could focus on the education, advancement, and well-being of this significant population, building it as a major asset for the region, not as an incapacitating liability.

- **Center for Educational Transformation:** This center would concentrate on the kinds of educational opportunities that need to be brought into play to prepare Phoenicians of all ages and backgrounds to participate in their knowledge-based future. Focusing on this goal would go a great distance in leading to reverse the negative trends of the Phoenix region having one of the highest high school dropout rates in the United States. There is a vicious cycle of many students who do not see the benefit of staying in high school since the most work available then is of low wage and with a limited future. At the same time, the Phoenix region cannot recruit the people who will be entrepreneurial leaders of the new economy from a community where they cannot find a capable workforce. Providing funding for raising education levels is one part of the answer. Perhaps more important though is providing learning that emphasizes critical thinking skills, problem-solving abilities, resourcefulness, and innovation, which together allow people to create their own capacities and set their own futures. Along with this is the need for a set of well thought out education options that dovetail with the requirements of both the citizenry and the regional enterprises.

- **Center for Gerontology**: A significant proportion of the Greater Phoenix population is retirees, a population that will grow in ever greater numbers as the "baby boomer" population moves into its retirement years. Phoenix could be a center for both life-long wellness and the availability of high quality treatment for this community cluster. This would be both a huge benefit to the resident population and an attraction to people from around the world seeking an extended and high quality lifestyle. Developments from this center would generate a vital flow of unique innovation, research, and development. However, at this point there is not a major research, preventive and treatment network program for wellness-oriented health care for among senior citizens in Greater Phoenix.

  Such a dynamic center would be a catalyst for attracting and retaining significant numbers of general and special skilled health care practitioners. It could also be important for raising reimbursement rates for state physicians so that they are competitive to other regions, a major reason for the current scarcity of specialists in Arizona. Health care providers individually or collectively could lead this effort to determine the necessary incentives to serve as a magnet drawing a continuing stream of quality health care practitioners. These practitioners and their related institutions could set the standard for high quality of life health care, generate the human and institutional resources to sustain and advance that care, and educate and lead others from around the world in this area.

- **A Future Center**: The future belongs to those who shape it. A Future Center will explore possible emerging trends and opportunities to experiment with prototype applications. These outcomes would be available to regional enterprises to develop further and find technologies and markets for broader scale implementation. Explorations at the Future Center would also identify and amplify the weak peripheral signals surface that are early indicators of emerging trends and issues, providing the region substantial lead time to redirect and reshape its energies and investments to take that nascent future into account. A Future Center is not just a physical and relationship phenomenon. It is also a mindset that requires going beyond conventional thinking and a culture of innovation to respond to conditions and prospects that do not yet exist. The future perspective creates a critical strategic advantage for the region by allowing its enterprises "to look backwards from the future" to see which of its current resources and structures need to be built up over time to prepare for anticipated needs.

Closing Thoughts

The Greater Phoenix region has begun the process that can lead it to be a Knowledge Capital. It has made some very key and strategic moves to bring in new technology sectors, reposition its major university assets, and generally decide that it is going to stake its future on becoming a Knowledge Capital. It has started to construct critical building blocks for being a significant, creative region.

The seeds have been planted, awareness is being raised, and important actions have been taken. Nonetheless, this transformation is a multi-year, multi-decade and multi-partner process. Will the seeds sufficiently root, bear fruit, be harvested, and be leveraged in such way that it changes the character, mindset, and nature of activities in the Greater Phoenix region? This is only something that the people of the Phoenix region and those who will be joining them over the coming decades can determine.

The Greater Phoenix region has been best at mapping out specific strategic thrusts. However, it is just starting to address the co-equal need of transforming its organizations into knowledge-based enterprises. If Phoenix is to make its mark in the world these policies and strategies must be enabled by enterprises that are characterized by high capacities for responsiveness and world-class performance.

If both dimensions are equally undertaken there is a good chance that Greater Phoenix will succeed as a knowledge capital. However, the world will not wait for the Phoenix region to make and act upon these crucial decisions. There are numerous other candidates who are also striving for the same role, mobilizing themselves, making the requisite investments in people and infrastructure, and committed to building their long-term knowledge-based futures. Time will tell how well Greater Phoenix makes sure that is creating its own future.

References

Davenport, Thomas O. (1999). *Human Capital: What It Is and Why People Invest It*, San Francisco, CA: Jossey-Bass.

Jacobs, Jane (1970). *The Economy of Cities*, New York: Vintage.

Saint-Onge, Hubert and Armstrong, Charles (2004). *The Conductive Organization: Building Beyond Sustainability*, Woburn, MA: Butterworth-Heinemann.

Chapter 12

A Capital System for Monterrey

Francisco Javier Carrillo, *The World Capital Institute and The Center for Knowledge Systems, Tecnológico de Monterrey, México*

Introduction

This chapter is a follow-up to Chapter 4. The purpose here is to illustrate, in the particular case of the city of Monterrey, the Generic Capitals System introduced there. The intention is that this list may help other cities develop a complete and consistent set of indicators, within a coherent and practical framework. This chapter contains mainly the hierarchical list of capitals or "social knowledge accounts" for Monterrey. Whereas this is an independent exercise, it makes reference to the formal initiative to develop Monterrey as a KC. The Project "Monterrey: International City of Knowledge" is one of five strategic initiatives of the 2004–2009 Nuevo León State Government Administration, http://www.nl.gob.mx/. The Project's objectives and main lines of action are described in the Project's Manifesto ("Monterrey: International City of Knowledge," CORPES, 2005), the Project's webpage http://www.mtycic.nl.gob.mx/index.html, and the document describing the five strategic initiatives, downloadable from http://www.nl.gob.mx/?P = intro_cd_conocimiento.

The Monterrey Capital System structure and definitions follow the Generic Capital System described in Chapter 4. This chapter includes version 1.0 of the taxonomy of knowledge capital accounts for Monterrey. At the uppermost levels, it follows exactly the generic structure described in Chapter 4. At the lowermost levels, it gets increasingly asymmetric and particular, just as each city's capital system is expected to do. Therefore, the levels of disaggregation are different for different capitals up to the eighth level, for example, in 1.1.1.2.3.4.2 "Technological: comparative advantages in the development of high value-added technologies."

Once a Capital Systems starts to operate, it keeps very dynamic throughout its life. Nevertheless, it keeps as a permanent base the generic structure of capitals introduced in Chapter 4 and reproduced in Figure 1. The version presented here is the hierarchical disaggregation of capitals (i.e., the social knowledge accounts) as of May 26, 2005. In this simplified version, investment and product capitals are nested within

Figure 1

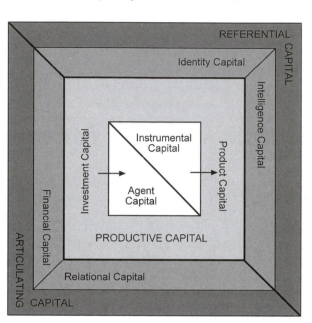

Generic Capital System. © F. J. Carrillo, 1998

financial capital. More recent versions treat these as level-1 categories, as in the original scheme, including all investment and product capital of both financial and knowledge base. Obviously absent are those capitals that do not apply to Monterrey, e.g., litoral extension or denominations of origin. While the list as presented here may be rather cumbersome to read as text, it is intended to be displayed as an outline[1], so that the list can be easily expanded and collapsed at will. At the most aggregate level the list corresponds with the Generic Capital System.

The list reported here includes (i) the capital decimal index, (ii) the capital name, (iii) the capital definition (in italics) in all cases up to level-4, and in some cases beyond, (iv) some capital attributes as further disaggregations with no numerical index, such as the entries below capital 1.2.1.1.1.1.1.1 "Social integration of women." In some cases, capital attributes are operationalized as indicators, like in 2.2.1.2.1.2.1.2 "Primary school," whose entries below are actual indicators. For each capital, a "Knowledge and Value Record" such as Figures 2 and 3 exemplify has been developed. Each record contains:

- The Capital decimal index and name
- The Capital attributes (major features)
- The Value Dimensions (at least one value element per attribute)
- The available indicators

---

[1] In the early years of the Capital System (see Chapter 4) we used the MORE™ Outline Program for Macintosh, now discontinued. That dedicated application allowed immediate conversion of the text outline to several graphic views. MS Office™ now provides text-only outline built-in capabilities.

Figure 2

"Knowledge and Value Record" Example A. © F. J. Carrillo, 2005

CAPITAL SYSTEM: Monterrey, International Knowledge City	
1.1.1.2.3.3	**Socioeconomic Differentiators**
Definition	Socioeconomic factors differentiating the city either as an established stereotype or as a statistically documented feature
Capital attributes	Hard working, industrious, thrifty, sparing, frugal, outspoken, and simple population
Value dimensions	Time destined to work; Outsiders perception of local character; Attractiveness for new business and business tourism
Indicators	(1) New business entrepreneurship (Latin American, LA, ranking: 1 lowest, 7 highest) • Monterrey 5.34 • Sao Paulo 4.56 • Santiago 4.45 • Caracas 3.01 (2) Time destined to work, Latin American ranking (11 or more daily hours) • Sao Paulo: 33% • Monterrey: 27% (3) Description of inhabitants as cheerful and optimistic people (LA) • Monterrey: 77% (highest) • Regional average: 57% • Sao Paulo: 33% (4) Business centers perceived as main touristic attraction (LA) • Monterrey: 47% (highest) • Santiago: 30% • Regional average 19% (5) Best city to do business in LA • Santiago—1 • Miami—2 • Sao Paulo—3 • Monterrey—4 (6) Importance of having contacts and belonging to social groups for a successful career (percentage indicates level of importance) • 91% Guatemala City • 84% Santiago • 83% Monterrey • 76% Mexico City (7) Size of Nuevo León State GDP = US$40, 464 million, equivalent to • Kwait • Morocco • Ucraine
Stakeholders	All citizens, Private Sector, State Government
Capital Angel	Nuevo León Economic Development Secretariat
Knowledge bases	INEGI, EGAP, Economic Analisis Department UANL, Nuevo León Chamber of Industry and Commerce
Sources	(1) Proteus Consultants, quoted in America Economia, May 2003 (2–6) Felipe Abarca: En busca de la ciudad creativa, Especial Ciudades 2005, America Economia Edición 299, pp. 30–39 (7) Clemente Ruiz Durán: SIREM/World Bank, April 2004 www.foroconsultivo.org.mx/eventos_realizados/nacional/ponencias/7_1_ruiz.pdf

Figure 3

"Knowledge and Value Record" Example B. © F. J. Carrillo, 2005

CAPITAL SYSTEM: Monterrey, International Knowledge City	
1.2.1.1.1.1.1	**Social Integration of Women**
Definition	Progress in gender equality
Capital attributes	Proportion of women with professional career, Proportion of women with executive positions, Proportion of women in high public offices, Relative income women/men
Value dimensions	Women in parliamentary seats, Women in legislative and executive positions, Professional and Technical female personnel, Women contributing to family income, Relative salary of women, Male/female income quotient, Women in labor force, Women in school, University degrees granted to Women
Indicators	(1) Women in parliamentary seats (percentage of total) • Sweden: 45.3% • Mexico: 15.9% • Monterrey: 28% (2) Women in legislative and executive positions (percentage of total) • Philippines: 58% • México: 25% (3) Professional and Technical female personnel (percentage of total) • Philippines: 62% • México: 40% (4) Women contributing to family income (percentage of total) • Sweden: 50% • Mexico: 49% (6) Estimated women salary (PPP US$) • Norway: $31356 • Mexico: $4915 (7) Estimated men salary (PPP US$) • Norway: $42340 • Mexico: $12967 (8) Women/men estimated salary • Kenya: 0.90 • Sweden: 0.83 • Mexico: 0.38 • Iran: 0.29 (9) Female labor force (as percentage of male rate) • Ghana: 98% • Sweden: 89% • Mexico: 48% • United Arab Emirates: 0.37% (10) Adult female literacy • Russian Federation: 99.5% • Mexico: 88.7% • Bangladesh: 31.4%
Stakeholders	All citizens, all civil rights organizations Women's rights organizations
Capital Angel	Nuevo León State Ombudsman
Knowledge bases	Council for Social Development of Women, Center for Social Studies of Gender, Family Justice Agency
Sources	(1) Juana Nava, Salto histórico de mujeres en Congreso de Nuevo León, www.cimacnoticias.com/noticias/03jul/03071602.html 30/07/05; (2–9) UNDP, Human Development Report 2004, United Nations Development Programme (6, 7) Table 24; (2, 3, 8) Table 25; (4, 5, 9) Table 27; (10) Table 26

- **The Stakeholders:** While the citizens are the ultimate stakeholders, there are specific agents who may have a significant role in identifying and developing each capital
- **Capital Angel:** Ideally, each capital should be looked after by some individual or entity particularly committed to it and responsible to update its record
- **Knowledge bases:** These are organizations or experts who can provide a deeper understanding of that capital
- **Sources:** The main references to substantiate the record's information.

Finally, the value computation system is under development, so that the whole system can be visualized through a dashboard and an Integrated Value Report. As mentioned before, the purpose here is to exemplify the application of the Generic Urban Capital System to a particular case. The Capital System can be visualized as a hierarchical tree with many branches (in fact, dedicated outlining software applications allow the outline text to be displayed in several graphical renderings: bottom-up, top-down, left-right, right-left, etc.). Each branch becomes thinner and thinner until it reaches the unitary point where a record compiles the ultimate value dimensions or variables and the understanding of these. Hence, we call these final individual entries "Knowledge and Value Record." Figures 2 and 3 provide two examples of such records, taken from Monterrey's Capital System. To give an idea of the possibilities, the Monterrey Capital System displayed below had 366 records (and therefore terminal points) at the time of writing, whose hierarchical structure can be compressed through the outliner to just half a page (say, levels 1 and 2) or zoomed at will at any desired level.

Hence, the purpose of this chapter is to illustrate the application of the Generic System of Capitals to a particular city. In the case of Monterrey, the focus has been in comparing each of the city's value dimensions with the highest value available anywhere in the world. The rationale is to assess the status of Monterrey as an "International City of Knowledge" as the official denomination claims. At the time of writing, this exercise remained an independent account of the value dimensions that can be recognized in the city's configuration and life. Even if there has been a continued collaboration with both public and private agents, as well as with the Project's and CORPES agency management, the taxonomy of capital accounts for Monterrey presented here remained an independent initiative. As such, this version as it stands constitutes no official document and implies neither an endorsement by nor an obligation to the State of Nuevo León or the City of Monterrey Governments.

THE CAPITAL SYSTEM OF MONTERREY "INTERNATIONAL KNOWLEDGE CITY"

The taxonomy of categories of Monterrey as a Value System
Version May 26, 2005

1   METACAPITALS
   1.1   Referential Capital. Value elements that allow the identification and alignment of all other capitals
      1.1.1   Identity capital. Internal value referents
         1.1.1.1   Inherited identity. Formal and informal elements, accumulated through the city's history, that contributed to determine its identity
            1.1.1.1.1   Name. Unequivocal character of the city's denomination and expression of its relative importance
               1.1.1.1.1.1   Foundational act
               1.1.1.1.1.2   Historical records of name evolution through history
               1.1.1.1.1.3   National and international name brand recognition

1.1.1.1.2   Rank. Monterrey's relative importance at both national and international level

    1.1.1.1.2.1   Federal Decrees stating the existence of the State of Nuevo León, its municipalities and cities

    1.1.1.1.2.2   National and international rankings by population, area, GNP, and GNPc

    1.1.1.1.2.3   Number of foreign consulates

1.1.1.1.3   Heraldry. Evolution and current status of the armorial ensign

1.1.1.1.4   Heraldic records. Archives related to the city's heraldry

1.1.1.1.5   Historic profile. City characterization through history, mainly as industrial city

    1.1.1.1.5.1   City chronicles

    1.1.1.1.5.2   Historical records

1.1.1.2   Current identity. Formal and informal elements, contributing to determine its current identity

  1.1.1.2.1   Current status. Current formal elements defining the city's identity. 1984 decree creating the "Municipios de la Zona Conurbada de Monterrey" area of the State of Nuevo León.

  1.1.1.2.2   Sense of identity and belongingness. Residents sense of identity and belongingness

    1.1.1.2.2.1   Sense of identity

Extent to which each inhabitant recognizes himself as a local citizen.
Extent to which Monterrey natives residing in another cities continue to regard themselves as "regiomontanas."

    1.1.1.2.2.2   Sense of belongness

Permanence of city natives
Permanence of immigrants
Proportion of native/immigrant residents
Immigrance rotation

  1.1.1.2.3   Differentiation. Formal and informal elements that are distinctive of Monterrey

    1.1.1.2.3.1   Marketed image. Idealized or official image of contemporary Monterrey

Summary of the city image as promoted by the Government

    1.1.1.2.3.2   Attractiveness factors. Formal and informal elements contributing to the decision by individuals, families, and companies to establish themselves in Monterrey

      1.1.1.2.3.2.1   For residence. Conventional elements in quality of life rankings

Population
Economy and employment
Cost of living
Education
Public health and medical services
Weather
Crime
Transportation
Entertainment

Art and culture
"Best city to live in" ratings

1.1.1.2.3.2.2   For career development. City conditions and attributes
for professional development

Openness
Formal job offer
Informal job offer
Best companies to work for index ratings
Professional and creative class migration
Relative salaries
Relative work benefits
Job rotation
Career opportunities

1.1.1.2.3.2.3   For business. Elements contributing to a company's decision to open, establish, move to, and stay in Monterrey

Direct foreign investment
Business migration
New business start-ups per year
Efficiency of new business set up formal process
International "best cities for doing business" rankings

1.1.1.2.3.2.4   For studying. Elements contributing to a prospective student's decision to stay or move to Monterrey for high
school and higher education

Quality of local schools and universities
National and international rankings of best schools and universities
National and international foreign student enrollment
Percentage of national and international foreign students

1.1.1.2.3.2.5   For entertainment and tourism. City attributes and conditions making it attractive for entertainment and tourism

Catalog on touristic attractions and infrastructure
Affluence of national and international tourism
National and international best city to visit rankings
Gross and per capita expenditure of city visitors
Presence and image in touristic information channels

1.1.1.2.3.3   Socioeconomic differentiator. Distinctive city features, both
as stereoptypes and statistical factors

1.1.1.2.3.3.1   Social differentiators

Average working hours
External perception of resident's character

1.1.1.2.3.3.2   Economic differentiators. Distinctive economic performance factors

GDP and GDPc
PIB per cápita
Productivity index
Savings capacity

Time to open a new business
Government efficiency

1.1.1.2.3.4   Core competencies: areas of outstanding performance at international level
1.1.1.2.3.4.1   Organizational: high performance organizational practices

World-class events held by the city
− 2002 UN Financing for Development World Summit
− 2004 Summit of the Americas

1.1.1.2.3.4.2   Technological: comparative advantages in the development of high value-added technologies
1.1.1.2.3.4.2.1   TICs

Investment in new TIC companies
Availability of TIC talent

1.1.1.2.3.4.2.2   Biotechnology

Investment in new biotech companies
Availability of biotech talent

1.1.1.2.3.4.2.3   Health sciences

Investment in new health companies
Availability of health science talent

1.1.1.2.3.4.2.4   Aerospace

Investment in new aerospace companies
Availability of aerospace science talent

1.1.1.2.3.4.3   Cultural: areas of outstanding performance

Museums and cultural spaces
Literary tradition
Forum Monterrey 2007

1.1.1.3   Prospected identity. Formal and informal elements composing its future vision
1.1.1.3.1   Vision. City's image of itself for 2006

"Monterrey 400: A history with a future" document, statements of Monterrey's Vision and Mission

1.1.1.3.2   KBD Strategy. Strategic knowledge-based development Plan
1.1.1.3.3   Knowledge Capital Accounts. Capital System and Integrated Value Report
1.1.1.3.4   Strategic perspective. KBD prospection of the city
1.1.2   Intelligence capital
1.1.2.1   City Intelligence System. Quality of the city's systems to sense, make sense of, and respond to agents and events which are significant to the city's welfare

Existence of government office with professional intelligence capabilities as a support to strategic planning and performance assessment
Existence of professional urban planning and studies, knowledge-based strategic development

1.1.2.2   Monterrey Future Center. Quality of the city's system to foresee and create its future

Existence of public and/or private future center
Existence and quality of regional and urban prospective studies

1.2   Articulation Capital. Value elements which make possible the interrelationship or exchange of value elements between each other
1.2.1   Relational Capital. The quality of the interaction between the city's internal significant agents, as well as between the city and its external significant ones
1.2.1.1   Internal. State of the interaction between significant internal agents
1.2.1.1.1   Social cohesion and urban integration. Strength of the relationship between social agents and quality of the conditions determining it
1.2.1.1.1.1   Structural aspects. Cohesion of economic sectors expressed throughout the capacity to associate, form clusters, reconvert industry and infrastructure and communications, as well as the improvement of the environment and of impoverished regions. Public strategy of social cohesion and its outcomes
1.2.1.1.1.1.1   Sociocultural cohesion
1.2.1.1.1.1.1.1   Social integration of women

Improvements in gender equality
Women in parliamentary seats
Percentage of executive and government offices held by women
Percentage of women in professions and technical jobs
Income comparison men/women
Total school and university women enrollment according to International Normalized Education Classification (INEC)
Percentage of women as contributing members to family
Income coefficient women/men
Economic activity of women
Women with professional career

1.2.1.1.1.1.2   Socioeconomic cohesion
1.2.1.1.1.1.2.1   Income distribution gap
1.2.1.1.1.1.2.2   Poverty indicators
1.2.1.1.1.1.3   Productive cohesion
1.2.1.1.1.1.3.1   Business agreements to improve productivity and competitiveness
1.2.1.1.1.1.3.2   Business agreements to improve the environment
1.2.1.1.1.1.4   Political cohesion
1.2.1.1.1.1.4.1   Political alliances
1.2.1.1.1.1.4.2   Dialogue channels
1.2.1.1.1.1.4.3   Conflict resolution mechanisms
1.2.1.1.1.2   Other aspects of social integration.
1.2.1.1.1.2.1   Quality of urban factors determining social conditions
1.2.1.1.1.2.2   Citizens coexistence and availability of open spaces and commons
1.2.1.1.1.2.3   Neighborhood integration
1.2.1.1.1.2.3.1   Enclosed urbanizations
1.2.1.1.1.2.3.2   Urban sprawl

1.2.1.1.2   Legality and egalitarianism. Social inclusion and law enforcement
1.2.1.1.2.1   Guarantee of constitutional entitlements
1.2.1.1.2.2   Equality of opportunities
1.2.1.1.2.3   Respect for human rights
1.2.1.1.3   Transparency. Advances in legislation and practices of access to information and social accountability
1.2.1.1.4   Corruption control. International transparency benchmarks
1.2.1.1.5   Governability. Strength of social institutions' international benchmarks
1.2.1.2   External. State of the interaction with significant external agents
1.2.1.2.1   Image. Quality of the public perception of Monterrey
1.2.1.2.1.1   National. City image national benchmarks
1.2.1.2.1.2   International. City image international benchmarks
1.2.1.2.2   Public and private networking. Quantity and quality of interactions with significant external agents
1.2.1.2.2.1   Official foreign affairs agencies
1.2.1.2.2.1.1   National and international city liaison offices
1.2.1.2.2.1.2   Consular and other external agencies established in Monterrey
1.2.1.2.2.2   Private and public networking
1.2.1.2.2.2.1   Economic freedom
1.2.1.2.2.2.2   Business communication and international collaboration competencies
1.2.1.2.2.2.3   Citizens communication and international collaboration competencies
1.2.1.2.2.3   Agreements. Participation in both significant international agreements and bilateral collaboration schemes
1.2.1.2.2.3.1   National

Northeast Region collaboration agreements
Bilateral State collaboration agreements

1.2.1.2.2.3 2   International

Number and importance of international and bilateral agreements

1.2.1.2.2.4   Monterrey Twin Cities
1.2.2   Financial Capital. Monetary denomination of all or some production value dimensions
1.2.2.1   Macroindicators. Set of economic indicators conventionally used for basic international comparisons
1.2.2.1.1   GDP, GDPc, Growth forecast
1.2.2.1.2   Industrial production
1.2.2.1.3   Consumer price index
1.2.2.1.4   Trade balance
1.2.2.1.5   Current account
1.2.2.1.6   Foreign currency reserve
1.2.2.1.7   Currency exchange rate
1.2.2.1.7.1   USA dollar
1.2.2.1.7.2   Euro
1.2.2.1.7.3   Yen
1.2.2.1.8   National treasury bonds
1.2.2.1.9   Stock Exchange Index

1.2.2.1.10   Interest rates
1.2.2.1.11   Inflation
1.2.2.1.12   Unemployment
1.2.2.1.13   Income salary
1.2.2.1.14   Budget balance
1.2.2.1.15   Sovereign debt
1.2.2.1.16   Investment risk qualification
   1.2.2.1.16.1   Country risk
   1.2.2.1.16.2   State risk
   1.2.2.1.16.3   City risk
1.2.2.2   Public accounts. The official accounts of each Mexican State and of the Nation as whole, held by the Federal Government

2   PRODUCTIVE CAPITALS

2.1   Investment Capital. Any value element contributed as a new production input
  2.1.1   Total R&D Expenditure and private/public proportion
    2.1.1.1   Private investment
      2.1.1.1.1   R&D Expenditure and propotion of total
      2.1.1.1.2   Risk Capital Investment
      2.1.1.1.3   Creation of Technology-based Businesses
    2.1.1.2   Public Investment
      2.1.1.2.1   R&D Expenditure and proportion of total
      2.1.1.2.2   Funds for Technology-based Business Creation
  2.1.2   Foreign Investment
    2.1.2.1   Private Investment
    2.1.2.2   International Agencies Funds
      2.1.2.2.1   Direct foreign investment
    2.1.2.3   Creation of Technology-based Businesses
    2.1.2.4   Risk Capital Investment
    2.1.2.5   Human Capital Attractiveness
      2.1.2.5.1   Creative Class Attractiveness
      2.1.2.5.2   Qualified Labour Attractiveness
2.2   Human Capital. Value-generating capacity of individual and collective social agents
  2.2.1   Individual base. Value-generating capacity of individuals
    2.2.1.1   Organic. Aspects of the individual's physical constitution, its developments and health condition which are determined by the environmental and social conditions and determine its organic integrity and overall potential
      2.2.1.1.1   Ethnic diversity. Ethnic composition of the State of Nuevo León's population
        2.2.1.1.1.1   Population of national origin

        Quantitative and qualitative variations in demography
        Social growth rate
        Immigration rate by state of origin
        Mexican indigenous population growth in Nuevo León

        2.2.1.1.1.2   Population of foreign origin

        Resident population by migratory status
        Resident population by country of origin and time of residence

2.2.1.1.2   Health and nutrition. Physical and mental welfare and individuals as well as nutrition habits

   2.2.1.1.2.1   Health. Physical and mental welfare of individuals

Life expectancy at birth
Life expectancy index
Infant mortality rate
Children with deficit in weight/age rate
Children with deficit in height/age rate
Children with deficit in weight/height rate
Children with low weight at birth

   2.2.1.1.2.2   Nutrition. Quantity and quality of food and drink intake with reference to the needs of human organism and its balance

Diet quality
Average diet
Proportion of individuals with balanced diet
Eating habits
Fat and carbohydrates intake per capita
Fast food and processed food consumption
Drinking habits
Soft drinks consumption

2.2.1.1.3   Socioeconomic. Economic base from which the State and city inhabitants have access to opportunities to develop their productive potential

GDP, per capita, distribution by social class
Economic participation rate
Week workload average
Income distribution
Poverty indicators

2.2.1.2   Intellectual. Aspects of intellectual and emotional development of individuals which are determined by the environmental and social conditions and determine its organic integrity and overall potential

   2.2.1.2.1   Normal capacities. Individual competencies and performance in the family, education, and production environments

      2.2.1.2.1.1   Family integration competencies. "Knowledge, capacities and skills aggregated to the effectiveness of attitudes and practice of families which facilitate and promote children's survival, development, protection and participation" (UNICEF).

         2.2.1.2.1.1.1   Paternal competencies

Provider responsibility
Home abandonment
Intrafamily paternal violence

         2.2.1.2.1.1.2   Maternal competencies

Provider responsibility
Home abandonment
Intrafamily maternal violence

2.2.1.2.1.1.3   Children competencies

Child development performance from birth through 3-year age
Lactancy, maternal and educational nursery, and child development
centers enrollment by municipality

2.2.1.2.1.2   Formative competencies. Amount of individuals and quality
of their performance in formal education institutions

2.2.1.2.1.2.1   School education system. Amount of individuals and quality of their performance in formal education institutions of
the school system

2.2.1.2.1.2.1.1   Kindergarten. Amount of individuals and quality of
their performance in kindergartens

2.2.1.2.1.2.1.2   Primary School. Amount of individuals and quality
of their performance in primary schools

Neat primary scholarization rate
Primary school repeaters
Rate of fifth grade achievers

2.2.1.2.1.2.1.3   Secondary school. Amount of individuals and quality
of their performance in secondary schools

Population in secondary school age
Neat enrollment rate by sex

2.2.1.2.1.2.1.4   High School. Amount of individuals and quality of
their performance in high schools

Number of students
Existence, approvals, failures, and graduates
Coverage at end of course by municipality and grade

2.2.1.2.1.2.1.5   Technical. Amount of individuals and quality of
their performance in technical schools

2.2.1.2.1.2.1.6   Higher education. Amount of individuals and quality
of their performance in higher education institutions

2.2.1.2.1.2.1.6.1   Undergraduate. Amount of individuals and quality of their performance in professional schools,
universities, and technical institutions

2.2.1.2.1.2.1.6.2   Graduate. Amount of individuals and quality of
their performance in graduate programs

2.2.1.2.1.2.2   Beyond school education system

2.2.1.2.1.2.2.1   Extra-school education system. Extracurricular education for population in schooling age

2.2.1.2.1.2.2.2   Continued education

2.2.1.2.1.2.2.3   Second chance education

2.2.1.2.1.3   Productive competencies. Amount of individuals and quality
of their performance in formal production activities

2.2.1.2.1.3.1   Knowledge intensive. Amount of individuals and quality
of their performance in formal production activities

Number of creative-class professionals
Personnel employed in R&D and technical activities

2.2.1.2.1.3.2   By job sector according to OIT 1988 classification

2.2.1.2.1.3.3 Managerial
2.2.1.2.1.3.4 Professional
2.2.1.2.1.3.5 Technical
2.2.1.2.1.3.6 Assistant
2.2.1.2.1.4 Lifelong and career development. Amount of individuals and quality of their performance in continued training and education after regular graduation and before retirement

Training enrollment
Adult education centers enrollment

2.2.1.2.2 Special capacities. Individuals with special capacities which require a different learning process and infrastructure

Total number of people with special capacities, per category and as a percentage of the population
Total number and percentage of people with special capacities enrolled in formal education
Total number and percentage of people with special capacities engaged in full employment

2.2.1.2.3 Knowledge citizens competencies (see Chapter 17, by America Martínez)
2.2.1.2.4 Sociocultural competencies. General level of cultural and civic performance
2.2.1.2.4.1 Social. Habits, civic culture, urbanism, including driving and waste-disposal habits
2.2.1.2.4.1.1 At home. Individual social behavior and neighbor relationships
2.2.1.2.4.1.2 Driving and transportation. Habits and behaviors related to transit (both drivers and pedestrians) and transportation
2.2.1.2.4.1.3 Public spaces. Habits and behaviors of individuals in public areas
2.2.1.2.4.2 Cultural. Cultural competencies of individuals, including artistic capacities and cultural patterns and attitudes such as reading habits, diversity tolerance, and safe-sex practices
2.2.2 Collective Base. Collective and team-based value-generating capacities
2.2.2.1 Organic. Structural human dispositions having an impact on the constitution of organizations or on their functions
2.2.2.1.1 Demographic structure. Statistical composition of the population by demographic factor
2.2.2.1.2 Public health. State of collective physical and mental welfare and conditions determining it
2.2.2.1.2.1 Social welfare. Coverage and quality of social welfare institutions

Births managed by health professionals
Urban population with access to adequate sanitation

2.2.2.1.2.2 Epidemiology. Public management of endemic diseases and health risks

TBC and other common diseases vaccination coverage
Public response capacity to epidemic hazards

2.2.2.1.2.3   High impact diseases. Deadly or severe avoidable diseases which depend on habits and affect large sections of the population, such as cardiovascular diseases, diabetes, and AIDS

Main causes of death
Percentage of deaths attributed to avoidable causes

2.2.2.1.2.4   Addictions. Narcotics, alcohol, and tobacco consumption

Volume of consumption and annual variation
Number of deaths caused by addictions

2.2.2.2   Intellectual. Knowledge-based, including emotional and cultural collective capacities
2.2.2.2.1   Cultural heritage. Social transmission of knowledge and values from generation to generation through uses and customs
2.2.2.2.1.1   Languages. Conservation and general level of proficiency

Spanish proficiency level
Mastery of a second language

2.2.2.2.1.2   Religions. Consistency with own religious beliefs and tolerance of other religious or nonreligious perspectives

Total number and percentage of catholic population over 5-years old
Total number and percentage of population over 5-years old from other religions
Total number and percentage of population over 5-years old with no religion

2.2.2.2.1.3   Arts. General aesthetic development and artistic expression capacity of the population
2.2.2.2.1.4   Handicrafts. Capacity to produce artisanal work with a distinctive local character
2.2.2.2.1.5   Customs. Distinctive live cultural practices
2.2.2.2.1.6   Dressings. Distinctive local dressing practices and production
2.2.2.2.1.7   Regional cuisine. Catalog of dishes or cooking styles and practices distinctive of the region
2.2.2.2.1.8   Celebrations and rituals. Former cultural practices kept by tradition
2.2.2.2.2   Socioeconomic environment. Collective dispositions to effectively engage in productive action
2.2.2.2.2.1   Competitiveness. Capacity to create and sustain a favorable environment to generate more economic value and social prosperity

City ranking in national and international benchmarks

2.2.2.2.3   Evolutionary capacities. Collective dispositions toward social learning and effective change
2.2.2.2.3.1   Cultural diversity. Richness of the city's cultural makeup
2.2.2.2.3.2   Tolerance. Capacity to relate empathically and assertively with people of a different racial, social, cultural, or economic background
2.2.2.2.3.3   Civic culture and citizen participation. General level of self-governance and initiative

2.2.2.2.3.4 Entrepreneurship. Collective capacity to create new high-value businesses

2.2.2.2.3.5 Innovation. Collective capacity to conceive and effectively develop new ways to add value in any relevant human activity

2.3 Instrumental Capital. The means of production through which other capitals leverage their value generation capacity

  2.3.1 Tangible. Material-based means of production through which other capitals leverage their value generation capacity

    2.3.1.1 Geographic

      2.3.1.1.1 Longitude and latitude. Longitude is the angular distance between 0° meridian (Greenwich) and a given point on the Earth's surface. Latitude is the angular distance between the Equator and a given point on the Earth's surface

      2.3.1.1.2 Orography, hydrography, geology, seismology, and soil composition. Geographic elements determining the physical setting of the city and its possibilities, such as accessibility, water resources, type of constructions, etc.

      2.3.1.1.3 Climate. Is the average state of meteorological elements in a region, considering a long period of time?

      2.3.1.1.4 Landscape. Aspect of natural surroundings

      2.3.1.1.5 Flora. Indigenous plant species

      2.3.1.1.6 Fauna. Indigenous animal species

      2.3.1.1.7 Other natural assets and liabilities

    2.3.1.2 Environmental

      2.3.1.2.1 Physical environment

        2.3.1.2.1.1 Air

          2.3.1.2.1.1.1 Air quality

          2.3.1.2.1.1.2 Air improvement programs

        2.3.1.2.1.2 Soil and vegetation

          2.3.1.2.1.2.1 Land use

          2.3.1.2.1.2.2 Soil pollution

          2.3.1.2.1.2.3 Waste management

        2.3.1.2.1.3 Water

          2.3.1.2.1.3.1 Natural systems

          2.3.1.2.1.3.2 Water quality

          2.3.1.2.1.3.3 Water pollution

          2.3.1.2.1.3.4 Water treatment and distribution

      2.3.1.2.2 Urban environment

        2.3.1.2.2.1 Urban landscape

        2.3.1.2.2.2 Architectural harmony

        2.3.1.2.2.3 Visual pollution

        2.3.1.2.2.4 Auditive pollution

        2.3.1.2.2.5 Olfative pollution

    2.3.1.3 Infrastructural

      2.3.1.3.1 Material cultural heritage

        2.3.1.3.1.1 Historical sites and archeological records

        2.3.1.3.1.2 Historic buildings and monuments

        2.3.1.3.1.3 Museums and retrospective collections

        2.3.1.3.1.4 Objects and samples inventories

        2.3.1.3.1.5 Other physical repositories where the object or medium (not the codified information that carries, if any) is the most value element

2.3.1.3.2   Underground infrastructure
   2.3.1.3.2.1   Pipelines
      2.3.1.3.2.1.1   Drinking water

      Coverage and quality of the drinking water distribution network
      Quality of drinking water

      2.3.1.3.2.1.2   Sewage
      2.3.1.3.2.1.3   Natural gas
   2.3.1.3.2.2   Wire networks
      2.3.1.3.2.2.1   Electric network
      2.3.1.3.2.2.2   Wired telephone network
      2.3.1.3.2.2.3   Wired telecoms network
2.3.1.3.3   Civil infrastructure
   2.3.1.3.3.1   Urban configuration
      2.3.1.3.3.1.1   Zonification, districts, neighborhoods
         2.3.1.3.3.1.1.1   Zonification
         2.3.1.3.3.1.1.2   District configuration
         2.3.1.3.3.1.1.3   Neighborhoods
         2.3.1.3.3.1.1.4   Housing
      2.3.1.3.3.1.2   Green and recreational areas
         2.3.1.3.3.1.2.1   Parks
         2.3.1.3.3.1.2.2   Natural reserves and protected areas
         2.3.1.3.3.1.2.3   Squares
         2.3.1.3.3.1.2.4   Sports centers
      2.3.1.3.3.1.3   Streets, avenues, and civil infrastructure
      2.3.1.3.3.1.4   Highways, fast roads
      2.3.1.3.3.1.5   Bridges and tunnels
      2.3.1.3.3.1.6   Natural hazards protection infrastructure
   2.3.1.3.3.2   Urban sprawl
      2.3.1.3.3.2.1   Massive popular housing
      2.3.1.3.3.2.2   Enclosed residential areas
      2.3.1.3.3.2.3   Urban gap
      2.3.1.3.3.2.4   Architectural eclecticism
      2.3.1.3.3.2.5   Density of visual pollution
      2.3.1.3.3.2.6   Disruption of natural landscape
      2.3.1.3.3.2.7   Automobile predominance
   2.3.1.3.3.3   Automobile infrastructure
      2.3.1.3.3.3.1   Vehicle census
      2.3.1.3.3.3.2   Traffic fluency
   2.3.1.3.3.4   Urban transportation
      2.3.1.3.3.4.1   Public transportation network
         2.3.1.3.3.4.1.1   Metro
         2.3.1.3.3.4.1.2   Buses
         2.3.1.3.3.4.1.3   Taxis
   2.3.1.3.3.5   Extraurban connectivity
      2.3.1.3.3.5.1   Airports
         2.3.1.3.3.5.1.1   National flights
         2.3.1.3.3.5.1.2   International flights
      2.3.1.3.3.5.2   Access to maritime ports
      2.3.1.3.3.5.3   Trains and buses terminals and stations
      2.3.1.3.3.5.4   Railroad network
      2.3.1.3.3.5.5   Road network

2.3.1.3.3.6   Communications
2.3.1.3.3.6.1   Surface mail and telegraph
2.3.1.3.3.6.2   Telecommunications
2.3.1.3.3.6.2.1   Intraconnectivity
2.3.1.3.3.6.2.1.1   Local radio network
2.3.1.3.3.6.2.1.2   Local TV network
2.3.1.3.3.6.2.1.3   Local data network
2.3.1.3.3.6.2.2   External Connectivity
2.3.1.3.3.6.2.2.1   Telephone network
2.3.1.3.3.6.2.2.2   National and international radio network
2.3.1.3.3.6.2.2.3   National and international TV network
2.3.1.3.3.6.2.2.4   National and international data network
2.3.1.3.3.6.2.2.5   Internet access
2.3.1.3.3.7   Crime prevention

Ranking in regional and international crime prevention index
Ratio of inhabitants/policemen
Coverage, quality of public and private crime prevention services

2.3.1.3.4   Productive Infrastructure
2.3.1.3.4.1   Industrial infrastructure. Installed capacity in investment and
productivity
2.3.1.3.4.2   Commercial infrastructure

Total sqaure meters of commercial premises, by level of services
Proportion of formal and informal commercial businesses

2.3.1.3.4.3   Service Infrastructure
2.3.1.3.4.3.1   Health and social welfare: land, buildings, installations,
equipment, furniture and tools for medical and sanitary
services

Census hospital beds
Public and private investment in health service infrastructure

2.3.1.3.4.3.2   Hotel capacity. Rankings in international benchmarks

Square meters of hotels by category
Hotel beds by category

2.3.1.3.4.3.3   Leisure and entertainment facilities

Total area of space for family recreation
Restaurants
Number of theatre, cinema, arenas, stadiums, and other spectacle
seats
Bohemian index
Number of places offering live music

2.3.1.3.4.3.4   Conferences, fairs and business events infrastructure.
Ranking in international benchmarks for business events.
2.3.2   Intangible. Knowledge-based means of production through which other
capitals leverage their value generation capacity
2.3.2.1   Social organization structure. Structural capacities of social subsystems
2.3.2.1.1   Social innovation system. Structural innovation capacity of social
subsystems

2.3.2.1.1.1   Civic innovation. Innovation capacity of NGOs

Annual NGOs growth
Total citizen participation in NGOs

2.3.2.1.1.2   Productive innovation. Innovation capacity of the private sector

New businesses incubation and creation
Proportion of high-value new business creation
Survival rate of new businesses after five years
Initial public offerings

2.3.2.1.1.3   Educational, scientific, and technological innovation. Innovation capacity of the education, scientific, and techno-logical establishment

Cycle life of university curricula
Scientific citations
Patents and licenses

2.3.2.1.1.4   Government innovation. Innovation capacity of the public sector

Legal reforms
Rankings in international government efficiency benchmarks

2.3.2.1.2   Civil organization system. Structural capacities of NGOs

Total registered NOGs
Citizen participation in NGOs

2.3.2.1.3   Productive System. Structural capacities of the private sector

Total ISO certified companies
ISO certifications by sector

2.3.2.1.4   Educational, scientific, and technological system. Structural capacities for education, science, and technology
2.3.2.1.4.1   Educational. Structural capacities of the educational system.
2.3.2.1.4.1.1   Kindergarten. Structural capacities of pre-school education

Students per teacher
Students per school

2.3.2.1.4.1.2   Primary. Structural capacities of primary education

Terminal efficiency
Failure rate
Ratio students:teacher

2.3.2.1.4.1.3   Secondary. Structural capacities of secondary education

Terminal efficiency
Failure rate
Ratio students:teacher

2.3.2.1.4.1.4   High school. Structural capacities of high school education

Certified teachers
Terminal efficiency
Failure rate
Ratio students:teacher

2.3.2.1.4.1.5   Vocational technical. Structural capacities of technical education

Certified technological institutions
Terminal efficiency
Failure rate
Ratio students:teacher

2.3.2.1.4.1.6   University. Structural capacities of university education
2.3.2.1.4.1.6.1   Undergraduate

Degrees granted
Graduates time to full employment

2.3.2.1.4.1.6.2   Graduate
2.3.2.1.4.1.6.3   Specialization programs

Degrees granted
Time to salary or position improvement

2.3.2.1.4.1.6.4   Master programs

Degrees granted
Time to salary or position improvement

2.3.2.1.4.1.6.5   Doctoral programs

Degrees granted
Time to research program, executive position, creation of own company

2.3.2.1.4.2   Scientific and technological. Structural capacities of the scientific and technological system
2.3.2.1.4.2.1   Publications
2.3.2.1.4.2.2   Patents
2.3.2.1.4.2.3   Investment in R&D
2.3.2.1.4.2.3.1   Public investment. Public expenditure in R&D as a percentage of GNP.
2.3.2.1.4.2.3.2   Private investment. Total private expenditure in R&D.
2.3.2.1.5   Government system. Structural capacities of government bodies
2.3.2.1.5.1   Legislative. Structural capacities of State and municipal legislative bodies
2.3.2.1.5.2   Executive. Structural capacities of State and municipal government agencies

Government efficiency
Accountability and performance of government bodies

2.3.2.1.5.3   Judiciary. Structural capacities of State and municipal judiciary bodies
2.3.2.2   Information and telecommunications infrastructure. Structural capacities, traditional and ICT-based for information and communications
2.3.2.2.1   Information platforms. Printed and electronic media containing information about civil society, private industry, education, and government
2.3.2.2.1.1   Manual information systems. Manual systems for recording, storing, retreving, processing, and distribution

2.3.2.2.1.2   Periodical publications. Diaries, newspapers, bulletins, and other periodical publications about civil society, private industry, education, and government

Number of periodicals and circulation
Newspaper-reading index
Ratio newspapers:inhabitants

2.3.2.2.1.3   Electronic information systems. Electronic systems for recording, storing, retreving, processing, and distribution
2.3.2.2.1.3.1   E-government

Coverage
Accessibility and usability
Content, Privacidad
Services
Participation

2.3.2.2.1.3.2   Electronic media. Electronic periodical publications about civil society, private industry, education, and government
2.3.2.2.2   Knowledge bases and systems. Records, archives, and collections sustaining the city memory
2.3.2.2.2.1   Physical-base records. Records in nonconventional documentary units, e.g., stone encriptions, codices, etc. where the content is the most valuable aspect
2.3.2.2.2.2   Records and archives. All records in formal document units
2.3.2.2.2.3   Digital memory. All records and document units containing information about the civil society, private industry, education, and government
2.3.2.2.2.4   Electronic databases. Data repository about the civil society, private industry, education, and government
2.3.2.2.2.5   Public information services. Information resources offered to the public by agents of the civil society, private industry, education, and government
2.4   Product. Output of the economy as a whole, and of its most important aggregated factors
2.4.1   Added Product
2.4.2   Productivity. By worker, unit of investment and resource
2.4.3   State and City Product

GDP
GDPc
GDP Index
GDP annual variation

2.4.4   Sector product
2.4.5   Tax collection. Coverage of taxable base
2.4.5.1   Net tax collection
2.4.5.2   Percentage collection per tax category
2.4.6   Fund delivery from migrant mexican workers to their communities of origin

Direct transfers from mexicans working abroad
Total volume of transfers and annual variation

Chapter 13

Rijeka: Increasing Efficiency of Intellectual Capital in City-Owned Companies

Karmen Jelcic, *IC Center, Croatia*

Rijeka—A Knowledge City, Ambitions, and Activities

Rijeka, a historic city located at the northern part of the Croatian coast, has been undergoing a period of fundamental change since 1997. Throughout centuries it was governed by Romans, Austrians, Hungarians, Italians, and Croats, each administrator leaving a trace on people's conceptions and activities. From 1719 it was a free port where many languages were spoken and various cultures met, shaping an open-minded environment for new ideas and concepts. During the 20th century, Rijeka was a typical industrial city, accommodating one of the largest shipyards in Croatia and a huge port stretching almost along the entire waterfront. Unlike other coastal towns it had no riviera; however, this shortcoming was compensated by Opatija, a resort, only a few kilometers away. While Opatija attracted tourists and citizens of Rijeka for leisure and fun, Rijeka sacrificed its charm and Mediterranean beauty to industry and port activities, the pillars of its existence at that time.

With diminishing importance of the port and local industry, the City Government started to redesign priorities. Increasing life quality of the citizens became a key priority. New regulations, e.g., prolonged closing times for cafes and restaurants increased the attractiveness of Rijeka's nightlife. Recognizable cultural manifestations, organized by the city, have been attracting more and more people each year. E-government has helped to enhance the quality of communication between city officials and citizens. Assigning of many waterfront kilometers for leisure purposes will increase the attractiveness of the city in the next few years. Another priority has been to create a supporting business environment for the development of small and medium enterprise and knowledge-based industry.

Due to its historic past and the process of redefining its image and goals, the City Government of Rijeka is open for new concepts and ideas, striving to become a knowledge city. This means supporting innovation and entrepreneurship through the system, not damping it by bureaucracy, promoting knowledge and ability as the new key production factors, valuing and rewarding economic achievements in order to motivate businessmen and raise the economic standard. It became the first city in Croatia, which started dealing with the issues of the knowledge economy (KE) and accepted to pilot a program, which aims at increasing the efficiency of national intellectual capital (IC) in state-owned companies through activities in selected companies owned by the city.

Context for the "Project of Increasing Efficiency of National Intellectual Capital (PIENIC)"

An international context for the project is provided by the European Union (EU), which is preparing the transition to the KE. According to the Lisbon Agenda issued in March 2000, "The EU is confronted with a quantum shift resulting from globalisation and the challenges of a new knowledge-driven economy. These changes are affecting every aspect of people's lives and require a radical transformation of the European economy . . . The Union has set itself a new strategic goal for the next decade: to become the most competitive and dynamic knowledge-based economy in the world."

As Croatia aims at becoming a member of the EU in a few years, it has to start aligning strategic goals, in this particular case, preparing Croatian economy for transition to the KE. According to the "National Programme for Joining the Union," the Lisbon Agenda has become one of the key documents for Croatia's economic development, thus providing the context and motivation for PIENIC in state- and city-owned companies.

Additional impetus came from three interesting initiatives within the EU. The first one was "The Value Added Scoreboard," which is issued yearly by the British Ministry of Trade and Industry, promoting value added and the efficiency of wealth creation as objective indicators of business success (http//www.dti.gov.uk). The second one was the "Intellectual Capital Statement—Made in Germany," which is a part of the nationwide project "Fit to Compete with Knowledge" and has been initiated by the Ministry of Economic Affairs in order to create a base for standardization with regard to IC reporting (www.bmwa.bund.de). The third one was the PRISM research project dealing with the role of intangible assets, with regard to business success of companies, cities, regions, and nations in contemporary economy (www.Euintangibles.net).

Next to the international one there was also a national context, which set the foundation for PIENIC, namely the first IC project in Croatia that focussed on awareness creation and education nationwide.[1] It was initiated by the Croatian Chamber of Economy and led by Dr. Pulic, president of the Croatian IC-association and the author of the VAIC™ (Value Creation Efficiency Analysis). It was realized by the IC-Center in Zagreb. Lectures were organized in all sixteen counties of Croatia and a handbook on IC basics was published and distributed for free.[2] Special focus was directed toward measurement of the efficiency of Croatian economy at national, regional, and company level. The methodology used to assess economic performance was the VAIC™.[3] It represents the Croatian approach to the development of measurement

---

[1] Bonfour, Edvinsson (2004). *Intellectual Capital for Communities, Nations, Regions, and Cities*, Burlington, USA: Elsevier Butterworth-Heinemann.

[2] Jelcic, Karmen (2002). *Handbook for IC Management in Companies [Prirucnik za upravljanje intelektualnim kapitalom u tvrtkama]*, Zagreb, Croatia: Croatian Chamber of Economy.

[3] More at www.vaic-on.net, VAIC™ is a Registered Trade Mark of International Business Efficiency Consulting, L.L.C.

tools capable of meeting the needs of KE. The first report "IC-Efficiency in Croatian Economy"—a summary of the principal results provided by the VAIC™ analysis—featured the economic performance of the national economy, the sixteen counties, and the 400 top Croatian companies from 1996 to 2000. For the first time, counties, cities, and companies had the opportunity to benchmark according to the criteria of value added and efficiency of value creation. Two more annual and three quarterly issues of intellectual capital efficiency reports followed. Slowly but steadily they have become accepted as relevant reference sources by business and political management. During the latest elections, local governments used those new criteria in order to present what they had achieved, in particular the ones who had increased the efficiency during their mandate.

According to the VAIC™ analysis, 210 companies in state ownership, which are of special interest to the state, contributed in the total value added of Croatian economy with a share of 24%.[4] Total efficiency of these companies was way below the Croatian average. Fifty companies barely created value added to cover wages and salaries, not to mention investments into the future. Calculations indicated that if those 210 companies achieved a 5% increase in efficiency, which would still be below the Croatian average, it would amount to US$12 million more value added. According to Leif Edvinsson, this unrealized value represents national capital in waiting.[5] As shown, companies in state or city ownership represent a significant potential for increase of value creation and efficiency and are therefore the primary target group for PIENIC.

In this national subcontext, the Town Administration Department of Entrepreneurship of the city of Rijeka, which promotes economic activities in order to ensure progress in the development of city economy, realized the importance of the above issue. City government decided to pilot the PIENIC project in city-owned companies, whereby the IC Center in Zagreb became a partner in its realization.[6]

Features and Goals of PIENIC

The Project of Increasing National Intellectual Capital Efficiency (PIENIC) has been developed by the IC-Center. It is the result of domestic and international knowledge sharing, year-long consulting with Croatian companies, insider information from managers, in particular those with experience in IC-projects, as well as profound insight into the business environment in Croatia. PIENIC offers a unique solution to an emerging need, which, paradoxically, has not been recognized as such by most companies, city officials, and government representatives.

PIENIC was primarily designed for state-owned companies that not merely need modern machinery but also modern ways of thinking and working in order to become and stay competitive. Many such companies have started copying western business models which are about to be outdated soon and thus cannot enable them to achieve their aim, competitiveness in the 21st century, which is characterized by KE. Therefore, these companies have to take new roads and find their own knowledge recipes.

---

    [4] The Efficiency of Intellectual Capital at national, regional and company level, (2003). Croatian Chamber of Economy.
    [5] Edvinsson, L. (2002). *Corporate Longitude, Navigating the Knowledge Economy*, Stockholm: BookHouse Publishing Sweden AB.
    [6] The IC-Center (CIK) is the only consultancy firm in Croatia specialized on Intellectual capital matters. (www.cik-hr.com). It is a branch office of the International business efficiency Center (IBEC, L.L.C.).

The main features of PIENIC are:

- explicit focus on value creation, in particular on value added and efficiency of value creation, in addition to cost control
- introduction of IC as key production factor
- implementation of new management and measuring tools (VAIC™ and PIKA™[7]), which are helpful in increasing value creation and efficiency and include IC
- education on the KE, the role of knowledge and IC, and international trends in the field of IC
- intellectual capital teams as the main drivers of change
- coaching instead of consulting.

The underlying logic is that only if political and company managements realize that business terms are changing and comprehend the significance of knowledge and IC—key value-creating factors—they will start dealing with this new issue and make it a priority issue.

Because of that, the first step is awareness creation and education. Unless people learn about the ways of managing and measuring this new key resource, they will not be able to cope with it successfully. Therefore, the basic PIENIC education program includes lectures on various IC-related topics, storytelling of domestic case studies, and success stories as well as the distribution of a handbook on managing IC in companies. The handbook is written in a manner that makes the IC concept easy to comprehend by a broad audience. We consider this to be very important, since all employees, who represent the human capital of companies and are therefore the moving force in the realization of the program, should understand what ICM is about and not merely the top and middle management.

The second step is measuring. As Lord Kelvin said over hundred years ago "When you can measure what you are speaking about and express it in numbers, you know something about it." The VAIC™-analysis is introduced as the appropriate measuring tool, enabling the monitoring of the companies' ability to create wealth as well as the performance of existing resources—physical and financial, but also IC.

The third step consists of workshops that deal with the visualization and analysis of a company's IC. The software tool PIKA™ has been designed to help achieve that. First, a questionnaire of 260 IC-related questions is filled out by the management and selected employees. This should provide information on how they perceive their company's handling of nonmaterial factors related to employee's knowledge and skills, values, networking, knowledge sharing, leadership, vision, corporate culture, customer focus, capability of innovation, and efficient value creation. Each question offers a choice of three answers. If, e.g., 30% choose Answer One, and 70% Answer Two the situation is quite obvious. Depending on the fact whether the answer chosen by the majority supports the company's goals, it is classified as a critical or noncritical factor. However, if the perceptions of the interviewed staff diverge, e.g., 30% choose Answer One, 30% Answer Two, and 40% Answer Three, it implies that there might be communications or transparency problems which also have to be dealt with. During workshops the participants analyze the results achieved and highlight positive, negative, interesting, or odd ones. In the software, a short text to each question from the questioner can be found

---

[7] PIKA™ is a Registered Trade Mark of International Business Efficiency Consulting, L.L.C.

which provides a kind of guideline with regard to modes of approaching this issue. A "key question" on each topic helps start the discussion on how things have been done so far, whether it supports future goals, why and how things could be done better in order to increase efficiency and effectiveness, which knowledge and expertise would be necessary to do better and whether it is available inside or outside the company. The key points of the discussion and the conclusions are implemented into the program. This way it is easy to print out a report featuring the context, the questions, results achieved by the questioner and discussion highlights related to the different IC factors and communicate it to interested parties. It is recommended to start with issues that are identified as key factors of business, in particular the critical ones, and to continue until all the topics featured in the software have been covered. This ensures continuity in dealing with intangible capital, which is very important during the first year, when it becomes either routine or obsolete in the view of management.

The fourth step of PIENIC encourages transformation into value-oriented business, which, in this case, means "to think more about how to create value and less of how to cut costs." Experience shows that managers tend to spend most of their time thinking about cost control and current business problems. Only few take the time to think and talk about the future or new concepts and possibilities which would enable them to create more value with existing resources. The bigger the value added cake the more there is to share for all the participants and less energy is spent on fights for the biggest share.

As with any other process, it will take time and effort to change this mental pattern, but a start has to be done at some point. If knowledge and IC are key value-creating factors of the KE, they have to be treated with the same attention and care as physical and financial capital. This implies that an orientation toward value creation in modern business is not possible without a strong focus on intangible business factors. However, as long as the significance of IC is underestimated, management rarely finds the time to think of and discuss the ways of utilizing this key resource in more effective and efficient ways. Finally, in order to achieve a successful transformation into value-oriented business, a supporting incentive and rewarding system has to be created. Most of the present ones in Croatian companies do not really reward the flexible, innovative, creative, proactive, and customer-friendly employees who are the value creators.

The fifth step is coaching. During the realization of PIENIC, the consultant team does not act as a problem solver. Company management is qualified and paid to do so and no consultant could know their company and its business environment better. What management needs is impetus to start dealing with issues they have not yet realized as critical to their business, advice on possibilities in dealing with it, new views of their business performance, education on relevant matters, a competent and motivated team force to overcome resistance, and experienced partners to support them when necessary. Because of various reasons, the word from an outsider is often accepted more easily than the one from an insider, which makes it sensible to bring in consultants from various fields of expertise.

Let us now turn toward the goals of PIENIC on the national scale: First, to start the realization of the program issued by the "National Competitiveness Council" in 2003, which so far has had little impact on business practice.[8] Secondly, to increase

---

[8] 55 Recommendations for the Increase of Croatian Competitiveness (2004). USAID and the Croatian National Competitiveness Councel, Zagreb.

the value creation efficiency of the state- or city-owned companies, which are performing below national efficiency level. For the city of Rijeka, this means a benefit of several million US$ extra income. Thirdly, to demonstrate that an increase in efficiency can be achieved without discharging employees, by better utilization of their intellectual potential. State-owned companies should be a role model for other companies in that matter. Fourthly, to contribute to a new and positive image of Croatia, and the city of Rijeka in particular. This image would be one of a trendsetter and knowledge region. Fifthly, to create an intellectual export product, since PIENIC can be sold to other cities and countries, once it has proved beneficial in business practice.

Case Study—Implementation of PIENIC in City-Owned Companies of Rijeka

As mentioned before, in Rijeka the initiative with PIENIC was taken by Town Administration Department of Entrepreneurship. Leading decision-makers were convinced of the relevance behind the IC issue and the opportunities of the project. It was agreed to pilot PIENIC in several companies, which are supervised by the City Government. In providing public service, such companies have to meet expectations of different parties (local government, companies, citizens, visitors) and perform to maximum public benefit. With this in mind, it becomes imperative that municipal companies become value oriented and start applying modern management methods and tools in order to lower costs and increase the level of service quality and value added for customers, employees, and the owner, the city of Rijeka and thereby all its citizens. The goal was a 5–10% increase of value creation efficiency and improvement of the companies' competitiveness, starting the process of continuous improvement of IC effectiveness and efficiency.

Although the City Government approved of the project, the initial meeting with CEOs was nevertheless a challenge. They not only had to accept the project, but had to also truly support its realization. Former experience with state-owned companies implied that strong resistance was to be expected from top and/or medium management. In some cases it was stated openly, which was the better option, since it created opportunity for dialog. The worse scenario was formal agreement and quiet boycott later on. In order to prevent this, we invited the IC director of a very successful Croatian state-owned company to the initial meeting. He made it clear that IC was a top priority issue for any company and that top management had to truly support PIENIC if it was to succeed. The argumentation, coming from a practitioner, turned most CEOs into allies. The next step could be taken.

At first, a cross-functional IC team was established in each company and assigned the following tasks:

(1) To be the main carrier of the IC project (measurement and continuous improvement of IC-effectiveness and efficiency, aided by the software packages VAIC™ and PIKA™)
(2) To become a nucleus, which would create internal and external awareness, as well as favorable conditions for IC-related action
(3) To organize education and discussions on IC and KE
(4) To become a reference center for issues regarding IC (literature, networks, experts, case studies, etc.)
(5) To become a force, which would initiate changes in thinking and doing and motivate other employees in doing so.

After a short period of adaptation to the new situation, all IC teams were highly motivated to learn and start working toward the achievement of goals. It was a challenge for them; their commitment and engagement show how much hidden potential there is in most employees once they receive the opportunity to act. This may be self-evident in many companies but in most of the state-owned Croatian companies there is still a strong hierarchical system, where employees are expected to follow orders from their superiors and execute given tasks, not to think or act in creative and innovative ways.

The IC teams shared an interesting experience: despite the support of their CEO, top and/or middle management resisted and obstructed the realization of the project. An explanation might be that the project brought change and more transparency to their line of business with less room for individual manoeuvres. It also meant accepting responsibility for their share in value creation or value destruction. Resistance, in various forms, also came from colleagues, subtle or open and hostile. Despite the fact that team members had to spend extra time on learning, meetings, and project-related tasks along with their regular activities, it did not earn them the respect of others. Most considered their engagement a waste of time, and the expenditures on books and technical support were not seen as investment in their company's future earnings capability, but as a waste of money. It is understandable that the previously mentioned situation affected the teams' motivation to be the carriers of change. Furthermore, there was no special incentive for the team members. It was agreed though that everyone participating in the project would receive a fair reward from the extra value added created during the project.

Before the teams started working with concrete IC issues, they had received education on what KE is about and which role knowledge and intellectual capital played. In this training, the following topics were addressed: theoretical and practical background of managing and measuring IC, basics on the concept of IC, learning organization, change management, introduction into project management, and human capital assessment. It was vital to make the audience understand that only a timely start would assure enough time for a relatively painless transformation from traditional to knowledge-based business. This in turn would enable the companies to face the upcoming challenges more successfully and possibly ensure the preconditions for a competitive player in the European arena. The future competitiveness, when Croatia enters the EU, is a hot issue for all Croatian companies. The EU competition which will set new business terms, for investors and shareholders with high performance expectations are a nightmare to state-protected and monopolistic companies.

In order to spice up theory, home case studies and success stories were told. The most impressive one in Croatia is the story of the shipyard "Uljanik," a state-owned company. Thanks to their explicit orientation toward value creation, IC-related activities, continuous education, process-oriented business organization, and determined management, it succeeded to become the second best shipyard in Europe after escaping bankruptcy several years ago. It is the only globally competitive shipyard in Croatia, and does not rely on state subventions for survival. Success of another company, "Cimos," the Croatian partner of the French car manufacturer "Citroen," is another story worth telling. Like in "Uljanik," the management implemented the IC concept successfully; continuously measuring value creation and efficiency, it improved business processes in a way that made them value adding and thus succeeded to increase their performance from year to year. The spirits of the audience listening to these stories were raised immediately, but in the discussion most of them doubted to be able to achieve similar results in their own companies since a small revolution, unlikely to happen, would be necessary. An argument in favor of this attitude also comes from the shipbuilding industry. None of the management teams of other shipyards in Croatia followed their colleagues' positive example and neither did the government impose radical changes in the mentioned direction, although most shipyards are a severe burden to the national budget.

The VAIC™ analysis, which was applied for measurement of economic success at national, regional, city, and company level for the past three years in Croatia, was introduced to the companies in Rijeka as well. This way, information regarding their ability to create value added and the efficiency of key resources were obtained. At first, a period of 3–5 years was analyzed in order to establish a trend and determine how well the companies were doing at the beginning of the project. Then the results were benchmarked against the national, regional, and sector efficiency levels, as well as against the performance of possible competitors or similar companies in the EU (assuming data was available) (Figures 1 and 2).

Figure 1

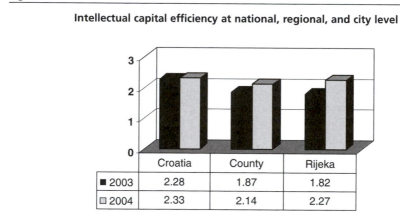

Intellectual capital efficiency at national, regional, and city level

	Croatia	County	Rijeka
■ 2003	2.28	1.87	1.82
☐ 2004	2.33	2.14	2.27

Figure 2

Increase of value added in %, national, regional, and city level

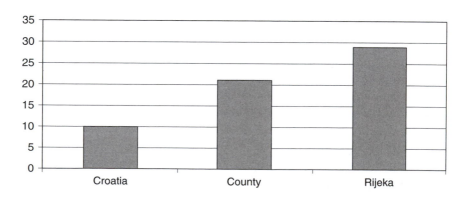

A VAIC™ software was installed in each company, enabling continuity in monitoring IC performance, supporting orientation toward value creation and efficiency. Team members working in accounting were trained for data input and result analysis. New projects were defined, in which efficiency would be monitored from the beginning to the end. Furthermore, they learned that it was beneficial to simulate VAIC™ parameters before contracting new projects, in order to control efficiency. Because the value creation analysis is not very complicated it was accepted quite easily as an additional tool providing insight into company's performance. It caused some fierce discussion and brought up vital issues, helping to eliminate circumstances causing value destruction not noticed before. There was also resentment regarding the new measuring and monitoring tool. It took some time until the management understood the benefits of measuring value added. That was easier to achieve with efficiency, since everybody could understand that it was better to achieve a higher return with the same resources.

We can say that PIENIC was a success in Rijeka, although it was not untroubled. The educational part was very well accepted by all parties; however, most companies would have preferred not to go beyond the point of education and measurement on company level. It was evident that action beyond that point was perceived as an intrusion into the manager's field of responsibility and that they felt as if their capability and credibility as leaders and businessmen had been at stake. In many cases, though, operational management and workers were much more eager to go on with the program than the leaders. Even more, they had many useful value adding ideas and written material, which were put aside in somebody's drawer. It became obvious that for many managers PIENIC seemed more a threat than an aid in achieving better business results. First, the new way of measuring and monitoring enabled insights, which were not favorable to all parties, in particular when applied inside the company. Secondly, it was unusual and uncomfortable to have teams discussing present practices openly and entering their findings and suggestions into a system, where they could be easily recalled. Thirdly, due to the unexpected transparence and interest of various parties, responsibility became an issue.

This project has shown that it is not likely that Croatian companies in state or city ownership would embrace changes easily, even if they were beneficial for the company. Since such companies receive subventions from their owners in order to be able to stay in business, they have little intrinsic intention to turn into companies which can compete in the open market, based on their value-oriented goals and business organization, motivated work force, and innovation capability.

Conclusion

The case study of PIENIC in Rijeka demonstrates responsibility on the part of the City Government of Rijeka to the shareholders of city-owned companies, the citizens, as well as long-sightedness in regard to strengthening those companies' future earnings capability. It also sends a nationwide signal toward political management, that they must start dealing with issues imposed by the 21st century economy if they want to secure the economic well-being of the cities, regions, and our nation.

Regarding the current political and economic situation it might be assumed that Croatian government and regional and local decision-makers would eagerly start to promote and support initiatives related to IC issues, in that way strengthening the capability of Croatia's economy to cope with challenges brought up by the KE. But up to this moment, initiatives as the one in Rijeka are isolated examples.

So far, there are no other official programs, aiming at the education of businessmen and those who create the economic environment, providing information on what KE is about and what its implications are for Croatia as a nation, its regions, cities and companies. Furthermore, no agreement has been achieved to systematically test new ways of measuring and reporting in order to establish a base for developing of national standards and for participating in the global quest for management and measurement tools suitable to meet the needs of KE.

For a country in transition, like Croatia, the KE could be its greatest opportunity to become a truly competitive player in the European and in the global market. Its strength is the human capital, the well-educated, engaged, flexible, and innovative working population. Unfortunately, many work in unsupportive environments with little or no opportunity to turn their intellectual potential into value. This points to the main weakness of Croatian economy, the structural capital: lack of explicit orientation toward value creation, old-fashioned ways of managing business, measuring tools, which do not encompass IC performance, an unproductive value system defined by our country's socialist heritage and the focus on individual benefit rather than on the benefit of the company and the entire community. The greatest threat facing the future prosperity of the Croatian economy is accounted to inadequate and late treatment of the aforementioned issues.

Chapter 14

An Experimental Aesthetic Audit of a City Within a City: The Case of Christiania

Raphaële Bidault-Waddington, *Laboratoire d'Ingéniérie d'Idées (LII), Paris, France*

An Original Case Study

Around 1971, a small group of hippies formed a squat on the edge of Copenhagen, abandoned by the Danish Ministry of Defence in the late 1960s, in order to create a "free city," which they called Christiannia. Being some of these settlers of Norwegian origin, the new city was apparently named after an ancient denomination of Oslo. Unlike many American or European hippie communes, which vanished almost as quickly as they appeared, Christiania found a viable and long-term way of operating. Over the years, the population of Christiania grew to 1000, houses were constructed, ancient buildings restored, and efficient public infrastructures were implemented. Furthermore, Christiania set up its own system of laws and developed its own central administrative system to manage its economy and offer public services such as mail, garbage collection and recycling, kindergarten, etc. Many activities (including illegal drug activities) and businesses bloomed, some of them becoming national corporations. An extremely rich and dynamic cultural life is the foundation of the city's unique and specific identity. Almost seen as a "hippie land" Christiania is physically characterized by its outdoor wall paintings, car-free streets and wild vegetation between buildings.

Despite several serious internal and external crises and several rounds of tough negotiation with the Danish Government over the years, Christiania survived and still functions as an independent city today. In about three decades, Christiania has remained a unique and autonomous self-managed city; has become the most visited area in Copenhagen; and has gained incredible international aura, worthy of a myth or an international brand, with support only from the Danish people and the media.

This shiny but slightly suspicious first portrait appeared as a tempting invitation to audit the "free city" as an interesting case of study.

The Method

Although generally associated with art practices, aesthetics consists in finding the brightest combination of intellect with matter, i.e., of intangible ideas with tangible elements according to time and space; it can thus be applied to the understanding of other areas of human activity. Mixing a wide range of vocabularies (economic, artistic, architectural, scientific, philosophical, sociological, sensory, etc.), the LII audit tends to highlight the intellectual aspect of tangible practices and to improve the aesthetic combination of both, in order to create high and sustainable value. If the initial focus of the laboratory was on corporations, the aesthetical assessment of Christiania is an experimental exercise to audit companies on the case of a city.

To pursue this audit, the LII used the Grid of Reading that it developed to assess companies and called *Mise en Perspective*. Built like a patchwork or a cubist portrait, it consists in observing and analysing the organization under 24 different angles in order to perceive its strengths and weaknesses, to measure its efficiency, dynamic, and potential of development, and finally to detect its implicit and explicit value and knowledge (Table 1).

These 24 facets correspond to 4 levels of reading:

(1) "Functional Architecture" will map the fundamental structure of the organization as an operating system designed according to six different axes. Here the audit will consist in assessing the efficiency of the processes in quite a quantitative way.
(2) "Cultural Style" will then offer a more qualitative approach of the whole system and will focus on every element that may define and differentiate the organization in a subtler way, so that less obvious yet strategic elements are not missed. The last of the six aspects considered in this second part will verify the general harmony of the organization as a sub-conclusion of part 1 and part 2.

Table 1: Grid of reading

Architecture	Cultural Style	Positioning	Mindscape
Physical organization	Qualified offer	In the branch of land administrations	Initial shuffle
Human organization	Qualified target	In its competitive environment	History and development dynamic
Transportation and flows	Behavior	In the natural environment	Decision-making and risk-taking aspects
Economic flows	Partners	In society	The name as a brand
Legal aspect	Management and authority	In the media	Knowledge and influences
Strategy	The general harmony	In history	Underlying project

(3) "Positioning" will assess how the organization interacts within its own context and along six different axes.

(4) Finally "Mindscape" will aim at having a deeper look at the intellectual capital of the organization, once again structured in six distinctive sub-parts. The last sub-part will conclude on the direction the organization is taking and the sense it is making.

Because the method is systemic rather than linear, the analysis can be read in any order. The result of the audit is normally delivered on a single graphic and dynamic board (1 m × 1.5 m) with 25 sub-parts in order to create a full panorama on the "organization in perspective" and so that it can be used as a convenient strategic management tool. Presented here is a linear and narrative translation of this board.

Sources of Information

Since Christiania has no central administration, no official documents are available except through the local newspaper. A large part of the information has been collected through interviews and working sessions with Christiania's lawyer, chief accountant, old and young residents, external workers notably involved in the city's cultural life, business managers, and visitors. Access has been possible to a few strategic documents such as a fresh study of the social structure of Christiania or historical studies thanks to two architects involved in negotiations with the Danish state and a Danish artist who completed a substantial investigation a few years ago. Finally, a photographic survey was used to qualify the cultural style.

Christiania in Perspective/Part I: The Functional Architecture

The Physical Organization

Because Christiania was originally a military base, it is a car-free enclosed area of about 40 ha and composed of two distinctive parts. A 20 ha square-shaped southern part is considered as the entrance and center of Christiania. It is separated from its surroundings by a brick wall on two sides of the square and by seawater canals on the two other sides. This area is about 10-minute walking distance from the city center of Copenhagen and gathers most of Christiania's facilities, shops, and activities. Most of the buildings are former military structures transformed into lofts, flats, concert halls, bars, restaurants, workshops, warehouses, shops, etc. To be noticed is the recently built skateboarding park in the central square. A few new wood houses were built in the 1970s and 1980s; from that period remain some train wagons transformed into small houses. Christiania counts 70 dynamic independent businesses and two daily open markets: the handicraft and tourist market, and the hash and marijuana market called "Pusher Street." Although touristy, Christiania has no hotel or hostel facilities.

Stretching north from the center along both sides of the canal is a long and thin piece of land, measuring 20 ha and separating Copenhagen from its suburbs and empty fields. This area resembles the country-side with scattered wooden residential houses, including some built around small brick former gunpowder houses in the 1970s and 1980s. Almost no activities take place in this very quiet and remote area except a couple of workshops, the kindergarten, and the pony club.

The far north exit gives access to a couple of fields and to the beginning of an abandoned industrial zone and harbor that are currently being transformed. In this way,

Christiania draws a bridge between Copenhagen's center and emerging neighborhoods. Regarding administration, the land is split into 13 sub-areas managed independently.

Human Organization: Residents, Workers, Visitors

About 900 people live in Christiania (650 adults and 250 under 18) with an average of 13 inhabitants per area. Since no building has been built since the early 1990s, the population is steady but aging and now far above national averages. Christiania agreed with the Danish state not to build any new house since 1992 so there is no place available to new residents, including the children of Christiania. This is one of the largest problems of Christiania and gives a strong sign of life decline in the city.

Because the original population of Christiania were squatters, hippies, and "all the black sheep of the country," the average educational level is well below the national level. Christianites are mostly independent workers (artists, freelancers, entrepreneurs, etc.), workers for small structures inside or outside Christiania including the Community's central system, or are social workers. However, the unemployment rate is higher than in Copenhagen.

The administration consists of a system of meetings, each of them dedicated to a specific field of decision-making: budget allocation, choice of new residents, infrastructure improvement, and business support. In each meeting, decisions have to be unanimously agreed upon to be implemented. Because there is no official authority, the decisions are implemented thanks to the goodwill of individuals.

About a hundred people come everyday to work in Christiania, mostly in the shops and in cultural and tourist activities. More than a million visitors come every year for a day or an evening, mostly during the summer time.

Transportation and Flows

Christiania is a car-free area and has low-tech transportation infrastructures. It has, however, a well-arranged garbage collection, and has even recently invested in a new technology to sort the garbage in 50 different product sub-families to facilitate its recycling. Christiania has also organized its own efficient post office and mail system.

Cars are a new problem because many Christianites now own cars and have to park them outside the car-free town. Visitors' cars also congest the circulation in the surrounding areas. There is thus an urgent need for parking facilities.

Information among residents circulates through word of mouth and through the weekly newspaper, the *Christianias Ugespejl*, which provides all the local news, announces local meetings, and discloses decisions and economic figures to everyone. Information is transparent, this being part of the requirements of the self-government policy. The connection among residents is very strong compared to most neighbors in Copenhagen or in other cities. The self-governance system encourages local involvement and exchange between residents.

Economic Flows

The global budget of Christiania is now about 17m DKK per year. One half is collected from the residents' fixed rent (there is no private property in Christiania), and the other half from businesses, which pay a yearly negotiated rent according to their profitability. Then the central account (Faelleskassen), pays 600 000 DKK per year to the Ministry of Defence as a land tax, now assimilated as a rent. Water and electricity bills regarding residency should amount to about 3m DKK. The total of business payments is 8.5 m DKK. Residents pay 1600 DKK per month: 700 DKK for the rent, electricity and water, and 900 DKK for local institutions and services (post office, garbage collection, kindergarten, building office, economy office, and area budget). The central economy meeting occurs once a month to dispatch the fund to the institutions.

All 70 independent businesses pay taxes and VAT to the Danish state as regular Danish corporations (1996 reglamentation). Then the Faelleskassen pays an estimated VAT for all the local services (about 150 000 DKK in 2002) with an emphasis on transparency. As there is no official authority in Christiania, those who neglect to pay are only "shamed" by being listed in the local newspaper and pressured to pay or move out by their neighbors. However, many residents do not pay their rent.

Further, Christiania keeps a capital of about 600 000 DKK, available as an internal insurance mutual fund in case of any emergency need. As a matter of fact, the economic model of Christiania is close to the style of the 19th-century farmer's mutual fund, totally independent from the Danish State, whose financial help has always been declined.

Pusherstreet's economy is totally autonomous from Christiania's economy and no drug money enters the Faelleskassen. It is almost impossible to get any figures about the volume of drugs sold and of money made through the deal. This money is probably immediately taken away from Christiania, if not away from Copenhagen and Denmark. The drug offer in Pusherstreet is very similar to the one of coffee shops in Amsterdam and probably comes from the same circuits.

Legal Aspect

Christiania is both legal and illegal. As a "free-city," it has positioned itself outside any legal frame and has built its own. Christiania's law is not written but oral, based on Scandinavian tradition. Only few oral rules have been implemented: no hard drugs, no weapons, no violence, no trading of buildings or residential areas. Aside from these few rules, there is absolutely no official authority.

However, although the Danish State has tolerated this parallel system over the last three decades, at the time of writing, it is now willing to re-integrate Christiania's administration and close the soft-drugs market. Consequently the national police forces have recently re-entered the area and the future of Christiania as a "free-city" is seriously threatened. Without a central strategy and authority, Christiania has real difficulties to cope with this hard pressure.

Strategy

As Christiania has no government, it does not have any central strategy. The strategy of Christiania is to let things grow in an organic and free-style way. The current crisis with the Danish state highlights an urgent need for a centralized projection of the existing city, which may, however, question the fundamental model of Christiania.

Christiania in Perspective/Part II: The Cultural Style

The Qualified Offer

Everything in Christiania has a magical touch as it mostly looks like a colorful hippie land. Buildings are old and valuable military brick building transformed into stylish lofts and workshops, original wood houses designed by hippie architects, or abandoned wagons transformed into small bohemian houses. Many walls including the one enclosing Christiania are painted with vivid colors and frescoes and give a strong visual identity.

Two styles correspond to the two generations of residents/cohabitants: the original hippie culture with psychedelic features dominates, but the street culture of the second generation, inspired by the 1980s and 1990s rap and graffiti culture is also quite strong and visible. The impressive skateboard park is the temple of this second generation.

In between buildings, nature has pursued its course so that Christiania looks like a countryside village with dirt paths, flowers, and trees everywhere. No barriers separate houses and buildings so that the entire space is accessible to visitors.

Shops are also symptomatic of the hippie culture with a lot of handicraft, recycling activities such as ancient oven restoration, furniture renovation, organic foods, etc. Tourist and entertainment spaces are blooming with music cafés, fancy restaurants, and several theater and concert places. The two open markets have specific offers: the handicraft market offers products from Christiania but also many "hippie flavored" products from many countries (Asia, Africa, and Latin America). The soft drugs market offers an extremely wide choice of hashish and weeds, like most coffee shops in Amsterdam.

Many Christianites started their own businesses and all of them have the same hippie touch. For example, the *Christiania Bikes* industry has patented bikes with a unique style and now exports worldwide.

The tourist attraction consists in visiting the area, safely and openly smoking a joint, and enjoying food and cultural activities such as music and live shows. All of them belong to an alternative hippie or more contemporary alternative culture so that visitors experience the strong feeling of diving in an alternative world and society, a "free-city."

The Qualified Target

Residents are the first "clients" of Christiania. The original residents of Christiania included hippies and other marginal population, who are still an important part of the community and are still involved in social activism. But through the years, the population of Christiania has gone through a gentrification process, becoming quite family oriented, and resembling more of a "bourgeois-bohemia" normalized population. The immediate consequence has been a major security improvement in the area. The subversive dimension of Christiania has shifted from the core to the surface of the city.

Christiania was quite an unsafe place until about 7–8 years earlier to the time of writing, when only young marginal males wanted to live or go there, and has since turned into a safe, attractive area. So, the other clientele of Christiania are tourists. Christiania is the second most touristic spot of Copenhagen and welcomes more than a million visitors per year. Since the hippie culture has been a worldwide visual cultural movement that brought in a utopian, festive, and "cool" spirit, everyone is enchanted by Christiania, from children to grandparents.

Behavior

Resistance is a key to understand Christiania's behavior. Like the nature around them, Christianites have always preserved their feeling of freedom and only regulate themselves in the case of an emergency and external requirement, especially the one of the Danish Government. Those moments have always been important moments of questioning. From an alternative structure it became a social experiment, then an example of ecological society. The current crisis should be appreciated as a necessary moment. When considering this model, one should also consider the social normalization dynamics, and perhaps focus more on the cultural paradigm.

Creativity, entertainment, and goodwill are the most important qualities of Christiania, even if the product of this creativity has slightly drifted from the artistic scene to the commercial scene. Like artists or entrepreneurs, Christiania does not like to be told what to do, but it has acknowledged the necessity of dialog and negotiation to preserve its existence. Christiania has thus cultivated a smart "wait and see" attitude, waiting for the outside to say "stop" to its uncontrolled, free, organic behavior.

Partying should be considered as a major motivation for Christianites. Each demonstration Christianites have organized has had a political dimension but always with huge parties and entertaining shows that have provided Christiania with a strong affective capital.

Partners

The media are Christiania's most important partners. Even if Christiania's aesthetics have aged and the city is not a source of new trends, all media keep on talking about Christiania. Media are Christiania's best weapon in its political battles with the Danish State. Being quite a closed society, it does not rely on other external sources and does not depend on anyone financially, except the international drug circuits, which may be considered as implicit partners.

Management and Authority

Christiania has no government, and regulates itself thanks to various forms of meetings. The Common Meeting is the most important one in making major decisions and planning the strategy, but the unanimity requirement blocks most decisions and ends up a "no strategy." Then local meetings, much smaller than the Common Meeting, deal with the current issues of each of the 13 areas on a concrete level. Each area has an average of 70 inhabitants so local meetings are almost like "building coops." The Economy Meeting, gathering one person of each area plus the central accountant, is the only efficient meeting.

General Harmony

Christiania is a strongly knitted fabric showing an original experimental pattern. Imagination, creativity, free styling, and roughness shape the pattern. The colors and texture are resistant, but this will not last forever if no care is given to it internally as much as externally. As the community is aging, it will probably find it increasingly difficult to resist. The result is self-normalization and the current generational issue can be analyzed as the opposition of a conservation dynamic versus a renewal dynamic.

Christiania in Perspective/Part III: Positioning

In the Branch of Land Administrations

The question is rather complex, as Christiania may be considered a neighborhood of Copenhagen, a city in a city or a state in a state. The status of Christiania is still unclear (public or private?). Its unique link to the branch is an agreement with the

Ministry of Defence to pay a tax to occupy the land. If this agreement may be assimilated as a rent, then Christiania could also be considered as a private park—public to visitors but private in its constitution. As Christiania looks like a young society, still in the process of defining itself, this position should be clarified in the future.

In Its Competitive Environment

As a park to visit, Christiania competes with *Tivoli Park*, both places registering the largest amount of visitors in Copenhagen. Tivoli generated more than 300m DKK of turnover, about 11m DKK of net profit and more than 5m of tax to the state. Tivoli is 150 years old and its total assets oscillate around 600m DKK. In terms of Knowledge Capital the question emerges: how much would the collective creation of Christiania be worth, as a social asset, after 30 years of existence?

As a neighborhood, Christiania competes with Vesterbro and Norrebro for their cultural scene but has substantially lost attractiveness. It has a strong success with tourists, but Danish emerging artists do not live or hang out in Christiania anymore.

As a residential area, rent in Christiania are about half compared to anywhere else in central Copenhagen, where prices have drastically increased since 2000. Christianites have, however, spent huge amounts of time and money to build residences or infrastructures that they do not own.

As a state, the comparison should be made on a legal level. Unlike the Danish State, which has an extended involvement in the life of the country, Christiania cultivates a minimal central system.

In the Natural Environment

The ground of Christiania is polluted with heavy metals and remaining of gunpowder. Nature has, however, been growing in a luxuriant way. It is part of the general organic development policy. The landscape of Christiania is extremely precious and exceptional in an urban environment. The shore and surrounding water could eventually be improved. As Christiania has been giving such a strong life to the originally deserted piece of land, it has built an implicit bridge between the city and the mostly abandoned industrial site behind it, all along Refshalevej and past Quintus Bastion. The fact that young artists from Copenhagen have started activities in this area confirms this urban dynamic that deserves proper planning.

In Society

As the Danish society is highly organized and planned, Christiania stands as the messy alternative spot, able to integrate some the country's fringe groups and it is the reason why Christiania has been considered as a social experiment. This "black sheep" integration process may not be as efficient as in 1980s or 1990s because of the general normalization process going on. But Christiania still brings hope to the Danish society as a tangible example of a "something else" or alternative system, and thus provides a very strong symbolic value.

On a more simple level, Christiania draws a lifestyle model where fun has kept a central position in the local way of living. Paradoxically, in Christiania, life is not considered as a painful battle but people are ready to struggle and work hard to enjoy life and have fun.

In the Media

The media are among Christiania's best partners. If local media have sometimes been critical, most of them generally support Christiania and regularly speak about it. Concerning the international media, their voice has been even more flattering, always describing Christiania as an extraordinary experiment or as a fabulous place that no one should miss visiting when in Copenhagen. All over the world, Christiania is promoted as the "cool" place in Copenhagen with nature around and soft drugs openly sold. Also, the more the Christiania is in crisis with the Danish Government, the hotter the subject is in the media.

In History

Denmark has a history of free lands that governments have allocated for different reasons, cultural or economic (e.g. concessions in the harbor to support international trade, other examples of temporary self-managed squatted place, etc.). The map of Christiania is also a remainder of Copenhagen's former "star shape" plan. The "bastion" brick buildings were fringing the city. Christiania, in some ways, cultivates this borderline position.

Regarding its political history, Christiania borrows from international 20th-century utopian ideas, from Communism to ultra-liberal anarchism, from Le Corbusier's architecture to the hippie movement. The ultimate historical value of Christiania is to be an exceptional living museum of 1970s' hippie culture.

Christiania in Perspective/Part IV: Mindscape

The Initial Shuffle

Cinematographer Nils Vest clearly explains in his documentary film *Christiania You Have My Heart* the initial shuffle of Christiania. The founders, most of whom remained anonymous, had a simple desire: "just building our own space." And they just did it. With energy and courage, they created a dynamic trend, built houses or temporary habitations, and, little by little, organized their common space. At a period of intense intellectual debate, their motivation was to get out of it, go for action, and build their own little dreamland.

The History and Development Dynamic

Along the way, some tried to take advantage of it, to get famous from it, or to project political ideology on it, but Christiania maintained a strict decision of being a place with no power and no authority. However, because the place had no authority, it became a favorable place for illegal activities, which were not part of the original intention. The soft drug market developed very quickly, along with hippie music, live performances, and other fringe activities. As the space was big enough, everyone could settle and no restrictions were made to new entrants. For a long time, the crime rate in Christiania was much higher than anywhere in Denmark, leading to some serious crises, always ending through negotiation with the Danish State. The current situation is a new step in this process.

Decision-Making and Risk-Taking Aspects

Decision-making is done through different meetings and is based on mutual agreement, goodwill, and common sense, thus leaving a great free space for individual creation, entrepreneurship, and pleasure. Strongly defending this model under legal threat from the beginning, Christiania proves its ability to take risks and resist pressure, notably thanks to media support and to the fact that it has no head government (leaving no grasp on it). The current aging problem of Christiania is questioning its ability to make decisions and to take risks.

The Name as a Brand

Christiania was named by the original squatters in reference to the ancient name of Oslo, to the area being called *Christianshavn*, and probably to the extremely non-conformist Danish Queen in the 17th century, who was peculiarly close to artists.

Christiania is now as much a symbol of a possible utopia as an international brand. Its associated logo is the three yellow dots on a red background flag. It has been chosen in reference to the three "i's" in the word "Christiania." Its colorfulness shows the playfulness of the free town, almost like a clown outfit. The three dots also evoke the idea of an adventure to continue (. . .) which is actually the case. The brand has a strong potential value to be developed through licences and incorporated tourist services.

Knowledge and Influences

The educational level in Christiania is much lower than in the rest of the country (no schools, no libraries); so its intellectual capital mostly lies in the freedom of its lifestyle and its entrepreneurial dynamic. Moreover, Christiania has been seen from outside as an exemplary case of a utopian city, a social experiment, an ecological citizenship, an anarchy, a communist community, an alternative political system, an artistic trend, a fictionalized place, a playground, a traditional picturesque Danish garden, etc., which provide Christiania with a speculative implicit symbolic value rather than an explicit intellectual capital.

The Underlying Project

The standard underlying project of a city is to provide a place: to live, work, and visit (for knowledge, tourism, entertainment, shopping, etc.) and Christiania's organization supports those three objectives. Its underlying project, however, includes a fourth function, which is to be a place to resist to global and social integration as an urban and lifestyle laboratory.

Christiania in Perspective/Part V: Conclusion

Final Diagnostic

Christiania is the fruit of a healthy, creative, and resistant dynamic. It has produced an original, valuable, and well-knit urban fabric that deserves the label "national asset."

Christiania is a wise, self-managed, self-normalizing, and self-funded long-term development project. Christiania is an inspiring, entertaining, and free-style model of entrepreneurship and lifestyle.

But Christiania is at the edge of legal survival and should pursue its legalization process with the Danish State by translating its existing system into a foundation. It needs to regulate an inter-generational issue by building new houses. It should adopt a fine branding strategy to protect itself from overconservative or commercial strategies.

Finally, Christiania should challenge itself culturally to avoid a slowly killing museumification process, notably by stimulating creative exchanges with other more up-to-date neighborhoods of Copenhagen and other international cities.

This final diagnostic has been developed into a full strategic recommendation in an Idea and Urbanism Competition launched by the Danish Government in 2004, regarding the future of Chistiania, in which it was awarded the 3rd prize.

Part Three: Perspectives

Chapter 15

How Much Does Urban Location Matter? A Comparison of Three Science Parks in China

Stephen Chen, *Australian National University, National Graduate School of Management, Canberra, Australia*

Introduction

The success of Silicon Valley in stimulating the development of new technology and new firms is now legendary, and although the area was not purposely created, many countries around the world have sought to emulate its success by creating areas designated as technology parks, science parks, or something similar. They have all been attracted by the apparent ability of such clusters of firms not only to support technological development through their innovative activity but also to generate employment and contribute to GDP growth (Porter and Stern, 2001). Examples of such parks include Cambridge in the UK, Sophia-Antipolis in France, Hsinchu Technology Park in Taiwan, and Tsukuba in Japan.

Studies of industry clusters have often shown that geographical concentration is one important feature that has contributed to their success. One argument is that specialized skilled workers and firms may be attracted toward a region once a critical mass of firms within the industry is attracted there. However, there are arguments that clustering in high-tech sectors may follow a completely different pattern. Such high-tech clusters often span across not only sectoral but also geographical boundaries. There is no longer a need for the geographical concentration of complete production as was previously the case. Instead knowledge flows and linkages have become key elements in knowledge-based production.

In response to this changed state of affairs, in the 1980s the Chinese government changed its policy of sustaining a National Innovation System (NIS) in favor of a Global-Regional Innovation System. This development in China was also driven by economic as well as political developments. First, China has adopted an economic policy of encouraging foreign direct investment (FDI). Second, it has accepted and encouraged close economic and industrial relations externally, with Hong Kong, Taiwan, Korea and to a lesser extent with Japan. Third, the Chinese government has pursued an internal policy of allowing more regional autonomy. These elements have come together to foster the development of regional innovation centers.

Beginning in the early 1990s, the central government established technology parks in 53 major Chinese cities. These parks resemble those in other parts of the world in aiming to build a concentration of high-tech firms drawing from the universities and businesses within or near the park. However, the evidence on performance is mixed (MacDonald and Deng, 2004). This raises several questions. First, do high-tech firms in these parks obtain benefits from their location in a major metropolis? Second, do science parks benefit the local economy? Lastly, how have the firms in these parks been able to benefit from knowledge spillovers such as those from universities and firms? From FDI. The example of Hsinchu demonstrates the importance of informal transnational networks. Have science parks in China similarly benefited from returning students?

Technology parks in China provide valuable opportunities to examine these questions. The heterogeneity of the host cities provides an opportunity to identify external economies, if any, and other features contributing to the success of technology parks in the region. This chapter examines these questions using data on three Chinese science parks and their host cities. The chapter is set out in the following way. Firstly, we review previous studies of science parks and industrial districts. Next, we examine the history and performance of science parks in three cities in China—Beijing, Shanghai, and Xi'an. Finally, we discuss the implications for research and policy making concerning science parks.

Review of Relevant Literature on Cities and Science Parks

The idea that the geographical concentration of firms can generate externalities through localization and agglomeration dates back to Marshall (1920). According to Marshall, three forces drive the formation and growth of regional clustering of industries: information exchange or knowledge spillovers, a shared labor pool, and the backward and forward linkages between firms in a large local market. Numerous studies have identified Marshall's external economies, in understanding and explaining industry concentration and the growth of cities (e.g., Glaeser et al., 1992; Krugman, 1993). Science parks are an attempt to create such externalities by design (Appold, 2003).

Despite the intense interest in science parks worldwide, findings on the actual performance of science parks are mixed (Lindelöf and Löfsten, 2003; Siegel et al., 2003). Storey and Tether (1998) argue that with the exception of France, the science parks in Europe have made only a modest direct contribution to employment, and the contribution to technology transfer was difficult to assess. Massey et al. (1992) argue that many science parks to be primarily a form of prestigious real estate with few productive synergies generated, and geographical proximity between a university and a science park seems to account for very little in promoting technology transfer. Similarly Westhead and Storey (1995) found that although a number of firms have located on a science park in order to be close to a university, the extent to which these university–industry links existed was less than that anticipated. This finding is also supported by Vedovello (1997) who shows, through a comparative analysis, that geographical proximity between partners is not an important influence for the existence or strength of formal links between university and industry.

One of the problems may be that different types of science park have different effects. Although most economic theory on geographic concentration of firms is based on Marshall's (1920) studies of industrialized cities in Britain, more recent research has identified many alternative forms of industrial districts. Markusen (1996) identi-fied four distinct types of industrial districts:

(1) the Marshallian or Italianate district, comprised of small, locally owned firms that make investment and production decisions locally,
(2) the hub-and-spoke district built around one or more major corporations,
(3) the satellite district, comprised of branch plants of multinational corpora-tions, and
(4) the state-centered district, centered on a major government tenant.

However, some have argued that Markusen's typology is not appropriate for the Asian context. Based on studies in Korea, Park (1996) suggests that districts move through distinct stages, based on the strength of network links. In the first stage, the branch plants of large multinational corporations dominate. National government directives support the growth of these satellites by providing affordable factors of production such as cheap land, plentiful labor, and tax breaks. The nation-state plays a particu-larly important role in Asian development by creating the zones, then placing and directing their occupants. In stage 2, the advanced hub-and-spoke stage, local suppli-ers and start-up companies that provide components to or buy products from the foreign-based multinationals join the network. In stage 3, advanced satellites, small new firms, and other spin-off businesses related to the multinationals produce goods using components obtained elsewhere, but new spin-off firms and local research and development (R&D) ties begin to appear. Stage 4 is dominated by pioneering high-tech domestic companies, with extensive locally embedded supply and market linkages not related to the multinationals. A distinctive feature of this stage is innovation based on local R&D, along with locally devised production and/or distribution systems. Walcott (2002) also identified an intermediate, bridge high-tech stage in Chinese science parks. "Bridge high technology" companies engage in local production inde-pendently of multinationals but depend on research and development advice, and finance obtained from local Chinese universities and related institutes. Examples from other countries include Taiwan's Hsinchu (Chen and Choi, 2004), Korea's Taeduck (Park, 2000), and Japan's Tsukuba (Castells and Hall, 1994).

Phelps and Ozawa (2003) have also argued that a different form of spatial agglom-eration is developing generally as economies move into the post-industrialization phase. Unlike traditional agglomeration around manufacturing towns, this focuses on global city regions that provide knowledge-intensive services as part of a global network.

Science Policy in China

The policy of science park building in China needs to be seen against a backdrop of the national science policy. Early attempts at a science policy in the People's Republic of China were driven by a planned economy approach, which the communist govern-ment copied from the Soviet Union. Although some changes took place after the break with USSR in the late 1950s, including attempts at decentralization and the loosening of centralized control during the Cultural Revolution, the Chinese government remained committed to a planned economy until major reforms in the late 1970s. The country pursued a policy of centralized control and self-reliance, refusing FDI. The situation has changed dramatically from the early 1980s, when the Chinese government departed from a policy of sustaining an NIS in favor of a Global-Regional Innovation System by allowing a massive inflow of FDI in selected regions.

Subsequently foreign companies have come to play a significant role in China's high-tech industrial development. One of the vehicles through which the Chinese government has pursued this goal is through regional science and technology parks (Wang et al., 1998). The science parks offer various policy incentives to encourage investment and new firm formation in the parks. For example, new firms are exempt from corporate income tax for two years; taxes are waived for the import of materials and parts used in producing goods for export; and intangible assets such as intellectual property can be capitalized.

The first technology park in China approved by the central government was established in 1988 in Beijing, centering on Beijing University, Tsinghua University, and many of the research institutes of the Chinese Academy of Sciences. In 1991, another 26 technology parks were approved by the State Council, followed by yet another 25 in the following year. Yanglin Agricultural Technology Park was established in 1997 bringing the total number of national technology parks to 53. In addition, various local governments have established a number of science parks. Most of the parks are located in coastal provinces (35) with only five located in the western part of China. Many parks (22) are hosted by the provincial capital cities or central government—supervised municipalities. Most of the host cities except Yanglin are also major metropolises with a strong industrial base. The heterogeneity of the host cities and the science parks in China provide a valuable opportunity to examine the relationship between science parks and their host cities.

Comparison of Three Science Parks

We examine next the performance of three major science parks in China and their relationship with the cities in which they are located.

Beijing

Beijing is the capital of China and the country's leading political, cultural, and international exchange center. Along with Shanghai, Tianjin, and Chongqing, Beijing is one of four municipalities in China that enjoy similar economic and administrative autonomy as provinces.

The biggest sector in Beijing is the tertiary sector, which accounts for 61.5% of Beijing's GDP, particularly banking and insurance, and social services, which account for 14.7% and 10.0%, respectively, for the city's GDP (Table 1).

In 2003, gross output of high-tech industry amounted to RMB152.1 billion, representing 39.9% of gross industrial output in 2003. Electronics and information technology firms make up the largest contribution (Table 2).

Table 1: Composition of industry in Beijing (in %)

	1990	2002	2003
Primary	8.8	3.1	2.6
Secondary	52.4	34.8	35.8
Tertiary	38.8	62.2	61.5

Source: Beijing Statistical Yearbook.

Table 2: Composition of high-tech industry in Beijing

	2002	2003
Total	100.00	100.0
Electronic and information	61.08	64.5
Biological and pharmaceutical products	6.52	10.5
New materials	8.37	10.2
Organic whole of light, machine and electricity	20.73	11.4
Others	3.31	3.4

Source: Beijing Statistical Yearbook 2004.

Of the 4,019 industrial enterprises, only 1,362 were state owned or state holding (Table 3). Non-state owned enterprises accounted for 46% of gross industrial output.

Beijing exports grew by 24.9% to US$7.4 billion in 2003. Japan was the largest overseas market, followed by the USA, Hong Kong, and Germany. Major exports included machinery and transport equipment, and finished products grouped by materials. Beijing's imports grew by 42.0% to US$11.6 billion in 2003. Japan is the leading source of imports, followed by the USA, Germany, and Hong Kong. Major import commodities were machinery and transport equipment, and finished products grouped by materials.

Beijing has the largest number of, and the most prestigious, institutions of higher education and scientific research in the country. There are 73 institutions of higher education (including the world famous Beijing and Tsinghua Universities). Twenty-two percent of the population of working age have a college degree or higher (Table 4).

Table 3: Enterprises by region (values in RMB100 million)

City	No. of Domestic Enterprises	Gross Output Value of Domestic Enterprises	No. of Foreign-owned Enterprises	Gross Output Value of Foreign-owned Enterprises
Beijing	3059	2473.23	960	1337.13
Shanghai	6808	4369.57	4290	5973.25
Xi'an	653	542.98	82	95.68

Table 4: Educational level by region (calculated from data in Sample Survey of Population Changes 2003)

City/Region	Percentage of College Graduates
Beijing	21.9
Shanghai	17.9
Shaanxi	7.6

Table 5: FDI by region (in 10,000 USD)

City	1990	2000	2003
Beijing	39,202	168,368	219,126
Shanghai	32,104	316,014	546,849
Xi'an	1,154	15,633	25,557

Among the world's largest 500 enterprises, 160 or so have invested in Beijing. In 2003, the utilized amount of FDI increased by 19.8% to US$2.1 billion (Table 5). Foreign investment mainly flows into Beijing's tertiary sector, which accounts for over half of the total foreign investment. Areas that attracted the largest share of foreign investment included: manufacturing; information transmission, computer services and software; real-estate trade; and tenancy and commercial services, etc. Hong Kong is the largest source of overseas investment in Beijing. Other major investors came from Korea, USA, Japan, Singapore, and Germany.

Science Parks in Beijing

Beijing has established a coordinated set of industrial districts composed of Zhongguancun Science Park, Beijing Economic-Technological Development Area, Beijing Tianzhu Export Processing Area, Central Business District, Financial Street, and Industrial Development Areas. The Zhongguancun Science Park was the first high-tech science park to be established at the state level in 1988 (Cong, 2001). It is actually composed of several areas: Haidian Development Area, Fengtai Development Area, Changping Development Area, Electronics Town Science and Technology Development Area, and Yizhuang Science and Technology Development Area. It is currently home to 8,000 high-tech enterprises, 180 enterprises of them with an income in excess of 100 million Yuan. Some world-class enterprises such as Lenovo (Legend), Founder, and some other enterprises have also set up businesses in Zhongguancun Science Park.

In addition to these state-funded centers, Beijing has set up 10 city-level and 50 town-level industrial development areas to especially absorb relocated urban industrial companies and foreign investment to develop processing and manufacturing industries. Zhongguancun has been very successful at attracting foreign investment (Wang and Wang, 1998; Zhou and Xin, 2003). The Beijing high-tech area houses over 1,400 foreign-funded enterprises, 43 out of top 500 in the world, R&D institutions run by Microsoft, IBM, Motorola, and 20 other multinational corporations, and about 1,200 enterprises launched by more than 3,600 former overseas students.

Shanghai

Located on the east coast of China, Shanghai is China's largest container port. Like Beijing, Shanghai is one of the four autonomous municipalities in China and has been the leading commercial and financial center of China since the last century. Shanghai has a total area of 6,300 km^2 and, with a population of at least 20 million people, is China's most populous city. Shanghai contributes 5.3% of the nation's GDP (RMB625.1 billion in 2003) and 8% of the nation's total industrial output value (RMB1,126.7 billion in 2003).

In 2003, Shanghai's industrial output reached RMB1,126.7 billion, and it is a national leader in the production of chemical fibers, ethylene, cars, program-controlled exchanges, power-generating equipment, and personal computers. The six key industries of Shanghai are automobiles, petrochemicals and fine chemicals, fine steel and iron, complex machinery, biomedicine, and electronic information. Together the six industries accounted for 63.4% of the total gross industrial output of Shanghai in 2003.

Shanghai has been undergoing major industrial restructuring over the last decade. One change has been the growth of the private sector (36% of the city's GDP in 2003 compared with 1% in 1978). The share of low value-added manufacturing has decreased significantly, particularly the textile and heavy-equipment manufacturing industries as many of them have relocated outside of Shanghai (Table 6).

Although low and medium value-added industries still account for the vast majority of Shanghai's industrial employment, Shanghai has made significant progress in developing its high-tech industries, such as computer, telecommunications equipment, and integrated-circuit (IC) manufacturing (Table 7). Shanghai's output of high-tech industries grew by 50.5% to RMB298 billion in 2003.

The service industries have also been growing significantly. Half of Shanghai's GDP is now attributed to service industries. Between 1980 and 2003, output of the service sector grew by 46 times. Financial industry; retail and wholesale; real estate; transport, warehousing and post; information transmission, computer service, and software; and hotel and eateries are the six major service sectors.

Shanghai is the second largest import–export center in China after Guangdong. Exports grew by 51.2% to US$48 billion in 2003 while imports grew by 57.4% to US$64 billion. Major export markets are the USA, Japan, and the EU. Major imports include electronics parts and components, textiles, plastic raw materials, automobile parts, and accessories. Major import sources were Japan, Taiwan, South Korea, Germany, and the USA.

Table 6: Composition of GDP in Shanghai (in %)

	1990	2002	2003
Primary	4.4	1.6	1.5
Secondary	64.8	47.4	50.1
Tertiary	30.8	51.0	48.4

Table 7: Composition of high-tech industry in Shanghai

	Growth (%)	Share	
	2003	2002	2003
Total gross output value	32.9	100.0	100.0
High and new technology industry	50.5	23.4	26.5
Electronics and information	67.8	14.0	17.7
Biology and medical technologies	18.6	1.93	1.7
Photoelectric, mechanical and electrical products	64.5	2.2	2.7

Source: Shanghai Statistical Yearbook 2003, 2004.

One of the biggest changes in Shanghai's economy in recent years has been the growth of foreign investment (Wei and Leung, 2005). Shanghai is a major destination in China for FDI, accounting for 10.2% of China's total FDI in 2003. The city's cosmopolitan character, sophisticated and affluent consumers, and highly educated and skilled labor force, as well as preferential policies toward foreign investors have made it highly attractive to overseas investors. Foreign investments in Shanghai have been mainly in industry (51.3% of FDI utilized from 1979 to 2003), although in recent years, thanks to liberalization in the services sector, foreign investment in the services sector has increased rapidly. In 2003, investment in the services sector amounted to US$3.3 billion, or 57% of the total utilized FDI. Hong Kong is traditionally the largest source of FDI in Shanghai. Shanghai has also become the favored place of residence in China for Taiwanese investors. In early 2004 it was estimated that more than 400,000 Taiwan residents were living in Shanghai, not counting those who come only for shorter stays. Other major investors in Shanghai are from Japan, the USA, Singapore, and Germany. Foreign-invested enterprises play an important role in Shanghai's economy, accounting for 47.9% of Shanghai's gross industrial output and 63.5% of its total exports in 2003. About 300 of the world's top 500 enterprises have invested in Shanghai, such as GE, Mitsubishi, Itochu, Siemens, Hitachi, and Carrefour.

Shanghai is home to 57 institutions of higher learning (including private universities and colleges and vocational ones) with 331,600 three- or four-year undergraduate students. Over 48,000 postgraduate students are studying in 51 research institutions for master's degrees (36,600) or doctoral degrees (12,300). Eighteen percent of the population of working age has a college degree or higher (Table 4).

Zhangjiang Hi-Tech Park

Shanghai is home to one-third of China's scientific research projects and forty-seven industrial parks, including two national-level science and high-tech parks. The largest is Zhangjiang Hi-Tech Park. Opened in 1992 it occupies over three square kilometers in the rapidly developing Pudong area, a formerly agricultural area located on the eastern margins of Shanghai. In the area are 13 schools of higher learning, including the Shanda University and the Pudong Foreign Languages School, and more than 400 educational organizations, as well as centers established by the Chinese University of Science and Technology, Fudan University, and Shanghai Jiaotong University. The science park houses a variety of incubators sponsored by several government entities intermix as well as numerous large multinational companies, from Revlon to Roche. Three Indian software giants—Satyam, Infosys, and TCS—established branches in Pudong, and it is now the area with the greatest potential for software development.

The park's two leading industries are information technology and modern biotechnology and pharmaceuticals, and its principal aim is to develop innovation and entrepreneurship. The park's main industries are supported by the park's national level bases: the National Shanghai Biotech & Pharmaceutical Industry Base, the National IT Industry Base, the National 863 Information Security Industry Base, and the National Technology Innovation Base. Two major IC manufacturers, the Semiconductor Manufacturing International (Shanghai) Corporation (SMIC), and the Shanghai Grace Semiconductor Manufacturing Corporation (GSMC) are located in Zhangjiang, and have attracted a large number of related enterprises to the park. Zhangjiang also houses more than 10 national-level pharmaceutical R&D organizations, including the Institute of Materia Medica of the Chinese Academy of Sciences, and the National Human Genome Center at Shanghai, and more than 90 well-known bio-pharmaceutical enterprises.

Xi'an

Xi'an is the capital of Shaanxi province, which is located in central China. A relatively underdeveloped province, Shaanxi has abundant reserves of coal, natural gas, petroleum, salt, and other nonmetallic minerals, which account for 24% of the province's total industrial output. While heavy industries account for over 69% of Shaanxi's industrial output, light industries, mainly textiles, food and beverages, electronics and telecommunications equipment, and pharmaceuticals, have gained in importance in recent years, particularly in Xi'an (Table 8).

Shaanxi produces the third largest number of graduates in R&D behind Beijing and Shanghai. Eight percent of the population of working age has a college degree or higher. The province is home to 29 state universities, 3 military universities, 66 private colleges, 126 technical schools, and 15 other institutions of higher education. The major local institute of technology is Xi'an Jiaotong University, which moved from its main campus in Shanghai in 1956 as directed by the central government.

Shaanxi ranks third in terms of overall R&D strength after Beijing and Shanghai. It has more than 2,000 science and technology research institutes. A largest number of R&D institutes and personnel are concentrated in Xi'an itself; it is a historic city with abundant cultural assets, including the famed terracotta army. Xi'an is the largest transportation, telecommunications, information, and finance center in central China, and is located roughly midway between the major cities of Beijing in the East and Chengdu in the west. The city covers an area of 10,108 km^2 and has a population of 6.9 million.

Xi'an developed as China's leading center for the defense industry following a decision by the central government in the 1950s to develop research and military centers in the interior. At that time the intention was to reduce China's vulnerability to airstrikes from the USA. Under the "Military-to-Civilian" initiative, a number of military enterprises in Xi'an have converted their technologies and production capacities to develop and produce products for commercial purposes. Xi'an's expertise in nuclear power and aviation dates from this period. Xi'an was also the launchpad for the central government's millennial Great Western Development (*xibu da kaifa*) campaign in 1999. Infrastructure development initiatives have concentrated on linking Xi'an with other development areas via a new railway to Nanjing and a projected new international airport.

Although not a major import-export zone, foreign trade in Xi'an has increased steadily from US$1,375 million in 1995 to US$2,309 million in 2003. Foreign direct investment has also increased significantly from US$11.54 million in 1990 to US$256 million in 2003 (Table 5).

Xi'an Hi-Tech Industrial Development Zone

Xi'an Hi-tech Industrial Development Zone (XDZ) was founded in May 1988, and was approved as a national development zone by the State Council in March 1991. Since 1994, XDZ has always been ranked among the top national high-tech development

Table 8: Composition of GDP in Xi'an (in %)

	1990	2002	2003
Primary	11.96	5.80	5.39
Secondary	43.05	45.2	44.15
Tertiary	44.99	49.00	50.46

Source: Xi'an Statistical Yearbook.

zones in China and in December 2002, XDZ was cited as one of the most vigorous six cities and areas in China by the United Nations Industrial Development Organization (UNIDO). Xi'an Hi-Tech Zone has around 5,000 enterprises (including 560 foreign-funded enterprises from 28 nations). The share of the three key industries and of others in Xi'an Hi-Tech Zone are:

- Electronics information 39.4%
- Optical-mechanical-electrical integration 35.2%
- Biological medicine 16.7%
- Others 18.7%.

XDZ has successfully attracted foreign investment from America, Japan, Hong Kong, and Singapore as well as from elsewhere in China. More than 30 foreign enterprises have moved to XDZ, including IBM, Intel, Bosch, NEC, and Honeywell. Seventeen companies have established R&D centers in the park including IBM.

Discussion and Conclusions

The three host cities thus show significant differences in their geographic location, nature of the local industries, and workforce (Table 9). These all affect the sources of technical knowledge available locally. However, what has been even more striking is the difference in the level of FDI in the three cities. Although all three cities have shown significant increases in FDI over the last 15 years, clearly Shanghai has a clear lead. These differences in local resources and FDI have clearly had an impact on the nature and performance of the science parks located in each city.

These differences between the three parks in terms of their firms and their external links have an impact on their performance according to various criteria. This is consistent with other studies that suggest that the performance of science parks varies considerably depending on their composition and strategy (Rabellotti and Schmitz, 1999). Thus, the Shanghai High-Tech zone houses the smallest number of high-tech firms of the three regions (Table 10) but demonstrates the highest performance of the three regions in terms of income per worker. Xi'an shows the lowest performance. The differences are even more striking when exports per worker are compared, when the performance of Shanghai is nearly 1000 times that of Xi'an. Of the three zones, Shanghai has shown the greatest improvement in productivity from 2000, when it lagged far behind Beijing. This probably reflects the greatly increased foreign investment and investment in new technologies that have taken place in Shanghai firms.

Firms in the high-tech zones have clearly made significant direct contributions to the local economy—44% of GDP in the case of Beijing, 20% in the case of Shanghai, and 43% in the case of Xi'an. The contribution is less in the case of Shanghai where the local economy is more diverse, and other parts of the economy such as retail have also shown rapid growth. Indirect benefits include attracting private investment and foreign investment. In the case of Shanghai, it was estimated that every one RMB of state investment attracted 14 RMB of private capital, and 99 RMB of foreign capital. In the case of Xi'an, state funding was 173 million RMB compared with private funding of 1.909 billion RMB and foreign investment was 877 million RMB at the end of 2003.

One clear conclusion from the three cases is that, unlike science parks in Europe and North America, the main benefit of the technology parks in China has not been external economies from collocation of firms within the park or within locality; rather they have been more successful in leveraging on linkages forged with FDI. This is not

Table 9: Productivity of high-technology enterprises in development zones

Development Zone	No. of High-Tech Enterprises	No. of Employees	Income (10,000 RMB)	Exports (1000 USD)	Employees per Company	Income per Worker (1000 RMB)	Exports per Worker (1000 USD)
2003							
Beijing	12,030	488,561	28,864,155	329,299	40.6	590.8	0.67
Shanghai	550	115,009	16,109,807	663,450	209.1	1400.7	5.77
Xi'an	2,537	167,390	6,264,743	33,363	66.0	374.3	0.20
2000							
Beijing	6,181	291,473	14,326,050	1,816,922	47.16	559.5	6.24
Shanghai	434	90,563	7,513,625	2,327,534	208.7	203.2	25.71
Xi'an	1,590	97,738	2,741,984	104,079	61.5	123.0	1.07
1993							
Beijing	2,674	91,145	1,363,765	108,932	34.1	15.0	1.20
Shanghai	178	55,264	763,481	70,686	310.5	13.8	1.28
Xi'an	800	20,808	119,993	1,137	26.0	5.8	0.05

Table 10: Contribution of high-technology development zones to local economy

	Beijing High-tech Output	GDP	% Contribution	Shanghai High-tech Output	GDP	% Contribution	Xi'an High-tech Output	GDP	% Contribution
1993	6,695	86,354	7.8	6,502	151,161	4.3	925	22,956	4.0
2000	91,038	247,876	36.7	67,477	455,115	14.8	19,163	64,326	29.8
2003	160,775	366,310	43.9	123,615	625,081	19.8	40,214	94,160	42.7

surprising since one of the aims of the Chinese government in setting up the parks was to attract foreign investment. One practical lesson from this study is that science park initiatives and policies to attract FDI are complementary in the case of China. Unlike Park's (2000) science parks in Korea, science parks in China are not progressing steadily away from reliance on foreign firms but seem to have jumped a stage on the back of FDI. They appear closer to Phelps and Ozawa's (2003) post-industrial form of agglomeration.

Another clear finding from the three cases is that the science parks have benefited the cities that host them. This implies that science park performance cannot be determined independently of the cities that host them, and suggests a need to consider the utilization of knowledge from science parks in the wider context of urban and regional planning.

Acknowledgments

The author gratefully acknowledges the assistance of Professor Wang Kanliang of Xi'an Technological University in providing data on Xi'an High Technology Zone.

References

Appold, S. (2003). Research Parks and the location of industrial research laboratories: An analysis of the effectiveness of a policy intervention, *Research Policy*, vol. 33, pp. 225–243.

Castells, M. and Hall, P. (1994). *Technopoles of the World: The Making of Twenty-first Century Industrial Complexes*, London: Routledge.

Chen, S. and Choi, C. J. (2004). Creating a knowledge-based city: The example of Hsinchu Science Park, *Journal of Knowledge Management*, vol. 8, no. 5, pp. 73–82.

Cong, C. (2001). Zhongguancun: China's Silicon Valley, *China Business Review*, vol. 28, pp. 38–41.

Glaeser, E. L., Kallal, H. D., Scheinkman, J. A. and Shleifer, A. (1992). Growth in cities, *Journal of Political Economy*, vol. 100, December, pp. 1126–1152.

Krugman, P. R. (1993). On the number and location of cities, *European Economic Review*, vol. 37, April, pp. 293–298.

Lindelöf, P. and Löfsten, H. (2003). Science park location and new technology-based firms in Sweden—Implications for strategy and performance, *Small Business Economics*, vol. 20, pp. 245–258.

MacDonald, S. and Deng, Y. (2004). Science parks in China: A cautionary exploration, *International Journal of Technology Intelligence and Planning*, vol. 1, no. 1, pp. 1–14.

Markusen, A. (1996). Sticky places in slippery space: A typology of industrial districts, *Economic Geography*, vol. 72, pp. 293–313.

Marshall, A. (1920). *Principles of Economics: An Introductory Volume*, 8th edition, London: Macmillan.

Massey, D., Quintas, P. and Wield, D. (1992). High tech fantasies: Science parks in society, *Science and Space*, London: Routledge.

Park, S. O. (1996). Networks and embeddedness in the dynamic types of new industrial districts, *Progress in Human Geography*, vol. 20, no. 4, pp. 476–493.

Park, S. O. (2000). Innovation systems, networks, and the knowledge-based economy in Korea, in Dunning, J. (ed.), *Regions, Globalization, and the Knowledge-based Economy*, Oxford: Oxford University Press, pp. 328–348.

Phelps, N. A. and Ozawa, T. (2003). Contrasts in agglomeration: Proto-industrial, industrial and post-industrial forms compared, *Progress in Human Geography*, vol. 27, no. 5, pp. 583–604.

Porter, M. and Stern, S. (2001). Innovation: Location matters, *MIT Sloan Management Review*, vol. 42, no. 4, pp. 28–37.

Rabellotti, R. and Schmitz, H. (1999). The internal heterogeneity of industrial districts in Italy, Brazil and Mexico, *Regional Studies*, vol. 33, no. 2, pp. 97–108.

Siegel, D. S., Westhead, P. and Wright, M. (2003). Science parks and the performance of new technology-based firms: A review of recent UK evidence and an agenda for future research, *Small Business Economics*, vol. 20, pp. 177–184.

Storey, D. and Tether, B. (1998). New technology-based firms in the European Union: An introduction, *Research Policy*, vol. 26, pp. 933–946.

Vedovello, C. (1997). Science parks and university-industry interactions: Geographical proximity between the agents as a driving force, *Technovation*, vol. 17, pp. 491–502.

Walcott, S. M. (2002). Chinese industrial and science parks: Bridging the gap, *Professional Geographer*, vol. 54, no. 3, pp. 349–364.

Walcott, S. M. (2003). Xi'an as an inner China development model, *Eurasian Geography and Economics*, vol. 44, no. 8, pp. 623–640.

Wang, J. C. and Wang, J. X. (1998). An analysis of new-technology agglomeration in Beijing: A new industrial district in the making? *Environment and Planning*, vol. 30, pp. 681–701.

Wang, S., Wu, Y. and Li, Y. (1998). Development of technopoles in China, *Asia Pacific Viewpoint*, vol. 39, no. 3, pp. 281–301.

Wei, Y. D. and Leung, C. K. (2005). Development zones, foreign investment and global city formation in Shanghai, *Growth and Change*, vol. 36, no. 1, pp. 16–40.

Westhead, P. and Storey, D. J. (1995). Links between higher education institutions and high technology firms, *Omega International Journal of Management Science*, vol. 23, no. 4, pp. 345–360.

Zhou, Y. and Xin, T. (2003). An innovative region in China: Interaction between multinational corporations and local firms in a high tech cluster in Beijing, *Economic Geography*, vol. 70, no. 2, pp. 129–152.

Chapter 16

Urban Concentration of European Business Services and the Role of Regional Policies

Luis Rubalcaba, *University of Alcalá and Servilab, Spain*
Rubén Garrido, *University Institute of Economic and Social Research, Servilab, Spain*

Introduction

Business-related services, and business services in particular, are key driving forces in the development of European cities and regions. These services act not only as followers of economic activity but also as a catalyst. They attract investment and help the growth of enterprises from all economic sectors (agriculture, industry, and services). Since enterprises need services to be competitive, regions, especially those less favored, need a certain endowment of them. High quality business-related services in a region attract investment from other sectors of the economy and create favorable conditions for regional development.[1] However, business-related services concentrate so much in some regions and cities that there is a clear lack of such services in many regions and countries. Trends toward decentralization are still much less important than trends toward more concentration.

The role of business-related services in regional and urban development has been recently recognized by policy makers at national and EU level. Business services have become part of innovation and business-support service activities promoted by local and regional authorities. However, there is still a lack of awareness about their overall importance at national and EU level. Only recently, services have been considered as a priority by the Commission in its guidelines for 2007–2013 programs.[2] There are two

---

[1] Wide literature from academic and policy studies has proven the key role of business services for regional development. See recent works by Daniels, Illeris, Wood, Rubalcaba, Bryson, Bonamy, Gadrey, Beyers, among others. See also the list of selected references at the end of this document.

[2] "Proposal for a regulation of the European Parliament and of the Council on the European Regional Development Fund" [COM(2004) 495 final, Brussels, 14.7.2004].

main reasons behind the lack of political attention regarding the role of business-related services in urban and regional development. On the one hand, there is a lack of data and reliable statistics and related studies, and, on the other hand, there is a materialistic view which insists in denying the added value generated by services, far apart from the tangible value which goods provide.

This chapter shows new evidence on the role of business-related services in regional development. It is based on new statistics (mainly the Audit Urban Eurostat project) and it has been written from the perspective of that service-oriented literature which considers services as fully productive activities. The positive recognition of services, as opposed to the negative perception of services, defining them not by what they are but by what they are not, indicates the role of co-production and integration in the rest of economic activities. As a result of this approach, a set of policy implications is discussed and some policy recommendations are provided in order to strengthen the role of services in the dynamic behavior and growth of cities and regions. The EU is taken as reference case study although the related conclusions could be, to some extent, applied to other geographical spaces in general.

The Links between Advanced Services and Urban and Regional Development[3]

Most of the empirical evidence collected in the related literature reports high concentration rates of business services in certain areas, cities, regions, or countries. Many differences can be observed depending on the type of services whereby these producer services as a whole do not contribute in a significant way to economic and industrial decentralization. Business services locate together in certain places where relative advantages are offered, being their concentration higher than that observed in other economic sectors. Some manufacturing or traditional service sectors are usually quite adapted to the economic bases and structures, but business services location shows impressive concentration of activity in some places while in other the opposite applies. In any case, the phenomenon is rather complex and a great deal of factors interact together. This has been indicated in some key studies on business service location: Marshall, Damesick, and Wood (1987), Coffey and Polèse (1987), Hansen (1990), Bailly, Coffey, Paelinck, and Polèse (1992), Moulaert and Gallouj (1993), Senn (1993), Baró, and Soy (1993), Marshall and Wood (1995), Cuadrado and Rubalcaba (1993), Daniels (1993), Cuadrado Roura and Del Río Gómez (1993), Bonamy and May (1994), Esparza and Krmenec (1994), Illeris (1994, 1996), Illeris and Phillipe, (1993), Rubalcaba (1999), Rubalcaba and Garrido (1998), Wood (2002), among others. Most of these works are mainly region-oriented, although some of them also deal with urban implications in similar directions as the ones undertaken in the recognized works provided by Sassen's chapter (1991) on producer services or by Castells' discussion (1989) about the dialectics between centralization and decentralization of services.

Accordingly, the concentration of business services as such can only be explained by a wide array of factors, whose effects vary (acting in a different way) depending on the specific content of every business service activity. However, common trends indicate

---

[3] Some of the ideas included in this section have been further developed in a previous work by Rubalcaba and Gago (2003). A recent work by Rubalcaba and Merino (2005) also stresses the importance of the links between business services and urban interrelations in conurbations like those existing in the Madrid region.

the remarkable contribution of business services to the establishment of new economic hierarchies and new central places in the global economy (Daniels, 1993). Globalization processes make services move according to new strategies, among which location is an important one. The presence of human resources, clients and information does matter as location factors. The risk of being located in the wrong place is increasing in the new global world. The opportunities created by globalization open up new scenarios where uncertainty and vulnerability are the natural context in which many enterprises work. Within a changing context and variable economic conditions, like the current worldwide recession, many agents try to reduce risks by following the leaders and finding locations where the greatest economic activity is concentrated. Needless to say, certain decentralization strategies reduce risks and uncertainty at some point, in the same way as manufacturing industries do when factories are transferred to developing countries. In this sense, a certain division of labor and feasible working distance through ICT make decentralization strategies possible. This happens mainly in two cases: namely in those services produced in a quite standardized way and in ICT-intensive services, and those suitable to be provided through electronic means. However, trends toward decentralization seem to be more than offset by concentration impulses. In any case, the location of business services is more complex because of the interaction taking place between industry, economic structures and the presence of multinationals (Illeris and Philippe, 1993), among other.

Table 1 presents a summary of factors explaining the key elements behind business services concentration or decentralization. These factors can be divided into five categories, according to different aspects of service provision. Firstly, those factors related to the geo-economic context; secondly, those related to environmental conditions; Thirdly, factors derived from market dynamics; and in the fourth place, those factors related to the entrepreneurial characteristics of firms. Finally, there is the very specific nature of services.

The geo-economic context is in its turn defined by several elements. Firstly, the classical transaction costs and opportunity costs that modify companies' behavior from the point of view of relative costs. Demand-oriented factors are mainly defined by proximity and location of current or potential clients (including here some of the still valid elements pointed out by the Christallian model, Ellger, 1997), and by the economic development and growth, of which income acts as a major indicator. The macroeconomic neoclassical perspective explains growth following the factor endowments given to a place. Production locates where relative scarcity (and relative high prices) is less important. Business innovative intensive services would concentrate where related productive factors—mainly human capital—are more abundant and cheaper. Of course, this neoclassical approach needs to be complemented by the new endogenous growth theories or evolutionist theories reinforcing the role of intangibles and knowledge-explanatory factors behind technological change and total factor productivity gains. As far as innovative business services are concerned, the attention should be focused on the quality of human resources, their level of skills and qualifications (Coffey and Shearmur, 1996; Illeris, 1996). Finally, the role of service economy as such is an important element concentrating business services, since they usually grow parallel to certain services, such as financial services, telecommunications, public administration services, or business services themselves, which turn out to be their main users.

Regarding the geo-economic factors explaining decentralization, neoclassical macroeconomic theories are based on decreasing marginal productivity, what makes the transfer to other places with major economic returns more profitable (as it can be derived from the Solow convergence model). From a microeconomic-based perspective, the decrease in both transportation and communications costs make decentralization

Table 1: Factors explaining business service decentralization or concentration trends

Toward Concentration	Toward Decentralization
Geoeconomic context	
Transaction and opportunity costs	Shrinking traveling costs
Proximity and client location	Shrinking communication costs
Income and economic development	ICT boost
Factor endowments	Decreasing marginal productivity
Productivity gains: skills and qualifications	Manufacturing economic bases
Service-oriented economy	
Environmental conditions	
Agglomeration economies	Environmental negative externalities
Innovative *milieu*	Rise of prices and costs in demanded areas
Urban and regional conditions	Other limits to agglomeration economies
Market dynamics	
Presence of multinationals	Factor mobility
Reputation	Market transparency
Uncertainty	Integration
Trade barriers	
Entrepreneurial profiles	
Requirement for co-ordination	Specialization processes
Integration and concentration of knowledge	Steps toward global strategies
Service nature	
Intensive interactive co-productions	ICT dominance of co-production
Short-time co-productions	Commodification processes
	Long-time co-productions

Source: Rubalcaba and Gago (2003).

easier, reducing opportunity costs. Nowadays, a major factor explaining decentralization is the predominance of ICT in many advanced services, as these new technologies make distance service provision feasible.

Together with these geo-economic factors, environmental conditions are also very relevant. Agglomeration economies have been quoted many times as service concentration factors, even if limits to agglomeration economies apply—particularly in some advanced business services (Moulaert and Gallouj, 1993; Marshall and Wood, 1995). Innovative services take comparative advantages from the innovative milieu or favorable urban and regional conditions. At the same time, some of these services can be produced in independent areas, where high prices, pollution, and congestion externalities can be avoided.

Market dynamics influence business services concentration too. The sole presence of multinationals makes a difference. Some cities, regions, and countries concentrating many multinationals are associated with a high level of reputation and prestige. The "follow the leader" effects (Daniels, 1993) are very important, especially in those contexts dominated by uncertainty. A firm reduces the risk of failure by locating offices in already tested places. On the contrary, mobility factors, human resources in particular, help to decentralize services. The economic market integration and market transparency make the decentralization of certain activities possible. Fair trade is a decentralization factor while trade barriers (legal, economic, cultural, etc.) normally trigger concentration of economic activities.

Entrepreneurial attitudes and organizations have also been studied as factors promoting concentration or decentralization trends in business services location. According to Bonamy and Valeyre (1994) there are two fundamental organizational features that help explain spatial dynamics: specialization and sharing out of tasks; and co-ordination and integration. A high level of specialization and a low need for co-ordination due to standardization of processes implying location is supported by sociotechnical and socioprofessional differences in the labor markets and the local and national systems of employment. They constitute activities that hinge on the guarantee of supply. On the other hand, more organic, integrated activities with more requirements for co-ordination are organized according to the amount of demand. Location in this case depends on the interaction between internal and external activities. The role of networks in service provision is also highly remarkable (May, 1994).

Changes in business organization have an important impact in urban structure. Technological changes in transport and communications have made changes in the organization of business production easier. If there are important location economies, enterprises can transfer their production facilities to highly specialized locations and concentrate management, strategy, and research tasks in other areas, mainly urban, with an important concentration of business services. As a result, the aforementioned organizational and market changes take a territorial dimension in urban areas: cities move from a sector-oriented to a function-oriented specialization, thus resulting in a clear division between manufacturing regions/cities and regions/cities serving as business centers. Since proximity is more important for the strategic functions of businesses (management, quality, innovation, etc.) than for production stages, changing from an urban, sector-oriented specialization to a function-oriented one encourages a greater concentration of services in the territory (Duranton and Puga, 2005).

Finally, the very nature of services influences business service location in a very remarkable way. Many services where interaction between supplier and buyer in the co-production process is intense require physical proximity, which does not determine but influences the location of headquarters and local offices close to the major potential or current markets. On the contrary, other services which are more suitable for ICT implementation and provision through ICT do not request high proximity requirements and tend to be very standardized or commodified. In relation to this, the traditional division between customized services, requiring proximity, and standardized services, enabling the division of labor and the division between production and distribution, is still valid. Nevertheless, some very customized services can be co-produced in a very distant way when complex processes require long-time or specialized co-productions; such is the case of some R&D services.

Figure 1 shows the uneven influence of the most commonly quoted location factors at different space levels. So far, some of the cross-section results are only hypothetical, but they present logical results. Urban concentration of services, innovative in particular, is highly dominated by demand and environmental conditions. From the point of view of information, the results are as expected. Those tasks requiring implicit information need a greater proximity between supplier and customer, a one-to-one contact. Therefore, ICT has a smaller impact and in such way the concentration is higher in the cities than in the regions. Regional concentration is more affected by economic income and supply factors. International comparison should consider the economic base in addition to supply factors. Items like human capital and the presence of multi-nationals are supposed to influence any geographical level to a similar extent. On the other hand, concentration within some city districts is highly determined by supply

Figure 1

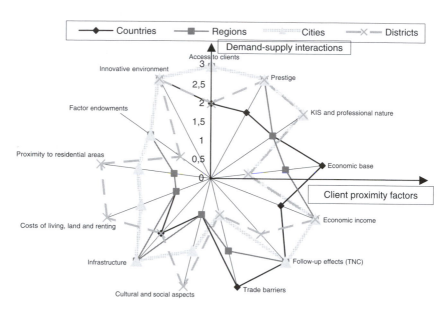

Factors explaining the geographical concentration of business services

factors and, only in certain advanced professional services, by elements of physical proximity with customers.

The traditional industrial pattern establishes that there are base activities and induced ones. The first category includes traditional industries, whilst the second covers most services. The first category is meant to attract the second, which is, in addition, very sensitive to distance and requires great proximity. This explanation establishes once more a hierarchy of central locations. However, the model has serious flaws (Jayet, 1994): the barriers between base and induced activities are vague and what is more, there are basic activities which can turn non-basic activities into their location criterion.

Business-related services can act as base activities when the effects of distance are reduced and those of scale are emphasized. This is compatible with the fact that the movement of business services is inscribed to a large degree in the pre-existing urban hierarchies and contributes to their reinforcement.[4] Hansen (1990) argued that "producer services—carried out both within manufacturing firms and by 'independent' enterprises—play a pivotal role in expanding the division of labor, productivity, and per capita income." This was supported by empirical analysis of metropolitan areas in major US regions and in the nation as a whole. It is obvious that, today, services can no longer be considered as mere followers of manufacturing industry, according to

---

[4] Jayet (1994) establishes three types of location: external (through Weber transport costs models, etc.); Hedonic, through external attributes that suppose implicit prices (due to organizational needs of the company, relationships with the local work market, etc.); territorialization (through the economic organization of the territory; milieus, industrial districts, etc.). This last approach grants an active role to the territory and the location possibilities of business services.

Figure 2

Percentages of employees working in knowledge-intensive services. Source: Hutchins and Parkinson (2004) based on Eurostat, Regions, 2003

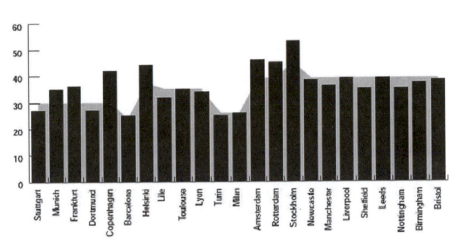

neo-industrial theses, but they represent, in Gadrey's words, "a decisive principle in the urban hierarchy of the metropolis" (1992, p. 120). He claims that business services

> are not only facilitators of economic activity, but also play a role in attracting other activities and export of services outside the city or region. [. . .] It could be argued that the majority of empirical studies carried out [. . .] from the sixties and eighties confirms the validity of this second concept (in comparison to neo-industrial theses) in developed countries.

Previous, related empirical works published in 1999 and 2003 (see reference list) include empirical evidence about the correlation between business services and economic development. Other recent evidence stresses the role of services in regional and urban competitiveness, through the growth of the new learning economy (OECD, 2001), and in innovation and competitiveness (Parkinson and Hutchins, 2004; Hutchins and Parkinson, 2005), although the linkage with core cities does not always have the expected intensity, given the main economic and performance indexes based on regional data (Figure 2). Recent statistical data allow us to have a better measurement of the role of services in urban development.

The Role of Private–Public Interactions in Business Services Growth

Leading cities and regions concentrate the majority of highly qualified business services in Europe due to the interaction between different agents creating a service economy at regional level: private business-related services suppliers, clients of services—users—, business-support services and the institutional framework. Concerning the last two actors it is important to notice that some of the most successful business service policies at regional level are found in those regions already leading the international concentration of business services. Therefore, this kind of service policies are not just "social" policies for less developed regions.

Less developed regions normally have an important lack of private business-related services, so the institutions and business-support services act sometimes as substitutes of private business-related services. As a result, the benefits of the complementarities between private and public-oriented services are less relevant than in more advanced regions. Moreover, developed regions export services to the rest of the regions and, in particular, to less developed ones. They also import services from other competitive regions where prices are lower. In this sense, less developed regions have the possibility to develop competitive advantages and exporting services to top regions, following the current examples provided by Ireland or India. There are opportunities for both competitive regions based on low wages and competitive regions producing high quality services.

To obtain these competitive advantages as well as the service endowments needed for local services users, policymakers promote interaction, which has already proven successful in regions with top business-related services: interaction between suppliers and clients, between public and private services, between best practices and failure practices. In such context a business-related services policy should promote both the supply and the demand of services, both private services and business services, and the transformation of bad practices into best practices. Figure 3 summarizes the aforesaid interrelations.

Summing up, the latter is an example of a complex, multidimensional process with a permanent feedback. Without any doubt, business services are nowadays a key factor: they improve business competitiveness and allow a better management of changes in an economic environment marked by the lack of stable demand, customisation, and an increasingly shorter product life. Therefore, those regions (and, more precisely, cities) with a good business services supply are better positioned to locate in their territory those business functions with greater added value. As a result of

Figure 3

The role of regional interactions and related policy needs in a service-informed and global economy

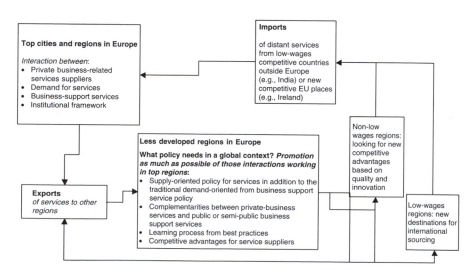

this, they will be able to offer a higher remuneration for their production factors (mainly work) than other areas where businesses are subject to a strong international competition led by prices. In this way, business services are identified as linking factors between the urban and regional environment and the new global economy.

The Urban Concentration of Business Services in Europe

Some Stylized Facts

The aim of this chapter is to point out some of the abovementioned aspects by using a new database applicable to European cities.

Table 2 shows some basic features of the main urban variables in relation to their level of inequality (taking dispersion as measuring factor) between the European cities and those we have considered as the most important cities.

First, the level of inequality in the main macroeconomic variables (population and GDPc) is highly noticeable. Urban Audit shows results for European cities with just over 50,000 inhabitants and those whose population clearly surpasses one million. The features of top range cities as opposed to the total are clear:

- Higher levels of population, positive dynamics in population growth, and less inequality in its dimensions.
- Less inequality also in the levels of income per capita.
- Generally speaking, regarding the production structure of cities, it can be said that the level of similarity is higher among top range cities than in the total, with clearly lower variation coefficients in almost all major economic sectors (with the exception of agriculture and hotel and catering industry).
- Data referring to business services activities are especially significant. The presence of services in these cities is 43% higher than in the total of the sample, with a level of dispersion notably lower.

These results would prove the importance of agglomeration economies, and, therefore, of proximity factors as key factors in service location. Figure 4 illustrates the correlation between the population and the importance of business services, showing

Table 2: Simple concentration (inequality) index in key urban variables

	No. of Cities Large Range	Variation Coefficient	No. of Cities Top Range	Variation Coefficient
Population	257	1.67	53	1.22
GDP per capita	146	0.90	53	0.39
% Agriculture	197	4.36	41	5.23
% Manufacturing	224	0.45	46	0.38
% Horeca	224	0.26	46	0.14
% Transport and communications	222	0.46	46	0.54
% Business services	222	0.46	46	0.23
% Social and public services	224	0.33	46	0.34

Source: Based on Eurostat data (Urban Audit data).

Figure 4

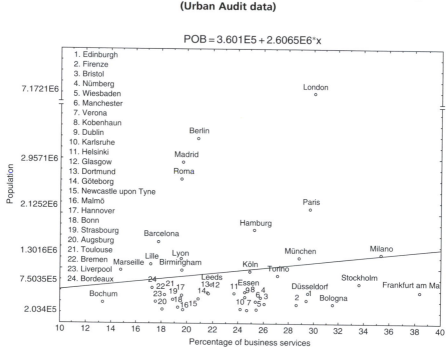

Location of business services and population. Source: Based on Eurostat data (Urban Audit data)

a clearly positive, though weak, relation. On the other hand, the relation between GPCpc and employment rate in business services is much more evident (Figure 5). It is not easy to draw conclusions on the causality in the relation, especially when some factors which can be used to explain the location of business services (human capital, proximity with high added value business, etc.) are concentrated in regions (and cities) with high income levels. The presence of business services guarantees a positive growth dynamic, which makes it very difficult to tell cause from effect. In any case, it goes beyond the objective of this contribution.

However, the importance of services, and especially of business services, and the income levels have a lot to do with the structural change taking place in the economies (especially in the most advanced ones).[5]

As a matter of fact, Table 3 shows some important correlations between the percentage of business services and some relevant variables of urban economic structure:

- Generally speaking, it is clearly evident that those cities with greater presence of business services have a more dynamic labor market, featuring a greater participation (activity) and better additional results (lower unemployment rates). This has a special significance among the 53 top-range cities selected for the sample in comparison to the rest.

---

[5] Garrido (2002, 2004) shows how Spanish regional growth can be explained by the structural change and the importance of services in this process.

Figure 5

GDP per capita and business services employment. Source: Based on Eurostat data (Urban Audit data)

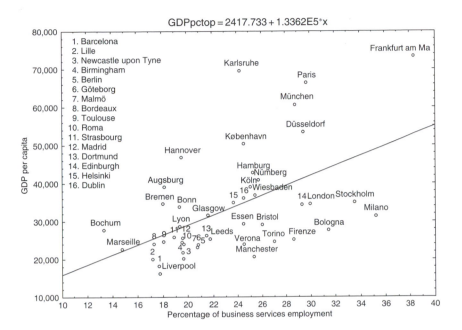

$$GDPpctop = 2417.733 + 1.3362E5*x$$

Table 3: Correlation between the importance of business services and some relevant variables

	Top Urban Areas	All Urban Areas
	% BS	% BS
Active population	0.4959 N = 40 p = 0.001	0.1491 N = 190 p = 0.040
Unemployment	−0.5626 N = 40 0	−0.3403 N = 184 0
% Manufacturing	−0.0514 N = 46 p = 0.734	−0.4854 N = 220 0
% Agriculture	−0.0146 N = 40 p = 0.929	−0.4537 N = 192 0
% Transport and Communications	0.0053 N = 46 p = 0.972	0.0696 N = 220 p = 0.304
% Social and Public Services	−0.5206 N = 46 0	−0.3083 N = 220 0

- In relation with the urban production structure, the results are equally interesting. There is a clear negative relation between business services and agriculture (for the whole of the sample) and between business services and industry. There is a similar relation with public services.
- For the reduced sample, the trends are the same, but the intensity is lower. In fact, the negative relation with industry is not important, which could indicate that, especially among top cities, there is a change from a model of sector-related specialization to a model of function-related specialization, with the presence of business services and industrial business developing activities of greater added value in these cities.

This would also justify the importance of intangible elements in goods and service production, which can be summarized in the need to integrate information to all production processes. Since information is increasingly important (information on new markets, processes, products, quality, innovation . . . , all of them intangible materials), the city becomes the perfect vehicle to spread out that information and represents a radical change in the concept of periphery (geographical) toward other concepts emphasizing accessibility as a key factor (European Commission, 2004). See Figure 6.

Bearing in mind that urban specialization is not sector-but function-related (Duranton and Puga, 2005), we could expect a higher concentration of business services in those cities with a clearly different role from that of the rest. For this purpose, ANOVA technique has been applied in order to spot the differences in the presence of

Figure 6

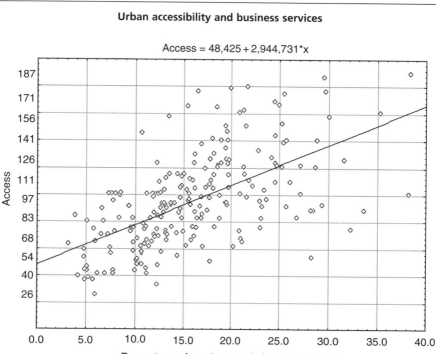

Urban accessibility and business services

Access = 48,425 + 2,944,731*x

Percentage of employment in business services

business services among capital cities and the rest and in those cities with a clear international orientation.

Figure 7 illustrates the analysis results and shows how the differences are not so noticeable regarding countries and their capital cities (the presence of business

Figure 7

The presence of BS and the type of city (capital or international)

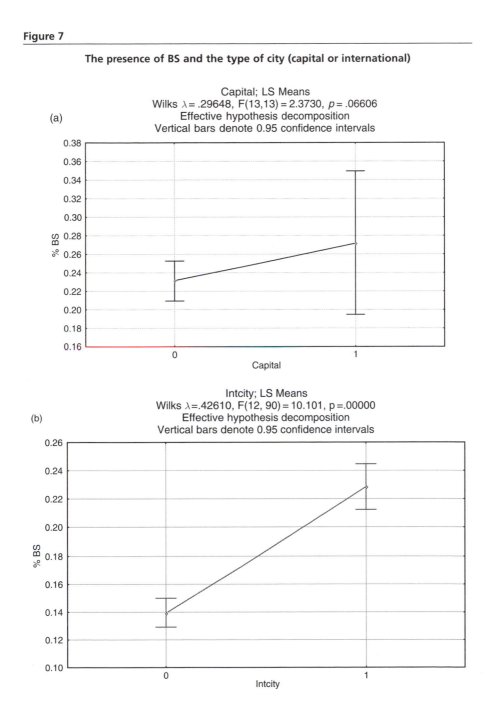

services has no statistic relevance) while it is clear that the cities with international orientation are those with the greater presence of business services. Besides, this would prove the importance of urban features while explaining the presence of business services and not an administrative decision (as it is the State Capital). Indeed, it would prove that inequalities can increase as far as countries will not have cities with such functions being able to attract or generate business services activities.

Toward an Exploratory Approach of Business Service Urban Location in Europe

All the previously analyzed elements allow us to provide a series of hints on factors which can explain, with a deeper analysis, a greater presence of business services. A joint analysis of all the information available in Urban Audit allows us to display the most important factors among those presented above. For this purpose, we have carried out a Principal Components Analysis (PCA) making possible the extraction of big factors to explain the differences in relation to the presence of business services (Table 4).

The four selected factors explain close to 70% of total variance (67%), which provides a very positive result given the 12 variables used in the analysis. The elements related to what we have named "connectiveness" are specially relevant. Connectiveness is a factor usually correlated in a positive manner with transport accessibility and the results of the labor market (employment rates). In this way, connectiveness can be defined as a dimension linking cities with the rest of the economic world. For this reason, an adequate provision of transport infrastructures can be at least as important as an adequate provision of advanced services for business.

Table 4: Principal components analysis: Results

	Factor 1 (Connectiveness)	Factor 2 (Size and Producer Services)	Factor 3 (Social and Public Services)	Factor 4 (Population Growth)
Population	0.354789	0.483674	−0.464618	
Population growth		−0.410832		−0.530871
GDP per capita	0.442278			−0.468550
Access transportation	0.794907			
Working force				0.521899
Unemployment rate	−0.831513			
% Business services	0.761523	0.450800		
% Manufacturing	−0.656874	−0.439428	−0.460124	
% Agriculture		−0.657882		0.502464
%Trasport and Communications	−0.426867	0.526364	−0.334301	−0.260929
% Social and public services			0.902084	
% Horeca services	0.603999	−0.499882		

Note: Coefficients of less than 0.3 are not plotted.
Source: PCA based on Eurostat data (Urban Audit data).

The PCA also points out that these services are correlated to urban dimension/size and the provision of other less advanced services for production. It is to be highlighted that these two urban dimensions (connectiveness and size/producer services) are correlated to social and public services or population growth. The most "quantitative" aspects of urban evolution would not be considering the most "qualitative" ones, linked to the connection of a city with its physical and knowledge-related environment, the real vertebrate axis of competition advantages in the international urban hierarchy.

Final Remarks and Policy Implications

Nowadays, business services have a great significance as activity sector, location factor for other activities, and as an element improving the competitiveness of the territory. The concentration of business services activities is highly noticeable and there are important difficulties to reduce inequalities in this field. This is specially significant as far as the lack of business services can imply the lack of possibilities to develop advanced activities which generate an important added value in the territory. Thus, we might be witnessing the configuration of a new regional periphery (of cities) which do not fulfil the basic functions for business (lack of international cities). Therefore, these cities are rather production centers and not centers for knowledge generation. Not only do these new peripheries represent a physical configuration, but they are also linked to the difficulties of information access and therefore to the role their cities play in the contact network of reference territories.

Resulting from the above, the relevance of business services, as an instrument for regional policy, is increasingly higher. This final section underlines the importance of the debate on how to improve the role of high quality business services in regional policy, guaranteeing complementarities and synergies between public and private services. To pursue this aim, there is a need for better information on ongoing initiatives, instruments and operational conditions as well as the underlying factors behind, respectively, success or failure of these actions. These can be the major four objectives of an urban and regional policy on business services.

(1) To design and put forward enterprises and regional and urban policies useful to increase the business services endowments in less developed regions and cities.
(2) To evaluate how current regional (structural funds, other regional policies) and enterprise policies (innovation policies, business-support services) can be used to promote more services and competitive services (quality, prices, employment) in European regions and cities.
(3) To benchmark best practices among member states, regional governments, and regional development agencies.
(4) To integrate policies toward private business-related services and policies toward business-support services in a comprehensive and complementary framework.

From these major policy objectives some concrete actions can be suggested. A first conclusion can be drawn from the complex and wide range of organizations providing business-related services in the regions. Besides private enterprises, there are technological and scientific parks, business innovation centers, incubators, research and training organizations, chambers of commerce, professional associations, etc. This disparity of instruments and forms gives a rich economic background for developing enterprise and regional and urban policies. Each body or organization is responsible for a certain level of integration between enterprises and regional development. It is important to promote the knowledge on the wide set of initiatives and instruments (e.g., subsidies, tax benefits, and public-financed services) that are useful to promote enterprises services, both for suppliers and clients. In this sense, a catalogue or register of different bodies and initiatives would be highly useful and appreciated by enterprises.

Not all initiatives promoting services produce the same results. Some are very successful, other obtain a moderate success. Some are a failure and waste of public resources. The differences in policy intervention (independence degrees of regional programmes), regional models (centralized, decentralized, private participation, etc.), and the balance between market failures and public failures (difficult to evaluate before, during, and after action takes place) all explain some of the unequal results of business-services promotion initiatives throughout Europe. Study actions would be required to understand the criteria defining success and failure in all these initiatives.

In particular, it is necessary to identify, analyze, and promote best practices for investment in business-related services in less favored regions in order to rationalize and consolidate present efforts based on the analysis of the needs of regional economic structures.

The role of structural funds in services should also be researched and evaluated. Should there exist certain possibilities of improvement and of making services more efficient within the different programmes, some action should be undertaken. Structural funds should promote, among their objectives, the best possible services in regions, from the point of view of both supply and demand, of the complementarity between public and private services, and of the ex-ante and ex-post evaluations based on specifically defined criteria for services.

As a consequence of former or ongoing initiatives, certain specific complementary actions could be evaluated. To start with, the promotion of training courses on initiative review programmes should be evaluated in order to encourage those obtaining better results and revise the approach of those involving under-utilized resources. The exploitation of synergies is also to be evaluated. We also need to identify the needs of companies and evaluate on a case-by-case basis the advisability of providing subsidies for customer companies or of promoting public or private supply of services. There is a need to determine the field of action for public services in accordance with competition rules. The participation of private agents in public and State centers, as well as self-financing should also be encouraged.

Figure 8 shows a full 3-type range of possible regional policies for business services, at regional, national, and EU level. It summarizes three main types of policies: first, those policies oriented to the promotion of better information, better statistics, and better knowledge about the topic; second, benchmarking and best practices of existing policies; and third, the support of competitive business-support services interacting in a synergetic way with the existing private business service sector. The axe related to better knowledge calls for action in the research world. Further research is needed to obtain a better understanding on the links between services, knowledge creation and diffusion, and urban dynamism and status within the global hierarchy of cities.

Figure 8

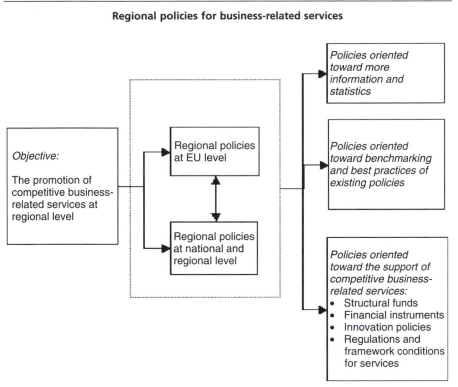

Regional policies for business-related services

References

Bailly, A., Coffey, W., Paelinck, J. H. P. and Polèse, M. (1992). *Spatial Econometrics of Services*. Aldershot: Avebury.

Baró, E. and Soy, A. (1993). Business service location strategies in the Barcelona metropolitan region, in Daniels, P. W. et al. (eds), *The Geography of Services*. London: Frank Cass.

Bonamy, J. and May, N. (1994) *Services et mutations urbaines*. Paris: Antropos, Economica.

Bonamy, J. and Valeyre, A. (1994). Services, relation de service et organisation, in Bonamy, J. and May, N. (eds), *Services et mutatons urbaines: Questionnements et perspectives*. Paris: Anthopos, Economica.

Castells, M. (1989). *The Informational City*. Oxford, UK, and Cambridge, USA: Blackwell.

Coffey, W. J. and Polèse, M. (1987). Trade and location of producer services, *Environment and Planning A*, vol. 19, no. 5, pp. 597–611.

Coffey, W. J. and Shearmur, R. G. (1996). The growth and location of high order services in the Canadian urban system, 1971–1991. North American Meetings of the Regional Science Association International. Washington, DC, 14–17 November.

Cuadrado Roura, J. R. and Del Río Gómez, C. (1993). *Los servicios en España*. Madrid: Pirámide.

Cuadrado, J. R. and Rubalcaba, L. (1993) Regional trends in business services supply in Spain, in Daniels, P. W. et al. (eds), *The Geography of Services*. London: Frank Cass.

Daniels, P. W. (1993). *Service Industries in the World Economy*. Oxford: Blackwell.

Duranton, G. and Puga, D. (2005). From sectoral to functional urban specialisation, *Journal of Urban Economics*, vol. 57, no. 2, March 2005, pp. 343–370.

Ellger, C. (1997). Planning Christallerian landscapes: The current renaissance of central place studies in East Germany, *The Service Industries Journal*, vol. 17, no. 1, pp. 51–68.

Esparza, A. and Krmenec, A. (1994). Producer services trade in city systems: Evidence from Chicago, *Urban Studies*, vol. 31, no. 1, February, pp. 29–46.

European Commission (2004). A Study on the Factor of Regional Competitiveness, Preparatory studies for the third cohesion report elaborate by Cambridge Econometrics, University of Cambridge and Ecorys-Nei.

Gadrey, J. (1992). *L'économie des services*. Paris: La Decouverte.

Garrido, R. (2002). *Cambio Estructural y Desarrollo Regional en España*. Madrid: Pirámide.

Garrido, R. (2004). El crecimiento regional en España: Convergencia relativa, divergencia absoluta, Papeles y Memorias, Real Academia de Ciencias Morales y Políticas.

Hansen, N. (1990). Do producer services induce regional economic development? *Journal of Regional Science*, vol. 30, no. 4, 465–476.

Hutchins, M. and Parkinson, M. (2005). Competitive Scottish cities? Placing Scotland's cities in the UK and European context, *Scottish Executive Social Research*. Edinburgh: Blackwell.

Illeris, S. (1994). La localisation des producteurs et utilisateurs de services, in Bonamy, J. and May, N. (eds), *Services et mutatons urbaines: Questionnements et perspectives*. Paris: Anthopos, Economica.

Illeris, S. (1996). *The Service Economy: A Geographical Approach*. Chichester: John Wiley & Sons.

Illeris, S. and Phillipe, J. (1993). Introduction: The role of services in regional economic growth, in Daniels et al. (eds), *The Geography of Services*. London: Frank Cass.

Jayet, H. (1994). Services et space, in Bonamy, J. and May, N. (eds), *Services et mutatons urbaines: Questionnements et perspectives*. Paris: Anthopos, Economica.

Marshall, N. and Wood, P. (1995). Services & Space, *Key Aspects of Urban and Regional Development*. Singapore: Longman Singapore Publishers.

Marshall, N., Damesick, P. and Wood, P. (1987). Understanding the location and role of producer services in the United Kingdom, *Environment and Planning A*, vol. 19, pp. 575–596.

May, N. (1994). Introduction, in Bonamy, J. and May, N. (eds), *Services et mutatons urbaines: Questionnements et perspectives*. Paris: Anthopos, Economica.

Moulaert, F. and Gallouj, C. (1993). The locational geography of advanced producer firms: The limits of economies of agglomeration, in Daniels, P. W. et al. (eds), *The Geography of Services*. London: Frank Cass.

OECD (2001). *Cities and Regions in the New Learning Economy*. Paris: OECD.

Parkinson, M. and Hutchins, M. (2004). *Competitive European Cities: Where do the Core Cities Stand?* Office of the Deputy Prime Minister, UK, London.

Rubalcaba, L. (1999). *Business Services in European Industry—Growth, Employment and Competitiveness*. Luxembourg: European Commission, DGIII-Industry.

Rubalcaba, L. and Gago, D. (2003). Location and role of innovative business services in European regions: Testing some explanatory factors, *The Service Industries Journal*, vol. 23, January.

Rubalcaba, L. and Merino, F. (2005). Urban demand-supply interactions in business services, *The Service Industries Journal*, vol. 24, January.

Rubalcaba, L. and Garrido, R. (1998) *Crecimiento y geografía de los servicios a empresas en el contexto de la nueva sociedad servindustrial: El caso de la Comunidad de Madrid*. Madrid: Comunidad de Madrid.

Sassen, S. (1991). *The Global City: New York, London, Tokio*. Princeton: Princeton University Press.

Senn, L. (1993). Service activities, urban hierarchy and cumulative growth, in Daniels, P. W. et al. (eds), *The Geography of Services*. London: Frank Cass.

Wood, P. (ed.) (2002). *The Business Service Revolution in Europe*. London and New York: Routledge.

Chapter 17

Knowledge Dissemination and Innovation in Urban Regions: An Evolutionary Perspective

Jan G. Lambooy, *Utrecht University and the University of Amsterdam, The Netherlands*

Innovation, Dissemination, and Urban Environments

A generally sustained assumption in modern economic theory is that innovation leads to productivity rise and to increased economic growth. This assumption is based on the idea that innovations are often organizational and technology-related improvements of processes and products that enhance the efficiency and effectiveness of economic organization and of production (Baumol, 2002). A second important assumption is that this process is connected with the nature of the dissemination (or diffusion) of the relevant knowledge via markets and networks of relations between innovating firms and universities and other research organizations (Baumol, 2002; Lambooy, 2003; Audretsch and Keilbach, 2004). Furthermore, in both regional and urban economics a third assumption is accepted, namely that this process of innovation, dissemination, and economic growth is favored by spatial clustering in those agglomerations that are involved in both a worldwide and an intra-regional division of labor, with a con-comitant specialization of firms and cities (Jacobs, 1961; Krugman, 1995; van Oort 2003; van der Panne, 2004). In this regard, it is assumed that innovation is—at least partly—influenced by, and dependent on, the kind of urban and social environment involved: It must be a "diversified" and "creative" environment, containing a diversi-fied knowledge base in research as well as various meeting places, and with a creative workforce (Jacobs, 1984; Florida, 2002; Storper and Venables, 2004). Innovation as an act of creating marketable novelties depends on creativity and on the generation, the dissemination, and the application of knowledge. Turning knowledge into commer-cially viable and socially accepted applications is not a one-dimensional and strictly technological road but involves various feedback mechanisms in which intermediaries and indirect links play a role.

The mechanisms behind the processes of the three assumptions are not always made explicit. However, there is at least one common line: In order to get the expected results, knowledge has to be generated, disseminated, and applied by entrepreneurs as "useful knowledge" (Mokyr, 2002; Audretsch and Keilbach, 2004). Knowledge has to be "on the move."

As Machlup (1962) contended, our economies are in a phase of transition to a knowledge-based structure, where innovations lead to an all-encompassing change in the sectoral composition. In this process of change, the basic units (in evolutionary economics: routines, habits, and firms) have to be adjusted, and sometimes even entire systems need to be redesigned. In the case of structural change, often caused by radical innovations, the networks and intermediaries have to adjust their place and function, and even a new architecture of functions and "routines" may sometimes be necessary to survive. Firms and other actors have the ability to create an organizational culture that filters information in an interactive learning process. Exchanging information in a learning process will change both the sender and the receiver of the information, as well as its content. The market mechanism and organizational configurations can influence the nature of the filtering process, but persons (intermediaries, gatekeepers) can do so as well. In this chapter the emphasis is on the influence of urban environments, networks, and patterns of knowledge dissemination on innovation and economic growth. In the first case, the kind of urban economies involved, "externalities" and "spill-over" have received much attention, whereas in the latter case the role of networks and of intermediary persons and structures is emphasized. Intermediaries can select information, alter its contents and then select the channels and the goals for transmission (Hagerstränd, 1952; Rogers, 1995). Insights from evolutionary economics and agglomeration economics will be used here, as well as modern network theory. The chapter ends with some general conclusions.

Networks, Innovation, and Diffusion

Innovation theory focuses rather on knowledge generation and the development of products and technologies, and not so much on organizational factors and dissemination (Sorenson and Fleming, 2004) or the role of urban environments. The diffusion of knowledge is more than the transfer of ideas, patents, or licenses from persons, firms, or departments to other persons, firms, or departments. It often depends on learning and interaction in networks (internal to the multi-locational enterprise, external among firms) and on the "channels of diffusion" (Pred, 1976). This process is embedded in social, institutional, and spatial structures. There are many kinds of channels, and diffusion can be "direct" or "indirect." In the case of personal contacts, the transfer of certain attributes occurs through contacts, although these contacts may not always be intentional, planned, or designed. This relates to the use of networks in diffusion analysis. Here it is argued that networks are organizational configurations with four functions: (1) to facilitate cooperation between persons and firms; (2) to transmit information and knowledge between economic actors (individuals, firms, governments), in order to enable them to use that information; (3) to provide connections or channels for the transfer of information and knowledge; and (4)—the oldest function—as markets to enable the exchange of goods and money. In general, the dissemination or transfer of novelties occurs in many kinds of networks. A network of innovators consists of nodes, links, and message contents. Sometimes, the transfer of information to partners in the process takes place in an indirect way, through intermediate structures or intermediary persons or firms. The concept of the node can be used for cities (cf. Hagerstränd, 1952; Pred, 1976) and for intermediate persons and structures (Lambooy, 2003), as well as for the diffusion from websites to persons (Barabasi, 2002). The diffusion of knowledge, in addition to networks, also needs primarily efficient markets and institutions (Baumol, 2002). However, networks can create the necessary channels for markets and institutions to function properly. Access to information is decisive for entrepreneurs to succeed in introducing novelties or innovations. However, access is often hampered, due to barriers in the selection environments. The selection of successful novelties occurs in the three selection environments: the markets (based on competition), the institutions (the set of rules that has to be followed by actors in markets), and the regional structures (dealing with the effects of spatial structure, distance (costs), and the advantages of proximity, measured by, for instance, external economies and social networks).

Successful novelties have to be accepted by others, first within the firm (or another kind of organization), then in markets, either within the same region or elsewhere. In the latter case, other kinds of institutions and markets can influence the chances of success and survival.

Many parts of the processes and structures involved are not well known yet. Hence, the outcome of the selection process for new ideas and products is unpredictable. Moreover, the mechanisms of knowledge transmission and the channels of knowledge diffusion in urban agglomerations are not known either. Distance is often assumed to be important in explaining externalities and spillover (Jaffe et al., 1993; van Oort, 2003), but it is generally accepted that urban regions play a significant role in the entire process of generation, dissemination, and application. Neither distance costs nor proximity as such is decisive, however, but rather the competences of individuals, the character of the cities involved (Jacobs, 1961; Florida, 2002), and the nature of (interregional) networks. This issue is developed in the theory of agglomeration economies (Krugman, 1995; van Oort, 2003).

Evolutionary economics focuses on the creation of novelties, more in particular on those that are commercialized: innovations in the Schumpeterian sense (Boschma and Lambooy, 1999). Other, noncommercialized novelties can be developed in cultural, biological, and political sectors. According to Florida (2002), creativity is a concept that encompasses more than knowledge, and the creative classes are decisive for the economic growth of urban regions. The next section provides a brief survey of the relation between innovation and the generation and dissemination of knowledge.

Innovation and the Generation and Dissemination of Knowledge

Innovation is the development and introduction of novelties, sometimes leading to radical system changes. We distinguish two phases in this innovation process:

(1) Invention, discovery, R&D: the incentive to innovate lies with the supply and demand side.

(2) Innovation defined as diffusion (transfer), adjustment, adoption and imitation: combined with application and introduction in the market.

In this iterative and interactive process, technologies, products, or services are relevant, but so is the need to continuously adjust organizations. Innovation and transfer are based on the creation and the dissemination of novelty, new knowledge, or the introduction of existing knowledge in organizations (mainly firms) in a new way. The result is that after a phase of increasing variation, the variation can be reduced due to "selection" by markets, institutions, or spatial contexts, which will mean the end of products or processes with a lower than expected "utility" (Mokyr, 2002: 5). If there are no cognitive and institutional barriers, and when markets function properly, successful innovations will rapidly disseminate. In this process, we can distinguish three main groups of knowledge workers:

(1) Knowledge generators, in research organizations and firms;
(2) Knowledge appliers, who "translate" ideas into products and services; and
(3) Knowledge disseminators, who are actively involved in the diffusion process.

Entrepreneurs, wholesalers, consultants or lawyers, as well as civil servants working in license and patent offices—they can all be disseminators.

Three attributes of persons (especially entrepreneurs) are often assumed to be at the origin of innovation: knowledge, creativity, and a risk-taking attitude (Audretsch and Keilbach, 2004). Although creativity and knowledge generation show a strong overlap, they are not identical and, besides, they are not always present in one person in combination with the necessary risk-taking attitude. Creativity is often connected with the competence to deal with nonstandardized problems and situations, leading to previously unknown solutions. This capacity is not always based on systematic knowledge generation; it is strongly personal, sometimes linked with tacit knowledge instead of codified knowledge. Tacit knowledge is knowledge tied to an individual, but this does not necessarily mean that it is not standardized or shared knowledge because many tacit activities are standardized (like with traditional handicraft activities) and do not lead to new perspectives. Risk-taking can be an attribute of both persons and financial organizations, like in the case of venture capital. With Mokyr (2002), Audretsch and Keilbach (2004: 60) contend that there is a gap between "knowledge" and "economic or exploitable knowledge." Mokyr (2002) distinguished between "science" proper and "science, ready to apply," for which he uses the letters Ω and Λ, respectively. It can be argued that entrepreneurs are the main actors in bridging the gap and driving the selection process in creating a diversity of knowledge. However, in mainstream economic theory entrepreneurs are often disregarded, as are consumers or, in general, the demand side (Baumol, 2002; van den Ende and Dolfsma, 2005).

Creativity and knowledge are increasingly seen as the basis of an entirely new episode of economic development. However, it is necessary to be somewhat cautious with that view, and a special observation has to be made concerning the concept of the "knowledge-based economy." It is sometimes suggested that this kind of economy is completely different from the "previous capitalist industrial society." Knowledge is then, often, defined as a separate production factor, next to capital and labor. However, this is beside reality, as Machlup (1962) already contended. Knowledge cannot be seen as dissociated from other production factors, from industrial goods and the market or capitalist system of production (Sokol, 2004). But knowledge cannot be found only in "the heads and hands of knowledge workers" (tacit knowledge), it can also be codified and can then be found in goods (e.g., in computers), or it can be "incorporated" in written statements (like books, patents). Codified knowledge, which is developed by knowledge workers, can also be used in mass production, and even simple goods can then be produced "smarter" than before. Still, they remain just goods, produced in a capitalist system where producers attempt to get high profits and better market shares. The same goes for the services. The current mainstream of innovation studies focuses on the relation between science and innovation. Sometimes, scientists, universities and other research institutes—not the interaction with other persons and structures—are seen as the only origins of innovation. This especially applies to radical innovations. A strong role of universities is generally assumed, measured in publications, patents, and licenses. The process can start from both the supply and the demand side. The latter occurs when people or firms become conscious of a problem, after which they, or others, attempt to solve this problem or to break down the barriers to further development.

The principal constituent elements of the iterative and interactive innovation process are:

(1) Consciousness of a problem
(2) A search process to solve the perceived problems
(3) Generation of knowledge
(4) Using and adjusting knowledge to find solutions
(5) Testing, reframing and developing applications
(6) Introduction in the market
(7) Selection of the successful solutions
(8) Evaluation and feedback.

In all these phases, interaction between the actors and with the nature of the diffusion channels and their social and urban contexts is important. Cooperation and association are seen as organizational venues to organize this process (Nooteboom, 2000).

It is true that most scientists can be seen as creative actors, but not always as innovators, because they are not involved in the application and commercialization on markets. Innovations tend to be analyzed as a supply side–based technological process with marketable outputs, based on scientific input. Yet, societal demand and political pressure can also lead to research and new ideas, as the pressure from consumer groups has proven. Nonaka and Takeuchi (1995) called this the "knowledge conversion process." Another perspective is to distinguish between the various stages of the dissemination process: generation, introduction, imitation, adoption, and adaptation. Many authors have argued that one of the principal ways of dissemination is through interacting with firms, purchasing from and selling to other firms, or cooperating in some way. An interesting channel of diffusion is through spin-off from a parent firm, when new enterprises emerge, based on former employees of that parent firm (Stam, 2003). This can mean new forms of cooperation and codevelopment, or it can lead to increased competition to select the surviving novelties or innovations.

Selection is an active process. The behavior of economic subjects is influenced by the nature of the regional environment. Currently, the ideas of Jane Jacobs are once more a rich source for considerations on this subject. In her earlier work, Jacobs contended that the most important environmental condition is differentiation, by which she really meant increasing variety and complexity, as she explicitly indicated in the last chapter of her book *Death and Life of Great American Cities* (Jacobs, 1961, 1984). The "emergence of new variations" of economic activity is crucial for the continued existence of a neighborhood, a city, or a region, and can later serve as a selection environment for further initiatives (Johnson, 2001). As Florida (2002) observes, a creative environment is favorable for economic growth.

The generation and diffusion of knowledge and innovation has to be seen as a "context-sensitive" process. In our case, contexts can be restricted to organizations, networks, or urban environments. In the case of demand-driven innovation, proximity to certain environments with politically innovative governments also can be important to foster research. The Californian attitude to the air pollution caused by cars in the congested region of Los Angeles has led to a politically translated demand from "air-consumers" for rules for car-builders to change their technologies and to reduce "gas-guzzling" and the size of cars. Currently, however, most studies focus on the relation between universities and other research organizations on the one hand and industrial firms on the other hand, because that is often the only part that can be measured by output, like patents.

Cities as an Evolutionary Selection Environment for the Creation and Diffusion of Knowledge

Three authors have been very important to the development of the theory of "agglomeration advantages." Adam Smith developed his idea of the "division of labor," an organizational view connecting improvements in technology with the specialization of knowledge. He contended that cities will expand only if they have an efficient division of labor, both internally and externally, in combination with trade with the specialists elsewhere. Marshall (1890) and Weber (1909, 1929) further developed the concept. Marshall emphasized the transfer of knowledge, largely of the "tacit" type and within the same sector. He argued that knowledge is "in the atmosphere." Intended and unintended transfers of knowledge went not only via direct contacts but also via the labor market when workers moved to other firms. Weber and, later, Hoover (1948) divided agglomeration advantages into two categories, the localization effects and the urbanization effects. The former could be acquired by the division of labor within the same kind of activities and by the cost advantages of scale, and the latter were acquired through the combined effects of the variety of different sectors. This would lead to cheaper inputs in the production processes of complementary activities due to the wide array of choices and the strong competition. Both kinds of advantages also benefit from the quality of improvements through technological and organizational innovation, due to the proximity to research centres and the availability of all sorts of networks, and resulting in a strong access to the sources of information and knowledge. Urban environments are especially advantageous in nonstandardized and nonvoluminous production and for knowledge-intensive services.

Empirical work shows that the regional environment has to be considered as an important condition for the transfer of knowledge for innovation purposes (Lambooy, 2000; Boschma et al., 2002). However, the concept of proximity is more complicated than can be indicated by using descriptions like "physical distance" and "distance costs." Cognitive and social factors are also important here (Boschma, 2005). Social factors can be measured in the effects of trust and reputation. Porter (1990) has developed the idea of a cluster of strongly interconnected and complementary firms, with relations crossing the boundaries of industries. He acknowledges that spatial proximity could be decisive for the successful survival of firms and clusters:

> My theory sees geographic concentration as part of the more general process by which advantage is created and sustained. [. . .] Geographic proximity also has important reputational effects that limit opportunistic behaviour. [. . .] These arguments also help to explain why external economies are most significant within a nation (or region within a nation) and not across nations. (Porter, 1990: 791)

Clusters have a basis in "region-specific" knowledge, resources, and institutions. One of the strong assets of clusters is that they offer many opportunities for the easy transmission of knowledge.

Selection and the capacity of actors to adjust (in time) to their (selection) environment are important for firms to find the right economic and spatial strategy. Changes in technology and in the economic production structure have gradually altered the locational configuration of firms, have changed the sectoral employment composition of the economy, and have had a stimulating effect on cities with headquarters. More in particular, the rise of the service sector and the offices, as employment and management centres, has been important in this regard. The indirect role of certain urban environments in the development of knowledge was already emphasized by the French geographer Jean Gottmann (1961), in his important study of the urbanized Atlantic seaboard of the USA, as well as by Jane Jacobs (1984) and by Richard Florida (2002). This approach is related to the shift in the composition of economic structure, from agricultural and manufacturing to various kinds of services, but also to the functioning of agglomeration economies. Jean Gottmann argued that, in the modern, large metropolitan areas, jobs in manufacturing would be replaced by employment in the "quaternary activities," with work mostly in offices and laboratories. In general, it can be argued that knowledge workers and the "creative class" have an impact on economic growth because they have a high level of education or because they possess many personally tied "tacit knowledge" competences. The direction of the causality (knowledge leading to economic growth, or economic growth leading to high levels of education) is not certain. In a broader perspective, the theory of agglomeration advantages can be used to explain the economic mechanism of the relations between economic growth and the cumulative attraction of cities on firms and knowledge workers, externalities and advantages of agglomeration (van Oort, 2003; van der Panne, 2004).

Many city governments attempt to acquire the status of "knowledge city," often without understanding what kind of knowledge city they want to be, or what strategy to follow. Although all urban regions contain "knowledge activities," not all cities can be "knowledge centres." Here we will not present a full typology but just indicate the various possible characteristics, on the basis of which urban governments can pursue their strategies.

There are various kinds of economic activities in which a city can specialize and excel. In the first place, we have to mention the general and differentiated global cities, with all kinds of economic activities and often of a high quality. Usually, such cities show a strong concentration of universities and top research centres, and they also have a variety of headquarters of global companies. The urban regions of New York, London, Tokyo, and Paris are examples of this type of city. Below this "upper class" the variety increases, depending on location and the specialization of activities. The second type of cities can be seen as "cities with specialised global activities." Cities like Singapore, Rotterdam, and Hong Kong have strong logistical and commercial functions. Frankfurt, Vienna, Geneva, Brussels, and The Hague have strong concentrations of international organizations. Cities like Boston and Cambridge (UK) display strong academic specialization. The third type of cities to be mentioned here are "cities with a primarily national character, with combinations of specialised activities." In that case, not one but several special economic activities are concentrated in one city. Examples are Milan, Birmingham, and München. Another kind of urban regions are the "formerly industrial cities," with examples like the Ruhr Area in Germany and the cities in the northern Rust Belt of the USA. However, a large variety of other types of urban regions can be distinguished as well, for instance "the recreational city" (like Las Vegas and Monaco).

All these types of urban regions have to develop their own policies to enhance their knowledge functions, including the construction of clusters and "channels of dissemination." Most often, their strategies focus on developing educational organizations, enhancing the cooperation between universities and firms, and developing international relations. Sometimes an explicit policy is pursued to promote a specific cluster, like a biotech cluster or an ICT cluster. In the previous decades, many countries and cities wanted to be new "Silicon Valleys," or to become a "techno-polis." Currently, the fashion is to foster the "creative class" (Florida, 2002). It can safely be said that especially the large, diversified metropolitan areas are the places where innovation and dissemination benefit most from the characteristics of an innovative environment.

Conclusions: Governments, Governance, and Knowledge

In regional and urban economics there is a link between economic growth and the generation and diffusion of information and knowledge in urban environments. Governments are essentially tied to their territories, while knowledge and innovation function in "functional networks" with links all over the world.

Evolutionary economics connects innovation with changing interactive, dynamic structures, consisting of cooperating partners in regional production. Governance systems, based on cooperation, enable economic actors to fully utilize and expand their competencies. They also encompass governments and organizations that specialize in building cognitive competencies (learning, research) and in setting up interfirm networks. This results in the anchoring of competencies in dynamic institutions and in facilitating the development of new firms, new products, new technologies, and new organizational structures (Lambooy, 1997, 2002, 2003). The role of, in our case, urban and regional governments can be important. Sometimes, a (national, regional, or urban) government attempts to be an intermediating structure, like in the theory on Regional Innovation Systems (Lambooy, 2003; Cooke et al., 2004).

Governments can indeed play a role in facilitating innovation processes by furthering education, research, and networks of dissemination, but here we have to make some observations. First, the sectoral composition of the economy and the kinds of entrepreneurship involved are sometimes difficult to change in the short run. Therefore, the role of governments is often directed to a future further away. Next, city governments do not always have the cognitive competencies to generate knowledge centres and to co-ordinate the development of modern knowledge cities. The process of innovation and knowledge dissemination is not always a consciously designed process but rather an emergent one, developing through creative researchers, entrepreneurs, self-organization, and serendipity (Lambooy and Boschma, 2001). Urban agglomerations have many advantages for specializations in old and new activities, although a certain historical development can lead to path dependency. Differentiated urban environments can further enhance the rise of research centres and of the "creative class." Cities in such environments often display a high share of business services, with much employment in design and in entertainment activities.

Bibliography

Acs, Z. J., D. B. Audretsch and M. P. Feldman. (1994). R&D spillovers and innovative activity. *Managerial and Decision Economics*, vol. 15, pp. 131–138.

Arthur, W. B. (1994). *Increasing Returns and Path Dependance in the Economy*. Ann Arbor: University of Michigan Press.

Audretsch, D. B. and M. Keilbach. (2004). Entrepreneurship and regional growth: An evolutionary interpretation. *Journal of Evolutionary Economics*, vol. 14, no. 5, pp. 605–616.

Barabasi, A.-L. (2002). *Linked: The New Science of Networks*. Cambridge, MA: Perseus Publishers.

Baumol, W. J. (2002). *The Free-market Innovation Machine*. Princeton: Princeton University Press.

Boschma, R. A. (2004). Competitiveness of regions from an evolutionary perspective. *Regional Studies*, vol. 38, no. 6, pp. 1001–1014.

Boschma, R. A. (2005). Role of proximity in interaction and performance: Conceptual and empirical challenges. *Regional Studies*, vol. 39, no. 1, pp. 41–46.

Boschma, R. A. and J. G. Lambooy. (1999). Evolutionary economics and economic geography. *Journal of Evolutionary Economics*, vol. 9, pp. 411–429.

Boschma, R. A., K. Frenken and J. G. Lambooy. (2002). *Evolutionaire Economie*. Bussum: Coutinho publishers.

Boschma, R. A., J. G. Lambooy and V. Schutjens. (2002). Embeddedness and innovation. In M. Taylor and S. Leonard (eds), *Embedded Enterprise and Social Capital*. Aldershot: Ashgate Publishing, pp. 19–37.

Cooke, Ph, M. Heidenreich and H.-J. Braczyk. (2004). *Regional Innovation Systems*. London: Routledge.

Deroïan, F. (2002). Formation of social networks and diffusion of innovations. *Research Policy*, vol. 31, pp. 835–846.

Florida, R. (2002). *The Rise of the Creative Class*. New York: Basic Books.

Frenken, K. and F. G. van Oort. (2004). The geography of research collaboration. In Ph Cooke and A. Piccaluga (eds), *Regional Economies as Research Laboratories*. Cheltenham: Edward Elgar, pp. 38–57.

Fujita, M. and J.-F. Thisse. (2002). *Economics of Agglomeration: Cities, Industrial Location and Regional Growth*. Cambridge: Cambridge University Press.

Gottmann, J. (1961). *Metropolis, the Rise of the North-Eastern Atlantic Seaboard*. Cambridge, MA: MIT-Press.

Hagerstränd, T. (1952). *The Propagation of Innovation Waves*. Lund: University of Lund.

Hoover, E. M. (1948). *The Location of Economic Activity*. New York: McGraw Hill.

Jacobs, J. (1961). *The Rise and Death of Great American Cities*. New York: Random House.

Jacobs, J. (1984). *Cities and the Wealth of Nations*. New York: Random House.

Jaffe, A. B., M. Traytenberg and R. Henderson. (1993). Geographic localization of knowledge spillovers as evidenced by patent citations. *Quarterly Journal of Economics*, vol. 63, pp. 577–598.

Johnson, S. (2001). *Emergence*. London: Penguin Books.

Krugman, P. (1995). *Development, Geography, and Economic Theory*. Cambridge, MA: MIT-Press.

Lambooy, J. G. (1997). Knowledge production, organisation and agglomeration economies. *GeoJournal*, vol. 41, pp. 293–300.

Lambooy, J. G. (2000). Learning and agglomeration economies. In F. Boekema, S. Bakkers, F. Rutten and K. Morgan (eds), *Knowledge, Innovation and Economic Growth*. Cheltenham: Edward Elgar, pp. 15–37.

Lambooy, J. G. (2002). Knowledge and urban economic development. *Urban Studies*, vol. 39, pp. 1019–1035.

Lambooy, J. G. (2003). The role of intermediate structures and regional context for the evolution of knowledge networks and structural change. Jena: Max Planck Institute. Papers on Economics and Evolution, No. 0309.

Lambooy, J. G. and R. A. Boschma. (2001). Evolutionary economics and regional policy. *Annals of Regional Science*, vol. 35, no. 2, pp. 113–131.

Machlup, F. (1962). *The Production and Distribution of Knowledge in the United States*. Princeton: Princeton University Press.

Marshall, A. (1890). *Principles of Economics*. London: Macmillan.

Mokyr, J. (2002). *The Gifts from Athena; Historical Origins of the Knowledge Economy* Princeton: Princeton University Press.

Nonaka, I. and H. Takeuchi. (1995). *The Knowledge Creating Company*. Oxford: Oxford University Press.

Nooteboom, B. (2000). *Learning and Innovation in Organisations and Economies*. Oxford: Oxford University Press.

Perroux, F. (1950). Economic space: Theory and applications. *Quarterly Journal of Economics*, vol. 64, pp. 89–104.

Porter, M. (1990). *The Competitive Advantage of Nations*. New York: Macmillan.

Pred, A. (1976). The interurban transmission of growth in advanced economies. *Regional Studies*, vol. 10, no. 9, pp. 151–171.

Pyka, A. and G. Kuppers. (eds) (2002). *Innovation Networks; Theory and Practice*. Cheltenham: Edward Elgar.

Rogers, E. M. (1995). *Diffusion of Innovations*. New York: Free Press.

Simmie, J. (ed.) (2002). *Innovative cities*. London: Spon Press.

Simmie, J. (2004). Innovation and clustering in the globalised international economy. *Urban Studies*, vol. 41, no. 5/6, pp. 1095–1112.

Sokol, M. (2004). The "knowledge economy": A critical view. In Ph Cooke and A. Piccaluga (eds), *Regional Economies as Laboratories*. Cheltenham: Edward Elgar, pp. 216–231.

Sorenson, O. and L. Fleming. (2004). *Science and the Diffusion of Knowledge*. Harvard Business School, unpublished paper.

Stam, E. (2003). *Why Butterflies Don't Fly*. Utrecht: NGS-series.

Storper, M. J. and A. J. Venables. (2004). Buzz: Face-to-face contact and the urban economy. *Journal of Economic Geography*, no. 4, pp. 351–370.

Törnquist, G. (1970). *Contactsystems and Regional Development*. Lund: University of Lund.

van den Ende, J. and W. Dolfsma. (2005). Technology-push, demand-pull and the shaping of technological paradigms. *Journal of Evolutionary Economics*, vol. 15, no. 1, pp. 83–100.

van der Panne, G. (2004). Agglomeration externalities: Marshall versus Jacobs. *Journal of Evolutionary Economics*, vol. 14, no. 5, pp. 593–604.

van Oort, F. G. (2003). *Urban Growth and Innovation; Spatially Bounded Externalities in the Netherlands*. London: Ashgate.

Weber, A. (1929). *The Theory of the Location of Industries*. Chicago: University of Chicago Press, Translation of Part 1 of the German edition of 1909.

Chapter 18

Knowledge Citizens: A Competence Profile

América Martínez, *Center for Knowledge Systems, ITESM*

Introduction

The present context of the knowledge society has concurrently brought considerable demands and, mainly, valuable growth and fulfillment opportunities for its constituents (Carrillo, 1999; OCDE, 2002; Bounfour and Edvinsson, 2005). This situation allows people to grow into new competences, incorporate themselves into and play a part in the construction of their environment. This involves development of their individual potential in interactions with others and the environment, and establishing person–context exchange dynamics (Martínez, 1999).

In this sense, the knowledge city (KC) and similar concepts acquire significance as context for the knowledge citizen (KCz) as well as a specific line of study. The importance of the relations between the development of societies and their human capital (Carrillo, 1999; Chen and Ju Choi, 2004; Bounfour and Edvinsson, 2005) leads to a deeper analysis of the KCz as an essential element of this alliance.

Specialized literature concurrently shows a growing presence of the topic of KCz competences (Schwartz, 2001; Carrillo, 2003, 2005; Hospers, 2003; Longworth, 2003; Ergazakis et al., 2004; Florida, 2004, 2005). Consequently, I feel it is time to design a profile that proposes ranks for these competences. The objective, therefore, is a KCz profile identifying categories for its different competences at the first and second segregation levels, with a definition of the types of competences, and the mastery required in each one.

Thus, this chapter is organized as follows: Competences of the knowledge citizen discusses citizen skills associated with the concepts of the knowledge city: learning city, creative city, and intelligence city. Competence categories address the ranks that stem directly from the field of workplace skills, identifying a number of criteria on which competence taxonomies are based. It also reviews different proposals in respect to the categories of citizen competences. Profile of the knowledge citizen describes a complete KCz profile, including the criteria and elements considered. The final section discusses several conclusions.

Competences of the Knowledge Citizen

Different concepts represent the current context of the KCz. Knowledge cities (Schwartz, 2001; Ergazakis et al., 2004; Carrillo, 2005) feature a growth based on the generation of value using all the common assets, with the purpose of achieving sustainable growth for the community (Carrillo, 2003). The creative city (Hospers, 2003) combines concentration, diversity, and a positive image of competitive urban areas, where a creative process emerges to create a compelling attraction for the creative class (Florida, 2004, 2005). In the learning city (Longworth, 2003) education is stressed as an ongoing process focused on developing the human potential to capitalize and integrate its economic, political, social, cultural, educational, and environmental capital. The intelligent city (Komnios, 2002), in turn, is a simultaneously real and virtual spatial entity. Clusters and organizations engaged in the research and development of innovative processes and products pertain to the real space, while the community's digital ability is engaged in administrating its knowledge, promote technology, and practice interactive communication in virtual space. Both pave the way for technological innovation. Likewise, in the intelligent city people are a basic component. The following section discusses the features of knowledge cities: creativity, learning, and the intelligent cities vocation, as well as the competences of the KCz derived from these contexts.

A number of trends related to the competences of a KCz stem from the principles of knowledge cities (Carrillo, 2002, 2003), such as those associated with knowledge, consolidation, and self-development/esteem/evaluation. He also assigns (2002) significance to competences that contribute to the consolidation of a knowledge city from the standpoint of the ability to define the city capital system; that is, to define the city's assets by means of a complete and orderly structure. Besides, Carrillo (op. cit.) emphasizes—as a part of a profile of the KCz—an attitude supported by values such as common well-being, respect, acceptance of diversity, and collaboration, to name a few, and those competences related with the identification and development of relations that are meaningful for the citizens themselves and their city.

Under the concept of learning city, Longworth (2003) highlights the participation of all city agents, their association and contribution to mutual interests, as well as collaboration and a shared sense of purpose with other cities.

Regarding the creative city, Hospers (2003) stresses the importance of having a KCz who is inquisitive, persistent, pursues different paths to find a solution, generates alternative options in response to a problem or situation, and develops an inventive ability to seek new ways of doing things. Likewise, given the attractiveness of the creative city (Florida, 2004), the large diversity resulting from visitors, workers, and other groups acquires relevance and, therefore, a trait of the KCz is respect for the variety of cultural practices of the citizens and his/her participation in this diversity. Hospers (2003) underlines that the creative city provides spaces where citizens can engage in direct interaction. This leads the KCz to develop tolerance, respect, and empathy through intercultural interaction and the establishment of interpersonal relations, and to show interest in understanding the cultures of other countries. Simultaneously, Hospers (2003) recognizes that in the creative city, physical spaces and other resources that encourage cultural activity are available to community groups and organizations. This is why abilities and values associated with artistic appreciation and sensitivity become prominent in the KCz profile. On the other hand, Longworth (2003) recognizes that environmental awareness is of essence in sustainability, and therefore it is a significant aspect of the life and profile of the KCz.

In turn, Schwartz (2001) points out that permanent learning in current knowledge societies is made possible through the existence of different options under a tacit recognition of knowledge and new certification strategies, as well as the presence of diverse modes of education (e.g., corporate universities, distance education), networking, and the creation of communities of practice. Under Longworth's (2003) approach to the learning city, the lifelong learning concept is central. This highlights a continuous learning process based on citizen needs. In turn, Hospers (2003), Schwartz (2001), and Komninos (2002) recognize the importance of making learning and distance interaction tools available to citizens. They stress access to new communication technologies for all, as instruments to acquire knowledge and facilitate interaction and innovation. Consequently, the skills to use and manage digital distance communication technology, to deliberately seek information, and to identify the appropriate sources gain prominence, as well as a respectful, empathetic attitude toward distance relations. In this context, according to Hospers (2003), oral and written communication skills in the English language are a necessity.

Another important feature (Hospers, 2003) is an effective collaboration among local political parties, government agencies, schools, and businesses. The creation of committees where all social parties are represented, as focused on issues and actions that serve the interest and benefit of the local people, is characteristic of creative cities. Based on these elements, a KCz requires competences related with the fulfillment of responsibilities and rights as citizens, such as participation in creating entities to provide representation. Hospers (2003) claims that a fundamental ingredient is civic participation with a committed social and political approach, a significant degree of understanding and updating of public life in the city, and values such as common well-being, social responsibility, commitment, and equity—part and parcel of the overall KCz profile.

The learning city (Longworth, 2003) likewise constitutes a context where both interactions and interdependences among the different agents become substantial. Therefore, it is desirable for the KCz to develop participation, collaboration, communication, and association skills as well as a shared sense of purpose.

It should be mentioned that Schwartz (2001) and Hospers (2003) acknowledge the importance of congruence between public policy and the development of a KC and, consequently, of the development of a KCz with competences that will allow him/her to design and implement policies that will lead to the development and maintenance of a KC. In his approach to learning cities, Longworth (2003) highlights the need to develop KCz leadership skills.

Identification of KCz competences in the specialized literature I have reviewed provides the initial sketch of a profile. Further down in this chapter, I discuss an overview of taxonomies in the field of workplace competence and general studies on the citizen profile.

Competency Taxonomies in the Field of Workplace Skills

Taxonomies addressed below are borrowed directly from the field of occupational competences. CINTERFOR reports that the taxonomy used by CONOCER—a Mexican competence standardization and certification agency—considers three types of aptitudes. The first type includes the basic competences or elementary behaviors required for any job. The second type relates to generic competences, meaning performances that, while applicable to different occupations, demand a degree specificity that depends on the particular activity. The third type consists of particular competences that relate to the performance shown in very concrete and specialized occupation fields (Argüelles, 1996).

The levels in National Vocational Qualifications (NVQ) UK, include a classification in terms of levels of performance in competences based on a number of variables: complexity of the activity, variety of functions, diversity of contexts, autonomy and responsibility of the incumbent, and the extent of the need to engage the collaboration of others and procure resources. Competence levels involve a progressive mastery of these variables as levels grow. The bottom one is the least complex and varied, and these variables grow up to the fifth level. These variables acquire higher significance in work styles based on knowledge (Heidenreich, 2004), whereas they demand considerable autonomy and involve highly complex problems and situations.

Another proposition applicable to the work environment (Martínez, 2001b) comprises categories from the viewpoint of awareness and mastery of a competence; the autonomy required for its performance; the need to interact with others; the degree of individual effort required to develop the competence; and the complexity of functions and features involved in organizing the competence. Considering these variables, the levels range from the most basic and simple to the most complex and demanding in any given competence. These categories are assistant, junior, senior, and expert. Other interesting proposals to classify competences take into account different criteria. Garavan and McGuire (2001), for instance, base their classification on the nature of the competence, namely technical skills, entrepreneurship, human interaction, attitudes, values, and mental fitness.

Hence, the multiple criteria used in the taxonomies reviewed above provide an input when competences are ranked under a complete profile. The following section is a review of the inputs provided by research of citizens in general.

Field of Citizen Competences

Of particular interest for this paper is a consideration of the different taxonomies of citizen competences (Delors, 1996; Audigier, 2000; OCDE, 2002; MEN, Republic of Colombia, 2004), whereas they provide input for thought in regards to KCz competences and their particular ranking.

DeSeCo, the Development and Selection of Key Competences study (OCDE, 2002), proposes three simultaneous, interrelated, and self-contained categories namely, acting autonomously, using tools interactively, and operating in socially heterogeneous groups.

Another study (Audigier, 2000) of citizen competences is the Education of Democratic Citizenship project (EDC), which ranks key competences under three large categories: cognitive, affective, and choice of values, and those related with action. Cognitive competences are in turn subdivided into four categories that respectively refer to legal and political nature; knowledge of the present world; procedural nature; and knowledge of the principles and values of human rights and democratic citizenship.

The EDC derives a second area from this last category. It includes two more ranks of competence: ethical and choice of values, and social. Two added categories are in turn derived from these two. On one hand are those focused on the ability to live with others, cooperate, and build and implement team projects, ensure co-responsibility and, on the other hand is the ability to solve conflict under principles of democratic law.

For the EDC, development of the key competences outlined above helps the citizen become a free, autonomous person aware of his/her rights and obligations to act in a democratic society.

Another effort focused on the development by Columbian children of citizen competences in school (MEN, 2004) proposes three large groups: competence for peaceful co-existence, competence for participation and responsibility, and competence for diversity, identity, and appreciation of differences. From each one of these three groups, five potential types of competences develop to shape a citizen, such as those related with particular branches of knowledge; exerting citizenship; and practicing cognitive, communicative, emotional, and integrating skills.

The last part of this section deals with elements generated by the work of the International Commission on the Education for the 21st Century (Delors, 1996), which among other research lines on education selected the one focused on citizenship to provide a four-pillar foundation for the necessary competences. These pillars stand for learning to know, learning to do, learning to live together, and learning to be.

After reviewing the contributions provided by taxonomies of competences in similar fields, I submit the KCz profile I have developed on the basis of the inputs discussed above.

A Knowledge Citizen Profile

Addressing the elements analyzed throughout this chapter, I propose a KCz profile built on an initial taxonomy of competences. To support my proposal, I should mention that the bases for the construction of this profile are borrowed from and agree with the ideas developed by the OCDE in DeSeCo (2002) in regard to the foundations of human rights principles, democratic values, and the objectives associated with sustainable development. Concomitantly, the proposed profile is based on the principles of a humanistic approach of workplace competences (Garavan and McGuire, 2001) that stresses orientation to the individual's self-control and self-regulation, as well as freedom and autonomy principles (Argüelles, 1999) and the means to develop the competences.

Although this proposal constitutes a taxonomy of the competences that make up the KCz profile, it also takes into account that a taxonomy varies with the predominant standpoint, whereas different classifications may be generated that depend on the basis of choice (Pinto, 1999). Therefore, a choice needs to be made regarding the selective parameters from which the taxonomy will derive. In this case, the selected criterion is functionality, with emphasis on the "pragmatic elements conditioned by the task where the classification and its presumed usefulness are inserted" (Pinto, 1999, p. 26). This is to say that the selective parameters on which the proposed taxonomy stands is the function of the particular competence. I have selected this criterion because it is present in the field of citizen competence classification (OCDE, 2002) and on account of the simplicity it provides for an integral visualization of the types of value contributions made by a KCz when he/she performs in his/her environment. It should be noted that this taxonomy considers a randomly sectioned performance that allows identification and comprehension of the essential elements that make up the KCz profile. Notwithstanding, I have considered the principle that performance is not simple and segmented but complex and integrated. Likewise, in the construction of this profile, I have assumed the co-existence and interdependence of the individual's personal and social aspects. My proposal features a strategic derivation stemming from the value aspects of the KC, and defines three levels of competence mastery.

The strategic branching of this profile means that classification of the competences therein is essentially bound to the value aspects of Knowledge Cities (strategic derivation of the competences). This allows for a better assurance of congruence between

KCz competences and KC values. Therefore, value aligning constitutes an essential aspect of competence identification (Carrillo, 1999; Martínez, 2001a).

My proposal contemplates value dimensions of knowledge cities (Carrillo, 2004) that explicitly incorporate all the value forms that are essential for the KC and, consequently, for its maintenance and development that must in turn be ensured by the competences of knowledge citizens. The capital system I took as a reference is depicted on Table 1, and it is presented in a detailed way in Chapter 4 of this book.

The strategic derivation leads to a taxonomy of KCz competences that is not necessarily linear (one-to-one). Categories are classified under three specific ranks focused on concrete fields of competence, and a general rank that underpins the specific competences, thus making up a profile with four categories, as shown in Figure 1.

Table 1: Capital system

Capital	Sub-capital
Metacapitals	Referential Capital
	Articulation Capital
Human Capital	Individual Basis
	Collective Basis
	Evolution Abilities
Instrumental Capital	Tangible
	Intangible

Source: Carrillo (2004).

Figure 1

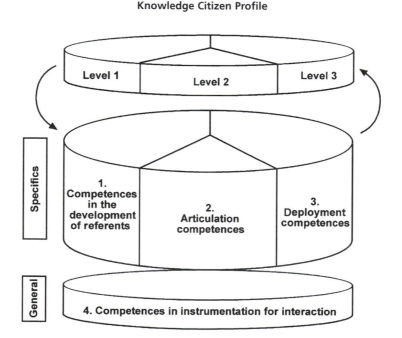

Knowledge Citizen Profile

The different competence categories stress a derivation from the fundamental value aspects that guide the entity, called metacapitals (Carrillo, 2004). This derivation becomes concrete in two of the three particular categories included in the profile: first, Competences in the development of referents and second, Articulation competences. In turn, the third one, Deployment competences, stems from human capital. Finally, Competences in instrumentation for interaction stems from instrumental capital, the only general category in this profile. The underlying logic in this taxonomy is first based on the fundamental relevance of the individuals' self-definition and self-construction from the viewpoint of his/her interaction with others; secondly, on the individual's involvement in his/her self-development and the development of the entity where he/she is a player; and, finally, on the means that support the individual's over-all performance. This branching out is shown in Figure 2.

Each competence category in the profile I propose is accompanied by its defi-nition and a general desegregation on Table 2. This KCz profile includes three

Figure 2

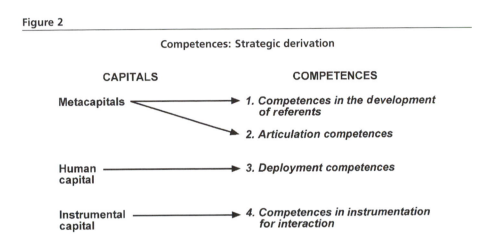

Competences: Strategic derivation

Table 2: Taxonomy of competences in the profile of the knowledge citizen and its general components

Competence Categories	Competences
	Specific
Development of Referents *Performance oriented to the determination, systematization, and implementation of all the value elements pertaining to the individual and the communities where he/she evolves (context).*	(1) Identity (self-knowledge and knowledge of context, choice of values, and construction and development of the personal identity and the context) (2) Value aspects (identification, implementation, and development of all the value elements that make up the personal/contextual identity) (3) Significant agents (identification of the agents that are relevant to all the elements of personal and contextual value, recognition of the agent–value connection)

Table 2: Taxonomy of competences in the profile of the knowledge citizen and its general components (*Continued*)

Competence Categories	Competences
Specific	
Articulation	
Performance oriented to the identification and development of significant personal relations, and similar relations with the community where the individual operates.	(1) Significant relations (assertive communication, negotiation, ability to relate with others, collaboration, co-responsibility, peaceful solution to conflict) (2) Civic responsibility (pursuit of social well-being, commitment, leadership, participation in citizen committees, knowledge and defense of own rights and responsibilities as well as those pertaining to the context) (3) Tolerance and solidarity (respect, empathy in cultural interaction and between genders)
Deployment	
Performance oriented to self-growth actions and actions to develop the community where the individual operates.	(1) Self-motivation (self-motivation, self-determination, autonomy and interdependence, acting as part of a context, and being a facilitator of others' learning efforts) (2) Attitude (innovation, inquisitiveness, perception of self-effectiveness, critical thinking, perseverance, self-reflection, pro-activity, intrinsic motivation, flexibility, tolerance for frustration) (3) Artistic sensitivity and creativity
General competences	
Instrumentation for interaction	
Performance oriented to the use, management, and development of support for the particular competences required to facilitate individual–context interaction.	(1) Available technology (employing and understanding the use, management, and development of hardware, software, and networks) (2) Language (use of language and symbols, fluency in oral and written English) (3) Resources (use and management of information and documents, deliberate search of information, optimizing physical and non-physical resources)

proficiency levels, which reflect how far an individual has progressed in each competence. The levels are based on three variables: awareness, or the extent in which the individual knows that he/she has developed a given skill; autonomy, or the extent in which the individual is able to perform on his/her own; and

Table 3: Competences in the knowledge citizen profile: Criteria and levels of mastery

Criteria	Level 1	Level 2	Level 3
Level of awareness (extent in which the individual knows whether or not he/she has developed a given competence)	Unconscious incompetence (unawareness of lack of competence)	Conscious incompetence (awareness of lack of competence)	Deliberately focused competence (directs and applies his/her competence in a conscious, deliberate manner)
Autonomy (extent in which the individual can perform independently)	The individual requires close assistance and counseling to develop the competence	The individual depends on guidelines	The individual is autonomous in his/her performance
Performance consistency (stability and repeatability of *n* individual's appropriate performance)	Performance is inconsistent	Performance shows some consistency	Performance is consistent

performance consistence, or the stability and repeatability of a person's appropriate performance. Table 3 shows the criteria used to determine proficiency levels and a definition of each.

Conclusions

The KCz profile proposed in this chapter is an initial step in the process of bringing together the advancements I have reviewed, which significantly contributed to identify KCz competences and generate a related taxonomy. They also allow us to capitalize the field of overall workplace skills and citizen research.

The profile likewise allows a complete and interrelated view of KCz competence and makes systematization of further development possible. The KCz profile, in this sense, constitutes an input for the design of learning scenarios that would influence an ongoing effort of KCz skills development by the KC.

One of the aspects I would consider a continuance of current progress is an ongoing development of the taxonomy of competences. This involves furthering the study, desegregation of these competences, as well as submitting the taxonomy all the involved agents for their consensus.

A further area of continuity would be scrutiny of the technical and methodological aspects of the profile with added rigor and empirical validation. Furthermore, a review is required of the use, meaning, evolution, and implications of concepts associated with city, knowledge city, citizen, and knowledge citizen and their bearing on the KCz profile, as a relevant line of research. Finally, it is of essence to apply the KCz profile at the time that learning experiences are designed, to pave the way for the development and evaluation of his/her competences with the ultimate purpose of having the KCz profile actually become a beneficial instrument for these citizens and their cities.

References

Argüelles, A. (1996). Competencia Laboral y Educación Basada en Normas de Competencia, *Editorial Limusa*, 319pp.

Audigier, F. (2000). Basic Concepts and core competencies for education for democratic citizenship, www consulted on March 2005, http://www.coe.int/T/e/Cultural_Co-operation/Education/ E.D.C/Documents_and_publications/By_Subject/Concepts/097_basic.asp#TopOfPage.

Bounfour, A. and Edvinsson, L. (2005). *Intellectual Capital for Communities, Nations, Regions and Cities*. Burlington, MA, USA: Elsevier. 338pp.

Carrillo, F. J. (1999). The Knowledge Management Movement: Current Drives and Future Scenarios. Memories of the 3rd International Conference on Technology, Policy and Innovation: Global Knowledge Partnerships: Creating Value for the 21st Century. www consulted on March 2005, sistemasdeconocimiento.org.

Carrillo, F. J. (2002). Capital systems: Implications for knowledge agenda, *Journal of Knowledge Management*, vol. 6, no. 4, pp. 3–5.

Carrillo, F. J. (2003). Conceptualización de Ciudades de Conocimiento, Technical Note. www consulted on March 2005, sistemasdeconocimiento.org.

Carrillo, F. J. (2004). *Journal of Knowledge Management*. Knowledge-based Development II: Knowledge Cities, vol. 8, no. 5, pp. 28–46.

Carrillo, F. J. (2005). Qué es la economía del conocimiento? *Transferencia*, vol. 18, no. 69, January, pp. 2–3.

Chen, S. and Ju Choi, Ch. (2004). Creating a knowledge-based city: The example of Hsinchu Science Park, *Journal of Knowledge Management*. Knowledge-based Development II: Knowledge Cities. vol. 8, no. 5, pp. 73–82.

CINTERFOR. 40 Preguntas sobre competencia laboral, www consulted on March 2005, http://www.cinterfor.org.uy/public/spanish/region/ampro/cinterfor/temas/complab/xxxx/esp/ index. htm.

Delors, J. (1996). La Educación Encierra un Tesoro. Ediciones UNESCO, 301pp.

Ergazakis, K., Metaxiotis, J. and Psarras, J. (2004). Towards knowledge cities: Conceptual analysis and success stories, *Journal of Knowledge Management*, vol. 8, no. 5, 5pp.

Florida, R. (2004). American's looming creativity, *Harvard Business Review*, vol. 82, no. 10, pp. 122–138.

Florida, R. (2005). *Cities and the Creative Class*, New York: Routledge, 198pp.

Garavan, T. and McGuire, D. (2001). Competencies and workplace learning: Some reflections on the rhetoric and the reality, *Journal of Workplace Learning*, vol. 13, no. 3/4, Proquest Education Journal.

Heidenreich, M. (2004). Knowledge-based work: An international comparison. University of Bamberg, Germany. *Management International*, Spring, vol. 8, no. 3; ABI Information Global.

Hospers, G. (2003). Creative cities in Europe: Urban competitiveness in the knowledge economy. Intereconomics, *Hamburg*, vol. 38, issue 5, September/October, pp. 260–269.

Komninos, N. (2002). *Intelligent Cities*, London: Taylor & Francis Group, 290pp.

Longworth, N. (2003). El aprendizaje a lo largo de la Vida. Ciudades Centradas en el aprendizaje para un siglo orientado hacia el aprendizaje. Paidós, 312pp.

Martínez, A. (1999). Competencia laboral y su contexto. Electronic version. Centro de Sistemas de Conocimiento. Nota Técnica CSC1999–01. http://www.sistemasdeconocimiento.org/p_csc3.html Producción Intelectual Notas Técnicas.

Martínez, A. (2001a). Un Modelo de Procesos Clave de Administración de Conocimiento. Transferencia, año 14, número 53, January, pp. 28–29.

Martínez, A. (2001b). Reporte Técnico. Capital Humano. Centro de Sistemas de Conocimiento. Documento Interno.

Ministerio de Educación Nacional (MEN), República de Colombia. (2004). Estándares Básicos de Competencias Ciudadanas, Serie Guías, n° 6. www consulted on March 2005, http://www.mineducacion.gov.co/index2.html.

OCDE. (2002). Definition and selection of competences (DeSeCo): Theoretical and conceptual foundations. www consulted on March 2005, http://www.portal-stat.admin.ch/deseco/ deseco_strategy_paper_final.pdf.

Pinto, M. (1999). *Manual de clasificación documental*. Ed. Síntesis, 298pp.

Schwartz, G. (2001). Knowledge city: A digital knowware. The construction of a knowledge-creating public space in Brazil. www consulted on March 2005, http://www.thinkcycle.org/tcfilesystem/download/development_by_design_2001/knowledge_city:_a_digital_knowware/schwartz_knowware.pdf.

The World Bank. (2003). Life Long Learning in Global Knowledge Economy, *Challenges for Developing Countries*, 141pp.

Chapter 19

Knowledge City, Seen as a Collage of Human Knowledge Moments

Ron Dvir, *Future Centers, Tel-Aviv, Israel*

Illustrations by Arye Dvir

Introduction

What Is a Knowledge City?

The emerging notion of "knowledge city" attracts considerable interest from city policy makers and researchers in the domains of knowledge management and knowledge-based development. The transformation into a knowledge city is seen by many actors in the urban development field as a possible solution to the sustainability challenges of the modern city and a recipe for citizens' prosperity (e.g., Ergazakis et al., 2004). And yet, the concept of "knowledge city" is in its infancy, and there are no agreed definitions of this term. Rather, there are several complementary perspectives from which to consider the concept, such as Urban Capital Systems (Carrillo, 2004), Regional Intellectual Capital (Bounfour and Edvinsson, 2005), Information Technology (Komninos, 2002), Urban Processes (Landry, 2000), and Urban History (Kunstler, 2004). Other researchers attempt to define the knowledge city through a checklist of desired characteristics (Ergazakis et al., 2004).

This chapter illustrates the knowledge city idea from a new perspective—one which connects to the daily experiences of the citizen.

What Happens in a Knowledge City?

We understand a knowledge city as a milieu which triggers and enables an intensive, ongoing, rich, diverse, and complex flow of knowledge moments.

A "knowledge moment" is a spontaneous or planned human experience in which knowledge is discovered, created, nourished, exchanged, and transformed into a new form. Nonaka and Konno (1998) suggested the cycle of four modes of knowledge conversion: socialization, externalization, combination, and internalization.

In our Knowledge City model, a Knowledge Moment happens at the intersection of people, places, processes, and purposes (Figure 1). In essence, the Knowledge Moment

Figure 1

The framework of the human knowledge moments scheme

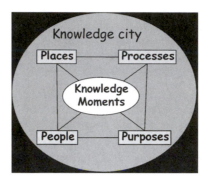

is a conversation between people in a particular place, using structured or unstructured processes aimed at explicit or implicit purpose.

- **People**: Knowledge Moments are human experiences that could (and should) involve the full range of any human being acting in the city—citizens and visitors; city officials, business people, and artists; local people and other cities' men and women; and young and old.
- **Places**: Knowledge Places are the spaces in which Knowledge Moments happen. A Knowledge City transformation strategy might include a plan to upgrade some of its existing (and frequently aging) institutions in order to provide richer context as knowledge places. For example, a city might redefine the roles of the library or museum to become knowledge-creation places. Traditionally, the term refers to physical places but virtual urban knowledge spaces (such as an urban citizens' portal) are also being experimented with (e.g., Bagir and Kathawala, 2004).
- **Processes**: Knowledge Processes can be well planned (e.g., a structured decision-making process) or unplanned (e.g., a spontaneous encounter). The more complex processes might involve many people, places, and Knowledge Moments.
- **Purposes**: All Knowledge Moments involve intrinsic motives of the actors, such as joy, engagement, and personal growth. Some are also related to specific, predefined external purposes (e.g., promotion of an economical objective of an individual, group of people, or the whole community).

The fundamental idea behind this model is based on the principles of co-evolution—through the dense stream of Knowledge Moments, all actors acting in the city co-evolve toward sustainablity.

How to Understand a Knowledge City?

There are several ways to explore and understand a Knowledge City using the Knowledge Moments lens:

1. **Wander around the city**: See what is happening and identify typical or exceptional Knowledge Moments.
2. **Follow several people for a day**: See how they spend the day and what they experience. Is the day full of Knowledge Moments? Does the city provide them with opportunities for such moments?

Figure 2

(3) **Follow a specific knowledge place during a whole day or week**: Is the place full of Knowledge Moments? Was new knowledge created, discovered, shared, and transformed into value?

(4) **Follow a specific knowledge process**: Who is involved? Who is not involved? In which places does it take place? What purposes does it serve?

As visualized in the following illustration, we suggest to understand the Knowledge City as a complex collage of interconnected Knowledge Moments which reflect the citizens reality (Figure 2). This metaphor is inspired by the book of Peter Cook, *The City, Seen as a Garden of Ideas* (2004).

A Collage of Knowledge Moments

A Note on Storytelling

Zarpom city does not exist. It was invented to illustrate the Knowledge City idea. However, many of the Knowledge Moments were not invented—they happened, or could have happened, in the many cities the author visited in his search for the conceptual meaning of Knowledge City. Similarly, the eight knowledge places will be familiar to the reader. Museums, libraries, town halls and schools exist in most cities, and some of them are already on a transformation path to becoming places that enable and trigger Knowledge Moments.

The City—History, Transformation, Citizens, and Knowledge Places

For many generations, the city of Zarpom enjoyed economic prosperity accompanied with social stability. In the last two decades of the 20th century, its traditional industrial base was quickly eroding, and in the process of globalization the economical restructuring had generated employment problems and a loss of jobs to lesser-developed countries with lower overheads and wages. A decline in the standard of living and an increase in social burdens followed. The young generation began to flee from the city. At the beginning of the third millennium, the new mayor, supported by an ambitious council, committed to reverse this vicious cycle of urban decline. They created a new strategy which they called "transforming Zarpom into a Knowledge City."

The city always had a well-developed urban infrastructure and wide range of public institutions. As part of the transformation strategy, many of them are now acting as "Knowledge Places": the city library, art museum, stock exchange, school, town hall, piazza, cafés, and the house of a typical family. The following map provides a schematic view of the city (Figure 3).

There are about 150,000 citizens. Our visit will introduce the reader to a dozen of them: including Ed, the commissioner for future generations; Jane, a chemistry student; Ruth, a 12 month baby; Barbara, a 14 years old; and Martin, the new mayor.

Urban Knowledge Diary

Table 1 is a chronology of one typical day at the city. For each of eight knowledge places, four snapshots of specific Knowledge Moments are briefly described.

Visiting the Knowledge City

The reader is invited to visit the Knowledge City and explore the collage of Knowledge Moments using four possible paths, of which three are illustrated in Figure 4:

(1) **Chronologically**: captures a snapshot of the city in the morning, afternoon, evening, and late at night.
(2) **Tracking places**: e.g., discover what happens in the library from morning until late night.
(3) **Following individuals**: for example, follow Barbara, a 14-year-old student, as she moves during the day between different knowledge places.
(4) **Following processes**: tracking separately each theme or story (the casino case, the networked library initiative etc.).

As the people, processes, and places intertwine, all of the alternative paths provide a rich understanding of the essence of the Knowledge City.

Figure 3

Eight Knowledge Places

The School

The school's new strategy redefined it as a "community center for values, education, and learning." It is open from early morning to late night (Figure 5).

Morning: Barbara (14) is one of the dozen members of the "19th century city exploration task force." Recently they have spent most of their school time on exploring the city's history. Barbara reports her discovery from last night's research in an old history book: the first lawn library in the continent was established in the city on 1814 (Figure 6). An idea emerges, and Barbara runs to the new library to discuss it with the librarians.

Table 1: The urban diary—a typical day in a Knowledge City

	School	Stock Exchange	Piazza	The Café	Town Hall	Library	Museum	Home
Morning	19th century exploration task—discovery!	Surprise—new IC screen	Knowledge City tour Encountering	Morning coffee—and the Casino Initiative (I)	Council meeting: "Knowledge City in action" program	Initiating the "City as a Public Library" project	Kindergarden week at the museum	Ideas pipeline
Afternoon	"The city as a Public Library" design meeting	When Jane met Roy	Human encounters	"The city as our office"	The Casino initiative (II)	"Writing a book together" workshop	Development workshop—museum as and innovation lab	Standing up for the first time
Evening	"My top five websites" fair	Public Monopoly evening	Piazza a la hyde park	Knowledge café event	The casino initiative (III): Emergency meeting	Intelligence query—Casinos and urban life	Future Images—Chemistry education 2020	Family Dinner
Night	"Time bank" activities	Public Monopoly evening	Egg-dropping competition	Two people, one bottle of wine	The casino initiative(IV): Citizen action group	Preparing the mobile library "Knowledge Bus"	Hard rock party and monthly White Night Rock party	Knowledge Cities Observatory

Figure 4

Figure 5

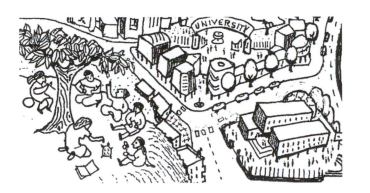

Figure 6

Afternoon: Barbara, Ronald, and Chris, the initiators of "City as Public Library" meet to promote the project. They act fast, and by tomorrow an invitation will be emailed to all the city citizens, calling them to register their books at the city book repository. The plan is to launch a pilot next week and start experimenting with the first public book exchanges. In six months, the "city as public library" will become a cornerstone of the evolving identity of the city as the "city of books."

Evening: The "My top five websites fair" opened in the afternoon and attracted more than one-hundred students and teachers (Figure 7). Experiences, recommendations, and hyperlinks were exchanged. Jane, participating from home, discovers some good sites she was not aware off—real pearls.

Night, late: The school "Time Bank" program was launched a year ago. The school community members, mostly school children and their parents and also other people from the neighborhood, were invited to register at the "knowledge yellow pages" service and specify their strength areas—specific domains where they could support someone else. Judo training, C++ computing, mathematics, chess, electricity maintenance, hair dressing—overall some 250 areas and more than 550 people enrolled at the program (Figure 8). For each hour contributed one hour credit is earned and can be consumed. Nicolas is at one of the classrooms, helping Steve overcome some algebra questions. Barbara, his daughter, will use the credit for a sculpturing lesson from Juan, another participant.

Figure 7

Figure 8

The Café

The Zarpom café is a "third place—one of those public 'great and good places' where people can gather, put aside their concerns of home and work, and hang out simply for the pleasure of good company and lively conversation" (Figure 9) (Oldenburg, 1989).

Morning: Shirley appreciates her daily visit to the café'—in the modern suburb she left a year ago, there were no "third places." In her newsletter she discovers a small article on a local entrepreneur's intention to turn the old textile factory into a casino. This rings alarm bells not only to her but also to several other early morning visitors at the other tables. Four of them agree to go to the town hall in the afternoon (Figure 10).

Afternoon: Three software programmers are already on their fourth hour and fifth coffee. Their company is experimenting with a new workplace design to replace their old offices. They call it "the city is my office." Every morning, each employee chooses where to work that day—from home, the library, the café, the community club—or at one of the few remaining offices in the small new office building the company rented. All they need is a laptop, wireless internet connection for each employee, coffee vouchers, and fresh thinking. Fridays are the official office days—all employees meet at the central office.

Evening: Every Thursday the café runs a "knowledge café" event. This is now a tradition here and in five cafes in other cities around the county. Tonight's question is "how to attract more tourists to the county." At the end, the six cafes exchange discoveries and ideas, using simple video conferencing.

Night, late: Two people at a side table, glass of wine, quite conversation (Figure 11).

Figure 9

Figure 10

The Town Hall

The new model of Zarpom governance is based on a visionary and energetic leadership in combination with a strong citizen-participation focus. The town hall, once a site for formal events and city officials' offices, is once again a place for the citizens (Figure 12).

Morning: The city council is discussing the "Knowledge City in Action" program, which serves as the strategic umbrella framework for city transformation. There is a hot debate—the mayor, Richard, suggests turning priorities upside down, and committing 75% of the program budget to educational activities. Most council members resist, believing that direct investment in knowledge-intensive industries will yield faster impact.

Figure 11

Figure 12

Afternoon: The job definition of Ed, the Commissioner for Future Generations, is "to ensure that current developments and decisions will not limit opportunities and possibilities of the future generations." Every day he understands a little more about what his title really means. Thirty minutes ago, Shirley rushed into his office with the casino story. She argues that the long-term damage might be significant. Fast action is needed—the council will make the decision next week. They phone the city intelligence centre at the library, and ask for fast initial information on similar experience of other cities (Figure 13). (Note: we follow here the example of retired Judge Shlomo Shoham, who pioneered this job title at the Israeli parliament in 2002.)

Evening: The word spreads to many citizens by email. The commissioner arranged an emergency open meeting to discuss the casino initiative. Two-hundred people arrive, listen to an initial intelligence report by the librarian, and explore the long-term implications. Ed seriously believes in applying the idea of the "Conversing City," although it can surface significant conflicts, which is the case tonight (Figure 14).

Night, late: Ed is still in the building with the citizen action group that started this morning at the café (Figure 15). Based on the voices heard at the evening meeting, they will challenge the new casino program at the council.

Figure 13

Figure 14

Figure 15

The Library

Any city needs an identity. One of the first steps in the city transformation program was to discover and leverage the uniqueness of the city. It took two months of conversations and workshops for an answer to emerge—Zarpom is now The City of Books. The library now invites conversations, music, activity, and all of the "quiet please" signs were removed. People still come to read and borrow books, but also to talk with old and new friends, create and discover (Figure 16).

Morning: Barbara rushes in with two of her colleagues to discuss their idea of turning the whole city into one big public library. Tom, the community intelligence

Figure 16

steward, buys in. "We have some 30,000 volumes, and can afford less than 600 new titles a year. But combing all private home libraries will mean a collection of maybe 1,000,000 books with thousands of new additions each year" (Figure 17). They agree that Barbara and her friends will start a pilot at their neighborhood to test the idea. Tom will help them browse the web for similar initiatives in other cities.

Afternoon: Today's workshop of the popular "writing a book together" series attracted some twenty participants (Figure 18). They work on coauthoring a book on the city's transformation over the last decade. The city library has already published ten books created through this workshop series—ranging from science fiction to "a home owners guide to a child" book. For many of the coauthors—so far frustrated writers, the program has helped them realize a dream. Tom believes that "a library should act not only as a temple of the human knowledge created in past generations"; like the old Alexandria library in its golden days, the library can be a place for nourishing new ideas.

Evening: Shirley, assisted by one of community intelligence stewards, explores how other cities were impacted by the presence of casinos, and how social risks have been

Figure 17

Figure 18

addressed. The information they discover will be the basis for the citizen action group started this morning at the café. The role for library staff members has been redefined in recent years, and now this place is the community intelligence center—adopting methods from the Technical and Business Intelligence centers in some of the larger city commercial businesses.

Night, late: Two staff members load books on an old truck (Figure 19). Tomorrow morning they will travel to the southern villages. The knowledge bus is part of the library strategy to reach all potential readers and extend this "knowledge place" beyond the city center.

The Museum

The City art museum was closed in the mid-1990s—it was too expensive to maintain, and received hardly any visitors, as was the case in other cities (Florida, 2002). Last year, as part of the Knowledge City strategy, the museum was reopened with the same old collections and staff—but in a new site—the old Under-roof Market, and with a completely new mission and atmosphere. The museum is now as much about the future as the past, as much about creation as exhibition, and as much about the art of living as ancient art (Figure 20).

Morning: This is "young generation" week at the museum; it is home to dozens of very young artists who left their kindergarten and moved to this wonderland for

Figure 19

LIBRARY GOES ON VILLAGE TOUR

Figure 20

a week. Tim (who is 5) and some friends work on a large sculpture of a child and mother. Yesterday, they toured the museum and discovered several interesting human body artworks, and found some really good ideas in works by Henry Moore and Dali (Figure 21).

Figure 21

Afternoon: The museum has defined one of its wings as an "innovation laboratory." Entrepreneurs or individuals, or groups are invited to use the space for several weeks or months to seed their ideas. The proximity to artworks adds a new dimension to the work. Today, the museum hosts Gregory and some friends who develop a prototype for radical, children's bicycles (Figure 22). Henrietta, an artist working as a museum guide, stops by for a minute with some of the kindergarten children visiting the museum. The children are curious, and Gregory and his colleagues have a completely new direction.

Evening: Chemistry professors, chemistry teachers, a medical doctor, a sculptor, a biotechnologist, students, school teachers, a philosopher—all gather to draw "future images" of Chemistry Education in year 2020. The results will be presented at the museum in the gallery of Future Images. Would they have an impact? It will be up to the participants to join forces and make a case for their ideas and take their vision forward.

Night, late: Hard rock party in the main exhibition space. Sixteenth century painted figures stare from walls at the lightly dressed dancers (Figure 23). The design gallery is noisy as well—tonight's "museum monthly white night seminar" is dedicated to "love vs. time." The participants will leave the place early next morning, after exploring . . .

The Piazza

The Piazza is the heartbeat of the city. This is the place for encounters, and spontaneous gatherings (Figure 24).

Figure 22

ANOTHER AMAZING INVENTION OF SCHOOL'S INNOVATION LAB

Morning: The Piazza is the departing point for the increasingly popular three-hour "Knowledge City Tour" (Figure 25). Ordinary tourists and officials from other cities alike come to see how the city is being transformed. The group climbs the bell tower, from where the guide points to some of the "knowledge places" that they will visit today—the library, the museum, the town hall, the old new industrial zone, the market and more.

Afternoon: The Piazza is filled with people going out for their lunch break. Some people meet old friends, some get into conversations with new friends, some read newspapers, some ideas are exchanged, some rumors emerge.

Evening: Was it a visitor to London's Hyde Park that brought the street debate tradition to Zarpom city perhaps twenty years ago? Today, as on every nice Tuesday evening, several speakers conduct loud debates with handfuls of opposers, supporters, and curious young and old people gathering around them (Figure 26).

Figure 23

Figure 24

Night, late: Tonight the bell tower has a new role. The competitors in the 3rd annual dropping-egg championship—young and old, professional hydraulic engineers and school students, artists and team of local politicians—climb up with sophisticated egg protection mechanisms embodying diverse technologies, hoping their egg will survive the 180-foot-long fall (Figure 27). A 35-year-old architect and his twins try their luck,

Figure 25

using an idea modified from Leonardo Da Vinci's parachute system. They have invested many nights over the last month in research, development, and testing. The four previous competitions have already triggered two pending patents, one popular toy, several improvements in products of local industries, thousands of broken eggs, and lots of fun.

Figure 26

The Stock Exchange

Zarpom stock exchange is the new heartbeat of the city's knowledge-based economic life—this is where ideas meet resources.

Morning: 09:01—Roy, a trader coming back from a long vacation, quickly scans the screens mounted on the walls of the trade room. What is this? He discovers a new screen, labeled "Intellectual Capital Index." It shows four indicators for each company already committed to this index: "human capital," "organisation capital," "renewal and innovation capital," and "relationships capital" (Figure 28).

Afternoon: Jane, who works for "City Ideas," an urban joint venture fund, meets with Roy. They discuss the commercial potential of the idea she submitted to the City Ideas Pipeline earlier today (Figure 29).

Evening: Richard, the owner of the pub on the stock exchange ground floor, is the spirit behind the monthly Monopoly competition (Figure 30). It looks like a hybrid of

Figure 27

traditional Monopoly and the popular SimCity computer game. The place is filled with business people eager to show off their skills, students ambitious to watch the experts, children coming to learn from tycoons, city planners coming to get some ideas, artists, and doctors.

Night, late: The game is still on. Over the night, more than fifty new startups were established, other companies went out of business, new approaches to taxpaying were explored, the university was privatized, and the city economy reshaped.

Home

"My home is my castle," says the Englishman. Home is also the place where much of our learning, discoveries, knowledge exchanges, ideas, and deepest inspirations occur. It is the site for endless amounts of Knowledge Moments. While many remain between the four walls of their houses, other moments extend to the whole city and beyond, through information technology (Figure 31).

Figure 28

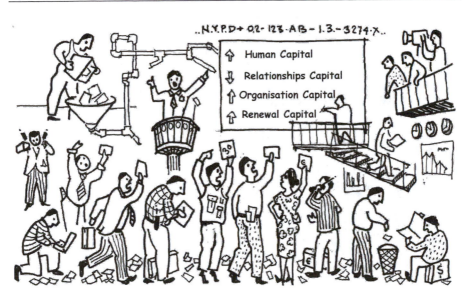

Figure 29

Figure 30

Figure 31

Morning: Jane logs onto the online "City Ideas Pipeline," a marketplace for citizens to publish and discover ideas, and to seek feedbacks, complementary ideas, potential collaborators, opportunity for investments, and more. Some ideas are commercial while others relate to social, educational, cultural, and political issues. Jane presses the "submit" bottom (Figure 32).

Figure 32

Afternoon: Baby Ruth (12 months) stands up for the first time, and falls backwards immediately (Figure 33). She tries again and again.

Evening: Dinner. This is the family time to tell small anecdotes from today's events, share frustrations, ask for advice, test an idea, laugh.

Night, late: Richard logs onto the internet. Tonight is the monthly Knowledge Cities Observatory online meeting (Figure 34). Mayors of Melbourne, Monterrey, Barcelona, Delft, Holon, Bangalore, and more than fifty other cities that define themselves as "knowledge cities" meet to learn from each other.

Figure 33

Figure 34

Conclusions

This collage of 32 Knowledge Moments demonstrated diverse human experiences, experienced in different places, by different people involved in different processes. A bird's eye view on these scattered moments suggests some insights about the essence of the Knowledge City. Each real world city is unique—there are no cities with the same history, mix of people, socioeconomic challenges. Each is unique, yet there are common characteristics.

Observations and Insights from Zarpom

Quality and quantity: A Knowledge City is about the quantity of the Knowledge Moments occurring within it—we argue that quantity creates quality and impact. The more opportunities for knowledge exchanges are created, the more opportunities for sustainable impact are generated.

Continuation and heartbeat: The stream of Knowledge Moments in Zarpom is continuous. A stream of ongoing encounters and Knowledge Moments is complemented by weekly or monthly events that act as the Knowledge City heartbeat.

Planned and spontaneous: It is the combination of planned and spontaneous Knowledge Moments that ensures the Knowledge City's vitality.

Breakthroughs?: Each of the operating principles of the knowledge places and processes are already practiced in most cities. It is the combination and intensity of already known principles that transform a city into a Knowledge City.

A sense of historicity: Some of the ideas demonstrated in Zarpom were practiced in old times and communities (e.g., the School's Time Bank), resembling the old goods barter economy. The modern Knowledge City can learn a lot from history's most innovative communities (Kunstler, 2004).

Roots: Zarpom is well rooted in its history, legacy and tradition. However, is it possible also to create an "instant" Knowledge City? There are several attempts, mostly in South East Asia, to build knowledge-based cities from scratch (Yang, 2005).

Future orientation: Although its historical roots are respected, Zarpom also has a strong future orientation. Some of the Knowledge Moments are related directly to concerns of the citizens about various long-term challenges, and result in practical action to secure the future.

Identity: Zarpom discovered its unique identity ("city of books") and now is leveraging it. This is a crucial challenge and critical success factor for any Knowledge City.

Governance: Zarpom practices a form of urban governance which is based on both strong and visionary leadership and commitment to citizen participation. This combination is manifested in many effective Knowledge Moments.

Multifaceted: As shown in the collage, the Knowledge City idea encompasses all aspects of the citizens' everyday life and well-being—urban economics, social challenges, personal relationships, arts, and education, for example.

Different scales: Knowledge Moments happen at all scales—from individual pause for reflection to big public events. However, even at the larger knowledge places and Knowledge Moments, the human scale is maintained, and the individual citizen "feels at home."

Dynamic flows: As demonstrated in the Zarpom story, many knowledge processes flow between places, involving different people at different phases.

Inclusive Knowledge City: The Knowledge Moments are not inclusive to the "knowledge workers," nor to the intellectuals. All can participate—citizens and visitors, young and old, industrialists, writers, and council members.

Speed: The flow between Knowledge Moments—from problem to idea to realization—is fast. The city economical infrastructure, participatory governance model, and open cultural climate all contribute to faster cycles and action. And yet, people—individuals and groups—have the time to reflect and deeply explore things which matter.

Information: Many Knowledge Moments involve the discovery of already existing (but frequently hidden) information, expertise and experience—and the conversion of it into action. A good knowledge place increases the chances of such discovery. Good information technology is important as well.

Transformation of existing places: Most Zarpom knowledge places are old institutions whose original role was enhanced to support the Knowledge City transformation. In many cases, it is a more sustainable approach than creating new places, with the potential to enable more interesting places to contribute to knowledge creation.

The role of architecture: The physical design of a place impacts the probability of Knowledge Moments, enables interesting flows, and highlights values. The city architects were major contributors to the transformation of many of Zarpom's aging institutions into vibrant knowledge places. They worked at all scales—from urban planning to detailed interior design. Architects enable the choreography and movement of knowledge, feelings, and ideas through and in between knowledge places (paraphrasing Lawrence Halprin, 1968).

Local and global focus: While many of the Knowledge Moments were focused on internal issues, Zarpom maintains strong knowledge-exchange relationships with other cities.

Serious play: Many of the Knowledge Moments at Zarpom involve playing and fun, e.g., the Monopoly night at the stock exchange. Play is an effective way to learn, discover, and explore unknown areas together.

Conversations: Most of Zarpom's Knowledge Moments are conversations, mostly between people, sometimes within people. Generalizing from this observation, the following insight come to the front of this story: The Knowledge City is a Conversing City.

Future Research

Zarpom was invented in order to illustrate a new perspective to the Knowledge City, and as an attempt to describe this idea in a form that connects to the daily experiences of each of us.

We suggest deepening the analysis of Knowledge Moments through comprehensive ethnographic study in which real Knowledge Moments, experienced by real people in real places will be explored. Such research would help addressing the following questions:

- What is the difference between a "Knowledge City" and a "regular city"?
- How does the intensity and characteristics of Knowledge Moments impact the sustainability of the city?
- What is the role of Knowledge Moments in the Knowledge City transformation strategy?
- How can urban places be redesigned and redefined in order to trigger and enhance Knowledge Moments? What would be the supporting knowledge places?
- Would a cross-cultural ethnographic study reveal the differences between Knowledge Moments experienced in different cultures?

Acknowledgment

The author wishes to thank Ed Mitchell who generously read proof this paper.

References

Bagir, M. N. and Kathawala, Y. (2004). Ba for Knowledge Cities: A Futurisitc Technology Model, *Journal of Knowledge Management*, vol. 8, no. 5, pp. 83–95.

Bounfour, A. and Edvinsson, L. (2005). *Intellectual Capital for Communities: Nations, Regions, and Cities*, Boston: Butterworth-Heinemann.

Carrillo, F. J. (2004). Capital cities: A taxonomy of capital accounts for knowledge cities, *Journal of Knowledge Management*, vol. 8, no. 5, pp. 28–46.

Cook, P. (2004). *The City, Seen as a Garden of Ideas*, New York: Monacelli Press.

Ergazakis, K., Metaxiotis, K. and Pasarras, J. (2004). Towards knowledge cities: Conceptual analysis and success stories, *Journal of Knowledge Management*, vol. 8, no. 5, pp. 5–15.

Florida, R. (2002). *The Rise of the Creative Class*, New York: Basic Groups.

Halprin, L. (1968). *Changing Places*, San Francisco: San Francisco Museum of Modern Art.

Komninos, N. (2002). *Intelligent Cities—Innovation, Knowledge, Systems and Digital Spaces*, New York: Spon Press.

Kunstler, B. (2004). *The Hothouse Effect*, New York: AMACON.

Landry, C. (2000). *The Creative City—A Toolkit for Urban Innovators*, London: Earthscan.

Nonaka, I. and Konno, N. (1998). The concept of "ba": Building a foundation for knowledge creation. *California Management Review*, vol. 40, no. 3, pp. 40–54.

Oldenburg, R. (1989). *The Great Good Place*, New York: Marlowe & Company.

Yang, A. (2005). Instant City, *Metropolis Magazine*, March, pp. 90–91.

Chapter 20

Reconstructing Urban Experience

Francisco Javier Carrillo, *The World Capital Institute and The Center for Knowledge Systems, Monterrey, México*

> My fears, indeed, concerned the past rather than the future
> H. P. Lovecraft, The Nameless City

Introduction

At the dawn of the Knowledge Cities Century, we are coming to terms with the realization that human destiny will unfold in cities. We are learning, too, that our capacity to shape such destiny will be determined by our self-knowledge as an urban species. This closing chapter aims at bringing into the Knowledge Cities (KC) debate the kind of transcendental options mankind faces in the urban arena. If cities can be conceptualized as value systems, we may wonder what is the space of possibilities for these as expressions of human potential and fate?

In order to conduct this analysis, we will look at the constituents of the urban experience and explore where the main constraints as well as the main possibilities may lie. We will look at some fundamental elements of urban life which perhaps were never the concern of early settlers and have yet to become categories of urban design. We will also look at some distinctive options which are emerging in the realm of contemporary urban experience, i.e., what it means living in a city and what it may evolve into. Contemporary urbanism is at the crossroads of several paths. Those paths are mostly mixtures of received paradigms of urban life and projections, mainly economic and technological, of ways to circumvent constraints to the limits imposed by those paradigms. It is this condition that has lead to identify a "crisis of traditional urbanistic instruments" (Vegara, 2002: 40).

According to Landry (2000: xiii), most people live in cities out of need, not desire: "in 1997 a survey showed that 84 per cent of people in the UK wanted to live in a small village, compared to 4 per cent who do." This implies that most people live in cities today because they have no choice. The majority may just take it for granted. This may also mean that increasingly, cities are becoming our societies' glorified jail, the aseptic grave of our utopias.

There is a conspicuous sense of inevitabilty in the paradigm of the megacity, the franchising of the urban experience and the trend toward global sprawl.[1] Cities have replaced nation-states in the leading role of economic globalization (Vegara, 2002: 35). Cities became the milieu of globalism (Muxi, 2004). Indeed, inevitability has pervaded urban globalization, insofar as "inevitability is the traditional final justification for failing ideologies" (Saul, 2004: 34).

From the perspective of KCs as value systems,[2] though, the space of possibilities is open to alternatives made possible by recombinations of all such value dimensions. And those dimensions are not only economic and technological but also increasingly knowledge-based, i.e., experiential.[3] This is the very core of the KCs and Knowledge Society's rationale.[4] This is the realization founding the insight that the history of the city may be just at the beginning.

Diversity of Urban Experiences

Living in a city is far from being a homogeneous experience. Indeed, each inhabitant of today's multiple and diverse cities lives each day through a particular array of experiences that not only may be common to others in many regards, but is also unique in many others. Puff pastry city is the multilayered environment of cultural, economic, sociological, scientific, and technological—amongst many—dimensions. But beyond the potentially infinite combination of urban experiences, the point here is to substantiate the vast richness of urban environments. What follows is an attempt to exemplify this variety by looking at some contemporary descriptions.

Weber's classical demarcation of urban settlements in terms of a value system based on trade and services—as opposed to a rural one, based on agriculture—is of limited use today. KCs, as social knowledge-based value systems, can have the most diverse basis of production (even agriculture, such as in flower production) so long as they are knowledge-intensive. What a common characterization of all contemporary urban experiences would be is the question we are addressing in this chapter.

In fact, "city" or "urban settlement" is rather limited terms for our purpose. When KCs were defined as a permanent settlement of relatively higher rank in which the citizenship undertakes a deliberate, systematic attempt to identify and develop its capital system in a balanced, sustainable manner (Carrillo, 2004: 34), the dimension of relative importance (by size or significance) was borrowed from numerous concepts of "city":

> Most definitions, unless referring to very particular usages (e.g.,: The City as London's financial district), convey the concept of a status granted to a relatively permanent, organized human settlement. *The Chambers Dictionary* includes as a definition the following: ". . . in various countries, a municipality of higher rank, variously defined . . . ." Thus, a generic concept of city can be synthesized as a self-governed human settlement that has been granted a special status by virtue of its relative size, population, merits or strategic importance. In short, a city is a relatively permanent human settlement of relatively high importance. (Carrillo, 2004: 28)

---

[1] Later in the chapter the concept of urban sprawl is discussed. For the time being, we can think of it as an *urban liability*, a physical or social condition that engenders a degradation of urban life.

[2] See Carrillo, 2004.

[3] See Carrillo, 1998.

[4] See Carrillo, 2002ᵃ.

Historically, the granting of such status by the commanding authority was the critical factor for city recognition. Even today, the functional category of city maintains this element of relative importance as a defining feature. Take the category of Metropolitan Statistical Area (MSA) as the unit of analysis defined by the US Office of Management and Budget (OMB) for government analysis and budgeting. An MSA is "(a place) that has at least one area of 50,000 or more population, plus adjacent territory that has a degree of social integration with the core as measured by commuting ties."[5] Sperling and Sander (2004) use indiscriminately MSA, metropolitan area, and metro area.

One of the dimensions brought out by this definition is the relation between the "core" of adjacent municipalities with other "cores." This applies to interstate, interregional, or even international overlaps. The options considered by Sperling and Sander are:

- One core to one county
- One core to many counties
- Many cores to one county
- Many cores to many counties.

These authors refer to the general practice of including the whole county when it makes contact with an urban nucleus, which leads to paradoxical results in those big largely uninhabited counties becoming part officially of a "metro area." Further, the concept of "Metropolitan Division" applies to concentrations of over 2.5 million with several clusters; and of "Micropolitan Statistical Areas" for urban nuclei between ten thousand and fifty thousand; whereas "Consolidated Metropolitan Statistical Areas" (CMSAs) stand for clusters of MSAs. Sperling and Sander's ranking includes the following typology of City Profiles:[6]

- National Center
- Regional Center
- Large City
- Small/Mid-size City
- Small Town
- Military Town
- College Town
- Capital City
- Beach Town
- Commuter Community.

With regard to comparative size, there are specific considerations, for boundaries are arbitrary and often fuzzy. Ranking cities by size reveals overlaps between several concepts applied to urban settlements: cities (administrative units), metropolitan areas (human settlements), agglomerations (population concentrations), etc. This becomes evident when trying to determine which is the largest city in the world. The World Gazetteer, http://www.world-gazetteer.com, makes a distinction between places and metropolitan areas. In terms of places, Shangai is No. 1 and Mexico City No. 12; whereas in terms of Metro Areas Tokyo is No. 1, New York No. 2 and Mexico City No. 3. For Thomas Brinkhoff, who runs the website http://www.citypopulation.de, the most populated agglomeration (agglomerations include a central city and neighboring

---

[5] OMB, 6/03, in Sperling and Sander (2004: 3).
[6] For descriptions and examples, see ibid., pp. 149–151.

communities linked to it by continuous built-up areas or by many commuters) is Tokyo, followed by Mexico City and Seoul.

On the other side of the spectrum with regard to size are micropolis: the dark-green middle ground between big-city life and country living. For a long time, according to the clear-cut distinction between urban and rural life (e.g., Max Weber's definition) you either lived in a metropolitan area or you did not. Since 2004, the U.S. Bureau of Census gathered data on micropolitan areas: locales with a core city of fewer than 50,000 and as small as 10,000 (Sperling and Sander, 2004: 4). The understanding of this type of community, with a dynamics of its own, might be related to important commercial and political phenomena, such as the rising of Wal-Mart or the re-election of George W. Bush (Gertner, 2004). This has fairly different meaning in other parts of the world, such as the affluent and much envied country life in Europe or the impoverished rural communities in developing countries. For New York's City Council Committee on Finance, the micropolis is considered an inner cluster or "city within the city" designated as Business Improvement Districts (BIDs).[7]

Another intermediate category is the city region: a surface within a radius of 100 km from the city center. The urban region or urban zone is a conglomerate similar to CMSAS, in that it includes a cluster of one or more cores with all the municipalities adjacent to them. This is also beyond Weber's original dichotomy in that a large rural territory might be incorporated into an urban demarcation.

Another interesting concept is that of urban networks. Rather than compact urban areas, these are both adjacent and discontinuous cities functionally connected for a specific purpose. Urban networks may be local, national, regional, continental, or eventually global. Traditional forms of networks are twin cities. Newer forms are cultural, political, or commercial urban networks, either contiguous or distant. Growing contiguity may lead to merged cities.

We can also find subcities (identifiable urban cores within larger metropolitan areas, e.g., Dallas-Forth Worth), intracities (innermost part of an urban-ringed configuration, such as Moscow and the ancient centers of oldest cities), cities within cities (The City as a distinctive part of London; Christiania in Copenhagen, Ciudad Universitaria in Mexico City or New York's BIDs mentioned above), city-states (from classic Greece to modern Singapore), or even states within cities (the Vatican in Rome). Each has its own structure and function and provides a distinctive set of experiences. Cities can also be monoproductive (i.e., largely based on a main product or service, like the College Town or the Military Town mentioned above). Alternatively, production areas may become functional cities (like Güller and Güller's Airport Cities).

In unfolding the multiple layers of the puff pastry city, Carlos García alternates between four perspectives, each associated to a formal discipline. From these perspectives, the reality of each city can be deconstructed. According to Garcia, the culturalist vision, based on history, provides the city of discipline, the planned city, and the posthistoric city. The sociological vision, based on economics and sociology, favors the global city, the dual city, the city of spectacle, and the sustainable city. The organicist vision, based on science and philosophy (hence, coming close to the concept of KC) reveals the city as nature, the city of bodies, and the lived city. Finally, the technological vision based on ICT brings the cybercity and the chip city. To these can be added all further visions, alternative discourses for identifying the city, identifying the multiple cities within each city, identifying the infinite cities in each urban resident.

---

[7] See the Committee's report available at http://tenant.net/Oversight/bid97/bid97.html.

Hence, the urban experience is a generic term for the plethora of possibilities resulting from the vast diversity of contemporary cities, times the many environments and levels of contact of each city, times its population, times the many experiential platforms of each citizen. Such term would include only the most recent possibilities, concentrated around the 19th and 20th century industrial city, which in a historical perspective accounts for only 0.5% of human presence on Earth, 2% of time since the establishment of the first Neolithic villages, and less than 4% of time since the foundation of the first urban settlements (Carrillo, 2004: 29). Thus, apprehending the universe of past and current urban experiences is a monumental undertaking.

Envisioning all future urban experiences is even more ambitious. Beyond the many perspectives on future cities (e.g., Hall et al., 2000; Moavenzadeh et al., 2002; Orr, 2004; see also many related websites[8]); there are a number of lines of evolution of urban life that are already transforming the meaning of urban experience in an unprecedented way:

- **The Megacity**: Most compelling is the degree of overcrowding that very large metropolis are experiencing, particularly in developing countries. What does urban planning mean in an agglomeration of over 20 million people? What is the meaning of company, community, or the others? There are already five such megalopolis (Tokyo, Mexico City, Seoul, New York, and Sao Paulo) and this dubious elite will soon be joined by several others: according to UN-Habitat's State of the World's Cities Report

  The world's urban population will grow from 2.86 billion in 2000 to 4.98 billion by 2030 . . . Most importantly, urban growth in middle- and low-income countries accounts for about 2 billion of this increase, suggesting that urban growth on a weekly basis will be close to 1 million persons, or a city the size of Hanoi or Pittsburgh each week. Much of this growth will be in cities over 1 million persons. The report notes that by 2003, there were 39 cities over 5 million in population and 16 over 10 million. (Ibid., Overview, p. 1)

- **The Metacity**: these are emerging trends of urban transformation opened up to Knowledge Societies[9] including, first, de-materialization (a lesser volume of material inputs and outputs); second, environmentalism (a greater concern with sustainability); third, experience upgrade (the rise of the k-worker and the k-citizen); fourth, virtuality (the capacity to attain a given result without the conventional material means); and fifth, essentialism (the understanding and pursuit of ever more fundamental values). To these I should add the new distributed platforms for collective knowledge construction, such as bloggs, wikies, and the open source movement.
- **The Multicity**: urban ubiquity, or living/acting in several cities simultaneously, is made increasingly possible by transportation and ICT. The international commuter, a reality that has existed for long among bordering binational settlements, has given rise to the jet-set commuter: that subset of the creating

---

[8] See, e.g., the following urbanists' visions and educational projects (there are plenty of the later available at the Internet): Future City Competition http://www.futurecity.org/; Future Cities and Virtual Cities Projects http://virtualcities.mcmaster.ca/; The Future Cities Project http://www.futurecities.org.uk/; Transport Research's Future Cities http://www.transportresearch.org.uk/FutureCities.htm; Superfuture Cities http://superfuture.com/city/home/; Pittsburgh's Future City Competition http://www.futurecitypittsburgh.org/; Melbourne's Museum Future Cities http://slf.org.au/futurecities/.
[9] For a further discussion, see Carrillo, 2004: 39–41.

class traveling weekly between distant cities thanks to a growing array of air-travel options. There is also the actual global citizen: people "floating" along several destinies worldwide for several purposes. But more ordinary, there is the ubiquitous citizen: constantly interacting with people and environments in several parts of the world through distributed work/learning/entertaining platforms. This means a lot more than accessing websites or databases whose physical location becomes irrelevant. It means real-time multi-media, multi-destiny online interaction with teamworks and communities in other latitudes and timezones.

The urban experience, therefore, is the rich combinatory potential generated by the uniqueness and complexity of each city on one side and the array of perceptual platforms of each citizen, on the other. Rather than describing or categorizing such possibilities, the attempt here has been to illustrate the complex and diverse universe of urban lives:

> Each city has its own character despite the expansion of trade marks and global corporations. There are cities of all sizes, forms and environments. Cities with towers that seem to reach the sky. Cities that never sleep. Cities of angels and devils. Shameless and vital cities or those where the memories of past glories lie buried under ruined façades. (Dodd and Donald, 2004: i)

Even the concept of Knowledge City has multiple predecessors. While the combinatory of related concepts has been explored before,[10] O'Mara (2005) offers a wide selection of concepts from which the idea of Cities of Knowledge is differentiated, as Longworth (1999) did before with the concept of Learning City and Komninos (2002) with Intelligent City. In making sense of the wide and diverse combinatory of city elements, we are searching for the essential ones that may allow us to redesign urban experience in new, unheard possibilities. This search and understanding the distinctive nature and novel promise of the Knowledge City are converging roads.

The Postindustrial City: Utopia and Reality

Françoise Choay, one of the pioneers of Urban Studies and Planning proposed two axis for the historiography of urbanistic ideas. In her classic 1965 book Urbanism, Utopias, and Reality,[11] she not only managed to capture the diversity of modern urban ideas from the Industrial Revolution through World War II, laid the foundations for the science of urbanism and inaugurated a critical discourse on the city as a manifestation of political and economic realities. She also identified a tension, an underlying contradiction at the core of the modern industrial city as the arena where human ideals come to terms with reality, as her title suggests. It is also the basis for her distinction between two streams of 19th century. "preurbanistic" thinking: one looking into the future, the other into the past.

Futuristic or "progressive preurbanism" denotes a universalism, the ambition to improve human life and to promote individual welfare, as exemplified by Charles Fourier, Robert Owen, and Pierre-Joseph Proudhon. Nostalgic or "culturalist preurbanism" sees the city as a cultural whole and finds its ideal in the organicism of the medieval city, as illustrated by the political-aesthetic proposals of William Morris and

---

[10] Carrillo, ibid., p. 33.
[11] L'Urbanisme, utopies et réalités, Paris: Editions du Seuil, 1965, et Collection Points essais, 1979.

John Ruskin. Even if Choay projected her urban paradigms into 20th century "urbanisitic" thinking (e.g., Le Curbousier[12] as progresist and Raymond Unwin[13] as culturalist) her dichotomy became harder to apply even to the earlier examples, since the implied contraposition became harder to sustain.[14]

What pervades from Choay's early work is her insight into the modern industrial city as the milieu of industrialization, as the breaking point of past and future, as the mirror where the best and worst of human nature is exposed, as the grounding of ideals into the lands of possibilities, as the affirmation of the local before the global, as the inescapable dialectic between the collective and the individual. This is perhaps the theme accompanying the postindustrial, postmodern city in search of its identity. The introduction to the 2004 Dialogue City and Citizens of the 21st Century held within the Barcelona Fórum Universal de las Culturas claimed: "Globalization is a future tense resulting from a problematic present. The city is the idealized past propelling us into a desirable future."[15]

The trouble with postmodernity is that nowadays neither the past is necessarily idealized nor is the future necessarily desirable. The postindustrial realities where the Knowledge City emerges call for a deeper, more lucid, and honest account of urban experience. The theatrical, megalomaniac setting that the globalized cosmopolis has become is at the edge of social and economic collapse. Muxi (2004) describes the "macdonaldization" and "disneylandization" of cities in terms of the banalization of architecture, the voyeurism and arrogance of power, and the narcissism of trade marks. The limits to current urban paradigms might well be both the limits of globalism as an ideology and the limits of unsustainable environmental and social practices.

No other reality indicates more brutally the pervasiveness of urban constraints than social exclusion. According to UN-Habitat, out of the world's urban population growth from 2.86 billion in 2000 to 4.98 billion by 2030, high-income countries will account for only 28 million out of the expected increase of 2.12 billion. In the section Cities and Globalization: A Race to the Bottom? UN-Habitat finds that "the 'fruits of globalization'—economic growth, rising incomes, and improvements in the quality of life—are rapidly being offset by the negative aspects of rapid urbanization: increased poverty, greater inequality, and the prediction that, by 2020, urban areas in the world's least developed regions will absorb nearly all of the global population increase predicted for the next three decades. This 'urbanization of poverty' is being propelled by a tremendous increase in the transnational movement of people and capital" (UN-Habitat, 2005).

In the recent United Nations SCO Report on adequate housing as a component of the right to an adequate standard of living, the Raporteur found that

> while the majority of the world's population lives in some form of dwelling, roughly one-half of the world's population does not enjoy the full spectrum of entitlements necessary for housing to be considered adequate. United Nations estimates indicate that approximately 100 million people worldwide are without a place to live. Over 1 billion people are inadequately housed. (UN Economic and Social Council, 2005: 2)

---

[12] (1887–1965).

[13] (1863–1940).

[14] E.g., Morris' political progresism is deeply rooted in medieval aesthetics, while Sitte's organiscism is revolutionary rather than nostalgic.

[15] La Ciudad: entorno de convivencia. Diálogo: "Ciudad y Ciudadanos del Siglo XXI". *Foro Universal de las Culturas*, Barcelona, September 8–12, 2004, available at: http://www.ggu.ua.es/documentos/Ciudad_y_ciudadanos%20del_siglo_XXI.pdf.

He also found that from the total of privately owned land, 75% is in the hands of 2.5% of landowners. He stressed that, currently, about a billion people live in impoverished slums and this could reach 2 billion by 2020.

The UN-Habitat Report claims in its summary that

> Under globalization, the spatial structure of cities is changing as new economic production patterns require more horizontal integration between functions in different sites, and as cities shift their attention to external locations and activities, resulting in new geographies and a "splintering" of earlier urban spatial patterns. The associated decentralization has major implications for the spatial configuration of cities, intensifying the process of metropolitanization and the related management problems. The report shows how poverty is increasing in many cities and how this is partly an outcome of the uneven costs and benefits of economic globalization. In addition, the report shows how urban poverty has been increasingly concentrated in particular neighbourhoods that have, generally, become the habitats of the urban poor and minority groups: racial minorities in some societies, international immigrant groups in others.[16]

The impacts of globalization in cities and the consequent degradation of human life is well captured by that fuzzy yet powerful concept of urbanism: sprawl. Often applied to the extreme, low-density scattering and horizontal spreading ("Los Angelization") of suburbs, it is also used in the opposite sense: monotony and crowdness in high-density neighborhoods. Like once said about pornography "it is hard to define but one can recognise when one sees it," urban sprawl is something going from the innocuous idea of "the expansion of a city and its suburbs into rural land and the periphery of the urban area" (Sperling and Sander, 2004: 58) to the very corruption of urban life, in aesthetic, moral, and social terms. Contrary to Sperling and Sander's view that "not all sprawl is bad" and even that such expansion is "a major factor determining an area's long-term quality of life,"[17] Swaback (2003) bluntly states that "people who are in total disagreement about anything to do with development easily agree that they hate sprawl" and that "we agree that sprawl is 'bad,' but because we don't know what it is, we don't know what we want to stop doing" (Ibid., p. 25). After a number of examples, Swaback arrives to the following description:

> Sprawl has little to do with density and everything to do with the production-driven, code-enforced absence of creativity. It is the artless sameness of uniformly sized lots, uniformly massed buildings, monotonously repeating designs and the automobile dependency that inevitably results from the absolute segregation of land uses. (Ibid., p. 32)

One may guess William Morris would have felt quite at ease with that definition and recognize himself as a sprawl-fighter in 19th century England. Hence, sprawl has to do with aesthetic and moral dullness as much as infrastructure and economic deprivation. It may happen in slums as well as in affluent neighborhoods. Sprawl has to do with human misery: "It stands in as a catchall for auto-centered development, scattered housing, strip malls, tract houses and anything else despised by urbanists and environmentalists" (*Architecture Magazine*, Dec. 2001)[18]. Sprawl is a degrading urban experience.

---

[16] General Overview Urbanization & the Economic Contribution of Cities.

[17] Surprisingly, though, Sperling and Sander rank the "Most Sprawl-Threatened Cities" (Table 3.3, p. 58) and those at the top of this list are at the very bottom of the overall ranking, i.e., are the worst cities. As an example, McAllen, Tx., which is top of the most-sprawl-threatened in the 200–500 k habs. range, gets an overall ranking of 317 out of 331 with a score of only 23.8 out of 100 (Table 2.2, p. 33).

[18] In Swaback, op. cit., p. 34.

Sprawl is the antithesis of urban utopia. This conclusion is consistent with Duany, Plater-Zyberk and Speck's downright contraposition between sprawl and urban ideals. In *Suburban Nation: The Rise of Sprawl and the Decline of the American Dream* (2000), they offer an analysis of sprawl and its components, before dissecting suburban life in the USA and exposing all its maladies. Suburban sprawl and the traditional neighborhood are set as polar opposites in structure, function, and spirit. Actually, the authors are amongst the cofounders of the Congress for New Urbanism,[19] whose Charter is virtually a manifesto against sprawl. If this sounds extremist, consider the following statement from the Bank of America, California's largest bank: "One of the most fundamental questions we face is whether California can afford to support the pattern of urban and suburban development, often referred to as 'sprawl,' that has characterized its growth since World War II" (1996). To a large extent, the New Urbanism movement[20] is a response against urban sprawl.

Understanding, rather than demonizing, sprawl is a challenge for KCs. The only meaningful replies are urban innovations, not regressions or denials of urban conditions. In fact, the degree of understanding of each city's own sprawl should be reflected in the city's Capital System (cf. Chapters 4 and 12), insofar as these constitute the "social knowledge accounts" reflecting all urban assets and liabilities. The Capital System becomes the new agora, where all value elements converge in an open, public manner. At this point, utopia can be restored in the postmodern city. Much as the classic urban ideal emerged and collapsed with the fate of the Greek city-states, the Knowledge City can restate the sense of the polis lost to the cosmopolis of globalism:

> The world of the polis had clearly given way to the world of the cosmopolis. And with that change from the smallness of the city-state to the immensity of the world-city, there were corresponding changes in the world view. The city-state was no longer run by citizens, citizens whose private and public duties were identical. In the world-state, bureaucrats and officials took over the duties formerly given over to citizens. Citizens lost their sense of importance as they became subjects under the control of vast bureaucratic kingdoms. From the face-to-face contact of the Athenian public Assembly, the people now became little more than numbers. As a result, they lost their identity. (Kreis, 2004: 7)[21]

City Identity and Urban Experience

Recovering each city's identity becomes paradoxically the best option to help each citizen to discover their own identity within it. According to Dodd and Donald "a city is more a spirit, a state of mind, than a series of norms and regulations or than considerations on the number of inhabitants" (2004: 8). In trying to capture the essence of each of the 250 cities selected from around the world, they offer a collage from each one, in which, besides a few general data, relatively objective elements such as history, topography and architecture are reported alongside subjective ones such as distinctive sounds, smells, sights, and the inhabitant's character. Their emphasis is precisely on the uniqueness of each city and the experience of it: "anything that contributes in making each city different and unique, specially in this times of globalization and international trade marks."

---

[19] http://www.cnu.org/.

[20] See, e.g., http://www.newurbanism.org, http://www.nutimeline.net and http://www.newurbannews.com/.

[21] The resonance of this with the EU's 2005 "Summer of discontempt" is striking.

The UN-Habitat Program makes clear what the space for urban planning is: "A city is both a territory and an attitude, and this attitude is culture" (2005, p. 2). Culture as expression of a city's identity is what Marco Polo was trying to convey to his sponsor The Kan when reporting on his travels, in that splendid exercise of imagination offered by Italo Calvino in *Le Cittá Invisibili*. Identity as the foundation of all urban value is what the Capital System is trying to capture: the protocapital or source of all capital (see Chapters 4 and 12).

Identity has not only a strong cultural value. It is more than a romantic quest. It is the basis for any serious strategy of urban planning and design in the advent of the KC. The capacity of each city to differentiate and brand itself is the beginning of KC management. This is why identity capital becomes the initial task in the identification and development of knowledge capital. In terms of Capital Systems, Identity and Intelligence, the two Referential Capitals, are the starting point for deploying the uniqueness of each city against the common categories of the Generic Capitals System (Chapter 4). These have been identified as the vertical (own) and horizontal (common) characteristics of modern cities (COTEC, 2004: 9).

Identity Management is now the first technical challenge for KCs. A number of resources and procedures to develop organizational and social identity are available. At the organizational level, the Center for Knowledge Systems[22] has developed an approach and tools for developing identity. The Capital Cities© Framework focuses on this as the initial task in KC strategic development. The Knowledge Cities Observatory[23] promotes identity development through its Identity, Value Mapping, and Indicators Systems for Cities Program.

Finding out, building, re-constructing,[24] and continuously evolving its identity is the first value dimension having an impact on the total worth of a KC. In fact, the quality of identity and intelligence capital leverages the value of all other capitals. Building a city's identity and upon it a city's capital system is the new solution point for the perennial tension between utopia and reality.

Reconstructing Urban Experience

Australian-American art designer Michael Dumlao keeps the website La Ciudad: Urban Identity in the Developing World,[25] where he displays multimedia resources on urban identity. Amongst these, Octavio Paz's urban poems are prominent. These remind us of the others as the unescapable urban nature of man, as that immense reality we may leave only to fall again into.

That the others are the most irreducible element of urban experience is more evident now than ever before. Given the relative availability of all other elements (such as basic services and telecommunications) in almost any corner of the world, basic urban experiences can be recognized in cases like the new British station in Antarctica or the

---

[22] http://www.knowledgesystems.org.
[23] http://www.innovationecology.com/kco.htm.
[24] Aleksandra Stupar has made valuable contributions to understanding the dynamics of urban identity evolution. In *(Re)creating the Urban Identity: The Belgrade Metropolitan Region at the Crossroads of the European Integration Flows* she illustrates dramatically how a city's identity (Belgrade) can be simultaneously battered by forces regime change, political realignment, civil war and supranational integration (downloadable at www.isocarp.org/Data/case_studies/433.pdf). In *Technology vs. Culture* she explores the impact of two other generic change forces on urban identity: technology and globalization.
[25] www.michaeldumlao.com/813/INDEX.htm.

Desert Knowledge Australia network. Today, the urban experience is defined by two elementary conditions: access to services and interaction with others, anywhere on Earth. Paraphrasing Paz, we may leave entirely a physical city but we carry with us our own urban experience as we remain attached to the others.

This may be a good summary of what this chapter—and to a large extent, this book—has dealt with, and the best way to bring it to an end. The other is the place where urban identity and personal experience meet, the place where utopia meets reality, the final reference for the city's capital system. The Capital System of the city becomes the knowledge and value mirror of a community, the true expression of its polis. As the language of social accountability for urban planning and policy deployment, the Capital System is the instrument to operationalize Swaback's planning ideal:

> Everything we plan, design and build should be conceived as a set of tools for enhancing human experience. The best planning and architecture becomes a living system that will be used, decorated and changed over time to support the needs and dreams of this and future generations. (Ibid., p. 223)

The UNDP Report on Cultural Liberty states: "Cultural liberty is a vital part of human development because being able to choose one's identity—who one is—without losing the respect of others or being excluded from other choices is important in leading a full life" (2004: 15). John R. Saul, in turn, points a core ability of global citizenship, "the basic philosophical test of functioning intelligence and ethics—the ability to imagine the Other."

Such ability has two experiential perspectives: the collective and the individual. The collective is on the urban design and policy side, whose limits are set by the organizational soundness of the city's government, as well as by the competence and commitment of its administrators (COTEC, 2004). While the strategic focus for policy development can be largely found in the international sustainability and social inclusion agenda; the new tools could be generated within the KCs framework. Thus, the collective dimension is largely public, political, and technical.

The individual perspective, on the other hand, belongs in the innermost constitution of human nature, in its possibilities to evolve on an urban environment. I have pointed out before the implications of coming to terms for the first time in human history with the self-imposed denial of our animal base along the lines of Griffith (2003) and the emerging picture of human nature provided by contemporary biological and social sciences of man (cf. Carrillo, 2004). Such a quest is taxed by the paradoxical inertias caused by ignorance and superstition upon the emerging knowledge societies. It requires to overcome the fear of finding out our true ancestry, the lowermost layers of our suburban undergrounds, much like the main character in Lovecraft's *Nameless City*. I have also pointed out the implications of bringing into urban discourse the interrelated contributions of the alterity (or otherness) studies and of the new sciences of consciousness, which are redefining empirically, conceptually, and morally our understanding of the construction of human identity (Carrillo, 2002). Altogether, these emerging perspectives may allow for the first time a self-conscious exercise of social design which departs from an understanding rather than a denial of the contradiction between what we strive to do and what we actually do (Griffith, 2003).

In short, whereas the challenges to KCs from the collective perspective are to a large extent public, objective, and increasingly accountable, even if still formidable (world poverty, environmental collapse, financial unstability, etc.) there is enough clarity on what the priorities for action are. If these look unsurmountable, the challenges to KCs from the individual perspective look even greater: to overcome for the first time in history the seeming contradiction between our biological buildup and our urban designs. The later might indeed prove the lead toward solving the former.

The global community is waking up to the Knowledge Cities Century with an urgency to understand and manage the social processes of an urban world. Furthermore, we face the need and opportunity to know ourselves in a way that enables the level of consciousness that a sustainable future requires. We may be running short of time and the option for a future may lie at the edge of human knowledge. Perhaps, if we are able to understand ourselves, we might start living our cities: Trieste, Zürich, Paris . . . and all of the others.

References

Bank of America. (1996). Beyond Sprawl: New Patterns of Growth to Fit the New California Originally published on the Bank of America's Web site. BankAmerica Corporation.

Carrillo, F. J. (2004). Capital Cities: a taxonomy of capital accounts for knowledge cities, *Journal of Knowledge Management*, vol. 8, no. 5, October.

Carrillo, F. J. (2002). Capital Systems: Implications for a Global Knowledge Agenda. *Journal of Knowledge Management*, vol. 6, no. 4, October, pp. 379–399.

Carrillo, F. J. (1998). Managing Knowledge-based Value Systems. *Journal of Knowledge Management*, vol. 1, no. 4, junio, pp. 280–286.

COTEC. (2004). La ciudad del conocimiento: La respuesta de la tecnología a los retos urbanos. Encuentros Empresariales COTEC. Madrid: Fundación Cotec para la Innovación Tecnológica.

Dodd, Philip and Ben Donald. (2004). *The Book of Cities*. London: Pavillion.

Duany, Andres, Elizabeth Plater-Zyberk and Jeff Speck. (2001). *Suburban Nation: The Rise of Sprawl and the Decline of the American Dream*. New York: North Point Press.

Gertner, Jon. (2004). The Micropolis. *The New York Times*, 12 December.

Griffith, J. (2003). *A Species in Denial*. Sidney: FHA publishing.

Komninos, Nicos. (2002). *Intelligent Cities*. London: Spon Press.

Longworth, Norman. (1999). *Making Lifelong Learning Work: Learning Cities for a Learning Century*. London: Kogan Page.

Hall, Peter G., Ulrich Pfeiffer and Sir Peter Hall. (2000). *Urban Future 21: A Global Agenda for 21st Century Cities*. London: E & FN Spon.

Kreis, S. (2004). From "Polis" to "Cosmopolis". History Guide, Lesson No. 9. Available at http://www.history guide.org/ancient/lecure 9b.html. Searched June 15, 2005.

Landry, C. (2000). *The Creative City*. London: Earthscan.

Moavenzadeh, Fred, Keisuke Hanaki and Peter Baccini. (2002). *Future Cities: Dynamics and Sustainability*. Netherlands: Kluwer Academic Publishers.

Muxi, Zaida. (2004). *La Arquitectura de l Ciudad Global*. Barcelona: Gustavo Gili.

O'Mara, Margaret P. (2005). *Cities of Knowledge: Cold War Science and the Search for the Next Silicon Valley*.Princeton, NJ: Princeton University Press.

Orr, David W. (2004). *Cities in Our Future: On Education, Environment, and the Human Prospect* (10th Anniversary Edition). Washington: Island Press.

Saul, J. R. (2004). *The Collapse of Globalism, Harper's*, vol. 308, no. 1846 (March), p. 33–43.

Sperling, Bert and Meter Sander. (2004). *Cities Ranked and Rated*, Hoboken, NJ: Wiley Publishing Inc.

Swaback, V. (2003). *The Creative Community: Designing for Life*. Phoenix, AZ: Charetauqua Press

UNDP. (2004). Cultural liberty in today's diverse world. UNDP: Human development Report 2004. Overview: Cultural Liberty.

UN Habitat. (2005). State of the World's Cities: General Overview. Urbanization and the Economic Contribution of Cities, Overview, p. 2.

Vegara, Alfonso. (2002). Ciudades en un mundo global. In Alicia A. Guajardo (ed.), *Análsis Estratégico del Area Metropolitana de Monterrey. Tecnológico de Monterrey*, pp. 35–52.

List of Contributors

Jon Azua (pp. 97–112), *Chairman, Enovatinglab, Bilbao, Spain.*

Raphaële Bidault-Waddington (pp. 177–187), *Laboratoire d'Ingéniérie d'Idées (LII), Paris, France.*

Francisco Javier Carrillo (pp. 43–58, 145–166, 273–284), *The World Capital Institute and The Center for Knowledge Systems, Monterrey, México.*

Jay Chatzkel (pp. 135–144), *Progressive Practices, Phoenix, Arizona, USA.*

Stephen Chen (pp. 191–204), *Australian National University, National Graduate School of Management, Canberra, Australia.*

Chong Ju Choi (pp. 87–96), *Professor of International Business, National Graduate School of Management, Canberra, Australia.*

Ron Dvir (pp. 245–272), *Future Centers, Tel-Aviv, Israel.*

Leif Edvinsson (pp. 59–73), *UNIC, Stockholm, Sweden.*

Kostas Ergazakis (pp. 3–15), *National Technical University of Athens, Greece.*

Søren Find (pp. 31–41), *Head of Section, Technical Knowledge Center of Denmark, Denmark.*

Pedro Flores (pp. 75–84), *Center for Knowledge Systems, Tecnológico de Monterrey, México.*

Blanca C. García (pp. 123–133), *Institute for Development Policy and Management (IDPM), School of Environment and Development, University of Manchester, UK.*

Rubén Garrido (pp. 205–222), *Professor of Economic Policy at the University of Alcalá and Director of the Regional Area at the University Institute of Economic and Social Research, Servilab, Spain.*

Hanah Hertzman (pp. 113–121), *CEO, Municipality of Holon, Israel.*

Karmen Jelcic (pp. 167–176), *IC Center, Croatia.*

Jan G. Lambooy (pp. 223–232), *Professor, associated with Utrecht University and the University of Amsterdam, The Netherlands.*

Maya Levin-Sagi (pp. 113–121), *Edna Pasher Associates, Tel-Aviv, Israel.*

América Martínez (pp. 233–243), *Center for Knowledge Systems, Instituto Tecnológico Y de Estudios Superiores de Monterrey, México.*

Samuel David Martínez (pp. 17–30), *Department of Computer Sciences, Tecnológico de Monterrey, México.*

Christian Wichmann Matthiessen (pp. 31–41), *Professor, Institute of Geography, University of Copenhagen, Denmark.*

Kostas Metaxiotis (pp. 3–15), *National Technical University of Athens, Greece.*

Carla C. J. M. Millar (pp. 87–96), *Professor of International Marketing & Management, University of Twente, Enschede, The Netherlands.*

Edna Pasher (pp. 113–121), *Edna Pasher Associates, Tel-Aviv, Israel.*

John Psarras (pp. 3–15), *National Technical University of Athens, Greece.*

Luis Rubalcaba (pp. 205–222), *President of the European Network of Services Research and Professor of Economic Policy at the University of Alcalá and Servilab, Spain.*

Annette Winkel Schwarz (pp. 31–41), *Director, Technical Knowledge Center of Denmark, Denmark.*

Caroline Y. L. Wong (pp. 87–96), *Australian National University, Australia.*

Index

Accessibility rights, 13
Advances services, 206–211
Aesthetic audit, 177–187
Agencies, 11
Agent capital management, 47
Agglomeration advantages, 228
Airports, 65
Articulation capital, 56
Atlantic Arc, 100
Audit Urban Eurostat project, 206

Ba, 69
Barcelona, 5–6, 27
Basque Country, 97–112
Beijing, 194–196
Beijing Economic-Technological Development
    Area, 196
Beijing Tianzhu Export Processing Area, 196
Bilbao, 27, 97–112
    Bilbao-Guggenheim effect, 98
    convergent strategy, 99–101
    differentiators, 112
    K-factor, 110–111
    strategy for excellence, 104–105
Birmingham, 27
Boston, 27
Buenos Aires, 27
Business Improvement Districts, 276
Business services, 205–222
    concentration, 208
        geographical, 210
        urban, 213–219
    decentralization, 208
    private–public interactions, 211–213
    regional policies, 221

Cafés, 118, 153–154
Capital angels, 149
Capital decimal index, 146
Capital systems, 48, 49–54, 238
    implementation, 75–84
    instrumentation, 81–83
    and knowledge cities, 79–81
Center for Citizen Participation, 142
Center for Construction and the
    Environment, 141–142
Center for Educational Transformation, 142
Center for Enterprise Performance, 141
Center for Gerontology, 143
Center for Hospitality and Tourism, 141
Center for NAFTA Performance
    Excellence, 140
Center for New Citizens, 142
Center for Technology and Innovation, 141
Charlotte, 77, 79, 81–82
China, 191–204
    science parks, 194–203
    science policy, 193–194
Choay, Françoise, 278–279
Christiania, 177–187
    cultural style, 181–183
        behavior, 182–183
        general harmony, 183
        management and authority, 183
        partners, 183
        qualified offer, 181–182
        qualified target, 182
    functional architecture, 179–181
        economic flows, 180–181
        human organization, 180
        legal aspect, 181

Christiania (*Continued*)
  physical organization, 179–180
  strategy, 181
  transportation and flows, 180
  mindscape, 185–186
  positioning, 183–185
    competitive environment, 184
    history, 185
    land administration, 183–184
    media, 185
    natural environment, 184
    society, 184–185
Cities General Intellectual Capital Model, 21
Cities Intellectual Capital Benchmarking
    System, 21
Cities Specific Intellectual Capital Model, 21
Citizen competences, 236–237
Citizens' rights, 13
City identity, 281–282
City of Children, 113–121
Coauthorship patterns, 37–40
Collection teams, 82
Committee on Singapore's Competitiveness, 89
Communications, 13
Comparative frameworks, 17–30
  models for, 20–23
Competences, 233–243
  fields of, 236–237
Competency taxonomies, 235–236
Competitiveness, 102
Concentration of services, 208
Contemporary Theory of the Firm, 50
Convergent strategy, 99–101
Country-building strategy, 109
Creapreneurship ©, 71
Creativity, 226
Curid, Elizabeth, 113

Decentralization of services, 208
Delft, 8–9
Development and Selection of Key
    Competences study, 236
Dialog, 103
Diffusion, 224–225
Dobelle, Evan, 98
Dublin, 8
Dynamics of exchange, 18

Economic growth theory, xiii
Economic science, 50
Edinburgh, 27
Education of Democratic Citizenship
    project, 236
Education/training, 13, 103
Engines of innovation, 126
Entrepreneurial partnerships, 128–129

European Commission, 3
European Union, xii
Euskopolis, 104
Evolutionary economics, 225
Evolutionary selection environments,
    228–229

Financial capital, 119
Financial support, 11
Florida, Richard, 17, 88
Freedom, 104
Future Center, 143
Futurizing, 59–60

Gehry, Frank O., 98
Generic capital systems
  basic assumptions, 54
  definitions, 54–55
  Monterrey, 145–165
Global networks, 135–136
Global public goods, 48
Global research centres, 31–41
  ranking, 35–37
Global Urban Observatory, 28
Globalisation, 207
Gottman, Jean, 228–229
Greater Phoenix, 135–144
  as knowledge capital, 139
  profile, 140
Grid of Reading, 178
Guggenheim-Bilbao project, 98–101
  benefits of, 102
Guggenheim Museum in Bilbao, 106

Health, 103
Henson, Scott, 19
Holon, 113–121
  financial capital, 119
  human capital, 116–117, 119–120
  initiatives, 114
  intellectual capital report, 115
  market capital, 117, 120–121
  process capital, 117, 120
  renewal and development capital, 117, 121
Home, 266, 268–269
Horn, Joe, 19
Hsinchu Technology Park, 191
Human capital, 20, 47, 56, 116–117, 119–120

IC Navigator Model for Municipalities,
    20–21
Image, 109
Information and communication technology, 87
Information rights, 13
Infrastructures, 109
Initiatives, 26–29

Innovation, 126, 223–232
  generation and dissemination of
    knowledge, 225–227
  networks, 224–225
Input capital, 54
Instrumental capital, 56–57
  management, 47
Intangibles, 60–61
Integrated Value Reports, 149
Intellectual capital, 43, 61–62, 77, 115
  inductive phase, 49
  Skandia model, 116–117
Intelligent capital, 56, 66
Intelligent cities, 19, 63–64
International Commission on the Education
    for the 21st Century, 237
Investment capital, 56

K-based value structures, 50–51
KC Capital System, 21–23
Key findings, 9–10
Key urban variables, 213
K-factor, 110–111
Knowledge-based development,
    75, 76–77
Knowledge-based economy, 87, 226
Knowledge-based strategies, 76, 79–81
Knowledge-based value systems, 44–49
  objects, agents and contexts, 44–46
Knowledge bases, 149
Knowledge cafés, 118, 153–154
Knowledge capitals, 135–144
  advantages of, 137
  bringing into existence, 137–139
  definition of, 135
  strategic plans for, 140–143
Knowledge cities, 77–79, 125–126
  benefits of, 5
  capital systems, 79–81
  context, 18
  definition, 4, 20, 245
  development, 11–13
  measurement of, 65–68
  operation, 13
  understanding, 246–247
  what happens in, 245–246
Knowledge citizens, 233–243
  competences of, 234–235
  profile of, 237–241
Knowledge conversion process, 227
Knowledge creation, 18
Knowledge dissemination, 223–232
Knowledge-driven global economy, 87
Knowledge exchanges, 64–65
Knowledge generation, 225–227
Knowledge harbours, 64–65

Knowledge management, xiii, 3, 75
  generations of, 46–49
Knowledge moments, 245–246
Knowledge places, 246, 249–269
Knowledge processes, 246
Knowledge society, 19
Knowledge zones, 70
Korea, 27

Lamm, Robert C., 107
Lapointe, Alain, 17
Leadership cultivation, 68–70
Learning cities, 19, 24
Libraries, 13, 257–259
London, 28
Longitude, 59–60

Malaga, 28
Manchester, 28, 123–133
  history, 126–129
Market capital, 20, 117, 120–121
Mataró, 28
Megacities, 34–36, 277
Metacapitals, 24, 54, 55–56, 149–155
Metacities, 277
Metaproductive capitals, 51–54
Metropolitan Statistical Area, 275
Metropolitan websites, 12
Millennium Village, 124
Mind Lab, 69
Momentum, 69
Monterrey, 145–165
  capital system, 149–165
Montréal, 7–8
Multi-ethnicity, 11–12
Multicities, 277–278
Munich, 7
Museums, 259–261

Networks, 224–225
New growth theory, xiii
North West Development Agency, 129

Objectives, 81
OECD, xii, 33
  Report on The Well-being of Nations: The
    Role of Human and Social Capital, 128
Optimism, 104
Output capital, 55

Participation rights, 13
Philadelphia, 28
Piazza, 261–265
PIKA, 170, 172
Poblenou 22@BCN, 81
Political/societal will, 11

Postindustrial cities, 278–281
Principal Components Analysis, 218–219
Private–public partnership, 211–213
Process capital, 20, 117, 120
Production capitals, 51–54, 55
Productive capitals, 56–57, 155–165
Productive Value Structures, 49–50
Progressive Policy Institute, 28
Project of Increasing Efficiency of National
    Intellectual Capital (PIENIC), 167–175
  context for, 168–169
  features and goals, 169–172
  implementation, 172–175

Ragusa, 62–63
Reclus-Datar group, 34
Regional Intellectual Capital, 245
Relational capital, 25
Renewal and development capital, 117, 121
Renovation and development capital, 20
Research cooperation, 37–40
Research excellence, 13
Research output, 34–36
Rijeka, 167–176
  PIENIC project, 167–175

Sao Paulo, 27
Schools, 249, 251–252
Science Citation Index, 32–33
Science parks, 191–204
Scientific wealth, 32–33
Self government, 103
Self-respect, 104
Shanghai, 196–198
Silicon Valley, 191
Singapore, 87–96
  culture and place, 92–93
  historical development, 89–90
  technology, 90–92
Skandia Future Centre, 69
Skandia model, 116–117
  focal areas, 116
  human capital, 116–117
  market capital, 117
  process capital, 117
  renewal and development capital, 117
Smith, Adam, 228
Social contracts, 138
Social Knowledge Capital, 43
Social welfare, 102–103
Society entrepreneurship, 70–72
Sophia-Antipolis, 191
Sprawl, 280–281
Stakeholders, 149

Stock exchange, 265–266
Stockholm, 6
Storytelling, 246–247
Strategic vision, 11
Strategy for excellence, 104–105
Subcities, 276
Super brains, 70
Sustainable cities, 130–131
System of Capitals, 23–24

Taxonomies, 235–236
Technopolis, 19
Territorial integration, 104
Town halls, 254–257
Tucson, 28

United Nations, xii
  Habitat Program, 279–280, 282
  Program for Development, 48
United Nations Organization, 3
UniverCities, 123–133
Urban accessibility, 216
Urban Capital Systems, 245
Urban capitals, 43–58
  definitions, 55–56
Urban environments
  business services, 213–219
  as evolutionary selection environments,
      228–229
  innovation and dissemination, 223–232
  key variables, 213
Urban experience, 274–278, 281–282
  reconstruction of, 282–284
Urban innovation engines, 12
Urban knowledge diary, 248, 250
Urban networks, 276
Urban units, 33–34
Urban/regional development, 206–211
Urbanization, xi

Value creation, 12
Value Creation Efficiency Analysis, 168–169
Value dimensions, 24–25, 146

Workplace skills, 235–236
World Bank, xii, 3, 28
World Economic Forum, 88

Xi'an, 199–200
Xi'an Hi-tech Industrial Development
    Zone, 199–200

Zhangjiang Hi-Tech Park, 198
Zhongguancun Science Park, 196